# LITTLE ROCK, U.S.A.

Edited by Wilson and Jane C. Record,
Sacramento State College.

It is important to remember that the incidents of the
school integration struggle in Little Rock are really
symbols of some of the gravest conflicts in our history.
State rights vs. federal rights, civil liberties, and
public responsibility for education are among the basic
issues involved.

This collection of materials for student analysis thus
opens up many paths of investigation requiring careful
appraisal of evidence, drill in organization.  Few
topics exist which offer more opportunities for exer-
cises in composition, more chances for development
of logical inquiry.

The tremendous variety of the documents will give
students practice in handling almost every kind of
bibliographical problem.

Your comments and suggestions will be welcome.

Sincerely yours,

*Howard Chandler*

# *LITTLE ROCK, U.S.A.*

# MATERIALS FOR ANALYSIS

*Interpreting Hamlet*

SELECTED AND EDITED BY

*RUSSELL E. LEAVENWORTH*

*The Voice out of the Whirlwind: The Book of Job*

SELECTED AND EDITED BY

*RALPH E. HONE*

*Little Rock, U.S.A.*

SELECTED AND EDITED BY

*WILSON RECORD* AND *JANE CASSELS RECORD*

# Little Rock, U.S.A.

## MATERIALS FOR ANALYSIS

---

Selected and Edited by

### WILSON RECORD, 1916 –
SACRAMENTO STATE COLLEGE

*and* JANE CASSELS RECORD

*Chandler Publishing Company*
660 MARKET STREET
SAN FRANCISCO 4, CALIFORNIA

Cover Photo: Wide World

# Foreword

In September 1957, at Little Rock, Arkansas, nine Negro teen-agers attempted to enroll at a previously all-white school. The story that followed had everything required for first-rate drama—violence, mob scenes, Presidential proclamations, troops with bayonets, summit conferences between the state of Arkansas and the United States of America—and it made headlines around the world.

We have here assembled facts and interpretations of the story. Our concern is not so much with what happened as with why it happened, what it signifies, and what its consequences will be. For that reason our collection of material begins with the Supreme Court's seminal school decisions of 1954-1955 and comes forward through the opening of Central High School in August 1959.

We could, of course, have picked a much earlier starting point, for history is a continuum and the roots of those September events reach back to the antebellum South and even further. Moreover, the story is not yet finished. But though our cut-off dates at each end are somewhat arbitrary so as to make the collection manageable, we believe that the material presented provides a wide-lens view of the Little Rock drama in its various dimensions—political, judicial, economic, ideological, psychological, sociological, religious, moral.

The readings are arranged in two sections. The first is designed to tell the story chronologically, from newspaper accounts, court records, and other documents. Official documents are reproduced, in whole or part, except where they are too cumbersome or repetitious, in which instances news summaries are substituted. The second section contains interpretive material, a spectrum of critical comment and opinion; the material was left ungrouped so that the student may do his own organization of the issues.

A table of contents in the usual form would require many pages. We have chosen, instead, to supply a "summary of contents." For Section I there is a list of the major events for the four principal periods. The reader may find this a handy chronology for placing any given incident in proper time relationship to the mainstream of events. For Section II there is a list of the people whose comments make up the "spectrum of opinion."

The readings included in this book are but a small portion of the vast sea of literature which has grown up around the desegregation problem in general and Little Rock in particular. Though our collection gives an adequate picture in the round, an interested reader may want to pursue some facet more intensively. In that case he should look through the voluminous bibliography published by the *Journal of Negro Education* in its quarterly issues. If the *JNE* is not available, he might consult the general guides to periodical literature which any library has. The *Race Relations Law Reporter* carries all the significant court decisions and many other documents. And the *Southern School News,* started in 1954 by a group of distinguished southern educators and journalists for the purpose of reporting objectively the consequences of the Supreme Court decisions, has an excellent month-to-month coverage of news items.

Some of the important supplemental books, periodicals, and articles are listed, in their customary place, at the end of this collection of Materials for Analysis.

Perhaps a paragraph about ourselves—specifically, our interest in Little Rock—is called for. We are native southerners, from Texas and Georgia, respectively, educated in southern schools and universities. Though we have lived in California for more than a decade, we have retained a live concern for, and close contact with, the south, through field trips, correspondence, and subscription to southern journals. The school crisis at Little Rock was, in our opinion, the most important single occurrence in the region during the 1950's.

Wilson Record
Jane Cassels Record

*Sacramento, California*
*August 15, 1960*

# SUMMARY OF CONTENTS

Move to Reopen Schools, July — NAACP Challenge to Pupil-Placement Law and Reopening of Central High against Segregationist Opposition, August

## II. THE MEANINGS OF LITTLE ROCK: A SPECTRUM OF OPINION

Observations on the Principal Parties and the Salient Issues of the Little Rock School Crisis, by Editors, Journalists and Other Writers, Educators, Lawyers, Businessmen, Housewives, Government Officials, Social Scientists, and Ministers. Some of the Commentators: Lillian Smith, James F. Byrnes, Harry Golden, Frederick Woltman, Harry Ashmore, Agnes Meyer, David Lawrence, Wilma Dykeman, Otto Klineberg, Herbert Ravenel Sass, Brook Hays, Virgil T. Blossom, James Jackson Kilpatrick, Colbert S. Cartwright, Fletcher Knebel, Relman Morin, Oscar Handlin, Kenneth B. Clark.

# SECTION 1

━━━━━━━━━━━━━━━━━━━━━━━━━━━━━━━━━━━━━━━━━━━━━━━━

# The Story of Little Rock:
# A Chronology of Events

# The Supreme Court's Opinion in the School Segregation Cases, May 17, 1954*

. . . THESE CASES [Brown v. Board of Education, Briggs v. Elliott, Davis v. County School Board, Gebhart v. Belton] come to us from the States of Kansas, South Carolina, Virginia, and Delaware. They are premised on different facts and different local conditions, but a common legal question justifies their consideration together in this consolidated opinion.

In each of the cases, minors of the Negro race, through their legal representatives, seek the aid of the courts in obtaining admission to the public schools of their community on a nonsegregated basis. In each instance, they have been denied admission to schools attended by white children under laws requiring or permitting segregation according to race. This segregation was alleged to deprive the plaintiffs of the equal protection of the laws under the Fourteenth Amendment. In each of the cases other than the Delaware case, a three-judge federal district court denied relief to the plaintiffs on the so-called "separate but equal" doctrine announced by this Court in Plessy v. Ferguson, 163 U.S. 537, 16 S.Ct. 1138, 41 L.Ed. 256. Under that doctrine, equality of treatment is accorded when the races are provided substantially equal facilities, even though these facilities be separate. In the Delaware case, the Supreme Court of Delaware adhered to that doctrine, but ordered that the plaintiffs be admitted to the white schools because of their superiority to the Negro schools.

The plaintiffs contend that segregated public schools are not "equal" and cannot be made "equal," and that hence they are deprived of the equal protection of the laws. Because of the obvious importance of the question presented, the Court took jurisdiction. Argument was heard in the 1952 Term, and reargument was heard this Term on certain questions propounded by the Court.

Reargument was largely devoted to the circumstances surrounding the adoption of the Fourteenth Amendment in 1868. It covered exhaustively consideration of the Amendment in Congress, ratification by the states, then existing practices in racial segregation, and the views of proponents and opponents of the Amendment. This discussion and our own investi-

---

* The unanimous opinion of the United States Supreme Court in *Brown v. Board of Education, et al.*, May 17, 1954, 347 U.S. 483. Reprinted from the *Race Relations Law Reporter*, February 1956, pp. 5-9. Footnotes and editorial contributions omitted with two exceptions.

gation convince us that, although these sources cast some light, it is not enough to resolve the problem with which we are faced. At best, they are inconclusive. The most avid proponents of the post-War Amendments undoubtedly intended them to remove all legal distinctions among "all persons born or naturalized in the United States." Their opponents, just as certainly, were antagonistic to both the letter and the spirit of the Amendments and wished them to have the most limited effect. What others in Congress and the state legislatures had in mind cannot be determined with any degree of certainty.

An additional reason for the inconclusive nature of the Amendment's history, with respect to segregated schools, is the status of public education at that time. In the South, the movement toward free common schools, supported by general taxation, had not yet taken hold. Education of white children was largely in the hands of private groups. Education of Negroes was almost nonexistent, and practically all of the race were illiterate. In fact, any education of Negroes was forbidden by law in some states. Today, in contrast, many Negroes have achieved outstanding success in the arts and sciences as well as in the business and professional world. It is true that public school education at the time of the Amendment had advanced further in the North, but the effect of the Amendment on Northern States was generally ignored in the congressional debates. Even in the North, the conditions of public education did not approximate those existing today. The curriculum was usually rudimentary; ungraded schools were common in rural areas; the school term was but three months a year in many states; and compulsory school attendance was virtually unknown. As a consequence, it is not surprising that there should be so little in the history of the Fourteenth Amendment relating to its intended effect on public education.

In the first cases in this Court construing the Fourteenth Amendment, decided shortly after its adoption, the Court interpreted it as proscribing all state-imposed discriminations against the Negro race. The doctrine of "separate but equal" did not make its appearance in this Court until 1896 in the case of Plessy v. Ferguson, supra, involving not education but transportation. American courts have since labored with the doctrine for over half a century. In this Court, there have been six cases involving the "separate but equal" doctrine in the field of public education. In Cumming v. Board of Education of Richmond County, 175 U.S. 528, 20 S.Ct. 197, 44 L.Ed. 262, and Gong Lum v. Rice, 275 U.S. 78, 48 S.Ct. 91, 72 L.Ed. 172, the validity of the doctrine itself was not challenged. In more recent cases, all on the graduate school level, inequality was found in that specific benefits enjoyed by white students were denied to Negro students of the same educational qualifications. State of Missouri ex rel. Gaines v. Canada, 305 U.S. 337, 59 S.Ct. 232, 83 L.Ed. 208; Sipuel v. Board of Regents of University of Oklahoma, 332 U.S. 631, 68 S.Ct. 299, 92 L.Ed. 247; Sweatt v. Painter, 339 U.S. 629, 70 S.Ct. 848, 94 L.Ed. 1114; McLaurin v. Oklahoma State Regents, 339 U.S. 637, 70 S.Ct. 851, 94 L.Ed. 1149. In none of these cases was it necessary to re-examine the doctrine to grant relief to the Negro plaintiff. And in Sweatt v. Painter, supra, the Court expressly reserved decision on the question whether Plessy v. Ferguson should be held inapplicable to public education.

In the instant cases, that question is directly presented. Here, unlike Sweatt v. Painter, there are findings below that the Negro and white schools involved have been equalized, or are being equalized, with respect to buildings, curricula, qualifications and salaries of teachers, and other "tangible" factors. Our decision, therefore, cannot turn on merely a comparison of these tangible factors in the Negro and white schools involved in each of the cases. We must look instead to the effect of segregation itself on public education.

In approaching this problem, we cannot turn the clock back to 1868 when the Amendment was adopted, or even to 1896 when Plessy v. Ferguson was written. We must consider public education in the light of its full development and its present place in American life throughout the Nation. Only in this way can it be determined if segregation in public schools deprives these plaintiffs of the equal protection of the laws.

Today, education is perhaps the most important function of state and local governments. Compulsory school attendance laws and the great expenditures for education both demonstrate our recognition of the importance of education to our democratic society. It is required in the performance of our most basic public responsibilities, even service in the armed forces. It is the very foundation of good citizenship. Today it is a principal instrument in awakening the child to cultural values, in preparing him for later professional training, and in helping him to adjust normally to his environment. In these days, it is doubtful that any child may reasonably be expected to succeed in life if he is denied the opportunity of an education. Such an opportunity, where the state has undertaken to provide it, is a right which must be made available to all on equal terms.

We come then to the question presented: Does segregation of children in public schools solely on the basis of race, even though the physical facilities and other "tangible" factors may be equal, deprive the children of the minority group of equal educational opportunities? We believe that it does.

In Sweatt v. Painter, supra [339 U.S. 629, 70 S.Ct. 850], in finding that a segregated law school for Negroes could not provide them equal educational opportunities, this Court relied in large part on "those qualities which are incapable of objective measurement but which make for greatness in a law school." In McLaurin v. Oklahoma State Regents, supra [339 U.S. 637, 70 S.Ct. 853], the Court, in requiring that a Negro admitted to a white graduate school be treated like all other students, again resorted to intangible considerations: "* * * his ability to study, to engage in discussions and exchange views with other students, and, in general, to learn his profession." Such considerations apply with added force to children in grade and high schools. To separate them from others of similar age and qualifications solely because of their race generates a feeling of inferiority as to their status in the community that may affect their hearts and minds in a way unlikely ever to be undone. The effect of this separation on their educational opportunities was well stated by a finding in the Kansas case by a court which nevertheless felt compelled to rule against the Negro plaintiffs:

> "Segregation of white and colored children in public schools has a detrimental effect upon the colored children. The impact is greater when it has the sanction of the law; for the policy of separating the races is usually interpreted as denoting the inferiority of the negro group. A sense of inferiority affects the motivation of the child to learn. Segregation with the sanction of law, therefore, has a tendency to [retard] the educational and mental development of Negro children and to deprive them of some of the benefits they would receive in a racial[ly] integrated school system."

Whatever may have been the extent of psychological knowledge at the time of Plessy v. Ferguson, this finding is amply supported by modern authority.* Any language in Plessy v. Ferguson contrary to this finding is rejected.

[Here, and on the next page, because they may be especially useful, two footnotes are included despite the general policy of omitting them.]

* K. B. Clark, Effect of Prejudice and Discrimination on Personality Development (Midcentury White House Conference on Children and Youth, 1950); Witmer and Kotinsky, Personality in the Making (1952), c. VI; Deutscher and Chein, The Psychological Effects of Enforced Segregation: A Survey of Social Science Opinion, 26 J. Psychol. 259 (1958); Chein, What are the Psychological Effects of Segregation Under Conditions of Equal Facilities?, 3 Int. J. Opinion and Attitude Res. 229 (1949); Brameld, Educational Costs, in Discrimination and National Welfare (MacIver, ed., 1949), 44–48; Frazier, The Negro in the United States (1949), 674–681. And see generally Myrdal, An American Dilemma (1944).

We conclude that in the field of public education the doctrine of "separate but equal" has no place. Separate educational facilities are inherently unequal. Therefore, we hold that the plaintiffs and others similarly situated for whom the actions have been brought are, by reason of the segregation complained of, deprived of the equal protection of the laws guaranteed by the Fourteenth Amendment. This disposition makes unnecessary any discussion whether such segregation also violates the Due Process Clause of the Fourteenth Amendment.

Because these are class actions, because of the wide applicability of this decision, and because of the great variety of local conditions, the formulation of decrees in these cases presents problems of considerable complexity. On reargument, the consideration of appropriate relief was necessarily subordinated to the primary question—the constitutionality of segregation in public education. We have now announced that such segregation is a denial of the equal protection of the laws. In order that we may have the full assistance of the parties in formulating decrees, the cases will be restored to the docket, and the parties are requested to present further argument on Questions 4 and 5* previously propounded by the Court for the reargument this Term. The Attorney General of the United States is again invited to participate. The Attorneys General of the states requiring or permitting segregation in public education will also be permitted to appear as *amici curiae* upon request to do so by September 15, 1954, and submission of briefs by October 1, 1954.

It is so ordered.

---

* "4. Assuming it is decided that segregation in public schools violates the Fourteenth Amendment.

"(*a*) would a decree necessarily follow providing that, within the limits set by normal geographic school districting, Negro children should forthwith be admitted to schools of their choice, or

"(*b*) may this Court, in the exercise of its equity powers, permit an effective gradual adjustment to be brought about from existing segregated systems to a system not based on color distinctions?

"5. On the assumption on which questions 4(*a*) and (*b*) are based, and assuming further that this Court will exercise its equity powers to the end described in question 4(*b*),

"(*a*) should this Court formulate detailed decrees in these cases;

"(*b*) if so, what specific issues should the decree reach;

"(*c*) should this Court appoint a special master to hear evidence with a view to recommending specific terms for such decrees;

"(*d*) should this Court remand to the courts of first instance with directions to frame decrees in these cases, and if so what general directions should the decrees of this Court include and what procedures should the courts of first instance follow in arriving at the specific terms of more detailed decrees?"

DOCUMENTATION SUITABLE FOR RESEARCH PAPERS

BIBLIOGRAPHY ENTRY

Brown v. Board of Education, et al., 347 U.S. 483 (1954). Excerpts reprinted from *Race Relations Law Reporter* in *Little Rock, U.S.A.*, ed. Wilson Record and Jane Cassels Record. San Francisco, 1960.

FIRST FOOTNOTE

*Brown v. Board of Education, et al.*, 347 U.S. 483 (1954), as reprinted from *Race Relations Law Reporter* in *Little Rock, U.S.A.*, ed. Wilson Record and Jane Cassels Record (San Francisco, 1960), pp. 2-6.

SUBSEQUENT FOOTNOTE

*Brown v. Board of Education, LRUSA*, p. ▉.

In the subsequent-footnote example this collection of Materials for Analysis is identified briefly as *LRUSA*. In such a position, following a first footnote that presents full information, the short form is self-explaining.

The same short form may be used in bibliography entries and in first footnotes if the bibliography contains appropriate explanation made by an entry in this form:

LRUSA. Short reference form for Record, Wilson, and Jane Cassels Record, eds., *Little Rock, U.S.A.*, which see herein at Record, etc.

The model documentation on p. 11 shows this short form in use.

## The Supreme Court's Supplementary Ruling in the School Segregation Cases, May 12, 1955*

THESE CASES were decided on May 17, 1954. The opinions of that date declaring the fundamental principle that racial discrimination in public education is unconstitutional, are incorporated herein by reference. All provisions of federal, state, or local law requiring or permitting such dis-

* The unanimous opinion of the United States Supreme Court in the supplementary ruling of 1955 (*Brown v. Board of Education, et al.*, May 31, 1955, 349 U.S. 294). Reprinted from the *Race Relations Law Reporter*, February 1956, pp. 11-12. Footnotes omitted.

crimination must yield to this principle. There remains for consideration the manner in which relief is to be accorded.

Because these cases arose under different local conditions and their disposition will involve a variety of local problems, we requested further argument on the question of relief. In view of the nationwide importance of the decision, we invited the Attorney General of the United States and the Attorneys General of all states requiring or permitting racial discrimination in public education to present their views on that question. The parties, the United States, and the States of Florida, North Carolina, Arkansas, Oklahoma, Maryland, and Texas filed briefs and participated in the oral argument.

These presentations were informative and helpful to the Court in its consideration of the complexities arising from the transition to a system of public education freed of racial discrimination. The presentations also demonstrated that substantial steps to eliminate racial discrimination in public schools have already been taken, not only in some of the communities in which these cases arose, but in some of the states appearing as *amici curiae,* and in other states as well. Substantial progress has been made in the District of Columbia and in the communities in Kansas and Delaware involved in this litigation. The defendants in the cases coming to us from South Carolina and Virginia are awaiting the decision of this Court concerning relief.

Full implementation of these constitutional principles may require solution of varied local school problems. School authorities have the primary responsibility for elucidating, assessing, and solving these problems; courts will have to consider whether the action of school authorities constitutes good faith implementation of the governing constitutional principles. Because of their proximity to local conditions and the possible need for further hearings the courts which originally heard these cases can best perform this judicial appraisal. Accordingly, we believe it appropriate to remand the cases to those courts.

In fashioning and effectuating the decrees, the courts will be guided by equitable principles. Traditionally, equity has been characterized by a practical flexibility in shaping its remedies and by a facility for adjusting and reconciling public and private needs. These cases call for the exercise of these traditional attributes of equity power. At stake is the personal interest of the plaintiffs in admission to public schools as soon as practicable on a nondiscriminatory basis. To effectuate this interest may call for elimination of a variety of obstacles in making the transition to school systems operated in accordance with the constitutional principles set forth in our

May 17, 1954, decision. Courts of equity may properly take into account the public interest in the elimination of such obstacles in a systematic and effective manner. But it should go without saying that the vitality of these constitutional principles cannot be allowed to yield simply because of disagreement with them.

While giving weight to these public and private considerations, the courts will require that the defendants make a prompt and reasonable start toward full compliance with our May 17, 1954, ruling. Once such a start has been made, the courts may find that additional time is necessary to carry out the ruling in an effective manner. The burden rests upon the defendants to establish that such time is necessary in the public interest and is consistent with good faith compliance at the earliest practicable date. To that end, the courts may consider problems related to administration, arising from the physical condition of the school plant, the school transportation system, personnel, revision of school districts and attendance areas into compact units to achieve a system of determining admission to the public schools on a nonracial basis, and revision of local laws and regulations which may be necessary in solving the foregoing problems. They will also consider the adequacy of any plans the defendants may propose to meet these problems and to effectuate a transition to a racially nondiscriminatory school system. During this period of transition, the courts will retain jurisdiction of these cases.

The judgments below, except that in the Delaware case, are accordingly reversed and the cases are remanded to the District Courts to take such proceedings and enter such orders and decrees consistent with this opinion as are necessary and proper to admit to public schools on a racially nondiscriminatory basis with all deliberate speed the parties to these cases. The judgment in the Delaware case—ordering the immediate admission of the plaintiffs to schools previously attended only by white children—is affirmed on the basis of the principles stated in our May 17, 1954, opinion, but the case is remanded to the Supreme Court of Delaware for such further proceedings as that Court may deem necessary in light of this opinion.

It is so ordered.

### DOCUMENTATION SUITABLE FOR RESEARCH PAPERS

BIBLIOGRAPHY ENTRY

*Brown v. Board of Education, et al.,* 349 U.S. 294 (1955). Excerpts reprinted from *Race Relations Law Reporter* in *Little Rock, U.S.A.,* ed. Wilson Record and Jane Cassels Record. San Francisco, 1960.

FIRST FOOTNOTE

*Brown v. Board of Education, et al.*, 349 U.S. 294 (1955), as reprinted from *Race Relations Law Reporter* in *Little Rock, U.S.A.*, ed. Wilson Record and Jane Cassels Record (San Francisco, 1960), pp. 7-9.

SUBSEQUENT FOOTNOTE

*Brown v. Board of Education, LRUSA*, p. ▮.

---

## The NAACP Program for Promoting School Desegregation, June 1955*

. . . FOR OUR PART, we must be prepared to meet the challenge in a forthright manner. Our branches must seek to determine in each community whether the school board is prepared to make a prompt and reasonable start towards integration of the public schools and whether it will proceed with good faith towards full compliance with the May 31 decision at the earliest practicable date. Promises unaccompanied by concrete action are meaningless; nor can there be concern with the attitudes of individuals towards a change in the school system. Segregated schools are illegal, and the Court is merely allowing school boards time to get their houses in order. It does not allow time to procrastinate, stall or evade. It is the job of our branches to see to it that each school board begins to deal with the problem of providing non-discriminatory education. To that end we suggest that each of our branches take the following steps:

1. File at once a petition with each school board, calling attention to the May 31 decision, requesting that the school board act in accordance with that decision and offering the services of the branch to help the board in solving this problem.

2. Follow up the petition with periodic inquiries of the board seeking to determine what steps it is making to comply with the Supreme Court decision.

3. All during June, July, August and September, and thereafter, through meetings, forums, debates, conferences, etc., use every opportunity to explain what the May 31 decision means, and be sure to emphasize that the ultimate determination as to the length of time it will take for desegregation to become a fact in the community is not in the hands of the

---

* From "A Directive to the Branches," adopted by an Emergency Southwide NAACP Conference in Atlanta, June 4, 1955. NAACP Pamphlet, 1955, pp. 14-16.

politicians or the school board officials but in the hands of the federal courts.

4. Organize the parents in the community so that as many as possible will be familiar with the procedure when and if law suits are begun in behalf of plaintiffs and parents.

5. Seek the support of individuals and community groups, particularly in the white community, through churches, labor organizations, civic organizations and personal contact.

6. When announcement is made of the plans adopted by your school board, get the exact text of the school board's pronouncements and notify the State Conference and the National Office at once so that you will have the benefit of their views as to whether the plan is one which will provide for effective desegregation. It is very important that branches not proceed at this stage without consultation with State and National offices.

7. If no plans are announced or no steps towards desegregation taken by the time school begins this fall, 1955, the time for a law suit has arrived. At this stage court action is essential because only in this way does the mandate of the Supreme Court that a prompt and reasonable start towards full compliance become fully operative on the school boards in question.

8. At this stage the matter will be turned over to the Legal Department and it will proceed with the matter in court. . . .

## DOCUMENTATION SUITABLE FOR A RESEARCH PAPER

BIBLIOGRAPHY ENTRY

*Directive to the Branches.* Adopted June 4, 1955, by an Emergency Southwide NAACP Conference in Atlanta, Georgia. NAACP Pamphlet, 1955, pp. 14-16. Reprinted in part in *LRUSA.*

FIRST FOOTNOTE

*\*Directive to the Branches,* adopted June 4, 1955, by an Emergency Southwide NAACP Conference in Atlanta, Georgia, as reprinted in *LRUSA,* pp. 10-11.

SUBSEQUENT FOOTNOTE

*\*Directive, LRUSA,* p. ▓.

The bibliography entry and first footnote above have the abbreviation *LRUSA,* explained on page 7 of this book. If the abbreviation is not used, the full form should be used as in the example on page 7.

## The Attitude of the Little Rock NAACP, February 1956*

". . . OUR objective is to secure the prompt and orderly end of segregation in the public schools. We want all children, regardless of race, to have the opportunity to go to the public schools nearest their homes. We seek an end to the hazards, inconveniences and discrimination of a system which now requires little children to pass each day several schools from which they are barred because of race and to travel nearly 10 miles to racially designated schools. . . .

"We are unwilling to connive by continued silence at such blows against the welfare of our young people, and so we have entered this suit.

"The school board has announced what it calls a "three-phase" plan for desegregation. It has, however, given no fixed dates for integration at any level and not even the vaguest target dates for integration at the elementary and junior high level. Meanwhile, it proposes to allow young children to endure indefinitely unnecessary hazards of needless daily travel. Its policy continues to exclude Negro boys from the training necessary for many important trades in technical fields. School authorities have refused relief even on these points and have thus driven us to ask the courts for needed relief for the children now in school."

### DOCUMENTATION SUITABLE FOR RESEARCH PAPERS

BIBLIOGRAPHY ENTRY

    *Arkansas Democrat,* Feb. 8, 1956, p. 1. Interview with J. C. Crenchaw. Excerpt in *LRUSA.*

FIRST FOOTNOTE

    *\*Arkansas Democrat,* Feb. 8, 1956, p. 1, interview with J. C. Crenchaw, excerpt in *LRUSA,* p. 12.

SUBSEQUENT FOOTNOTE

    *Crenchaw interview, LRUSA, p. ■.

The clipping containing this interview was supplied to the editors of this collection without its heading, hence this unusual organization of the documentation details.

---

* From a statement by the president of the Little Rock NAACP, the Rev. J. C. Crenchaw, February 8, 1956, as reported in the *Arkansas Democrat,* February 8, 1956, p. 1. An account of the suit and the school board's plan follows on pp. 19-26.

## The Southern Manifesto, March 12, 1956*

THE UNWARRANTED decision of the Supreme Court in the public school cases is now bearing the fruit always produced when men substitute naked power for established law.

The founding fathers gave us a constitution of checks and balances because they realized the inescapable lesson of history that no man or group of men can be safely entrusted with unlimited power. They framed this constitution with its provisions for change by amendment in order to secure the fundamentals of government against the dangers of temporary popular passion or the personal predilections of public office holders.

We regard the decision of the Supreme Court in the school cases as a clear abuse of judicial power. It climaxes a trend in the federal judiciary undertaking to legislate, in derogation of the authority of Congress, and to encroach upon the reserved rights of the states and the people.

The original Constitution does not mention education. Neither does the Fourteenth Amendment nor any other amendment. The debates preceding the submission of the Fourteenth Amendment clearly show that there was no intent that it should affect the systems of education maintained by the states.

The very Congress which proposed the amendment subsequently provided for segregated schools in the District of Columbia.

When the amendment was adopted in 1868, there were 37 states of the union. Every one of the 26 states that had any substantial racial differences among its people either approved the operation of segregated schools already in existence or subsequently established such schools by action of the same law-making body which considered the Fourteenth Amendment.

As admitted by the Supreme Court in the public school case (*Brown v. Board of Education*), the doctrine of separate but equal schools "apparently originated in *Roberts v. City of Boston* . . . (1849), upholding school segregation against attack as being violative of a state constitutional guarantee of equality." This constitutional doctrine began in the North—not in the South, and it was followed not only in Massachusetts, but in Connecticut, New York, Illinois, Indiana, Michigan, Minnesota, New Jersey, Ohio, Pennsylvania and other northern states until they, exercising

---

* Signed by 19 senators and 82 house members from 11 Southern states and issued March 12, 1956. Reprinted from *Southern School News,* April, 1956, p. 2.

their rights as states through the constitutional processes of local self-government, changed their school systems.

In the case of *Plessy v. Ferguson* in 1896 the Supreme Court expressly declared that under the Fourteenth Amendment no person was denied any of his rights if the states provided separate but equal public facilities. This decision has been followed in many other cases. It is notable that the Supreme Court, speaking through Chief Justice Taft, a former president of the United States, unanimously declared in 1927 in *Lum v. Rice* that the "separate but equal" principle is ". . . within the discretion of the state in regulating its public schools and does not conflict with the Fourteenth Amendment."

This interpretation, restated time and again, became a part of the life of the people of many of the states and confirmed their habits, customs, tradition and way of life. It is founded on elemental humanity and common sense, for parents should not be deprived by government of the right to direct the lives and education of their own children.

Though there has been no constitutional amendment or act of Congress changing this established legal principle almost a century old, the Supreme Court of the United States, with no legal basis for such action, undertook to exercise their naked judicial power and substituted their personal political and social ideas for the established law of the land.

This unwarranted exercise of power by the court, contrary to the Constitution, is creating chaos and confusion in the states principally affected. It is destroying the amicable relations between the white and Negro races that have been created through 90 years of patient effort by the good people of both races. It has planted hatred and suspicion where there has been heretofore friendship and understanding.

Without regard to the consent of the governed, outside agitators are threatening immediate and revolutionary changes in our public school systems. If done, this is certain to destroy the system of public education in some of the states.

With the gravest concern for the explosive and dangerous condition created by this decision and inflamed by outside meddlers:

We reaffirm our reliance on the Constitution as the fundamental law of the land.

We decry the Supreme Court's encroachments on rights reserved to the states and to the people, contrary to established law and to the Constitution.

We commend the motives of those states which have declared the intention to resist forced integration by any lawful means.

We appeal to the states and people who are not directly affected by these decisions to consider the constitutional principles involved against the time when they too, on issues vital to them, may be the victims of judicial encroachment.

Even though we constitute a minority in the present Congress, we have full faith that a majority of the American people believe in the dual system of government which has enabled us to achieve our greatness and will in time demand that the reserved rights of the states and of the people be made secure against judicial usurpation.

We pledge ourselves to use all lawful means to bring about a reversal of this decision which is contrary to the Constitution and to prevent the use of force in its implementation.

In this trying period, as we all seek to right this wrong, we appeal to our people not to be provoked by the agitators and troublemakers invading our states and to scrupulously refrain from disorder and lawless acts.

### DOCUMENTATION SUITABLE FOR RESEARCH PAPERS

BIBLIOGRAPHY ENTRY

"Southern Manifesto, March 12, 1956." Reprinted from *Southern School News,* April 1956, p. 2, in *LRUSA.*

FIRST FOOTNOTE

*"Southern Manifesto, March 12, 1956," reprinted from *Southern School News,* April 1956, p. 2, in *LRUSA,* pp. 13-15.

SUBSEQUENT FOOTNOTE

*"Southern Manifesto," *LRUSA,* p. ▩.

In place of *Southern School News,* the abbreviation *SSN* may be acceptable in the above examples.

These examples are models for other material from *Southern School News* in this collection.

## Segregationist Rally, March 20, 1956*

AT A segregation rally March 20 in the Jacksonville High School gymnasium near Little Rock, a White America leader, Amis Guthridge of Little

* *Southern School News,* April 1956, p. 8. Items from *Southern School News* are hereinafter identified by the initials *SSN* and the date, in brackets at the end.

Rock, said progress in the movement to maintain segregation had been such that he was confident the opponents of integration have the support of the state's public officials.

"We are not going to have trouble with public office holders, now that they know what we want," he said.

At previous segregation rallies, Gov. Faubus had been strongly criticized and there were indications that the anti-integration groups would offer a candidate for governor this summer. Faubus is expected to seek another term. . . . [*SSN* April 1956, p. 8]

## DOCUMENTATION SUITABLE FOR RESEARCH PAPERS

BIBLIOGRAPHY ENTRY

"Segregationist Rally, March 20, 1956." Reprinted from *SSN*, April 1956, p. 8, in *LRUSA*.

FIRST FOOTNOTE

\*"Segregationist Rally, March 20, 1956," reprinted from *SSN* April 1956, p. 8, in *LRUSA*, pp. 15-16.

SUBSEQUENT FOOTNOTE

\*"Segregationist Rally," *LRUSA*, p. ■.

These examples are models for other material from *SSN* in this collection.

---

## Governor Faubus's Statement, March 22, 1956

ON March 22, Gov. Faubus announced that a five-man committee, which had studied, with his blessing, Virginia's efforts to avoid or delay integration, had decided to initiate two acts (interposition and pupil assignment). . . .

"Integration is a local problem and can best be solved on the local level according to the peculiar circumstances and conditions of each local school district.

"The people of the state are overwhelmingly opposed to any effort to bring about sudden and complete integration."

. . . "Time is needed, in fact is absolutely necessary, to allow the citizens to cope with the most difficult problem that has faced the people of the state in many years. . . .

"I ask the cooperation of all the people," he said, "in upholding law and order and in preserving the peace and harmony that has prevailed." [*SSN* April 1956, p. 8]

## Resolution of Methodist Women's Society, March 22, 1956

ON March 22 at Malvern a resolution on integration was adopted at the annual meeting of the Woman's Society of Christian Service of the Little Rock Methodist Conference. It read:

"We recommend to this body that it call upon the governor of our state to appoint a committee made up of Christian citizens of integrity of both races to study and make recommendations that would guide the people of our state in lessening racial tensions in many areas of our common life, including desegregation of the public schools." [*SSN* April 1956, p. 8]

## Other Church Activity, April 1956

ON APRIL 19 at Rogers [Arkansas], the state Disciples of Christ (Christian Church) adopted a resolution urging all citizens to "exert their efforts toward orderly compliance" with the Supreme Court ruling against school segregation. The resolution urged candidates for public office "not to center their campaign for election upon issues which divide one race from the other and tend to fan flames of fear and hatred, but to discuss the vital issues confronting all citizens regardless of race."

On April 21, the official board of the First Methodist Church of England [Arkansas] announced it had adopted a resolution opposing desegregation and taking issue with Methodist groups which have gone on record as opposing segregation. . . .

The Greater Little Rock Ministerial Alliance, composed of white ministers, approved April 23 a proposal to merge with its Negro counterpart, the Interdenominational Ministerial Alliance of Greater Little Rock.

The Negro group had approved the plan April 9. The merger, which would unite 60 white and 30 Negro ministers, will become effective if both

For model documentation see page 15 or page 16.

groups approve a proposed constitution at meetings in June. [*SSN* May 1956, pp. 10-11]

## Bus Desegregation, April 25, 1956

OFFICIALS of the Citizens Coach Co., operator of the bus system at Little Rock and North Little Rock, announced April 25 that in view of the Supreme Court decision, enforced segregation of passengers would end immediately. The mayors of both cities said the police would "pay no attention" to mixed white and Negro seating. [*SSN* May 1956, p. 11]

## Baptist Action, June 27, 1956

A RESOLUTION opposing racial integration in the South was adopted June 27 at Little Rock by about 3,000 delegates to the annual convention of the American Baptist Association, which represents 3,000 churches in 24 states, mostly in the South. There was only one nay vote.

The resolution, drawn by Rev. L. D. Foreman, pastor of Antioch Baptist Church at Little Rock, said integration was both ungodly and unlawful.

It also said that a great segment of the Negroes in the South did not want integration. . . . [*SSN* August 1956, p. 3. This group is not to be confused with the Southern Baptist Convention, which has 30,000 churches and more than 8,000,000 members.]

## Negro Resolution, July 4, 1956

ON July 4 at Little Rock, about 30 Negroes attending a state meeting sponsored by the Interdenominational Ministerial Alliance of Greater Little Rock, a Negro group, adopted a resolution which:

1) Expressed confidence in the integrity of the decisions of the Supreme Court and said, "We view with alarm the attacks on this, the highest court in the land, and deem such attacks as un-American and a suggestion of subversiveness as well as conducive to destruction of law and order . . . the companions of communism and communistic thinking. . . .

Rev. Edgar N. French, a leader in the Montgomery, Ala., boycott, spoke at the meeting. He said a "brand new Negro has risen in the South, and the Negro is not satisfied." He called for passive resistance to segregation, warning against violence. "We're not afraid any more," he said. "We must not hate." [*SSN* August 1956, p. 3]

## Gubernatorial Campaign, July 1956

THE THREE major candidates for governor in the Arkansas Democratic primary hammered on racial segregation as one of the major campaign issues during July. . . .

[Former State Senator Jim] Johnson accused Faubus of "pussy-footing" on the integration question and said Faubus had waited for sentiment to develop before taking a stand on the issue. . . .

On July 9 at Pine Bluff, Faubus said that segregation was a minor issue because all of the candidates agreed on the subject. Some of the audience booed, but the booing turned to cheers when Faubus quickly added that there would be no breakdown of the state's traditional segregation pattern. . . . [*SSN* August 1956, p. 3]

## Statements by Arkansas Senator and National School Leader, August 1956

ON Aug. 20, in a speech before the Northwest Arkansas Dental Society Convention at Fort Smith, Sen. John L. McClellan, (D., Ark.) assailed the Supreme Court as "nine men lacking in judicial capacity."

The greatest danger facing the United States today, McClellan said, "is a Supreme Court that departs from the fundamentals of law and imposes personal opinions on interpretations of the law."

On Aug. 1, in an interview at Little Rock, Dr. Paul Misner of Glencoe, Ill., president of the American Association of School Administrators, said that local communities should have the autonomy to decide the racial segregation issue in their public schools.

He said that his organization had adopted a policy that education "is a matter of local responsibility and control." [*SSN* September 1956, p. 15]

## The Federal District Court's August 1956 Decision in the Little Rock School Case*

. . . THERE is no dispute between the parties as to the facts. They are as follows:

---

For model documentation see page 15 or page 16.

---

\* *Aaron v. Cooper*, August 28, 1956, Civ. No. 3113, U.S. Dist. Ct. E. Ark. Excerpts reprinted from the *Race Relations Law Reporter*, October 1956, pp. 853-

(1) The adult petitioners and minor plaintiffs are each citizens and residents of the City of Little Rock, Pulaski County, Arkansas, and are each members of the Negro race. The defendants are the Little Rock School District, its Board of Directors and its Superintendent. This is a class action by plaintiffs seeking integration of public schools in the Little Rock School District.

(2) The Little Rock School District contains 32.9 square miles. It was created in 1870 and since its inception the various schools in the District have been operated on a segregated basis.

On May 20, 1954 (three days after the Supreme Court rendered its decision in Brown v. Board of Education, 347 U.S. 483) the Little Rock School Board adopted a statement concerning "SUPREME COURT DE-CISION—SEGREGATION IN PUBLIC SCHOOLS." This statement was released for publication on May 23, 1954, and, inter alia, it provided:

". . . Until the Supreme Court of the United States makes its decision of May 17, 1954 more specific, Little Rock School District will continue with its present program.

"It is our responsibility to comply with Federal Constitutional Requirements and we intend to do so when the Supreme Court of the United States outlines the method to be followed.

"During this interim period we shall do the following:

1. Develop school attendance areas consistent with the location of white and colored pupils with respect to present and future physical facilities in Little Rock School District.
2. Make the necessary revisions in all types of pupil records in order that the transition to an integrated school system may serve the best interests of the entire school district.
3. Make research studies needed for the implementation of a sound school program on an integrated basis. * * *"

(3) The School Board instructed the Superintendent, the defendant, Virgil Blossom, to prepare a plan for the integration of the schools in the Little Rock School District. Such a plan was prepared and approved by the Board on May 24, 1955 (seven days prior to the supplemental opinion of the Supreme Court in Brown v. Board of Education, 349 U.S. 294). The plan is as follows:

---

860. The action was brought by Mrs. Aaron and others against Mr. Cooper and the other members of the Little Rock School Board, hence the designation *Aaron v. Cooper.* Further litigation in the Little Rock school cases is compiled and indexed under this heading in legal records.

### "LITTLE ROCK BOARD OF EDUCATION
### "PLAN OF SCHOOL INTEGRATION—
### LITTLE ROCK SCHOOL DISTRICT

"The Supreme Court decision of May 17, 1954, which declared segregated schools unconstitutional has placed before us the most difficult educational problem of our time. A careful analysis of the following has been made.

1. Financial ability of Little Rock School District to integrate its schools.
2. Adequacy of present school facilities plus those to be added from $4,000,000.00 bond issue of March, 1953, plus the amount of money to be realized from the sale of the *'old Peabody School Site'* on West Capitol Ave.
3. Proper time and method for the integration of the schools of Little Rock School District *in a manner consistent with the law as finally interpreted by the Supreme Court and acceptable to both races.*

"Our review of the three questions raised, reveal the following facts and opinions.

1. Integration of its schools by Little Rock School District will probably place *no serious additional* financial burden on the School District.
2. The facilities of Little Rock School District will be inadequate at the junior and senior high school levels until such time as the three senior high schools and six junior high schools are ready for occupancy.
3. It is our opinion that the proper time for, and method of integration is as follows:

A. *Time of Integration*

Integration of schools in Little Rock School District *cannot be accomplished until completion of the needed school facilities* (three senior high schools and six junior high schools) *and specific decrees have been formulated by the U.S. Supreme Court in the pending cases.*

B. *Method of Integration*

The method of changing from segregated to integrated schools should not be attempted simultaneously in grades one to twelve. Due to the complexity of this problem, an orderly systematically planned process should be followed.

In Little Rock School District our research and study causes us to believe that the following plan charts the best course for all concerned.

1. In our opinion integration should begin at the senior high school level. (Grades 10-12) *(First phase of program)*

2. Following successful integration at the senior high school level, it should then be started in the junior high schools. (Grades 7-9) *(Second phase of program)*

3. After successful integration in junior and senior high schools it should be started in elementary schools. (Grades 1-6) *(Third phase of program)*

*(Present indications are that the school year 1957-58 may be the first phase of this program.)*

"The Board of Education's reasons for the adoption of this plan of integration are as follows:

1. Since our school system has been segregated from its beginning until the present time, the time required in the process as outlined should not be construed as unnecessary delay, but that which is justly needed with respect to the size and complexity of the job at hand.

2. It is ill advised to begin this process with inadequate facilities.

3. It is unwise to begin integration until the Supreme Court gives direction through its interpretation of the specific cases before it.

4. By starting integration at the senior high school level the process will begin where fewer teachers and students are involved.

5. In the adoption of a plan of integration ((1) senior high school (2) junior high school (3) elementary schools) of sequential order, we provide the opportunity to benefit from our own experience as we move through each phase of this plan, thus avoiding as many mistakes as possible.

6. The establishment of attendance areas at the elementary level (Grades 1-6) is most difficult due to the large number of both students and buildings involved. Because of this fact it should be the last step in the process.

"We sincerely solicit your understanding and cooperation in the implementation of this plan in order that the interests of all children may be better served.

## LITTLE ROCK BOARD OF EDUCATION

William G. Cooper, Jr., President
Mrs. A. E. McLean, Vice President
Mrs. Edgar Dixon, Secretary
Dr. Edwin N. Barron
Foster A. Vineyard
R. A. Lile"

(4) Since the adoption of the plan, Mr. Blossom has read and explained the plan to approximately 125 to 150 groups in an effort to obtain public acceptance of its provisions and the resulting orderly integration of the schools.

Foremost among the problems of the Little Rock District are those of finances, structural organization, enrollment, and the selection and training of an adequate staff. These problems are not new, but they will be greatly accentuated by integration. By its plan the School Board is seeking to integrate its schools and at the same time maintain or improve the quality of education available at these schools. Some of its objectives are to provide the best possible education that is economically feasible, to consider each child in the light of his individual ability and achievement, to foster sound promotion policies, to provide necessary flexibility in the school curriculum from one attendance area to another, to select, procure, and train an adequate school staff, to provide necessary in-service training for the school staff, to provide a necessary educational program for deviates (mentally retarded, physically handicapped, speech correction, etc.), to provide the opportunity for children to attend school in the attendance area where they reside, to foster sound administrative practices, to maintain extracurricular activities, to attempt to provide information necessary for public understanding, acceptance, and support, and to provide a "teachable" group of children for each teacher. With regard to the latter objective, it is the policy of the Board to group children with enough homogeneity for efficient planning and classroom management.

(5) As of May, 1956, the number of Negro students in the Little Rock School District was as follows: Grades 1-6, 3,303; Grades 7-9, 1,252; Grades 10-12, 929; or a total of 5,484.

The number of white students on the same date was as follows: Grades 1-6, 9,285; Grades 7-9, 3,831; Grades 10-12, 3,126; or a total of 16,242.

The Negro students had 118 teachers for grades 1-6; 42 teachers for grades 7-9; and 25 teachers for grades 10-12.

The white students had 294 teachers for grades 1-6; 145 teachers for grades 7-9; and 108 teachers for grades 10-12.

The pupil-teacher ratio for all students was approximately 26-1 in senior high and junior high, and 30-1 in grade school.

At the present time there are three high schools in the District. Central High School was built in 1926, is presently an all-white school, and will accommodate 2,500 to 2,600 students. Technical High School was built in 1944, is now an all-white school, and will accommodate 225 to 250 students. Horace Mann High School was built in 1956, is now an all-Negro school, and will accommodate 925 students. Construction has begun on the West End High School, which will accommodate 925 students and which should be completed about July 15, 1957.

The School Board intends to start integration at the high school level (grades 10-12) in the fall of 1957. In accord with this plan the Board has completely reorganized its attendance areas. At present Central and Technical High Schools have a city-wide attendance area for white students, and Horace Mann High School has a city-wide attendance area for Negro students. Under the new plan Technical High School would remain a city-wide school for all students, but Central and Horace Mann High Schools, together with the new West End High School, would each have separate attendance areas. At this time there are no Negro students residing in the West End High School attendance area, but there are both Negro and white students residing in the Central and Horace Mann High School districts.

There are now six junior high schools in the District, and another one will be needed in the near future.

(6) In preparing for integration school authorities have taken a number of steps, including the establishment of attendance areas, study of aptitudes of the children, starting of the in-service program for staff members, new promotion policies, program of information to members of the community, harmonizing student records, continuation of building program, administrative studies, and work on the guidance program.

(7) As stated in the plan and established by the evidence, the Board intends to start integration in the fall of 1957 at the high school level. The reason for starting at the high school level is that fewer students, teachers, buildings, etc., will be involved. The school authorities hope to be able to learn by experience and to be better able to enter the next phase of the plan.

The second phase of the integration plan would start two or three years after the first phase, i.e., in 1959 or 1960, and would include grades 7-9 (junior high).

The final phase of the plan would start two or three years after the start of the second phase, and would include grades 1-6. In other words, complete integration would be effected not later than 1963.

(8) The Superintendent, Mr. Blossom, along with all the other defendants and the staff of the defendant district, has worked diligently in a good faith effort to prepare and to effectuate a plan of integration that will be to the best interest of all parties and to the public.

Mr. Blossom is a highly qualified and experienced school administrator and has given much thought and study to the myriad problems relating to integration. He has had the cooperation of the Little Rock School Board in his effort to achieve integration without lowering the quality of education offered to all the school children. . . .

In the case of Briggs et al. v. Elliott, one of the original cases before the Supreme Court, the three-judge court sitting in the Eastern District of South Carolina, upon a remand of the case, said: (132 F. Supp. 776) [of the Supreme Court and its decision]

> "It has not decided that the federal courts are to take over or regulate the public schools of the states. It has not decided that the states must mix persons of different races in the schools, or must require them to attend schools or must deprive them of the right of choosing the schools they attend. What it has decided, and all that it has decided, is that a state may not deny to any person on account of race the right to attend any school that it maintains. This, under the decision of the Supreme Court, the state may not do directly or indirectly; but if the schools which it maintains are open to children of all races, no violation of the Constitution is involved even though the children of different races voluntarily attend different schools, as they attend different churches. Nothing in the Constitution or in the decision of the Supreme Court takes away from the people freedom to choose the schools they attend. The Constitution in other words does not require integration. It merely forbids discrimination. It does not forbid such segregation as occurs as the result of voluntary action. It merely forbids the use of governmental power to enforce segregation. The Fourteenth Amendment is a limitation upon the exercise of power by the state or state agencies, not a limitation upon the freedom of individuals.
>
> "The Supreme Court has pointed out that the solution of

the problem in accord with its decision is a primary responsibility of school authorities and that the function of the courts is to determine whether action of the school authorities constitutes 'good faith implementation of the governing constitutional principles.' "

.    .    .    .    .    .    .    .    .    .

Learned counsel for plaintiffs earnestly contended in their oral argument that the defendants had not made a prompt and reasonable start toward full compliance with the May 17, 1954, decision of the Supreme Court; that additional time should not be allowed the Board of Directors until and unless a reasonable start toward full compliance had been made, and that in this instance such a start had not been made by the defendants. . . .

The testimony of the defendant Superintendent of Schools, Mr. Virgil Blossom, is convincing that not only he but the other defendants have acted in the utmost good faith. . . .

This court is of the opinion that it should not substitute its own judgment for that of the defendants. The plan which has been adopted after thorough and conscientious consideration of the many questions involved is a plan that will lead to an effective and gradual adjustment of the problem, and ultimately bring about a school system not based on color distinctions.

IT IS ORDERED AND ADJUDGED that the plan of school integration of the Little Rock School District officially adopted by the Board of Directors on May 24, 1955, be and same hereby is in all things approved, and that the prayer of the complaint of the plaintiffs for a declaratory judgment and for injunctive relief be and is denied.

IT IS FURTHER ORDERED AND ADJUDGED that jurisdiction of this case be and is retained for the purpose of entering such other and further orders as may be necessary to obtain the effectuation of the plan as therein outlined and set forth.

This 28 day of August, 1956.

## DOCUMENTATION SUITABLE FOR RESEARCH PAPERS

BIBLIOGRAPHY ENTRY

*Aaron v. Cooper,* Aug. 28, 1956, Civ. No. 3113, U.S. Dist. Ct. E. Ark. Excerpts reprinted from *Race Relations Law Reporter* in *LRUSA.*

FIRST FOOTNOTE

> *Aaron v. Cooper*, Aug. 28, 1956, Civ. No. 3113, U.S. Dist. Ct. E. Ark., as reprinted from *Race Relations Law Reporter* in *LRUSA*, pp. 19-26.

SUBSEQUENT FOOTNOTE

> *Aaron v. Cooper, LRUSA*, p. ▓.

---

## Three Segregation Measures in November Election, 1956

THREE PROPOSALS—a constitutional amendment, an initiated act and a resolution—designed to maintain segregation in public schools were approved by heavy margins in the Nov. 6 general election in Arkansas. . . .

The official vote count on the three anti-integration proposals was:

Amendment 47 to nullify the Supreme Court's desegregation decisions —185,374 for and 146,064 against.

Initiated Act No. 2 to assign pupils to schools on factors other than race—214,712 for and 121,129 against.

Resolution of interposition placing Arkansas on record against desegregation—199,511 for and 127,360 against. . . .

State Education Commissioner Ford said he thought the assignment act was "definitely a good law." He said it would help districts which want to keep their segregated schools. The act gives local school boards authority to assign pupils to specific schools for a variety of reasons—except race. [*SSN* December 1956, p. 8]

## Offer of Arkansas Council on Human Relations, January 1957

THE January issue of a newsletter distributed by the Arkansas Council on Human Relations, a pro-integration group, contained this report:

"Teams of Christian ministers representing some 10 communions are being formed across the state. Each team (one white minister and one colored) stands ready to speak before any church or church-group on the general theme: 'A Christian Views Race Relations Today.' " [*SSN* February 1957, p. 4]

---

For model documentation see page 15 or page 16.

[The Arkansas Council on Human Relations is a small private group affiliated with the Southern Regional Council.]

## Four New Segregation Laws, February 1957

FOUR BILLS designed to maintain racial segregation in public schools were passed in February by the Arkansas General Assembly. All had the support of Gov. Orval E. Faubus, who signed them into law.

The measures (1) create a state sovereignty commission with investigative powers; (2) require registration and periodical reports of persons and organizations working for racial integration; (3) relieve school children of compulsory attendance in racially mixed public schools; and (4) authorize school districts to hire legal counsel to defend school board members and school officials. [*SSN* March 1957, p. 13]

## Circuit Court of Appeals Approval of Integration Plan, April 29, 1957

THE Eighth Circuit Court of Appeals at St. Louis announced April 29 that it had approved the Little Rock school board plan to integrate the city's public schools gradually during the next six years. . . .

Wiley A. Branton of Pine Bluff, Negro attorney who was assisted by Thurgood Marshall of New York City, said he hadn't decided whether to appeal to the Supreme Court.

Branton said he was pleased by "some aspects" of the appeals court decision. The decision, he said, would force the school board to stick by its announced decision to integrate, no matter how long it takes.

"The courts have given us a cloak of protection against some die-hard, anti-integration groups who might still try to delay integration," Branton said. . . . [*SSN* May 1957, p. 2]

## Teacher Pay in the School Year 1955-1956

A STATISTICAL summary published by the state education department showed the difference between the average salary of Negro and white teachers [in Arkansas] was less in 1955-56 than in former years.

White teachers, averaging $2,375, drew $272 more than Negro teachers, who averaged $2,103. In 1954-55, the average pay for white teachers was $2,338 and for Negro teachers $2,043, a difference of $295.

Teaching positions for 1955-56 totaled 14,512 of which 11,538 were white and 2,974 were Negro. The total white enrollment was 316,709 and the Negro enrollment was 102,000. The total expenditure per child in average daily attendance was $162. The expenditure for white schools was $171 and for Negro schools $134. In 1954-55, total expenditures per child in average daily attendance was $156, with $166 for white schools and $125 for Negro schools.

State Education Commissioner A. W. ("Arch") Ford told *Southern School News* that "There will be a significant reduction in the difference between white and Negro teacher pay in the 1957-58 school year because many superintendents have talked to me about setting up for the first time a single scale for white and Negro teachers." [*SSN* May 1957, p. 2]

## *Details of Little Rock Integration Plan*

LATEST figures show the new Central High attendance area has 1,712 whites and 200 Negroes. The Horace Mann area has 328 whites and 607 Negroes. The new high school attendance area has 700 whites and 4 Negroes.

Under the district's transfer rule, which was in effect several years before integration became a question in the courts, pupils are allowed to transfer for educational reasons to any school if they do not create problems of crowding.

Under this transfer rule, [Supt.] Blossom expects that most of the white pupils in the Horace Mann area will transfer to Central High. And he expects that many of the Negroes in the Central High area will transfer to Horace Mann.

No teachers are involved. All Horace Mann teachers will be Negroes. All teachers at Central High and the new high school will be white.

Transportation problems, of course, are expected to be a major factor in the decisions of Negroes who elect to attend Central High. In addition, some courses at Central High which are not offered at Horace Mann may pull a few Negro pupils.

Few or no whites are expected at Horace Mann—at least the first year. Social considerations probably will override the attraction of proximity.

This is said to make the Little Rock plan essentially a voluntary sys-

For model documentation see page 15 or page 16.

tem—yet one which provides full and equal educational opportunities for Negro pupils at the high school level, with the exception of proximity in some cases.

The problem of white pupils who might object to mixed classes will be a consideration only at Central High. And if those white pupils do not wish to attend classes with Negroes, they can transfer to the new high school, which will be all-white or nearly so.

Blossom said overcrowding was not expected to restrict the free use of the transfer rule. Horace Mann has room for 1,000 pupils. Central High now has 2,600 pupils. The new high school has room for 1,000 pupils. In each, there is more than enough room for all pupils in the attendance area. . . . [*SSN* May 1957, pp. 2-3]

## Christian Church Convention Protest against Segregation Laws, May 1957

THE STATE convention of the Arkansas Christian Churches [Disciples of Christ] opened May 6 at Hot Springs with the Rev. William L. Miller Jr. of Rogers, convention president, telling about 500 delegates from 75 congregations that some churches which "yell violently" about gambling and liquor issues maintain a "deafening" silence on racial matters.

Miller said, "Let us with the boldness of a Peter or John tell our representatives and senators . . . that God hath made of one blood all nations on Earth.". . .

Delegates . . . unanimously adopted a resolution protesting segregation legislation passed in the 1957 session of the Arkansas General Assembly. . . . [*SSN* June 1957, p. 8]

## Citizens Council Plea for Defiance of Court, May 1957

. . . GOV. ORVAL FAUBUS was asked by the Capital Citizens Council of Little Rock to "order" Negroes and whites to attend separate schools at Little Rock next fall despite federal court approval of the Little Rock plan to begin desegregation at the high school level. [*SSN* June 1957, p. 8]

## Baptist Minister's Sermon against Segregation, May 21, 1957

THE Baptist minister who devoted his May 21 sermon to a condemnation of racial segregation and prejudice is the Rev. Nolan P. Howington. His

2,700 member church [First Baptist Church, Little Rock] is one of the largest Baptist congregations in the state.

Howington took his position despite the Arkansas Baptist State Convention's avoidance of the race issue at its annual meetings since the 1954 Supreme Court decision. The Baptist Convention is the largest religious organization in Arkansas that has not endorsed the court's desegregation decision. Many Arkansas Baptist pastors have criticized the Supreme Court ruling. . . .

Howington said later the response from his congregation to the sermon was "surprisingly good.". . . [*SSN* June 1957, p. 8]

## A Negro Leader and Two Segregationist Spokesmen on the Possibility of "Trouble," June 1957

. . . LESTER B. GRANGER of New York City, executive director of the National Urban League [a Negro organization], predicted in an interview at Little Rock that Little Rock schools would be integrated "without serious trouble" in September.

"There has always been an atmosphere of mutual respect and friendship among the races at Little Rock, and for that reason I believe that integration in the schools will be accomplished in an orderly way.". . .

Granger's prediction that Little Rock schools would integrate without trouble was challenged by Robert Ewing Brown, president of the Capital Citizens Council of Little Rock, a pro-segregation group. . . .

"The Negroes have ample and fine schools here and there is no need for this problem except to satisfy the aims of a few white and Negro revolutionaries in the local Urban League and the National Association for the Advancement of Colored People," Brown said.

Brown blamed Gov. Faubus for aiding integrationists by his silence. He said the governor had promised last year to protect the people against mixed schools. . . .

Amis Guthridge, a Little Rock attorney and a leading member of pro-segregation groups in Arkansas, . . . said there would be "hell on the border" in Little Rock in September if the schools integrated. He said that "there will never be integration in Little Rock public schools.". . . [*SSN* July 1957, p. 10]

For model documentation see page 15 or page 16.

## *Radio Minister's Opposition to Integration, July 17, 1957*

ON July 17 at Little Rock, at a meeting of the Capital Citizens Council, the Rev. J. A. Lovell of Dallas, Texas, a radio minister, told about 250 persons who attended the meeting:

"If the integration of the races continues while the Supreme Court and other public officials keep their weak-kneed attitude, there are people left yet in the South who love God and their nation enough to shed blood if necessary to stop this work of Satan," Lovell said. "We won't take this lying down."

Lovell said violence would be avoided if possible. . . . [*SSN* August 1957, p. 7]

## *Further Segregationist Protest, June-July 1957; School-Board Policy on Social Activities in Integrated Schools, July 1957*

A SEGREGATION leader, Amis Guthridge of Little Rock, an attorney and a director of the Capital Citizens Council, appeared before the Little Rock school board June 27 to ask for separate schools for white children who don't want to attend with Negroes. . . .

Guthridge was accompanied by the Rev. Wesley Pruden, pastor of the Broadmoor Baptist Church, who asked the board what its policy would be regarding the admission of Negroes to dances and other social functions at desegregated schools. . . .

On July 27, the board released its written answer to the questions raised by Pruden. The board said:

(1) Social functions which involve race mixing will not be held; (2) boys and girls will use regular facilities provided for school programs; (3) integration of the PTAs is a matter to be decided within those organizations; (4) all pupils will use restroom facilities regularly provided; (5) teachers can and will avoid situations such as love scenes in class plays featuring students of different races; (6) it would not "make projections on matters that do not exist," in response to the last query concerning hypothetical court rulings concerning future social situations. . . . [*SSN* August 1957, p. 7]

## *Georgia Governor at Segregationist Dinner, August 22, 1957*

MARVIN GRIFFIN of Georgia praised about 350 persons attending a $10-a-plate Capital Citizens Council rally Aug. 22 as "a courageous bunch of patriots." The Georgia governor received a standing ovation when he defied the federal courts to order integration in Georgia on what he called the premise that the federal government contributes a small amount of food to the school lunch programs.

"If they try to tell us then to integrate the races, I will be compelled to tell them to get their blackeyed peas and soup pots out of Georgia," he said.

He said the effect of the 1954 Supreme Court ruling against school segregation had not been felt in Georgia—"and that fact is no mere accident." Griffin continued:

"The determined and cooperative efforts of a dedicated people, a steadfast General Assembly and an administration committed unequivocally toward preservation of our cherished institutions—all of these working in concert have stemmed the tide.". . . [*SSN* September 1957, p. 7]

## Negro Conduct Recommendations for Integrated Schools, August 25, 1957

ABOUT 200 Negroes, some of them school children, were told by a panel of Little Rock Negro ministers and laymen Aug. 25 that they could help make school integration work by observing Christian principles. Frank W. Smith, one of the speakers, advised Negro students entering the integrated schools to remember that "it is not cowardly to ignore slurring remarks."

"The Scriptures tell us to turn the other cheek," he said. "Remember that prayer is always in order.". . . [*SSN* September 1957, p. 7]

## Legal Moves to Block Integration, August 29-30, 1957

SEGREGATIONISTS, suddenly strengthened by an assist from Gov. Orval Faubus, won a short-lived victory Aug. 29 when the Pulaski County Chancery Court issued a temporary injunction against integration of Little Rock public schools.

Next day a federal judge held the injunction invalid and enjoined all persons from interfering with the Little Rock integration plan. [Judge Ronald N. Davies of Fargo, N.D., temporarily assigned to the U.S. District court in Little Rock]

That rapid-fire legal skirmish climaxed a two-week flurry of litigation in both federal and state courts with integration of the state's biggest school

For model documentation see page 15 or page 16.

system and four other districts scheduled for early September. In addition to the segregationists' action, court rulings were sought by the Little Rock school board, a group of Negro ministers, the state attorney general and a professed neutral.

The suits included:

1) A request for a chancery court declaratory judgment on whether Arkansas segregation laws are superseded by federal laws.

2) A federal court action filed by 10 Negro ministers seeking to have the state segregation acts declared unconstitutional.

3) A move for a temporary injunction from chancery court to block the scheduled integration of Little Rock Central High School.

4) A mandamus action intended to force Little Rock school officials into allowing white students to transfer from Central High to all-white schools, if they wish. . . .

Gov. Faubus testified in the Aug. 29 chancery court hearing that he thought the present was one of the worst times possible to integrate. He said he had personal knowledge revolvers recently had been taken from students, both white and Negro. He was not asked to elaborate.

(Asked Aug. 30 about the governor's testimony, Little Rock Police Chief Marvin Potts said: "Let's say I haven't heard what Gov. Faubus says he has heard.")

Faubus said that "in my judgment the sentiment within the past three weeks has changed." He said that "one thing that triggered" what he called the rise of anti-integration feeling was a speech by Gov. Marvin Griffin to the Capital Citizens Council Aug. 22. "People are coming to me and saying if Georgia doesn't have integration, why does Arkansas have it?" he said.

Judge Reed ruled: "In view of the testimony and the show of the threat of violence, riots and bloodshed, and particularly in the opinion of Gov. Faubus, I feel I can only rule to grant the injunction."

The courtroom applauded. . . . [*SSN* September 1957, p. 6]

## *Editorial on Law Observance, September 1, 1957\**

IN HIS clear and forthright ruling in the Little Rock school case Federal Judge Ronald N. Davies has swept away the legal confusion generated by the apparent conflict between state and federal laws.

The judge ordered the Little Rock School Board to proceed on sched-

---

\* "A Time of Testing," *Arkansas Gazette*, page 1A, columns 6-7. Judge Davies had just overruled the chancery court's injunction.

ule with its plan for limited, gradual integration at the High School level—and he enjoined "all persons, in any manner, directly or indirectly, from interfering with the plan of integration as approved by the United States District Court."

This means that on Tuesday some 15 Negro children will be enrolled at Little Rock Central High School along with more than 2,000 whites. There are those who have suggested that this cannot be done without inciting the populace of this city to violence. They have, we believe, too little faith in the respect of our people for law and order.

We do not believe any organized group of citizens would under any circumstances undertake to do violence to school children of any race. And if there are any individuals who might embark on such a reckless and indefensible course we have no doubt that our law enforcement officers can and will preserve order.

This is a time of testing for all of us. Few of us are entirely happy over the necessary developments in the wake of changes in the law. But certainly we must recognize that the School Board is simply carrying out its clear duty—and is doing so in the ultimate best interests of all the school children of Little Rock, white and colored alike.

We are confident that the citizens of Little Rock will demonstrate on Tuesday for the world to see that we are a law abiding people.

## DOCUMENTATION SUITABLE FOR RESEARCH PAPERS

BIBLIOGRAPHY ENTRY

"A Time of Testing." *Arkansas Gazette,* Sept. 1, 1957. Reprinted in *LRUSA.*

FIRST FOOTNOTE

*"A Time of Testing," *Arkansas Gazette,* Sept. 1, 1957, as reprinted in *LRUSA,* pp. 34-35.

SUBSEQUENT FOOTNOTE

*"A Time," *LRUSA,* p. ▨

These examples are models for other material from newspapers in this collection.

## The Governor's Proclamation, September 2, 1957*

WHEREAS, The Governor of the State of Arkansas is vested with the authority to order to active duty the Militia of this State in case of tumult, riot or breach of the peace, or imminent danger thereof; and

WHEREAS, it has been made known to me, as Governor, from many sources, that there is imminent danger of tumult, riot and breach of the peace and the doing of violence to persons and property in Pulaski County, Arkansas;

NOW, THEREFORE, I, Orval E. Faubus, Governor of the State of Arkansas do hereby proclaim that a state of emergency presently exists and I do hereby order to active duty Major General Sherman T. Clinger, the Adjutant General of Arkansas, the State Militia units consisting of the Base Detachment of Adams Field and the State Headquarters Detachment at Camp Robinson, and any other units which may be necessary to accomplish the mission of maintaining or restoring law and order and to preserve the peace, health, safety and security of the citizens of Pulaski County, Arkansas.

IN WITNESS WHEREOF, I have hereunto set my hand and caused the Great Seal of the State of Arkansas to be affixed. Done in office in the City of Little Rock this 2nd day of September, 1957.

s/ Orval E. Faubus
Governor

### DOCUMENTATION SUITABLE FOR RESEARCH PAPERS

BIBLIOGRAPHY ENTRY

Faubus, Orval E., Governor. Proclamation, September 2, 1957. Reprinted from *Race Relations Law Reporter,* October 1957, in *LRUSA.*

FIRST FOOTNOTE

*Governor Orval E. Faubus, Proclamation, September 2, 1957, reprinted from *Race Relations Law Reporter* in *LRUSA,* p. 36.

---

* Reprinted from the *Race Relations Law Reporter,* October 1957, p. 937. This proclamation sent National Guard troops to Central High School on the evening of September 2, 1957 (Labor Day), before school was scheduled to start on September 3.

SUBSEQUENT FOOTNOTE
  *Faubus, Proclamation, September 2, 1957, *LRUSA,* p. ▉.

‖‖‖‖‖‖‖‖‖‖‖‖‖‖‖‖‖‖‖‖‖‖‖‖‖‖‖‖‖‖‖‖‖‖‖‖‖‖‖‖‖‖‖‖‖‖‖‖‖‖‖‖‖‖‖‖‖‖‖‖‖‖‖‖‖‖‖‖‖‖‖‖‖‖‖‖‖‖‖

## The Governor's Explanation, September 2, 1957

... THIS is a decision I have reached prayerfully. It has been made after conferences with dozens of people and after the checking and the verification of as many of the reports as possible.

The mission of the State Militia is to maintain or restore order and to protect the lives and property of citizens. They will act not as segregationists or integrationists, but as soldiers called to active duty to carry out their assigned tasks.

But I must state here in all sincerity, that it is my opinion—yes, even a conviction, that it will not be possible to restore or to maintain order and protect the lives and property of the citizens if forcible integration is carried out tomorrow in the schools of this community. The inevitable conclusion, therefore, must be that the schools in Pulaski County, for the time being, must be operated on the same basis as they have been operated in the past. . . . [*SSN* October 1957, p. 1; part of report of Faubus television speech explaining his reasons for sending the National Guard to Central High School]

[For model documentation, see page 15 or page 16. Material from *SSN* hereafter in this collection will not have directions concerning documentation.]

## Statement of the Mayor of Little Rock

IF IT were not for my own respect for due process of law, I would be tempted to issue an executive order interposing the city of Little Rock between Gov. Faubus and the Little Rock school board.

The people of Little Rock recently had a school board election and elected by an overwhelming vote the school board members who advocated a projected court-approved Little Rock plan [of gradual integration]. . . . [*SSN* October 1957, p. 1]

## School Board's Petition to Federal District Court, Asking Instructions, September 3, 1957*

PETITIONERS, the defendants in this suit, were proceeding in conformity with the plan of integration approved by the decree of this Court entered on August 15, 1956, when, on Monday, September 2, 1957, the Honorable Orval Faubus, Governor of the State of Arkansas, placed the Arkansas National Guard around Central High School in the City of Little Rock, spoke to the public of threatened violence, and stated that the public schools of Little Rock were to be operated as they had been operated in the past.

In the light of those actions, petitioners caused the following statement to be published:

"Although the Federal Court has ordered integration to proceed, Governor Faubus has said that the schools should continue as they have in the past, and has stationed troops at Central High School to maintain order.

"In view of this situation, we ask that no Negro students attempt to attend Central or any white high school until this dilemma is legally resolved."

Petitioners caused the said statement to be published because, in the exercise of their best judgment, they determined that an emergency existed; that it was the wise course to follow as regards the welfare and educational standards of both white and Negro pupils; and at the time of making their decision it was impossible to appear before this Court to seek instructions.

WHEREFORE, Petitioners ask that this court exempt them from any charge of contempt and instruct them as to whether they should recall the request that "no Negro students attempt to attend Central or any white high school until this dilemma is legally resolved."

DOCUMENTATION SUITABLE FOR RESEARCH PAPERS

BIBLIOGRAPHY ENTRY

Little Rock Board of Education. Petition to U.S. Dist. Ct. E. Ark., September 3, 1957. Reprinted from *Race Relations Law Reporter*, October 1957, in *LRUSA*.

---

* Reprinted from the *Race Relations Law Reporter*, October 1957, pp. 937-938.

FIRST FOOTNOTE

> *Little Rock Board of Education, Petition to U.S. Dist. Ct. E. Ark., September 3, 1957, reprinted from *Race Relations Law Reporter,* October 1957, in *LRUSA,* p. 38.

SUBSEQUENT FOOTNOTE

> *Little Rock Board of Education, Petition, September 3, 1957, *LRUSA,* p. ▉.

## From a Telegram Sent by Governor Faubus to President Eisenhower, September 4, 1957*

. . . THE QUESTION at issue at Little Rock this moment is not integration vs. segregation. . . .

The question now is whether or not the head of a sovereign state can exercise his constitutional powers and discretion in maintaining peace and good order within his jurisdiction, being accountable to his own conscience and to his own people. . . .

I am reliably informed that federal authorities in Little Rock have this day been discussing plans to take into custody, by force, the head of a sovereign state. . . .

I have reason to believe that the telephone lines to the Arkansas executive mansion have been tapped—I suspect the federal agents. The situation in Little Rock and Arkansas grows more explosive by the hour. This is caused for the most part by the misunderstanding of our problems by a federal judge who decreed "immediate integration of the public schools of Little Rock" without hearing any evidence whatsoever as to the conditions now existing in this community. . . . If these actions continue, or if my executive authority as governor to maintain the peace is breached, then I can no longer be responsible for the results. The injury to persons and property that would be caused—the blood that may be shed will be on the hands of the federal government and its agents. . . . As governor of Arkansas I appeal to you to use your good offices to modify the extreme stand and stop the unwarranted interference of federal agents. . . . [*SSN* October 1957, pp. 1-2]

---

* On the night of September 3 the district court had ordered the school board to proceed with its integration plan as scheduled. The following morning Negro students, who had stayed away from Central High School on September 3, reported to school and were refused entrance by National Guardsmen, whereupon Federal Judge Davies asked U.S. Attorney General Brownell to investigate the situation.

## From President Eisenhower's Telegram Replying to Governor Faubus, September 5, 1957

. . . THE ONLY assurance I can give you is that the federal Constitution will be upheld by me by every legal means at my command.

There is no basis of fact to the statements you make in your telegram that federal authorities have been considering taking you into custody or that telephone lines to your executive mansion have been tapped by any agency of the federal government.

At the request of Judge Davies, the Department of Justice is presently collecting facts as to interference with or failure to comply with the district's court order. You and other state officials—as well as the National Guard which is, of course, uniformed, armed and partially sustained by the [federal] government—will, I am sure, give full cooperation to the United States District Court. [*SSN* October 1957, p. 2]

## Events at Central High School, September 4, 1957*

THE FIRST Negro applicant to try to enroll at Little Rock Central High School yesterday, Elizabeth Eckford, 15, was twice blocked from entering the grounds, walked calmly down two blocks then sat out 35 minutes of vocal abuse while waiting for a bus to go home. . . .

Elizabeth, who wore tinted eyeglasses and carried books in her arms, alighted from a public transportation bus at Thirteenth Street and Park Avenue at 7:58 A.M. and walked a block to Park Avenue and Fourteenth Street.

When she approached the Guardsmen at the corner they drew together and blocked her entrance to the sidewalk. She crossed the street and started walking south on Capitol Avenue across the street from the front of the school. Before she had taken 25 steps she cut into the street and walked back to the line of Guardsmen. It was then that a crowd of 200 saw her and rushed to the scene.

The girl, silent and looking straight ahead, walked at a brisk pace down the line of troops. The crowd walked along with her and began a stream of cat-calling.

A woman told her to "go back where you came from," made a lunge at the girl and was pushed back by a Guard officer. Another in the crowd said, "you've got a better school than ours so why don't you go to it."

---

* *Arkansas Gazette,* "Attempts of Negroes to Enter School," September 5, 1957, p. 1A. For model documentation see p. 35.

When she made an attempt in the middle of the line to cross onto the school grounds and again was stopped by Guardsmen some one shouted "don't let her in our school—that 'nigger'."

She crossed Park Avenue and sat down on a bus stop bench at the northeast corner of Capitol and Sixteenth Street. There a crowd of about 50 supplemented by several Central High School students who had left the grounds pressed closely.

She told newsmen she had "nothing to say." The abusive shouts from the crowd continued. A Guard officer told the crowd to move back from the bench and it complied. . . .

The heckling of Elizabeth continued and a white woman who identified herself as Mrs. Grace Lorch stood behind her at the bench. Mrs. Lorch said she "thought I would stay with her—after all she's just a kid."

Mrs. Lorch became the object of vocal abuse from the crowd of other whites. Two white women, the most vociferous, asked her name and address but Mrs. Lorch refused to tell them. When the heckling became more heated a Little Rock city detective moved them back.

At Mrs. Lorch's suggestion, she accompanied the girl across Sixteenth Street to the southeast corner at another bus stop. The crowd followed and the heckling became more heated. Mrs. Lorch told reporters she thought Elizabeth was "in a state of shock." She decided to call a taxi and when she asked someone to phone, everyone in the crowd refused. Mrs. Lorch turned around to walk the ten feet to the front of the drug store where there was a phone and was pushed slightly when she walked through the crowd. At the door she found that the store was not open. When she returned, a bus was coming and Mrs. Lorch boarded it with the girl.

It was during the time Mrs. Lorch was with the girl that the seven prospective Negro students made their efforts to cross the line and were told that they couldn't by the troop commander, Lt. Col. Marion Johnson, who said that he was acting under Governor Faubus' orders to keep them out. . . .

## Denial of Petition to Suspend Integration Temporarily, September 7, 1957*

. . . WHAT did the testimony this morning disclose? Beyond the bald and unsupported statements in the petition, only the testimony of the Little

---

* From a statement by Federal District Judge Davies at a hearing on the School Board's petition of September 3 for a temporary suspension of the integration order, September 7, 1957. Reprinted from the *Race Relations Law Reporter*, October 1957, pp. 940-941. The petition is at p. 38 above. For model documentation see p. 19.

Rock superintendent of schools was offered, and that bore upon the desirability of the proper education of children in the Little Rock schools with which sentiments we all must agree.

The testimony and arguments this morning were, in my judgment, as anemic as the petition itself; and the position taken by the school directors does violence to my concept of the duty of the petitioners to adhere with resolution to its own approved plan of gradual integration in the Little Rock public schools.

It must never be thought that this court has not given careful consideration to this problem and all that it entails, but it must never be forgotten that I have a Constitutional duty and obligation from which I shall not shrink. . . .

The chief executive of Little Rock has stated that the Little Rock police have not had a single case of inter-racial violence reported to them and that there has been no indication from sources available to him that there would be violence in regard to this situation. . . .

The petition of the Little Rock school district directors and of the superintendent of the Little Rock public schools for an order temporarily suspending enforcement of its plan of integration heretofore approved by this court is in all things denied.

## Statement of Eight (out of Ten) Little Rock Aldermen, September 8, 1957

As THE duly elected aldermen of the City of Little Rock, Arkansas, we are closer to the sentiments of the people than any other public officials. We know that there was, and still exists, racial tension between our people because of the United States Supreme Court's decision concerning our schools. We believe that Gov. Faubus took the proper course in calling out the Arkansas National Guard in this crisis to protect the lives and property of all our people. We commend him for his prompt action and sincerely hope that we will be permitted to work out our own problems within due process of law and without outside intereference. We know that this is the desire of the overwhelming majority of the citizens of Little Rock. [*SSN* October 1957, p. 2]

*Interview with a Student Leader in Central High School, September 1957\**

*Q.* How long do you think this tension is going to last?

*A.* It's up to Governor Faubus.

*Q.* If you had your say, speaking personally, the Negro students could come to the school tomorrow?

*A.* Sir, it's the law. We are going to have face it sometime.

*Q.* Do you think the day is going to come when your school is going to be integrated?

*A.* Yes.

*Q.* Are you opposed to integration yourself?

*A.* If it's a court order we have to follow it and abide by the law.

*Q.* Would you mind sitting next to a Negro in school?

*A.* No. . . .

*Q.* Do you have any Negro friends?

*A.* No, sir.

*Q.* Have you done any soul searching at all about the segregation problem as a whole?

*A.* Not particularly.

*Q.* Would it make a big difference to you if you saw a white girl dating a Negro boy?

*A.* I believe it would.

*Q.* It would?

*A.* Yes, sir.

*Q.* Why?

*A.* I don't know. I just was brought up that way.

*Q.* Do you think Negroes are equal in intelligence and physically to white people?

*A.* That's just a matter of opinion.

*Q.* What's yours? You are person of some significance. You are the president of the student body.

*A.* If they have had the same benefits and advantages, I think they're equally as smart.

*Q.* Do you respect the Supreme Court?

---

\* From a Mike Wallace television interview with Ralph Brodie, president of Little Rock's Central High School Student body, as reprinted in the *Arkansas Gazette,* September 10, 1957, p. 4A. For model documentation see p. 12.

*A.* I certainly do.

*Q.* Do you believe all Southerners should live by the law of the land?

*A.* I don't see why we shouldn't. We've been living under it all our lives.

## From President Eisenhower's Statement Following a Conference with Governor Faubus at Newport, R.I., September 14, 1957

AT THE request of Gov. Faubus, of Arkansas, I met with him this morning in a constructive discussion regarding the carrying out of the orders of the federal court in the matter of the high schools of Little Rock.

The governor stated his intention to respect the decision of the United States District Court and to give his full cooperation in carrying out his responsibilities in respect to these decisions.

In doing so, I recognize the inescapable responsibility resting upon the governor to preserve law and order in his state. I am gratified by his constructive and cooperative attitude at our meeting. I have assured the governor of the cooperation of federal officials . . .

I am sure it is the desire of the governor, not only to observe the supreme law of the land but to use the influence of his office in orderly progress of the plans which are already the subject of the order of the court. . . . [*SSN* October 1957, p. 2]

## From Governor Faubus's Statement Following His Conference with President Eisenhower at Newport, R.I., September 14, 1957

. . . THIS TRIP to Newport has been worthwhile from my point of view. I recognize that the situation called for clarification and I assured the President of my desire to cooperate with him in carrying out the duties resting upon both of us under the constitution of Arkansas with the requirements of the federal Constitution.

I have never expressed any personal opinion regarding the Supreme Court decision of 1954 which voted integration. That is not relevant. That decision is the law of the land and must be obeyed. . . .

The people of Little Rock are law-abiding and I know that they expect to obey valid court orders. In this they shall have my support. In so doing, it is my responsibility to protect the people from violence in any form. . . .

When I assure the President, as I have already done, that I expect to accept the decisions of the court, I entertain the hope that the Department of Justice and the federal judiciary will act with understanding and patience in discharging their duties. [*SSN* October 1957, p. 2]

## Negotiations and Discussions at Newport and in Little Rock, September 1957*

AT NEWPORT, Governor Faubus, in his usual unhurried way, stressed the importance of the time element—a way should be found, he felt, to get federal-court "relief" for Little Rock until the Supreme Court had ruled on the validity of the State constitutional amendments and statutes—"interposition" and several other measures—approved either by the people of Arkansas in the 1956 election or the Arkansas General Assembly in 1957. The President conceded that time is a factor but thought that the matter fell so completely within the jurisdiction of the courts that little could be done by the Executive in that regard. . . .

. . . I remember how emphatic the President was in assuring the Governor that he regards the States as responsible for maintaining law and order and that the Governor's primary responsibility should be respected. "I do not criticize you for calling out the Guard—our only difference is that I would have given them different instructions.". . .

I had the feeling when the meeting ended that we were leaving loose ends, and wish now that an afternoon session had been set up. There was unfinished business. Still I can see why the President would think that the matter had been sufficiently explored and that the conclusions, which were later in the day put in writing, were sufficient.

My doubts about the adequacy of these conclusions were based on the desire to see a carefully drawn up agreement approved by all parties. I had come to Newport confident that such an agreement could be reached and both the President and Governor Faubus acted in a manner that strengthened that opinion. What made me uneasy, however, was the uncertainty about the "time element" that both sides agreed was the key to a final solution.

The rigidity of [Attorney General] Brownell's position on this factor gave me some forebodings, but I was still hopeful of working out a time-

---

* From "The Inside Story of Little Rock," by Brooks Hays, at that time Congressman from Arkansas, in *U.S. News & World Report*, March 23, 1959, pp. 124-132. The material is from Mr. Hays's book, *A Southern Moderate Speaks* (Chapel Hill: University of North Carolina Press, 1959). Mr. Hays was at that time also president of the Southern Baptist Convention.

table with the Governor when we returned to Little Rock. It is obvious to me now that this step should have been taken at Newport, where the conditions for a settlement were generally favorable. . . .

There is some logic to the argument that *temporarily*—but only temporarily and very briefly—[the Governor] could order the Negroes to be excluded without defying the Federal Government. At times, during all of these rapidly shifting situations, I wished the Governor were a lawyer. I saw so clearly the necessity of compliance with valid court orders, by changing the Guard instructions or substituting State police, that I persisted in efforts to interpret the problem to him in terms that would fit into his own moderate views of State sovereignty.

But he had too few political advisers who sympathized with those moderate views. Some of them exploited fully his promise not to force integration upon an "unwilling" community. Some of these advisers were from eastern Arkansas, where it must be conceded that there is a complex and delicate race problem. I was handicapped greatly by not being able to confront those who were, in my absence, canceling my arguments. . . .

I became very fond of the Governor during our long vigils at the Mansion. He called me his bishop—he is a Baptist—and I know he gave ear when I tried to picture the grandeur of the other course of defiance, defiance of the interpositionists—or nullificationists, to be more accurate. . . .

On Monday [September 16], the Governor indicated his willingness to send the National Guard home, provided that the target date for admission of Negro students was changed to a later date, possibly as early as September 30. He was quite concerned, however, that the constitutionality of the Arkansas sovereignty laws be determined as soon as possible, so he would not be caught between conflicting directives concerning his lawful actions. By negotiation with various prominent people in both public and private life, I arrived at this proposed course of action for the Governor:

1. That he write a letter to the parents of the Negro children asking them voluntarily to keep their children out of school until a set date arrived—we had assurances they would agree;

2. That he guarantee to use his influence to create a peaceful atmosphere;

3. That he see that the local school authorities provide private tutors for the nine Negro children during the interim period; and

4. That he pledge to use his office to insure the peace after the given deadline for admission.

One of the major stumbling blocks was the attitude of the Justice Department, which would make no commitment not to take Faubus to court. While this Department was also determined not to wait for State-court action on the sovereignty laws, it did indicate that federal action might be withdrawn once the school was integrated.

The Governor would not write such a letter under those conditions. . . .

. . . I also knew that the President would listen to [Presidential Secretary Sherman] Adams's counsel of moderation as long as there was a chance for conciliation but that, if that chance appeared to be fading, the counsel of Brownell, who apparently favored ultimate, extreme federal action, would gain the upper hand. . . .

I was determined not to make any contacts with the NAACP officials, either national or local. I disagreed with their tactics and, in the Little Rock situation, I could not even discuss the question with them without appearing to approve projection of the national organization into Little Rock's difficulties. . . .

[The remainder of this article appears below at pp. 57-59 under the heading "The Eve of the School Opening, September 22, 1957."]

## DOCUMENTATION SUITABLE FOR RESEARCH PAPERS

BIBLIOGRAPHY ENTRY

Hays, Brooks. "The Inside Story of Little Rock." *U.S. News & World Report,* March 23, 1959, pp. 124-132. Reprinted in *LRUSA.*

FIRST FOOTNOTE

*Brooks Hays, "The Inside Story of Little Rock," *U.S. News & World Report,* March 23, 1960, pp. 124-132, reprinted in *LRUSA,* pp. 45-47.

SUBSEQUENT FOOTNOTES

*Hays, *op. cit., LRUSA,* p. ■.
*Hays, "The Inside Story," *LRUSA,* p. ■.
*Hays, *LRUSA,* p. ■.

These examples are models for other material from magazines in this collection.

## An American Legion Resolution, September 8, 1957*

WHEREAS one of the principles on which the American Legion was founded as stated in the preamble to our constitution is to maintain law and order and whereas our comrade legionnaire, the honorable Orval E. Faubus, governor of Arkansas, has exercised the right and duty given him by the constitution of the state of Arkansas by calling on units of the Arkansas National Guard to protect life and limb and property in an emergency at Little Rock and whereas this action demonstrates to a high degree the qualities of full intelligence, integrity, resourcefulness and courage and loyalty to duty. Now, therefore, be it resolved that the Fifth District, Department of Arkansas, American Legion, extend to the governor our sincere congratulations and commendations upon his historic and courageous action; and be it further resolved that a copy of this resolution be forwarded to the *Arkansas Gazette* and a copy to the Department commander of the American Legion for personal transmittal to the governor.

## Foreign-Relations Effects of Integration Trouble†

SECRETARY OF STATE John Foster Dulles said today that the Little Rock integration trouble and other integration problems in the South "are not helpful to the influence of the United States abroad."

Dulles was asked to comment on reports that problems at Little Rock and other Southern cities were being broadcast widely not only by the Soviet Union but by the friends of the United States.

"I haven't read the reports but I have no doubt that this is true," Dulles said.

Radio Moscow has been chirping happily about the troubles of integration.

On September 4 a Moscow home broadcast stated: "A detachment of National Guardsmen, 250 strong and armed with rifles, guns, truncheons, and tear gas grenades, took up position yesterday in front of the

* Adopted by the American Legion, Fifth District, Department of Arkansas, at Lopanto, Arkansas. Reprinted from the *Arkansas Gazette,* September 9, 1957, p. 7A. For model documentation see p. 12.

† *Arkansas Gazette,* "Dulles Says U.S. Damaged Abroad," news story from Washington, D.C., September 10, 1957, published September 11, 1957, p. 2A. For model documentation see p. 35.

building of Little Rock Central High School. Negro children came to the school. The governor of the state, Orval Faubus, sent troops to prevent these children from proceeding to the School when the governor's detachment lined up in front of the School. A crowd of racialists gathered in the street of the town and hoisted the Confederate flag under which their ancestors nearly a century ago fought for the preservation of slavery in the United States.''

## *Negro Views on Integration, September 1957\**

THE BALDING stocky white man pointed a finger excitedly.

"You newsmen are missing the real story," he said. "The Negroes don't want integration any more than we white folks do.

"Why don't you talk to them? Pick out any group. . . . You'll find out what I know."

The Associated Press followed the suggestion of the man in the angry crowd at Little Rock Central High, the school kept segregated by Governor Faubus and the Arkansas National Guard.

But the results did not show what the segregationist said he knew.

Nineteen Negroes were interviewed, some in their homes, some at their jobs. They were rich and poor, with elegant furniture and threadbare rugs. Some spoke with college accents, others mumbled. A few were grandmothers, two were old maids. One man shoveled dirt for a plumber, another headed a large school.

Only two—both over 70 years of age—favored continued separation of the races in the schools of Little Rock. Three others would not say. The rest—in one degree or another—favored integration right now.

Many admitted though that they would hesitate to send their children to a school guarded by grim men with guns and angry men with shouts. They do not want to hurt their children. But a surprisingly large number said perhaps it would be better to get the hurt over with as soon as possible.

Older Negroes like a 70-year-old general clean-up man echoed the sentiments of white segregationists.

"Lots of folks don't agree," he said, "but God made you a white man and made me a colored man and said we should be in different places."

---

\* *Arkansas Gazette,* "Little Rock Negroes Give View on School Integration Dispute," by Stan Meisler, Associated Press, September 15, 1957, p. 7A.

"There'll always be trouble," said a 72-year-old washing and ironing woman as she sat sadly on the porch of her tattered home. "They'll be fussing and spatting and throwing things at each other in school if they're together."

But almost all others wanted integration. Some felt it was the right thing. Others felt that Negro schools in Little Rock were not up to par. But they had varying views about trouble at Little Rock.

"Trouble?" laughed Will Reece proudly. "I don't believe there is going to be any trouble after the 20th."

Reece, 54-year-old uncle of a girl turned away from the school by the Guardsmen, meant that he was sure that the Federal Court at a September 20 injunction hearing would force Mr. Faubus to remove the Guard.

"Naturally if my child went to school one day and a mob turned him back, I'd be hesitant about telling him to come back the next day," said a 47-year-old letter carrier, father of a two-year-old boy. "But somebody has to come back day after day, and the sooner you get it over with the better."

"I'm for integration," said a 43-year-old school teacher as she helped her 11-month-old boy try to walk. "But if it means bloodshed, I don't think it's worth it."

Then she looked at her child and added: "Somebody has to be a martyr."

"They say wait until the trouble is over," said Mrs. Eldora Seaton, a 65-year-old grandmother of a high school student. "All right, let's wait— if the wait isn't going to be too long."

Tommy King, a 47-year-old plumber's assistant, had a clear formula: "No, I wouldn't send my children if there was trouble. I wouldn't even send you. When you see a man with a gun you walk the other way."

Oscar Eckford Sr., an elderly storekeeper and grandfather of one of the children who wanted to enter Little Rock Central, said he thought his granddaughter "did the right thing." But he stressed the need for good will between the races and said "among Negroes, humbleness is a way of life."

There are several new schools for Negroes at Little Rock and the thought of leaving them for an older white school does not appeal to all Negroes.

A 15-year-old junior at Horace Mann High School had no intention of leaving but he would not object if white students enrolled at his school.

The principal of a Negro school explained that it would not be good policy for him to express a personal opinion.

But as the newsmen left he added quietly: "I have the same personal viewpoint about this situation that any other loyal American who fought in World War II should have. That's all I can say."

Most Negroes interviewed were unafraid to tell what they thought. Many confidently identified themselves. Almost all co-operated easily.

But one young woman announced shrilly: "If it's about integration I don't want to talk about it. I'll be glad when this is over, one way or another."

She obviously spoke for more people, white or Negro, than herself.

## DOCUMENTATION SUITABLE FOR RESEARCH PAPERS

### BIBLIOGRAPHY ENTRY

Meisler, Stan. "Little Rock Negroes Give View on School Integration Dispute," *Arkansas Gazette*, September 15, 1957 (Associated Press). Reprinted in *LRUSA*.

### FIRST FOOTNOTE

*Stan Meisler, "Little Rock Negroes Give View on School Integration Dispute," *Arkansas Gazette*, September 15, 1957 (Associated Press), reprinted in *LRUSA*, pp. 49-51.

### SUBSEQUENT FOOTNOTES

*Meisler, *op. cit.*, *LRUSA*, p. ■.
*Meisler, "Little Rock Negroes," *LRUSA*, p. ■.
*Meisler, *LRUSA*, p. ■.

These examples are models for other newspaper reports in this collection that carry a writer's name and are credited to a press service.

---

## Negro Students during Wait, September 1957*

"WE'RE waiting patiently but naturally we're a little restless."

That was how one of the nine Negroes barred from Central High

---

* *Arkansas Gazette*, "Nine Negroes Marking Time until CHS Dispute Settled," by Ed Martin, Associated Press, September 16, 1957, page 5B. For model documentation, see the immediately preceding material in this collection.

School by National Guardsmen described the students' attitude toward the present deadlock of federal and state authorities.

The third week of classes begins today at Central High for about 2,000 white pupils. But apparently the Negroes—3 boys and 6 girls—will spend the day at home again.

Are they studying on their own while waiting to be admitted?

Some are trying to work from some textbooks they had bought for the school term, some are keeping up their reading and some are just postponing everything until they can find out if and when they can go to Central High.

Elizabeth Eckford, the 15-year-old girl who tried unsuccessfully several times to walk between helmeted riflemen at the school on the morning of September 4, is particularly anxious to get started at Central.

She wants to take a speech course which is not available at the city's Horace Mann High School for Negroes, where the 11th grade girl went last semester.

Ernest Green, 16, the only senior among the nine Negroes, hopes he won't be too far behind when he begins class work again.

"I'm trying to dig into my books while I'm waiting," he said.

Green, who was named to the National Honor Society while attending Little Rock's Negro school last year, is a holder of the Boy Scout Eagle Badge. He plans to study electrical engineering at college.

Jefferson Thomas, 14, who will be a freshman in the high school, said he has been doing some reading and getting in a little baseball practice.

Asked if he planned to take up any school sport if he gets into Central, the 10th grader replied:

"Well, I don't guess there'll be much chance to. They told us at Dunbar (the Negro junior high school) that Negroes wouldn't take part in any sports activities at Central the first year."

Here's how the others are spending the days of waiting: Minnie Jean Brown, 16, an 11th grader, is brushing up on her French in preparation for a course she hopes to take.

Selma Mothershead, another 16-year-old 11th grader who likes to crochet, is spending some of her time in pursuing this hobby.

Fifteen-year-old Terrance Roberts, who is also in the 11th grade, said he is merely "marking time." Terrance, an all-A student last semester, is helping his mother take care of six younger brothers and sisters while he waits for a decision on the integration impasse.

Jane Hill, 15, and Carlotta Walls and Gloria Ray, both 14, three 10th graders who attended Dunbar together last year, are doing a little studying but have not attempted to try to get very far.

Gloria said she hopes she will be able to keep up with everyone else in math, her most difficult subject, when she starts classes.

Mrs. William B. Brown, mother of Minnie Jean, said her daughter and the other children were "let down pretty badly" after the Guardsmen turned them back from the school. All attempted to get in on the same day that Elizabeth tried it.

"They were very excited before registration," Mrs. Brown said. "They were so sure this thing would all be taken care of and thought they would be accepted."

## Court Opinion Instructing National Guard Not to Prevent Integration, September 20, 1957*

11. THE City of Little Rock has a long history of peaceful and amicable relations between the white and Negro races. Approximately 20 per cent of the population is colored. The Negroes reside in scattered sections of the city, and some neighborhoods are composed of both white and colored residents. For at least twenty-five years there has been no reported incident of violence arising from racial tension, either between adults or between children of school age. In January 1956, the city public transportation system abolished the previously existing arrangement of seating whites and Negroes in separate sections of the buses. No incident of violence as a result of this change has come to the attention of the city authorities.

12. In preparation for the carrying out of the school plan at the senior high school level at the opening of the fall term, 1957, the superintendent and the principals of the senior high schools arranged for colored students who reside in the Central High School attendance area to elect whether or not they desired to attend that school. Approximately forty to fifty such students elected to attend that school. Their records were carefully studied by the school authorities. They approved the applications of thirteen of these colored students on the basis of their scholastic ability, their general deportment, their character and their health, determining that these thirteen students were particularly well suited to make the adjustment involved in their attending a school theretofore composed solely

---

* From the Federal District Court's opinion, in enjoining the governor and the National Guard from further interference, September 20, 1957 (Friday). Reprinted from the *Race Relations Law Reporter,* October 1957, pp. 959-962. For model documentation, see p. 19.

of white children. The superintendent and the high school principals held several meetings with these students and their parents to prepare them for the adjustments necessary to their attending Central High School.

All steps necessary to the transfer of these students and their enrollment in Central High School were completed before the opening of the fall term, 1957. Four of these thirteen colored students chose not to transfer to Central High School. Consequently, the carrying out of the school plan for this term involved the placing of only nine colored students in a student body of approximately 2,000. The faculty and the white student body at Central High School were prepared to accept the 9 colored children as fellow students.

13. On the evening of September 2, 1957, the Governor of Arkansas and the Adjutant General of Arkansas, who is the commanding officer of the Arkansas National Guard (acting under orders issued to him by the Governor), stationed units of the Arkansas National Guard at the Little Rock Central High School. Those guardsmen were under the command of Lieut. Col. Marion E. Johnson. On September 2, 1957, the Governor of Arkansas issued to the Adjutant General an order directing him to place off-limits to white students those schools for colored students and to place off-limits to colored students those schools theretofore operated and recently set up for white students; and that this order was to remain in effect until the demobilization of the guard or until further orders. This order was in effect at the time of the hearing in this case on September 20, 1957.

14. Up to this time, no crowds had gathered about Central High School and no acts of violence or threats of violence in connection with the carrying out of the plan had occurred. Never the less, out of an abundance of caution, the school authorities had frequently conferred with the Mayor and Chief of Police of Little Rock about taking appropriate steps by the Little Rock Police to prevent any possible disturbances or acts of violence in connection with the attendance of the nine colored students at Central High School. The Mayor considered that the Little Rock Police Force could adequately cope with any incidents which might arise at the opening of school. The Mayor, the Chief of Police, and the school authorities made no request to the Governor or any representative of his for state assistance in maintaining peace and order at Central High School. Neither the Governor nor any other official of the State Government consulted with the Little Rock authorities about whether the Little Rock Police were prepared to cope with any incidents which might arise at the school, about any need for state assistance in maintaining peace and order, or about stationing the Arkansas National Guard at Central High School.

15. The fall term at Central High School began on September 3, but none of the nine eligible colored students appeared at the school that day because they had been advised not to do so since the National Guard was stationed at the school. On the evening of September 3, however, these students were advised by school officials to attend Central High School the next morning.

16. On the morning of September 4, 1957, the units of the National Guard at the Central High School, acting pursuant to the Governor's order, stood shoulder-to-shoulder at the school grounds and thereby forcibly prevented the nine Negro students, who were eligible under the School Board's plan to attend that school, from entering the school grounds. At that time, a crowd of spectators congregated across the street from the school grounds. No acts of violence were committed or threatened by the crowd, although some of them made rude and disparaging remarks about the colored students. The guardsmen made no effort to disperse the crowd or to assist and protect the colored students in their efforts to enter the school. They did not prevent any white students from entering the school. The evidence indicates that the Arkansas National Guard, which is composed of 10,500 men, could have maintained peace and order without preventing the eligible colored students from attending Central High School.

.  .  .  .  .  .  .  .  .  .  .  .

18. Since September 2, and up to the time of the hearing in this court on September 20, 1957, the units of the Arkansas National Guard have remained at Central High School and have continued to prevent eligible Negro students from attending the school, pursuant to the order issued to them by the Governor of Arkansas through the Adjutant General of Arkansas. . . .

### CONCLUSIONS OF LAW

.  .  .  .  .  .  .  .  .  .  .  .

2. The Governor of Arkansas, as chief executive and commander in chief of its military forces, has a vital interest in the maintenance of law and order and broad discretionary powers to suppress insurrection and to preserve the peace. Article VI, Section 4, of the Constitution of the State expressly provides that:

> "The Governor shall be commander-in-chief of the military
> and naval forces of the state, and may call out such forces to exe-

cute the laws, suppress insurrections, repel invasions or preserve the public peace."

Section 5 provides that:

"It shall be the duty of the Governor to see that the laws are faithfully executed."

As the chief executive of the state, he is appropriately vested with the discretion to determine whether an exigency requiring military state aid for that purpose has arisen.

3. The Governor does not, however, have lawful authority to use the National Guard to deprive the eligible colored students from exercising their right to attend Central High School, which right is guaranteed by the Federal Constitution, the school district plan of integration and the court's orders entered in this cause. If it be assumed that the Governor was entitled to bring military force to the aid of civil authority, the proper use of that power in this instance was to maintain the Federal Court in the exercise of its jurisdiction, to aid in making its process effective and not to nullify it, to remove, and not to create, obstructions to the exercise by the Negro children of their rights as judicially declared.

## *Withdrawal of the Guard, September 20, 1957\**

GOVERNOR FAUBUS early last night ordered Arkansas National Guard troops away from Little Rock Central High School, thus ending his 17-day military encounter with federal authority.

He said he would comply for the time being with the Federal Court injunction and would "do everything in my power" to keep the peace at the School.

After his speech over radio and television he was asked if that meant that he would use the State Police to keep order.

"What I do now will be determined by the events that transpire," he answered. . . .

## *Mayor's Warning, Governor's Departure, September 21, 1957†*

. . . THE MAYOR urged Little Rock residents to accept integration peacefully at the School and warned that "local law enforcement officers" would

---

\* *Arkansas Gazette*, Sept. 21, 1957, p. 1. For model documentation see p. 12.
† *Arkansas Gazette*, Sept. 22, 1957, p. 1. For model documentation see p. 12.

be on hand [tomorrow—Monday] to deal with persons who didn't. . . .

Governor Faubus . . . flew to [Sea Island] Georgia yesterday to attend the Southern Governors' Conference.

His departure left Lieutenant Governor Nathan Gordon as the State's acting chief executive. Mr. Faubus said he had conferred with Gordon but had offered him no suggestions for dealing with the integration issue.

At Atlanta the Associated Press reported Governor Faubus said last night he thought there would be violence if Negro pupils attempted to attend classes at Central High School this week. . . .

The Little Rock School Board yesterday reaffirmed its position that Central High was open to white and Negro students alike as ordered by the Federal Court. But the Board again left it up to the Negroes to decide when and if they should enroll.

## *The Eve of the School Opening, September 22, 1957*\*

. . . IN THE meeting [with Mayor Mann and several other Little Rock leaders on Sunday, September 22] at the Woods residence I do not recall that Governor Faubus was mentioned. It was assumed that the obligation for policing rested on Mayor Mann. I was asked about the White House or Justice Department plans for supplementing local police facilities, but I could bring very little light to bear on that question. I knew, of course, as many others did that the Department of Justice had not approved use of deputy marshals.

We discussed the propriety of using the Marine Corps Reserve component in Little Rock—most of whose members were local veterans and enrollees. Another possibility discussed was a request to be made of Lieutenant Governor Gordon to appeal for federal military assistance in suppressing a riot if real trouble should develop. Also one of the group mentioned that a small assignment of the Air Force Military Police, based 12 miles away, might be sufficient if they were legally available.

In August the President had said in a news conference in Washington that he could not conceive of a situation in which he would send federal troops into a State to enforce integration orders. For this reason, perhaps little thought had been given by anyone to the use of outside federal troops

---

\* This is the continuation of the magazine article by Congressman Hays, pp. 45-47 above, placed here because of the date and events it discusses. For documentation, see p. 47.

to supplement local forces. Troops at Camp Chaffee, Ark., may have been mentioned in this conference, but they were not thought of as importations, and anyway a request of the State government, temporarily under Lieutenant Governor Gordon's direction, for help was regarded as a condition to federal military assistance. There were many precedents for such help. I am sure that no one in the group at that moment anticipated the dramatic and frightening appearance of paratroopers at Central High School within 60 hours. . . .

To all appearances, this mayor's conference on Sunday was for the sole purpose of laying plans to prevent violence. The bitterest opponent of Mayor Mann could have found nothing to condemn in his expressed purposes, unless one wanted violence for the accomplishment of a desired end. No one in the group knew what Daisy Bates of the local NAACP proposed to do, and no one volunteered to advise her. . . .

In the late afternoon of that Sunday, Virgil Blossom met me in the Sam Peck lobby with this question: "Should I talk with Judge Davies about the necessity of having U.S. marshal deputies accompany the nine Negro students into the Central High School?" I thought it would be proper in the unusual circumstances for him to approach the judge. Within a few minutes he reported back to me that the judge would not talk to him—he merely referred him to U.S. District Attorney Osro Cobb. Blossom then called Cobb, but the district attorney thought he would have to have specific authority from the Department of Justice to seek an order from the federal judge for United States marshal's deputies' help in protecting the Negro students.

I called Sherman Adams to ask if he could get such clearance. This illustrates how determined I was to channel everything through Adams. I had brought him into the matter in the first place and I did not propose to bypass him or confuse the situation by multiple contacts, though I was sorely tempted to do so in order to spare him the discomfort of these continued appeals for information.

Adams called back to give me a telephone number at which Cobb could reach a responsible top official of the Department of Justice, adding that he thought the matter could be worked out. . . . Cobb told me that he did not get the authority from the Department when he called that Sunday afternoon for further instructions as to Blossom's request for marshal's deputies to escort the Negro students. The local policemen, officers and men, had balked at "escorting." They pledged to do their duty in preventing violence if the Negroes showed up, but as to escorting —"No, don't ask that," and they meant it. . . .

There were speculations as to what might have happened "if":

If the Governor had not gone away, and if he had sent State police to patrol actively the school area—he had never said he would not;

If it had not been a bright clear day—it had rained hard the two previous days;

If the fire chief had responded to Mayor Mann's request for the use of the fire hose;

If Judge Davies had ordered the United States marshal to assist the local police and add to his force of deputies;

If there had been a permanent federal judge presiding who had been appointed from the district; and

If the situation had arisen after, instead of before, the new city-manager form of government had been installed. . . .

During the month of September, no Negro voices were heard except those of NAACP leaders. The Negro community seemed to be in silent retreat and they have remained silent. Almost by default, Mrs. Daisy Bates, the local chairman, spoke for them. Her aggressiveness did not reflect the temperament of the majority of Little Rock Negroes, but her views on the school question obviously had their support. I did not hear from my old associates on the Urban League board, which I had helped organize as an effective social-service agency during the 1930s. . . .

The Negroes seemed unable to put forward the kind of leaders who could speak with their full confidence and with an authentic voice. There are such Negro leaders, but extremism among the Negroes had the same intimidating influence that it had with many of the white population, and they were not heard. . . .

## Events at Central High School, September 23, 1957 ("Black Monday")*

A HOWLING, shrieking crowd of men and women outside Central High School, and disorderly students inside, forced the authorities to withdraw eight Negro students from the school today, three and one half hours after they entered it.

At the stroke of noon, Mayor Woodrow Wilson Mann radioed to police officers on the scene telling them to tell the crowd:

---

* From the Associated Press report by Relman Morin, who won a 1957 Pulitzer Prize for this story, here reprinted from the *Sacramento Bee,* September 23, 1957, pages 1, A7. For model documentation see p. 51.

"The Negro students have been withdrawn."

Almost immediately, the three Negro boys and five girls left the school under heavy police escort. The officers took them away in police cars.

Crowds clustered at both ends of the school set up a storm of fierce howling and again surged toward the lines of policemen and state troopers.

Again, they were beaten back.

The explosive climax came after the school had been under siege since 8:45 when the Negroes quietly walked through the doors.

The [city] police, armed with riot guns and tear gas, had the crowd under control.

Inside, meanwhile, students reported seeing Negroes with blood on their clothes. Some whites who came out—in protest against integration—told of wild disorder, with policemen chasing white students through the halls and attacks on Negroes in the building.

The break came shortly before noon.

Superintendent of Schools Virgil Blossom said he asked Gene Smith, assistant chief of police at the scene, if he thought it would be best to pull out the Negroes.

Smith said he did.

Mann's announcement, ordering the police to notify the crowd, came minutes afterward.

Three newspapermen were beaten by the crowd before the sudden turn in the situation.

They are Paul Welch, a reporter, and Gray Villette and Francis Miller, photographers. All are employed by Life magazine.

A man smashed Miller in the face while he was carrying an armful of camera equipment. Miller fell to the ground, bleeding profusely.

All morning, the people had been threatening newsmen. "We ought to wipe up the street with these Yankee reporters," a man said.

Even after the Negroes left the school, the crowds remained.

Teenagers in two automobiles cruised on the outskirts before the withdrawal of the students.

During the hours while the Negroes were in the school, between 30 and 50 white students left.

One girl, Sylvia Jones, said she signed out and when asked her reason, said simply "Integration."

The crowd yelled, cheered and applauded each time a white student left the school. "Don't stay in there with them!" people yelled.

Women were hysterical.

Four Negroes were beaten and some arrests were made before the eight students went into the school.

It was a frightening sight.

The drama packed climax of three weeks of integration struggle in Little Rock came just after the buzzer sounded inside the big 2,000 pupil school at 8:45, signaling the start of classes.

Suddenly, on a street leading toward the school, the crowd spotted four Negro adults, marching in twos down the center of the street.

A man yelled, "Look, here they come!"

They were not the students. One appeared to be a newspaperman. He had a card in his hat and was wearing a camera.

I jumped into a glass windowed telephone booth on the corner. The scene was clearly visible. As the crowd surged toward the four Negroes, they broke and ran.

But they were caught on the lawn of a home nearby. Whites jumped the man with the camera from behind, rode him to the ground, kicking and beating him. They smashed the camera to bits.

This, obviously was a planned diversionary movement to draw the crowd's attention away from the school.

While I was dictating what I saw, someone yelled:

"Look, they're going into the school!"

At that instant, the eight Negroes—three boys and five girls—were crossing the schoolyard toward a side door at the south end of the school.

The girls were in bobby sox and the boys were dressed in open shirts. All were carrying books.

They were not running, not even walking fast. They simply strolled toward the steps, went up, and were inside before all but a few of the 200 people at that end of the street knew it.

Some did see the Negroes, however.

"They've gone in!" A man roared, "Oh, God, they're in the school!"

A woman screamed. "Did they get in? Did you see them go in?"

"They're in now!" some other men yelled.

"Oh, my God!" the woman screamed. She burst into tears and tore at her hair.

Hysteria swept the crowd. Other women began weeping and screaming.

At that moment, a tall, gray-haired man in a brown hunting shirt jumped on the barricade with others holding him. He yelled, waving his arms:

"Who's going through?"

"We all are!" the people shouted.

They broke over and around the wooden barricades, rushing the policemen.

About a dozen policemen were in that corner of the street.

They raised their billy clubs. Some grabbed men and women and hurled them back. Two chased a dark haired man who slipped through their line like a football player. They caught him on the schoolyard, whipped his coat down his arms, pinning them, and hustled him out of the yard.

The weeping and screaming went on among the women.

A man said, "I'm going in there and get my kid out."

An officer gritted, "You're not going anywhere."

Two ambulances rolled up. Nobody was in them.

Suddenly, another roar—and cheering and clapping—came from the crowd. A white student, carrying his books came down the front steps.

He was followed by two bobby sox girls. In the next few minutes, other students came out.

"There's not much education goin' on inside there now," one of the boys who came out told reporters.

A moment later, two policemen suddenly raced into the building through the north door. When they came out, they were holding a girl by both arms, rushing her forcibly toward a police prisoner's wagon.

For an instant, it looked as though the crowd would try to break the police lines again to rescue her.

But they put her in the car and drove swiftly down the street, past the barricade at the south end.

Screams, catcalls and more yelling broke out as the car, whipping dangerously close to the people and the barricades, raced down the street.

A man, distraught, came sprinting after it. "That's my kid in there," he yelled. "Help me get my kid out."

But the car was gone.

The eight Negro students slipped into the school this morning while a group of Negro adults fought the angry crowd of whites to divert their attention.

Reporters who caught just a glimpse of the students as they were rushed into the building through a side door said nine had entered but the school office said the number was eight.

The well executed plan of diversion held the crowd's attention long enough for the Negro students to be driven onto the campus and whisked through the side door. . . .

## Removal of the Negro Students, September 23, 1957*

. . . DESPITE the uproar on the outside, there was no serious trouble when the Negro students attended classes inside the building. In one class, two or three white students walked out when a Negro student was seated. In another class, almost half of the white students walked out. There was a good deal of noise in the halls. Slurring remarks were occasionally made to the Negro students, and sometimes several boys would block the passage of a Negro boy or girl through a doorway. One white girl slapped a Negro girl, who turned and said, "Thank you," and then walked on down the hall. A dozen white girls walked out when a Negro girl signed up for their gym class. On the other hand, many students spoke words of welcome and encouragement to the Negro children and urged them to "stay and fight it out." One white girl later told reporters there was "very little trouble at all" and that most of her classmates were "disgusted" with students who walked out. The great majority of students acted with dignity and tact.

About an hour after classes started I received a telephone call from Mayor Mann expressing alarm and suggesting the Negro students be removed.

"Why?" I asked.

"There'll be a riot," he said.

"Let's get Gene Smith's opinion," I said. "If he says the Negroes should be removed for the safety of all, I'll agree."

An hour later the mayor called again and renewed his suggestion. I telephoned the assistant chief of police at the school about eleven-thirty.

"We've got things under control," Smith told me, "but if the crowd keeps on growing it could be difficult."

"What about the lunch hour when classes are out—or after school?"

"That's what is worrying me," Smith replied. "Some of these people might try to follow the Negro students home. It might be wise to take them out now."

"All right," I said. "Go ahead and do it."

---

* From an account by Superintendent Virgil T. Blossom in "The Untold Story of Little Rock," *The Saturday Evening Post*, June 13, 1959, p. 102. For model documentation, see p. 47.

### President Eisenhower's Emergency Proclamation, September 23, 1957*

. . . PRESIDENT EISENHOWER denounced the "disgraceful occurrences" at Little Rock, threatened to use "whatever force may be necessary" to enforce the law and the court's order and issued a proclamation commanding all persons obstructing justice to cease and desist and disperse.

### President Eisenhower's Order of Federal Troops to Little Rock, September 24, 1957†

PRESIDENT EISENHOWER, informed that a mob had gathered in defiance of his "cease and desist" proclamation, ordered Federal troops into Little Rock and federalized the Arkansas National Guard, thus removing it from Gov. Faubus' command. One thousand members of the 327th Airborne Battle Group of the 101st Airborne Division were flown to Little Rock from Fort Campbell, Ky. . . .

### From President Eisenhower's Speech to the Nation, September 24, 1957‡

FOR A FEW minutes this evening I should like to speak to you about the serious situation that has arisen in Little Rock. To make this talk I have come to the President's office in the White House. I could have spoken from Rhode Island, where I have been staying recently, but I felt that, in speaking from the house of Lincoln, of Jackson and of Wilson, my words would better convey both the sadness I feel in the action I was compelled today to take and the firmness with which I intend to pursue this course until the orders of the federal court at Little Rock can be executed without unlawful interference.

In that city, under the leadership of demagogic extremists, disorderly mobs have deliberately prevented the carrying out of proper orders from a federal court. Local authorities have not eliminated that violent opposition and, under the law, I yesterday issued a proclamation calling upon the mob to disperse.

---

* *World Almanac*, 1958, p. 45.
† *World Almanac*, 1958, p. 45.
‡ Broadcast over radio and television networks; here reprinted from *U.S. News & World Report*, October 4, 1957, pp. 64-65.

This morning the mob again gathered in front of the Central High School of Little Rock, obviously for the purpose of again preventing the carrying out of the court's order relating to the admission of Negro children to that school.

Whenever normal agencies prove inadequate to the task and it becomes necessary for the executive branch of the Federal Government to use its powers and authority to uphold federal courts, the President's responsibility is inescapable.

In accordance with that responsibility, I have today issued an executive order directing the use of troops under federal authority to aid in the execution of federal law at Little Rock, Ark. This became necessary when my proclamation of yesterday was not observed, and the obstruction of justice still continues. . . .

Our personal opinions about the decision have no bearing on the matter of enforcement; the responsibility and authority of the Supreme Court to interpret the Constitution are very clear. . . .

It was my hope that this localized situation would be brought under control by city and State authorities. If the use of local police powers had been sufficient, our traditional method of leaving the problem in those hands would have been pursued. But when large gatherings of obstructionists made it impossible for the decrees of the court to be carried out, both the law and the national interest demanded that the President take action. . . .

The very basis of our individual rights and freedom rests upon the certainty that the President and the executive branch of Government will support and insure the carrying out of the decisions of the federal courts even, when necessary, with all the means at the President's command.

Unless the President did so, anarchy would result.

There would be no security for any except that which each one of us could provide for himself.

The interest of the nation in the proper fulfillment of the law's requirements cannot yield to opposition and demonstrations by some few persons.

Mob rule cannot be allowed to override the decisions of our courts.

Now, let me make it very clear that federal troops are not being used to relieve local and State authorities of their primary duty to preserve the peace and order of the community. Nor are the troops there for the purpose of taking over the responsibility of the school board and the other responsible local officials in running Central High School. The running of our school system and the maintenance of peace and order in each of our States are strictly local affairs, and the Federal Government does not interfere, except in very special cases and when requested by one of the several States. In the present case, the troops are there, pursuant to law, solely for the purpose of preventing interference with the orders of the court.

The proper use of the powers of the executive branch to enforce the orders of a federal court is limited to extraordinary and compelling circumstances. Manifestly, such an extreme situation has been created in Little Rock. This challenge must be met and with such measures as will preserve to the people as a whole their lawfully protected rights in a climate permitting their free and fair exercise. . . .

The decision of the Supreme Court concerning school integration, of course, affects the South more seriously than it does other sections of the country. In that region I have many warm friends, some of them in the city of Little Rock. I have deemed it a great personal privilege to spend in our Southland tours of duty while in the military service and enjoyable recreational periods since that time.

So, from intimate personal knowledge, I know that the overwhelming majority of the people in the South—including those of Arkansas and of Little Rock—are of good will, united in their efforts to preserve and respect the law even when they disagree with it.

They do not sympathize with mob rule. They, like the rest of our nation, have proved in two great wars their readiness to sacrifice for America.

And the foundation of the American way of life is our national respect for law.

In the South, as elsewhere, citizens are keenly aware of the tremendous disservice that has been done to the people of Arkansas in the eyes of the nation, and that has been done to the nation in the eyes of the world.

At a time when we face grave situations abroad because of the hatred that Communism bears toward a system of government based on human rights, it would be difficult to exaggerate the harm that is being done to the prestige and influence—and, indeed, to the safety—of our nation and the world.

Our enemies are gloating over this incident and using it everywhere to misrepresent our whole nation. We are portrayed as a violator of those standards of conduct which the peoples of the world united to proclaim in the Charter of the United Nations. There they affirmed "faith in fundamental human rights and in the dignity and worth of the human person," and they did so "without distinction as to race, sex, language or religion."

And so, with deep confidence, I call upon citizens of the State of Arkansas to assist in bringing to an immediate end all interference with the law and its processes. If resistance to the federal court order ceases at once, the further presence of federal troops will be unnecessary and the city of Little Rock will return to its normal habits of peace and order— and a blot upon the fair name and high honor of our nation in the world will be removed.

Thus will be restored the image of America and of all its parts as one nation, indivisible, with liberty and justice for all.

Good night and thank you very much.

### DOCUMENTATION SUITABLE FOR RESEARCH PAPERS

BIBLIOGRAPHY ENTRY

Eisenhower, Dwight D., President. Speech concerning troops in Little Rock, as printed in *U.S. News & World Report,* October 4, 1957. Reprinted in *LRUSA.*

FIRST FOOTNOTE

\*President Dwight D. Eisenhower, speech concerning troops in Little Rock, as printed in *U.S. News & World Report,* October 4, 1957, reprinted in *LRUSA,* pp. 64-67.

SUBSEQUENT FOOTNOTES

\*Eisenhower, *op. cit., LRUSA,* p. ■.
\*Eisenhower, speech concerning troops, *LRUSA,* p. ■.
\*Eisenhower, *LRUSA,* p. ■.

These examples are models for other speeches in this collection.

---

## *Little Rock Reactions to President Eisenhower's Federalization of the Arkansas National Guard, September 24, 1957\**

STUNNED by the rioting and strife of the last 24 hours, people in Little Rock reacted with surprise and relief today to the announcement that President Dwight D. Eisenhower has ordered federalization of the Arkansas National Guard.

---

\* From the Associated Press report by Relman Morin, here reprinted from the *Sacramento Bee,* September 24, 1957, pages 1, A6. For model documentation, see p. 51.

It was electrifying news here and apparently came as a complete surprise to officials in the Capitol and officers of the guard.

"My God, has he done that?" ejaculated Claude Carpenter, one of Governor Orval E. Faubus' key aides when informed by the Associated Press today. . . .

Faubus is flying back to Little Rock from Sea Island, Ga., where he has been attending the southern governors' conference. . . .

Faubus has been insisting the president has no authority to move in on the danger ridden Little Rock situation. He said federal troops could be brought in only at his request and that he had no intention of making any such request.

The news came while the hard pressed Little Rock police were cracking down with a genuine get tough policy today.

At the Central High School, focal point of the 22 day old racial controversy, they scooped up 11 persons, including two youths who appeared to be of high school age. All were white men.

That brought the total of arrests for two days to 44, including both whites and Negroes.

All but one were booked on charges of inciting to riot, carrying a weapon, or disturbing the peace.

Motorcycle policemen and police squad cars raced all over the city today. They were stopping and searching automobiles and frisking people for weapons.

At the high school about the same size crowd as yesterday's gathered an hour or so before the final buzzer rang for classes to begin this morning.

The police there moved quickly—and in complete contrast to their actions when the rioting broke out yesterday—by picking up known agitators early.

Fewer students reported for school this morning—but how many failed to appear could not be determined.

At Central, no Negro students showed up.

(According to the United Press, Mrs. L. C. Bates, state president of the National Association for the Advancement of Colored People, announced nine Negro children will attend the Central High School tomorrow, if the national guard, now federalized, can start protecting them then.

("The president's action has given us, and certainly the nine Negro children, renewed faith in the constitution," she stated.)

City policemen and state troopers were busy last night answering calls reporting fights between whites and Negroes. Most of them turned out to be of minor importance.

A gang fight between about 50 Negro and white teenagers touched off what may have been the most serious incident. State Trooper Louis Cone reported that when he told a car occupied by two Negro men and three women to "move on," the driver attempted to run him down.

Cone, who was knocked down by the automobile, said he jumped up, fired two shots at the fleeing car and then gave chase in his own automobile. A city policeman also fired a shot, he stated, and two city police cars joined in the chase.

Pursuit ended at a deadend street about 12 blocks away, when the Negroes' car bounced into a yard and smashed into a fence.

The police booked Curtis Patrick, 22, of Little Rock, for disturbing the peace. They also booked Clarence R. Sanders, 29, of Bunkie, La., an airman stationed at Little Rock Air Force Base, for disturbing the peace, carrying a concealed weapon—officers said he had a metal club—and assault with a deadly weapon. The latter charge stemmed from the attempt to run down Trooper Cone, who suffered a bruise on a leg. Saunders was fined $300 and given 90 days in jail.

No one was injured by the gunfire.

The three women in the car were taken to a hospital for treatment of cuts and bruises. They are Patrick's mother and sister—Rosalee Hubbard, about 50, and Robbie Lee Belt, 19,—and Catheryn Ransom, all of Little Rock.

The police said blows were struck in the Main Street gang fight but apparently no one was hurt seriously. The incident occurred at a drivein cafe—a hangout for white teenagers.

One white man, Dan Dinkins, 47, was treated for lacerations of the face and a depressed skull fracture after being hit on the head by a hurtling stone.

A 50 car cavalcade forming in downtown Little Rock was described by officers as "just a bunch of kids." They broke it up.

Between eight and 10 Negroes were arrested. The police reported no arrests of white men.

"Negroes, armed with all types of weapons, including pistols and razor blades, are attacking whites. . . . throwing stones, breaking car windshields and throwing bottles into doors of houses," an officer said.

Newsmen who drove by car through Negro districts found them uniformly dark and silent. Where a house was lighted, the lights were switched off at the approach of the car.

The aftermath of yesterday's violence stirred a storm of biting statements, claims and counterclaims.

"We are a disgraced city because of a handful of people," declared Mayor Woodrow Wilson Mann.

Lieutenant Governor Gordon called the mayor "a liar" and stated he would not recall the national guard to restore order without a written request from Mann, because, he added, he would not "take Mann's word for anything. Yesterday, to be polite, I said his statement was not correct. Today I say he is a liar."

This referred to a report, denied later by the mayor, that he had asked Gordon for help from the national guard. Mann said—during the earlier stages of the dispute in Little Rock—that he knew of no threat of violence over integration, and that it was unnecessary for Faubus to call out the troops.

Virgil Blossom, superintendent of schools, gave a description of events inside the high school yesterday after the nine Negro students entered which coincided with reports by the Negroes themselves—minor scuffling.

White students who came out reported seeing Negroes with blood on their clothes and told a tall story of taking one Negro boy by the arm and forcibly walking one half the length of a corridor in an attempt to get him out the door.

Terrance Roberts, 15, one of the Negroes, said he was pushed around but not harmed. A white girl said there was very little trouble at all.

## From a Talk to the Student Body of Central High School, September 25, 1957*

. . . WHAT does all this mean to you students? You have often heard it said, no doubt, that the United States is a Nation under law and not under men. This means that we are governed by laws, properly decided upon by duly constituted authority, and not by the decrees of one man or one class of men. Since this is true, it means that we are all subject to all the laws, whether we approve of them personally or not, and as law-abiding citizens, have an obligation in conscience to obey them. There can be no exceptions; if it were otherwise, we would not be a strong Nation but a mere unruly mob.

I believe that you are well-intentioned, law-abiding citizens, who understand the necessity of obeying the law, and are determined to do so.

--------

* By Major General Edwin A. Walker, commanding the federal forces, as reported by the United Press; here reprinted from the *San Francisco Chronicle*, September 26, 1957. For model documentation see pp. 12 and 51.

You have nothing to fear from my soldiers, and no one will interfere with your coming, going or your peaceful pursuit of your studies.

However, I would be less than honest if I failed to tell you that I intend to use all means necessary to prevent any interference with the execution of your school board's plan. This is what I have been ordered to do, and I intend to carry out my orders. Those who interfere or disrupt the proper administration of the school will be removed by the soldiers on duty and turned over to the local police for disposition in accordance with the laws of your community.

One last word about my soldiers. They are here because they have been ordered to be here. They are seasoned, well-trained soldiers, many of them combat veterans. Being soldiers, they are as determined as I to carry out their orders. However, as I stated before, the law-abiding people have nothing to fear from them. They have been carefully instructed not to molest any law-abiding citizen in his person or property, and they will obey these orders.

Since a peaceful atmosphere must be maintained in the school and its vicinity, it may be necessary for them to issue instructions concerning such things as loitering, assembling in large groups, and otherwise making it difficult for them to perform their duties. I earnestly ask that you co-operate, for your own benefit and ours. . . .

*Events in the Vicinity and in Central High School, September 25, 1957\**

To the people of Little Rock, the quiet tree-shaded corner has been known for years as "Fourteenth and Schiller."

The intersection, surrounded by neat homes and tidy lawns, has its counterpart in the residential neighborhoods of every city in America. As long as they can remember, people have been crossing it daily without giving it a second thought.

To the U.S. Army's 101st Airborne Division, "Fourteenth and Schiller" became "Roadblock Alpha." It bristled with bayonets. The only way you could get through—unless you had business in the area—would be to fight some of the toughest men ever to wear an American uniform.

On that first day, Sept. 25, 1957, nobody tried it.

---

\* "I Saw It Happen in Little Rock," *U.S. News & World Report,* an independent weekly news magazine published at Washington, October 4, 1957, pp. 37-41. Copyright 1957 United States News Publishing Corporation. For model documentation see p. 47.

A small crowd of curious people gathered at "Roadblock Alpha" the first thing in the morning—most of them just to see what was going on.

Lieut. William Ness stared at the crowd, and said: "Either you move or we'll move you."

They moved.

Throughout the day, all along Fourteenth Street and all along Schiller, little knots of citizens formed to talk things over. Passing by, you could overhear such remarks as these:

A man in shirt sleeves: "They're trying to cram this thing down our throats."

A woman: "The South has been occupied again."

Another man: "What are they trying to do to us? Bayonets ain't the way to do it."

These troopers meant business. With bayonets ready, they kept people on the move. To resist meant trouble, and nobody doubted it.

Sometime during the morning, a squad of troops moved down the street with a crowd dispersing rapidly in front of them. One man moved out ahead, and soldiers ran after him. Swirling out of the crowd came a teen-age girl, shrieking at the top of her voice:

"You leave my daddy alone! That man's my daddy! You leave him alone!"

She was 15-year-old Luanne Montgomery, a sophomore at Central High School, who had walked out of class because she didn't want to go to school with Negroes. The troopers had ordered her father to move, and pressed him because he wasn't moving fast enough. He wasn't arrested. But his daughter was almost hysterical.

Halfway down the block from Schiller, on Fourteenth Street, Paul Downs, of Springdale, Ark., stood in front of a house, clutching a bandaged arm. He said the bandage covered a bayonet wound. Here is his story:

"I was standing on the corner with other people when the troops came up and told us to move away. Well, I didn't move right away. 'I'm from the South,' I said, 'and I don't move very fast.'

"Before I knew it, the bayonet went into my arm right to the bone. So I got out of there fast. The doc put four stitches in my arm, and here I am back again."

Mr. Downs, 35, is a salesman who spent 13 years in the Army and saw service both in World War II and in Korea.

"All I ask," he said, "is that these troops use some discretion in this thing."

As he talked, a crowd began to gather. Behind the crowd came the troops. They took Mr. Downs away, and his listeners moved on.

Apparently C. E. Blake, a railroad man from North Little Rock, didn't move quite fast enough, either.

At one point, a crowd started forming near "Roadblock Alpha." Troops moved in and grabbed several young men, obviously the leaders. They were marched off to a detention compound.

A short time later, the crowd started jeering. Paratroopers moved forward with fixed bayonets. Mr. Blake, in the crowd stood stock still. The troopers advanced. The tip of a bayonet pricked Mr. Blake's shirt. He grabbed at the rifle, as if to push it away, and a scuffle developed.

Suddenly the butt of a M-1 rifle smashed against Mr. Blake's forehead. He went down, blood flowing from a gash just above his left eye. His wife stood over him, screaming. The troopers moved on. A friend took Mr. Blake to a hospital.

Through most of the day, Little Rock was a city of tense and jumpy people. Nerves were tightest in the school neighborhood. For example—

• A group of people stood near an intersection, silently watching troops hurry past "on the double." Suddenly, from the rear came the sharp clang of metal striking metal. A wave of apprehension swept the crowd. Everybody turned to see what was going on.

It was just two workmen putting up a "No Parking" sign.

• Several teen-agers with "ducktail" haircuts and long sideburns lined a curb making wisecracks at a detachment of troopers. The officer in charge snapped a command. A squad formed, bayonets ready, took one step forward and, in unison, yelled "Hah!" The youngsters scattered like startled rabbits.

• A reporter knocked at a door near Central High School and asked the woman who answered if he could use the telephone.

"Look at the blood on my steps," she said. "Just look there at the blood. The Yankee soldiers did that. Who are you for, anyway? If you're for Eisenhower, you can't use this phone."

Just a few minutes before, a man had been clubbed with a rifle butt while standing in her front yard.

At times, it was a city of wild rumors, too—

Somebody said a man had been bayoneted in the head while he stood on the porch of his own house. Nobody ever located him.

Somebody said fighting had broken out between white boys and Negro workers at a construction site in another part of town. It hadn't.

Somebody said that, inside the school, squads of armed troopers accompanied each Negro child to all classes. Others said they didn't. Troops were stationed inside the school throughout the day, though.

And it was a city beset with moods that ranged from apprehension to cold anger—

• A woman stood in a doorway, looking at Central High. "This is the grimmest day of my life," she said. "I didn't sleep a wink last night."

• Once a crowd, fleeing before the bayonets, dashed to the porch of a private home. A woman, trying to shoo them away, pleaded: "Don't get me in trouble! We want no trouble!"

• A young man glared at the troopers—from a safe distance—and said: "If they'd put their guns down and come across the street, we'd show 'em who's tough around here."

Something happens to you when you find yourself in close company with a bayonet. This happened to a member of the Board of Editors of "U.S. News & World Report":

"I was near the edge of a skirmish line of troops moving down the street with fixed bayonets. One of the paratroopers swerved toward me, apparently bound to clear me out of the neighborhood.

"It happened in an instant. Somebody yelled: 'Hey, he's all right. He's one of the newsmen!' The soldier swerved aside, missing me by a couple of inches.

"For a couple of seconds I was staring at the business end of a 101st Airborne bayonet, and it wasn't a very pretty sight."

It was 9:22 A.M.—40 minutes after the final bell had rung to start the day's classes at Central High.

Racing along Park Street came an olive-drab car—big enough to hold the nine Negro students the U.S. Army was taking to school. Jeeps filled with paratroopers escorted the car.

The cavalcade braked to a stop at the long walk leading up the concrete steps to the main entrance of the school. Three hundred fifty soldiers surrounding the school came to attention.

Paratroopers in full battle dress formed a tight guard around the staff car. The Negro students filed out of the car and started up the walk.

Across the street a group of white students chanted: "Two, four, six, eight—we ain't gonna integrate."

At 9:24 A.M. the Negroes crossed the threshold of the school. With military precision, it had taken the 101st Airborne Division two minutes to integrate Central High.

A junior-high-school football game was in progress at Central High stadium when the 101st Airborne took over in the dark of the night.

The troops went about their business exactly as they would advance to "secure" occupied territory. They moved in silently and deployed "on the double" to block all entrances to the high school. Through the gloom that contrasted with the nearby floodlights at the stadium, the soldiers hurried to their chores, unreeling wire for field telephones and setting up a field headquarters. Squads of paratroopers marched rapidly around the school, dropping off guards at each entrance.

Within minutes, combat troops had "secured" the area.

There are Negro troops in the 101st Airborne, but the Army announced they weren't on duty as guards or patrols when their division integrated Central High.

Military authorities decided to use the Negroes, along with white soldiers, as a reserve force.

Here and there, tempers grew short as the day wore on.

A Negro delivery boy came pedaling down Schiller Street on a bicycle. A crowd of white boys spotted him. The Negro dropped his bicycle and ran into a nearby house. Some of the white boys dashed to the porch behind him. Others pulled knives and slashed his bike tires to ribbons.

Within minutes, a squad of troopers rushed to the scene. An officer went to the door, and said: "Come on out, sonny—we'll take you where you want to go." The boy and his bicycle were piled in a jeep and driven away.

Two Negro boys sauntered down a street near a group of white teenagers. Things happened fast. Soon the Negroes were running, with the white boys in full chase. One of the Negroes grabbed a rock and threw it. A white boy seized his wrist, spun him around—and the fight started.

Almost instantly, the soldiers were there. They arrested one of the white boys and sent the Negroes on their way.

Maj. James Meyers, of San Antonio, Tex., watched a crowd of citizens at Fourteenth and Schiller streets—the Army's "Roadblock Alpha."

He said something to a private, who picked up a microphone and told the bystanders: "The 101st Airborne Division is here to enforce law and order. You are instructed to disperse and return to your homes."

"Go to hell!" a man in the crowd yelled.

Major Meyers picked up the microphone and said, matter-of-factly: "If you do not disperse now, it will be necessary for us to disperse you. We do not want to take this action."

A few people edged away, but most remained.

The major walked over to a radio jeep, called headquarters, and said: "Would you dispatch one platoon from Bravo Company to 'Roadblock Alpha'?"

Soon a column of paratroopers came along the street "on the double."

The Texas major called the column to a halt, picked up the microphone, and said: "Once again, you are ordered to disperse peacefully and return home."

"Why don't you go home?" someone called.

The major waved a command to the troops. Instantly, they split into two groups. One trotted down Schiller Street. The other advanced straight across the intersection, bayonets level. The people retreated.

The paratroopers fanned out the width of both streets and advanced at a steady pace. One group of bystanders dashed to a porch, shouting: "We live here." The troopers swept by and continued their march. Soon it was all over. With impassive, methodical efficiency, the 101st Airborne had cleared "Roadblock Alpha."

A couple of blocks from Central High School a teen-ager sat in a jeep under the guard of two soldiers. He had been arrested after an incident involving some of his friends, who now stood 50 feet away, down the street.

"Jump out and run," somebody yelled to him.

"I can't," he answered back. "I can't, I can't."

An officer walked up to the jeep, stuck his face up to the boy's face and said: "Do not get out of this jeep. I repeat, do not get out of this jeep and run away. Do you understand?"

"I understand," said the youngster. And there he stayed until the jeep carted him away to a prisoners' compound on the playing field behind Central High.

Only once that anybody noticed did the grim, businesslike discipline of the paratroopers crack.

A squad that had broken up a fight between white and Negro boys was marching away, in front of a crowd. From the crowd came jeers and catcalls. A sergeant darted his eyes in the direction of the noise and muttered:

"I wish I could—I could go over there and take any three of them and break them in two with one hand."

But he didn't break stride. Nobody in the squad glanced his way. It was as though the remark had never been made.

At 3 o'clock the school day was over.

Probably never before in U.S. history has a school let out amid such a scene as that at Central High. Three hundred and fifty soldiers in full battle gear surrounded the school and its neighborhood, ready for action. Jeeps rolled along the streets. Walkie-talkie radios cracked with military messages. A helicopter roared back and forth at an altitude of only 200 feet as the children trooped out.

But nothing happened. The white students poured out of the school much as they would on any school day—chatting, laughing, outwardly unconcerned. The Negro students were taken out through a side door and left in Army vehicles.

What did the white students think of their first day in mixed classes?

One boy said: "I don't like this integration stuff, but I'm not going to fight about it."

Said another: "We're against it, but there's nothing we can do about it."

A sophomore girl said: "Everything went off fine. At lunch some white boys and girls asked the colored students to eat with them, and they did."

Another girl: "I don't care if they come to school if I don't have to eat with them and undress with them in the locker room."

One boy shrugged his shoulders: "The school year is ruined."

What sort of school day had it been? This came from sophomore Bobby Rhoads as he walked down Park Street on his way home:

"I think all this troop business is stupid. I don't want this integration any more than anyone else, but it looks like it's bound to come.

"It was pretty hard to get anything done in school with everything else that was going on. That helicopter kept buzzing around over the roof all the time and it was hard for us to pay attention."

By nightfall, Little Rock's streets were quiet. The crowd that had formed and disbanded at "Roadblock Alpha" off and on through the day finally thinned to nothing. Only the troops remained.

Somebody asked an officer how long he thought the troops of the U.S. Army would be on duty at Central High.

"Indefinitely," he replied. "We stayed in Germany 15 years."

*Student Comment on September 25, 1957\**

A 16-YEAR-OLD white girl, a junior at Central High School, today made a tearful plea for parents to stay home and let pupils work out integration at the school.

"If parents would just go home and let us alone, we'll be all right," said the youngster, who declined to identify herself. "We just want them to leave us be. We can do it."

The brown-haired girl, shaking with emotion, told reporters she had been warned by another student not to attend classes today or "I was going to get it." She spoke to newsmen during the noon hour, after crossing alone through the line of soldiers in front of the school.

"We don't want it," she said, referring to integration. "Nobody wants it. But it's got to be."

The girl, one of 1250 pupils who remained in the 2000-student school, said she spoke for herself but indicated her sentiments were shared by others who attended school today.

She said the Negro pupils were "very well received" and there was "only one girl that kind of sneered up."

She described an incident that occurred in the lunch room at noon time when a "Negro boy was sitting by himself at a table and a white boy and girl, very high class, went down and asked the Negro very politely to go over and sit with them." She said the Negro boy got up, grinned and seemed "very thankful."

Clutching her hands tightly in front of her, and reminding photographers not to take her picture the girl said, "As long as I need education, I'll go to this school. As long as they keep parents back, the mob back, we'll be all right."

THE NINE Negro students who attended Central High School today for their first full day's session reported they were pleased with their reception by the school's white children.

The nine, taken to classes in an Army station wagon convoyed by two jeeps filled with soldiers, returned at mid-afternoon to the home of Mrs. L. C. Bates, State NAACP president. There they were met and taken home by their parents.

---

\* *San Francisco Chronicle*, September 26, 1957. Two stories: first by New York Herald Tribune Service, second by United Press. For model documentation, see pp. 12 and 51.

Elizabeth Eckford, 15, described Central as "just like any other school."

Gloria Ray, who celebrates her 15th birthday tomorrow, said she had made several "good" friends among the student body at Central today.

One of the girls said she was standing in a line at the cafeteria when one of the white girls invited her to join her at a table with another group of white girls.

"They were all so nice," she said. "They treated us like celebrities."

Melba Pattillo said, "Gosh, everyone was so friendly. We didn't think it would be nearly this nice. A lot of kids knew my name and introduced themselves. We got along real fine."

Ernest Green was more interested in learning about the soldiers than in commenting on his first day at integrated Central High.

"Man," he said, "when I go into the Army, I'm enlisting in the 101st (airborne division). I'm gonna be a paratrooper and go to Fort Campbell, Ky."

## *Inside Central High School, October 1957*

CLASSES went on more or less as usual at Little Rock Central High School with nine Negro students attending under the protection of federal troops. Early in October the students took their six-week tests. No results were released but most students seemed to think they were doing as well, or better, than usual. . . .

The work of some students suffered because of their absences. Most of these were those who took part in a student walkout and those who were suspended for incidents involving the Negro students. The walkout, promoted by the League of Central High Mothers, was considered a flop even by the students who participated. Only about 50 left the school on Oct. 3. The enrollment at the school is 1,973. The Mothers League had expected at least 200 to 250 to walk out. . . .

The student newspaper, the *Tiger,* urged students to "maintain a sensible, peaceful neutrality." Later on it said, "All that the history books will have to say about the events at Little Rock during the 1957-58 school term has not been written; no one knows what new developments will arise in the next few weeks and months. But another sort of history, of more importance to us personally, is our scholastic record. This should receive our full attention, regardless of the events that have taken place or will take place, and regardless of our personal feelings toward what has happened during this historic year at Little Rock Central High School."
[*SSN* November 1957, p. 6]

## Community and Church Action, October 1957

TWENTY-FIVE prominent business and professional men of Little Rock signed a statement Oct. 2 saying, "We believe that the people of the city of Little Rock, regardless of their feelings on the subject of segregation: (1) Believe in and are dedicated to government by law and order. (2) Detest and condemn violence. (3) Have faith in the use of democratic legal processes for settlement of differences. (4) Need a period of continual calm consideration of all facts and circumstances."

They therefore called on the people to uphold those "who enforce laws without reservation" and to condemn the threat, encouragement or use of violence. Some of the 25 are known to harbor strong segregationist feelings. Nine civic organizations adopted the statement.

A mass attempt to solve the Little Rock problem with prayer took place Oct. 11 and 12. Twenty-four Baptist ministers (only one a member of the Southern Baptist Convention) sponsored a prayer meeting the night of Oct. 11 for those who believe in segregation. Thirty-eight ministers and about 600 persons attended. The next morning 84 Little Rock churches, both Protestant and Catholic, and synagogues held prayer services for a peaceful solution. Between 6,000 and 7,000 persons attended. Churches at Hope, Crossett, Camden, Fayetteville and Hot Springs held similar prayer services the same day.

At a meeting of the state Baptist Student Union Convention, 359 out of 360 attending voted for a statement of beliefs stating that the Christian position in racial relations was to uphold the law of the land and abstain from violence. [*SSN* November 1957, p. 6]

## Failure of Attempt to Mediate between Governor Faubus and President Eisenhower, October 1957

THE FIRST thing to be done at Little Rock, apparently, was to get the federal troops out of town. Five members of the Southern Governors Conference were selected to talk to President Eisenhower about that but one of them, Gov. Marvin E. Griffin of Georgia, didn't attend the conference.

On Oct. 1 the other four met the President at the White House. They were Gov. Theodore McKeldin of Maryland, Gov. Luther Hodges of North Carolina, Gov. Frank G. Clement of Tennessee and Gov. LeRoy Collins of Florida, all Democrats except McKeldin. Hodges, the chairman, dealt with Gov. Faubus of Arkansas by telephone during the meeting.

During the afternoon conference the four governors presented to Eisenhower the Faubus position. The way the President understood it was given in his statement at the end of the meeting: "At the meeting the governors informed the President that the governor of Arkansas had authorized them to state he was prepared to assume full responsibility for maintaining law and order in Little Rock and in connection herewith will not obstruct the orders of the federal court." As soon as Faubus issued such a statement, the President said, he would have the troops withdrawn.

Within two hours Faubus put out his statement. It said it had never been his intention to obstruct the court order, that he would not obstruct the court order and that this had been his stand all along.

This did not satisfy Eisenhower: "The statement issued this evening by the governor of Arkansas does not constitute in my opinion the assurance that he intends to use his full powers as governor to prevent the obstruction of the orders of the United States District Court." He wouldn't withdraw the troops.

What went wrong? The White House said only that there were "many things" wrong with the Faubus statement.

Faubus said he had done what he had said he would do but that he was beginning to doubt that any agreement could be reached as long as Atty. Gen. Herbert Brownell Jr. and the "palace guard" were telling Eisenhower what to do.

The four governors on the committee were specific. They said Faubus had changed his statement after both sides had agreed to the wording verbatim of both the Eisenhower and Faubus statements. Specifically, McKeldin said, Faubus added the words "by me" to the sentence ending "the orders of the federal court will not be obstructed by me." Faubus, however, said those two words were in his statement as agreed to by telephone in advance.

Two days later Eisenhower described two conditions under either of which he would pull out the troops. The first was unequivocal assurance that court orders would not be obstructed and that peace would be maintained. The second was for conditions at Little Rock to develop so that local police could carry out the court order.

Faubus, reading this, said that his "by me" statement was the unequivocal assurance.

A few days later the governor said it looked to him as if the federal troops would be needed as long as the Negro students were attending Central High. Thereafter no known attempts were made to resolve the crisis as the relations between the state and federal authorities drifted to lower and lower levels. [*SSN* November 1957, pp. 6-7]

## Charges and a Resolution, October 1957

FIRST, Gov. Faubus said that swarms of FBI agents were working in Little Rock and holding teenaged girls incommunicado for hours while questioning them. FBI Director J. Edgar Hoover said this was a "falsehood."

Then the governor said that federal troops, on duty inside Central High as a protection for the Negro students, had entered the girls' dressing room where the girls, both white and Negro, change clothes for physical education classes. The White House said this charge was vulgar and untrue. Army Secretary Wilber M. Brucker said it was vulgar and unsupported. . . .

Toward the end of the month the Arkansas County Judges Association adopted without dissent a resolution commending Faubus for his stand at Little Rock and criticizing the President for sending federal troops. This association is recognized as one of the most powerful political groups in the state. . . . [*SSN* November 1957, p. 7]

## Inside Central High School, November 1957

MRS. MARGARET C. JACKSON, president of the Mothers League of Central High School, [said], "There is great resentment against the Negroes inside the school. The white children are determined to get them out of there."

At the school, classes were going on and teachers were giving grades. The armed guard was gradually being reduced. The Negro students lost the military escort which had been delivering them to and from school, and inside the school the soldiers quit trailing them from class to class. . . .

When integration took place Sept. 25 hundreds of paratroopers from the 101st Airborne Infantry Division were on guard. They were with the nine Negro students from their homes to the school, between classes and back to their homes. Then the Arkansas National Guard, on federal duty, took over some, then more, and finally all of the guard duty. Half the 1,000 paratroopers at Little Rock were sent back to Fort Campbell, Ky., then all but 225 were sent back and the last of them left Little Rock on Nov. 27. All but 900 of the 10,500 federal Guardsmen were returned to the state. Late in November only a handful of soldiers was at the high school each day—one or two on each floor of the five-story building, and a few patrolling in pairs on the campus.

Early in November two white girls and one Negro girl were involved in a bumping or shoving incident. All three were lectured by school officials, who called it the kind of trivial thing that happens anywhere there are 2,000 adolescents in one building. Later a white boy in the senior class struck one of the Negro boys and was suspended for a few days.

Students interviewed know of similar incidents that never made the papers: A white girl spitting in the face of a Negro girl; a Negro girl's gym shoes thrown out a window; hissing and remarks at the Negroes in the crowded halls.

They report these other incidents: In a spelling match a white team captain picks a Negro as first choice for his side; a home room class invites a Negro to read the Bible; a Negro student giving an extemporaneous talk, tells how her mother worried and struggled with a diet, finally gained five pounds and quit it, and the white students were "rolling in the aisles" with laughter.

In general the Negro students now go it alone. For a time a few white students tried to be friendly. The whites were ostracized by other whites and such fraternization as having lunch with the Negroes soon ended.

Nearly all the students know of talk about students organized to hurt the Negroes as soon as the troops are pulled out. Only one girl was found who actually knew any of the students supposed to be in on the plan. . . .

. . . Some teachers believe the Negroes in their classes tend to raise the level of work because the whites don't want to make lower grades.

Some teachers tried "talking out" the integration problem, others chose not to have it brought up in class. Neither method seems to have worked much better than the other. Teachers are aware of tension in the school and in themselves.

Many students voiced resentment at what happened to their school. This was especially prevalent among seniors. Among them the attitude was to make the grades and get out.

Another idea that several students expressed was that everything would have been better if the whole thing had been left to the students themselves to handle. [*SSN* December 1957, p. 2]

## Political Trends, November 1957

. . . IN LATE November the Associated Press surveyed political observers around the state and came up with the conclusion that for now at least Faubus is in an ideal position in state politics. That is, if he ran for a third term and the election were now a tide of segregation votes would sweep him in.

In Little Rock segregationists brought the issue of race into a city government election and very nearly won it with a surprising show of strength....

An examination of the vote by boxes showed that the Good Government slate got its victory margin in the boxes where the Negro vote was heaviest and in Pulaski Heights, the "silk stocking" section where most of the city's well-to-do whites live. [SSN December 1957, pp. 2-3]

## Student and Teacher Opinion in December 1957*

... CONSIDERABLE amount of remarks, "Hey, nigger" when the Negroes walk around the corridors. Several have been run into "on purpose" and their books knocked out of their arms. Most of this seems to be done by sophomores and juniors, not the seniors. There may be some prejudice in this since it [the information] came from a Pulaski Heights kid—but she said that the Heights kids have pretty well been minding their own business. Points out that the sophomores and juniors came from West Side Junior High and East Side Junior High—most kids from the Heights area in the 10th and 11th grades have gone to Hall High School. I don't think there's any doubt, though, but that the resentment of the Heights area and the fact that Hall got off without any Negroes has led to some of the troubles within the school....

Reportedly the most unpopular [Negro] is Minnie Brown—known as "The Big M" because of her size. Termed "the type who would cause a fight," Minnie, it seems, talks back (the others don't) and reportedly sometimes not in a very lady-like manner. Minnie is supposed to have asked a white boy in a classroom to move his foot. He refused. She stepped on his foot and he slapped her. She went rushing outside for her 101st guard, the teacher told him to stay outside, that that was her classroom and that she would take care of the situation. He did and she did. The kid telling me about it said the white boy was the type who would have slapped any girl—white or black.

Minnie has everybody interested in her now—she sings and [reportedly] is trying out for a talent assembly (later it turned out this wasn't true) which will be held soon. The kids are wondering what will happen. "If she gets on there will be boos and nobody will applaud. If she doesn't the NAACP will say she has been discriminated against." ...

The boys dress "real nice but the girls are sloppy." Seems they wear

---

* From notes of *Arkansas Gazette* reporters, who talked with students and teachers outside the school; here reprinted from *Southern School News*, January 1958.

colored socks and nobody, but nobody, wears anything but white socks. . . .
[Mathilda Tuohey]

. . . THE Negroes are fitting in fairly well. They are being accepted as
individuals. One girl, I hear, is fitting in particularly well. "The kids are
nice to them but they're just not included" in a lot of gatherings, a student said. . . .

They have not been seen at any all-school dances although this type
of social affair almost doesn't exist any more. Most of the dances and
parties are given by the numerous social and honor clubs. . . . The Negroes
like to take part in school activities and show a great spirit toward football
games. They all wore the school colors to school during Color Week preceding the Pine Bluff game. They have said they wanted to make football
trips on the numerous buses the white students take to each out-of-town
game but the Negroes have not gone.

At the Pine Bluff game at Pine Bluff some Pine Bluff High School
students got paint and wrote signs such as "niggers" and "integration" over
the Little Rock buses. At nearly every stop in Arkansas of the buses, people
have tried to strike up conversations with the white students about the
Negroes. Mostly old men at small towns are interested. The old men ask
if the Negroes are causing any trouble. If they are, the men said, the men
will come to Little Rock and "kill them niggers" for you. . . .

[A] white girl in gym class tossed one of the shoes of Minnie Brown
(Negro) out the window and Minnie cried. This is a common occurrence
even among whites. The white girls like to throw other white girls' shoes
out of the window just to be playing. . . . [Jerry Dhonau]

. . . [ONE teacher said] she felt that learning, on the whole, if anything
was better this year than in other years. Any individuals who had difficulty
had it because of absences. She said there had been more absences from
flu than from integration objections. . . .

[She] and also other teachers had appealed to the pride of the students, urging them that the best way they could overcome the bad publicity
the school had received was to work hard and make a good record. Said
the students had responded to the challenge. Said also that better learning
may have resulted from fact that there were few social activities during
first weeks of school and so fewer distractions from studying. . . .

. . . Central High is quieter in halls and rooms than ever before. . . .

[Another teacher said] she and many at Central High were much
agitated over things that have been in papers. Said teachers had told her
of incidents, prefacing story with remark "Now you won't see *this* in the

paper." One was the case of two white girls quarreling, parting with remark they would see each other after school and settle the matter. One of
the girls went on to her locker, somebody tapped her on shoulder, and
wham she got it in the eye. Her opponent had decided not to wait. Another
story—a white girl was loaded with books waiting for hallway traffic to
thin so she could get into class. Somebody, accidentally or on purpose, hit
her arm and all the books went flying. The girl just picked them up and
went on to class. Her point, of course, is that the incidents if they had
involved Negroes would have been blown out of proportion when they
might just have been run of the mill accidents or ordinary boorish-
ness.

"In any population of 2,000 you will find a small percentage of hoodlums," she said.

. . . Had observed two or three homerooms where Negroes are: In
these rooms there were intelligent youngsters who were courteously and
helpfully helping the Negro students get into the routine of things. One
teacher said she had one of Negro students, no smarter than rest, but who
was seriously interested in learning. He's going to raise tone of whole
class, teacher said.

Mother of a white student told her this—there was a problem in class
no one could solve. Teacher went around room and finally came to Negro
student who said: "I think I can." And he did get the answer, impressing
the class no end. . . . [Martha Jean Douglas]

ONE teacher who said she had accepted integration as "what had to be"
and who counseled her students from the beginning to keep level heads
now says she isn't so sure.

"It has been the nastiest thing ever to come into my life and to say it
hasn't affected our school work would not be true," she said. . . .

"We had a test this week—the same test was given two weeks earlier
last year," she said. "I don't think it's the children's fault. We just haven't
been able to move." . . .

Is it active resistance to the Negro students that is keeping her white
students from making good progress? "No. It's more the atmosphere."

Are the white students mean to the Negroes? "No, they aren't mean,
they just aren't accepting them."

Had her students ever talked about it? "We discussed every angle
there was. I felt that was the best thing to do—go ahead and try to have
some sensible discussions about it. I think pretty soon after we had the talks
the furor began to subside and everybody got a little tired of it. . . ."

Another teacher said that since the mobs have been dispersed from before the school, the school is back to normal. He said that the pace of learning is about the average for this time of year. . . .

[ONE white girl student] says that there are some, "just a few," who speak to Negroes in hall, class and sometimes in cafeteria. Said that "we let these know that they better stop this." Said that teachers lecture students about behaving but adds "nobody is listening to that stuff." Says that pupils spit at Negroes, knock books out of arms in crowds and let them "know that whites don't want them." She says that a "bunch of good fellows are sworn in" to beat up the Negroes when the soldiers leave. . . . [Charles Albright]

## The Negro Students in December 1957

HOW IS IT for the Negro students at Central High School? They say they are lonely, sometimes scared, proud, determined to stay and believe they are doing all right learning.

They have found some white students hostile to them, a few friendly, some curious but mostly disinterested. In school they live in an unpleasant atmosphere because only the hostile whites have anything to do with them. The friendly and the curious now leave them alone because of the threatening attitude of the other whites.

All nine are above average in intelligence and made good records in Negro schools. They are the survivors of 60 Negroes who applied for admission to the previously all-white high school. They come from homes generally above the local Negro average financially and from parents probably better educated than most local Negroes. Eight of them are natives of Little Rock, the ninth was brought here at the age of 3.

They are very reluctant to talk to reporters. Their parents and the NAACP help protect them. During the Christmas holidays, a *Southern School News* reporter couldn't get a single one of them on the telephone ("Can't come to the phone now," "Just going out," "Nothing new to say," etc.) Not all of their parents are NAACP members.

Their parents also do not want to be identified in print because of the fear that it will hurt their chances of keeping or getting jobs. Some of them say they have received threats by telephone.

Six of them are girls and three are boys. Five girls are in the 11th grade, one is in the 10th. One boy is in each of the 10th, 11th and 12th grades. [*SSN* January 1958]

## Increasing "Incidents" at Central High School, January 1958

JANUARY was a month of racial incidents and bomb scares at Little Rock Central High School and once a stick of dynamite though without cap or fuse was found in the school. It was the worst month for "incidents" since nine Negroes were integrated there last September. . . .

Minniejean Brown, Negro student suspended in December two days before the start of Christmas vacation for throwing a bowl of chili on a white boy, was reinstated Jan. 13. She missed nine days of school.

Darlene Holloway, a white girl, was suspended Jan. 10 after a shoving incident involving Elizabeth Eckford, Negro. . . .

At the end of [January] the school board issued a statement defining disciplinary policy and evaluating the behavior of Central High students. That evaluation said that the behavior of the majority of the students and the cooperation of most of the parents had been above reproach. It called for the cooperation of everyone. . . . [*SSN* February 1958 p. 12]

## New Negro Group Meets, January 9, 1958

A NEW NEGRO organization, the Greater Little Rock Improvement League, held its first public meeting Jan. 9. About 50 persons attended including Mrs. L. C. Bates, state NAACP president. The Rev. Oliver W. Gibson, president and organizer, outlined the aims of the League as about the same as those of the NAACP. The difference, he said, is in the method of achieving the aims. Gibson said the League would try to earn for Negroes their rights and privileges without the use of court litigation. Mrs. Bates wished them well. Two weeks later the League met again with about 20 present but this meeting was closed to the press. [Earlier the Reverend Mr. Gibson had described his group as agreeing with NAACP objectives but taking a "more moderate stand." Disagreeing with some of the NAACP'S methods, his group would try to solve problems "through reason and understanding."] [ *SSN* February 1958, p. 13]

## Anti-Integration Rally, January 14, 1958

WHITE CITIZENS COUNCIL members and friends filled the biggest downtown Little Rock hotel ballroom the night of Jan. 14 for a program headed by Roy V. Harris of Augusta, Ga. . . .

Harris said that race-mixing in southern schools had been brought to a halt and that Little Rock was proof of that. "Little Rock has Ike over a barrel," he said. "If the people of Little Rock stand pat and he is forced to keep troops here from now on, he soon will be the laughing stock of the nation and the world." . . . [SSN February 1958, p. 12]

## *School Board's Petition for Postponement, February 20, 1958*

THE LITTLE ROCK school board asked the federal district court Feb. 20 to postpone integration at Little Rock Central High School.

Events surrounding Little Rock Central High School built themselves toward a climax in February. It came on Feb. 20 when the school board went back to federal district court and asked for a postponement of the desegregation order.

The developments in the climactic week were these:

Friday, Feb. 14—Supt. Virgil T. Blossom recommended that Minnijean Brown, one of the nine Negro students, be expelled.

Sunday, Feb. 16—In both Little Rock newspapers the school board published as an advertisement a school board statement on disciplinary policy, saying that it must provide an educational program and that if this means unruly students must be expelled, it will expel them.

Monday, Feb. 17—School board expelled Minnijean Brown.

Wednesday, Feb. 19—The Walter C. Guy committee, a group of 25 prominent Little Rock businessmen organized last October, recommended that the school board ask the federal court for a delay.

Thursday, Feb. 20—The board petitioned the court for a postponement. . . . [SSN March 1958, p. 1]

## *Expulsions and Suspensions, February 17, 1958*

DISCUSSING her expulsion with a reporter, Minnijean [Brown], 16, a junior in school, said, "I just can't take everything they throw at me without fighting back.

"I don't think people realize what goes on at Central," she said. "You just wouldn't believe it. They throw rocks, they spill ink on your clothes, they call you 'nigger,' they just keep bothering you every five minutes."

"The white students hate me," she said. "Why do they hate me so much? I didn't realize how deep that phrase [white trash] affects white people."

On the day that Minnijean was expelled the school board suspended three white students. Sammie Dean Parker, a girl, and Howard Cooper were suspended for exhibiting printed cards "One Down, Eight to Go." Billy Ferguson was suspended for pushing one of the Negro girl students. . . . [*SSN* March 1958, p. 1]

## Editorial Comment from Little Rock and Moscow, February 1958

HARRY S. ASHMORE, executive editor of the *Arkansas Gazette* of Little Rock, blamed lack of leadership at Washington and in the South for the showdown between state and federal forces at Little Rock. At no time, he said in a speech at Harvard University, did President Eisenhower use the moral force of his office to persuade southerners of the justice of the course the Supreme Court was requiring of them. He also criticized the federal government for leaving it up to the Little Rock school board to carry out the integration order "against impossible odds."

Radio Moscow, giving its version of the incidents and troubles during January at Central High School, included the statement that Elizabeth Eckford, one of the Negro students, had been murdered. At Little Rock, Elizabeth laughed at the report. [*SSN* March 1958, p. 3]

## Boycotts and Counter-Boycotts

A HARVARD University professor of social psychology, Thomas F. Pettigrew, recently spent three weeks in Little Rock examining attitudes on the integration situation. He reported in a television interview at Boston that both boycott and counter-boycott were at work.

He said the business of the men's clothing store owned by James T. Karam, a friend of Gov. Faubus and described in some quarters as a leader of the violence at Central High last September, had suffered. Karam's Main Street store once did a thriving business with Negro customers and this is reported to have dropped. His store burned in December but he is rebuilding it now.

Pettigrew also mentioned boycotts of a bakery and the *Arkansas Gazette*. The bakery was involved because a high school-age daughter of its owner was quoted as favoring integration and because a member of the Little Rock school board is employed there. The *Gazette* has supported the school board's plan of gradual integration and opposed the action of Gov. Faubus. Segregationists reportedly wrote letters to *Gazette* advertisers

threatening to boycott them if they continued to use the *Gazette*. . . .
[*SSN* March 1958, p. 3]

## Report on Central High School in March 1958*

. . . LITTLE ROCK Central High School, which had its thirtieth birthday last
November, is an impressive structure physically, rising like a small, regal
university in yellow-bricked grandeur on spacious landscaped grounds.

The school accommodates 2,000 students in 100 classrooms built on
seven levels; its enormous auditorium holds the entire school population.
The second level is the busiest—since most of the basic-skills classrooms
are on this floor, as are also the offices of school officials, the auditorium
and bookstore. Various shop-work classes, laboratories, music and art
rooms, gym and lunchrooms are distributed on the other levels. The great
attraction of Central is its advanced instructional and activities programs
(many of which, incidentally, are not available at the all-colored Horace
Mann High School). . . .

[In] the classrooms, as one moved about the different levels of the
school, normalcy seemed the pattern. In one class of some twenty young-
ters, the gray-haired teacher was discussing college placement procedures.
Terrence Roberts, a junior, one of the Negro children, sat among the students, sharing their quiet attention to their teacher's advice.

Down in the boys' gym, Jefferson Thomas, youngest of the three
Negro boys among the group, played with the volley-ball team. The only
qualification visible here was that of skill, as young Thomas dashed about
with the others, catching and tossing the ball while the instructor stood
by.

Particularly in a physics laboratory did one get an impression of harmony inside the classroom. Here the only senior of the Negro group, Ernest
Green, who will be graduating in June, sat beside a white boy in his class,
working on small motors, generators and electricity. Ernest and the white
boy occasionally exchanged murmured comments on a problem, or helped
each other, or looked sheepish when some idea didn't work out.

But outside the classrooms there is an all too noticeable difference in
atmosphere. In the corridors, as classes were belled to change, uniformed
guardsmen, singly and in pairs, moved among the students. The token
number of guards, inside the school or cruising in jeeps on the outside, are

* From Gertrude Samuels, "Little Rock: More Tension Than Ever," *New York
Times Magazine,* March 23, 1958, pp. 23ff. For model documentation see p. 47.

estimated at thirty. In the congested corridors one senses the tension that the Negro newcomers and many others must feel.

For in contrast to most students, the Negroes walk alone, silently, rapidly, a little scared, looking to neither right nor left as they make for their next classes. They are watchful on the steps where several have met with "accidents." They keep their eyes peeled for the known segregationists. In the chatter and laughter of the corridors, this observer saw no white student stop to talk or smile with them. . . .

[A] small mob of militant segregationist students, inside the school, is in control. It is estimated at between fifty and 100 students, or less than 5 per cent of the school population. They appear to be directed by adults on the outside. . . .

This small, hard-core mob is easy to spot, both white and Negro students tell you in interviews outside the school, and several were suspended briefly for their cruelties. Most of them, sadly enough, are in the vernacular, "lower-class whites" who come from marginal homes and neighborhoods and harbor general social grievances; the Negro is apparently a handy target for their hostilities.

At Ponders, a corner ice-cream, coke and sandwich shop opposite the school, you run into four youngsters of this group. They bear an astonishing resemblance to the tough-gang appearance of New York's problem children, a sort of Southern counterpart, down to their blue jeans, leather jackets, duck-tail haircuts, large-buckled belts and cigarettes.

"You can't print what I'd like to say about them jigs," one of them says in answer to a question.

"I have nothing to say to you," another said scornfully. "I'm a segregationist and you're from New York." . . .

And one boy added: "We don't need knives like your kids in New York. If I need to use anything, I use these." He shoved one foot up on the table; it wore a heavy leather cowboy-style boot. . . .

Some of the white students are uninterested in the plight of eight Negro pupils in a population of 2,000; either from indifference, or in self-defense, they ignore the Negroes, rather than risk being called "nigger lover" or being ostracized socially or worse. Some reflect the views of most respectable people here who do not belong to the extremist group but do not oppose it either, since emotionally they are in sympathy with its objectives ("They don't bother us because we don't talk to them." . . . "They've got their own schools, so why don't they stay there?" . . . "Well, they better not try to come to our dances.")

But there are others—no one can estimate how many—who would

accept the Negroes but fear to make life more dangerous for them by avowing such friendships. For example, Ernest Green receives notes privately from white students who write that they "regret the situation" and tell him to keep his chin up.

And one white student, who, in her own words, has become a "marked woman" since she befriended a Negro last year, is unafraid to speak up. Her mother, a newspaper woman, added briskly that she'd "disown the child if she hadn't shown some guts." She is Robin Wood, a 17-year-old beauty, whose fair hair, dimples, sparkle and outstanding scholarship have so far proved more than a match for her detractors.

"We were pretty calm about integration last summer," Robin said, "and I thought, 'Good old Little Rock, we'll be the leaders.' Then Faubus called out the troops and we were shocked. Then when Terrence came to English class, a boy and a girl walked out." Later, she loaned Terrence her algebra book and was promptly called "nigger lover" by someone who carefully explained to her that "anyone who's a nigger lover is either ignorant or a Communist."

One day she tore off the school bulletin board segregationist literature that had been smuggled onto it by the hard-core group, including a "Daisy Bates—WANTED" sign. Recently, she was told by a dancing partner, "You'd better not run for vice president of the Student Body because you're a moderate."

"I thought that the majority of the people were on my side," Robin went on. "But I think that the fence-straddling kids have gone over to the segregationists. If the moderates had spoken up for law and order and squelched the ones making the trouble, I think we would have won—but it looks like the other side is going to win. . . .

## New School Proposal

A NEW school plan designed to restore racial harmony to Arkansas and to place the matter of segregation-desegregation on a voluntary basis, outside the courts, was offered at Little Rock. It was the work of Herbert L. Thomas Sr., a Little Rock insurance executive with a long record of civic service in his city and state. . . .

. . . Gov. Faubus would be asked to help the Little Rock school board maintain discipline at Central High the rest of the school year so that the troops could be withdrawn immediately; the eight Negroes at Central High would finish the school year there, then be returned to the Negro high school; the state Board of Education would appoint an interracial commission, which would have no official authority, to advise and consult with local school districts on their integration problems. "In those communities where circumstances warrant complete or partial desegregation, the commission could help resolve the attendant problems in such a way as to secure sufficient community support to make compliance workable. In areas where, for perfectly valid reasons, desegregation is not now practical the commission could promote the improvement of educational facilities where such improvement is needed."

Faubus has not committed himself for or against the Thomas plan. Both Little Rock newspapers, morning *Gazette* and afternoon *Democrat,* which also had approved the Little Rock school board's plan, came out for the Thomas plan. . . .

On the other hand, the NAACP, the Capital Citizens Council, the state association of Citizens Councils, the Mothers League of Central High School and Jim Johnson of Crossett, a segregationist leader, all came out immediately against it. . . . [*SSN* May 1958, p. 6]

## *White House Statement on Removal of Troops, May 8, 1958**

SINCE last September the federal government has stationed soldiers at the Little Rock (Central) High School to prevent obstruction of the orders of the United States District Court.

Since the summer recess starts at Central High School on May 28 and since there will be no further present need for the Guardsmen, I have directed they be released May 29.

Following that date I trust that state and local officials and citizens will assume their full responsibility and duty for seeing that the orders of the federal court are not obstructed.

The faithful execution of the responsibility will make it unnecessary for the federal government to preserve the integrity of our judicial processes.

## *Reprisal against Negro Student's Mother, May 1958†*

THE MOTHER of one of eight Negro students attending integrated Little Rock Central High School was told her teaching contract at a North Little

---

* Released by James C. Hagerty, Press Secretary to the president; here reprinted from *Southern School News,* June 1958, p. 10.

† From "Intimidation, Reprisal, and Violence in the South's Racial Crisis," published in 1959 jointly by the American Friends Service Committee, the National Council of the Churches of Christ in the USA, and the Southern Regional Council. For model documentation see p. 11.

Rock Negro elementary school had not been renewed. Mrs. Lois Patillo, mother of 15-year-old Melba Patillo, taught at the Jones elementary school for seven years. The school superintendent said Mrs. Patillo was one of several teachers whose contracts were not renewed because of "problems" which he said were strictly personal matters. An NAACP official quoted Mrs. Patillo as saying the superintendent told her he should have been consulted about the enrollment of her daughter at Central High last fall.

## Graduation at Central High School, May 1958

LITTLE ROCK Central High School peacefully graduated 602 seniors on May 27—one of them a Negro—after eight months and six days of integration protected by federal troops. Local police and the troops gave heavy protection at the graduation ceremonies but only one minor incident occurred. . . .

As the graduation dates drew near—baccalaureate on Sunday, May 25 and commencement Tuesday, May 27—considerable tension developed in Little Rock.

The school board and Supt. Virgil T. Blossom announced that they were determined to have a normal and dignified graduation. To insure that, two steps were taken. One was to restrict the activity and coverage of both reporters and photographers at the ceremonies. The other was to have extra police available in addition to the soldiers. . . .

Both services went off quietly but leaving the baccalaureate service a boy in the senior class spat in the face of a Negro girl in the party with Ernest Green and was promptly arrested by Little Rock policemen. During commencement there was no incident, not even a boo. . . .

J. W. Matthews, principal at Central High, announced that all eight of the Negro students had made passing grades and that one of them, whose name he wouldn't give, had made the honor roll. Mrs. Bates of the NAACP said the honor roll student was Carlotta Walls, a sophomore. . . . [*SSN* June 1958, p. 10]

## Newspaper Awards

THE *Arkansas Gazette,* morning newspaper at Little Rock, won two Pulitzer Prizes for its handling of the Little Rock school crisis. One went to Harry S. Ashmore, executive editor, for his editorials defending the Little Rock school board's gradual integration plan and criticizing Gov. Faubus for interfering with troops. The other was for the paper's news coverage. A third Pulitzer went to Relman Morin of the Associated Press for his story on the violence last Sept. 23 at Central High.

*The Guardian,* weekly newspaper of the Catholic Diocese of Little Rock, won a national first prize from the Catholic Press Association for an editorial published Sept. 20. The editorial said both Little Rock newspapers, the *Gazette* and *Democrat,* helped set the stage for trouble at Little Rock by the way they reported the news. It said both papers lacked "objective reporting and circumspect editing."

The Columbia University graduate school of journalism gave its first Columbia journalism award to J. N. Heiskell, editor and president of the *Arkansas Gazette,* May 29 for his "singular journalistic performance in the public interest" during the Little Rock school crisis. [*SSN* June 1958, p. 10]

## From the Court Decision Permitting Postponement of Integration for 2½ Years, June 20, 1958*

. . . IT IS the theory of the Board, reflected in its pleadings, evidence and briefs, that the plan of integration which it adopted in 1955, upon the assumption that it would be acceptable and workable, has broken down under the pressure of public opposition, which opposition has manifested itself in a number of ways hereinafter mentioned, and that as a result the educational program at Central High School has been seriously impaired, that there will be no change in conditions between now and the time that school opens again in September, 1958, and that if the prayer for relief is not granted the situation with which the Board will be confronted in September will be as bad as, if not worse than the one under which it has labored during the past school year, and that it is in the public interest that the requested delay be granted.

While the plaintiffs deny, at least formally, that the educational standards at Central High School have been impaired, it seems to us that their fundamental position is, that even if it be assumed that everything

---

* From the opinion of United States District Court Judge Harry J. Lemley. A native Arkansan, Judge Lemley had been appointed a few months earlier and had thus replaced Judge Ronald N. Davies, who had been temporarily transferred from North Dakota to fill a vacancy; Lemley's appointment had been hailed by Governor Faubus and other opponents of the integration plan. The text of Judge Lemley's remarks is here reprinted from the *Race Relations Law Reporter,* August 1958, pp. 630-641, without the footnotes. In the text, "the Board" is the Little Rock School Board; "the plaintiffs" are the representatives of the Negro parents and students who had brought suit to restrain the Board from postponing integration. For model documentation see p. 19.

that the Board alleges is true from a factual standpoint, nevertheless the Board's difficulties stem entirely from popular disagreement with the principle of integration, which disagreement does not form a proper legal basis for permitting the Board to postpone the operation of its plan. . . .

In addition, the plaintiffs contend that the Board does not actually stand in need of any relief. As touching the situation inside the school, they urge that the Board could have solved its problems during the year just past had it taken a firmer disciplinary stand, and that if such a stand is taken this fall the problems can still be solved; . . .

Those conflicting theories present two basic questions for our decision, namely, whether or not this Court, sitting as a court of equity, has the power to grant the relief sought, and, if so, whether or not the Board has made a showing sufficient to justify the granting of that relief. In that connection we might call attention to the fact that in the prepared statement that we read at the preliminary proceeding held on April 28 we took occasion to say, among other things: ". . . let me make it clear that if the Board makes a case for relief under the law and the evidence, then appropriate relief will be granted. But, on the other hand, if the Board fails to make a case, either from a legal or a factual standpoint, its petition will have to be denied."

As to the first question, there can be no doubt that this Court has "jurisdiction," in the sense of "power to act," to grant the relief sought. . . .

To hold that once a plan of integration has been approved and ordered into effect by a federal court, all of the details of that plan, including the commencing date and the rate of progress toward complete elimination of compulsory segregation, become immutably fixed would negate the concept of equity's "practical flexibility" in shaping its remedies, and would be an unwarranted limitation upon its "facility for adjusting and reconciling public and private needs." . . .

At the hearing on the petition, which extended from June 3, into the afternoon of June 5, the Board called to the stand its president, Mr. Wayne Upton, its Superintendent of Schools, Mr. Virgil T. Blossom, certain members of the administrative staff of the high school, and certain classroom teachers. While the attorneys for the plaintiffs diligently cross-examined the main witnesses called by the Board, they did not put on any proof of their own tending to contradict the factual aspects of the testimony of the Board's witnesses, but confined their evidence to the testimony of two expert witnesses, namely, Dr. Virgil M. Rogers, Dean of the School of Education of Syracuse University, Syracuse, New York, and Dr. David G. Salten, Superintendent of Schools at Long Beach, Long Island, New

York. Those witnesses gave it as their opinion in general that to grant the petition would be unnecessary and undesirable, and that the Board should keep its plan in operation while using stricter disciplinary procedures against those in the school who might become involved in racial incidents such as were described by the Board's witnesses; and they also were of the opinion that stricter procedures should have been used during the past session. . . .

It is important to realize, as is shown by the evidence, that the racial incidents and vandalism which occurred in Central High School during the past year did not stem from mere lawlessness on the part of the white students in the school, or on the part of the people of Little Rock outside the school; nor did they stem from any malevolent desire on the part of the students or others concerned to bomb the school, or to burn it down, or to injure or persecute as individuals the nine Negro students in the school. Rather, the source of the trouble was the deep seated popular opposition in Little Rock to the principle of integration, which, as is known, runs counter to the pattern of southern life which has existed for over three hundred years. The evidence also shows that to this opposition was added the conviction of many of the people of Little Rock, that the Brown decisions [Supreme Court decisions of 1954 and 1955] do not truly represent the law, and that by virtue of the 1956-57 enactments [of the Arkansas Legislature], heretofore outlined, integration in the public schools can be lawfully avoided.

In this connection, the president of the Board, Mr. Upton, testified that between the spring and fall of 1957 there was a marked change in public attitude towards the plan, that persons who had formerly been willing to accept it had changed their minds and had come to the conclusion "that the local School Board had not done all it could do to prevent integration, . . ."

Mr. Blossom further testified that the opposition to integration and the feeling that it was not required at this time had been greatly strengthened by numerous newspaper articles and advertisements, and by circulars and cards distributed in Little Rock, copies of which were introduced in evidence. Without prolonging this opinion by undertaking to abstract or quote from individual exhibits, we may say that we agree with Mr. Blossom's appraisal of their effect. . . .

. . . And Mr. Blossom expressed the opinion that the doubts and questions in the minds of many people were honest ones, and that it was his opinion that the great majority of the people of the community, from the contacts he had had with it, do not favor integration. . . .

Getting back to the effects of the events of the past school year on the educational program at Central High School, we find more specifically that those events have had a serious and adverse impact upon the students themselves, upon the class room teachers, upon the administrative personnel of the school, and upon the over-all school program. In addition, said events have cast a serious financial burden upon the school district, which it has had to meet at the expense of normal educational and maintenance functions.

As far as the students themselves are concerned, we think it obvious that the incidents and conditions that have been described could not have been good for them emotionally; but aside from that, their education has certainly suffered and under existing conditions will continue to suffer, as is shown by the testimony of the classroom teachers called by the Board.

For example, Mr. W. P. Ivey, who has taught mathematics in the Little Rock School district for 34 years and who has been on the faculty of Central High School ever since that school was opened in 1927, testified that the presence of the Negro students created a tension on the part of both students and teachers that was noticeable every day, and that this tension impaired his ability to teach and the receptivity of his students. On cross-examination he stated that the final results obtained by him in his classes were not as good as they had been in prior years, as evidenced by his tests and also by comparison of the grades made in his classes which included Negro students with the grades made in his classes not attended by any of the Negroes.

Another member of the faculty who described the adverse effect that the presence of the Negro students, and all that went with it, had on educational standards was Mrs. Govie Griffin, who has taught chemistry for 13 terms at Central. The subject that she teaches is an elective course, taken principally by those who plan to go to college and who presumably are interested in mastering the subject. It was her observation that the presence of the troops in the school, their standing outside of class-room doors during recitations, and their actions in walking up and down the halls, occasionally dropping their clubs, all had a disturbing effect on pupils and teachers alike. Due to that situation and the prevailing tension and unrest, the amount of subject matter that she was able to offer in her chemistry course was so seriously curtailed that she had to request that standard achievement tests usually given at the close of the school year be not given; and her request was granted. . . .

As to the effect of the events of the past session on the classroom teachers and administrative staff personally, the observations and experiences of Mrs. Elizabeth Huckaby, vice-principal for girls, who has been at Central since 1930, are informative. She stated that normally in addition to her administrative duties she taught two English classes, but that during the past year she has been compelled to give up those classes and to devote all of her time to administrative duties, and that from 75 to 90 percent of her time was devoted to problems created by integration. These problems, and the unrest and tension in the school had an adverse effect upon her nerves and physical well being. She testified that apprehension over existing conditions caused her to lose sleep, which problem she had never had before; that she had no social life because of her exhaustion at the end of each day, and that on week ends she and her husband would go to the country and relax, and that by noon on Sunday she "would begin to revive enough to face the next week." Mrs. Huckaby also observed that other teachers were likewise suffering ill effects; she stated that some would come to her trembling, and that others would come weeping because of the events that were transpiring, and she pointed out in this connection that teachers in the main are not accustomed to violence.

Mrs. Huckaby's testimony as to the effect of the integration problems on the classroom teachers was corroborated by that of Mrs. Margaret Ryman, a mathematics teacher, and of Mrs. Shirley Stancil, a guidance counsellor, and likewise by the testimony of Mr. Blossom. The latter stated that one of his greatest concerns during the year was the health and welfare of the teachers, and that he felt very strongly that the teachers were under more strain than the students since they had upon their shoulders the responsibility for the physical welfare and educational progress of every student in the school, and that "they took that responsibility to heart and it affected many of them and that was reflected in many of the conferences I had with them as individuals."

The tension and strain to which the administrative staff were subjected did not terminate with the close of the school day. Mr. Powell stated that on a typically difficult day his phone would commence ringing as soon as he got home from school, the calls coming from people desiring various types of information; that he has spent as much as three hours on certain days "answering the telephone, or in making calls or dodging calls;" that he has had to work long hours during the evenings and nights on many occasions, and that his social life and normal rest had been interfered with to a definite extent during the entire school year.

Along the same lines Mr. O. W. Romine, Director of School Plant Services for the entire school district, testified that under normal conditions he worked from eight in the morning until five in the afternoon, and that after hours' duty was rare. During the past year, however, he had been on call 24 hours a day, and had received hundreds of calls at all hours of the night; on many occasions when his telephone had rung, and he had picked up the receiver, he found no one on the line. At one stage of the troubles he was away from home so much at night that he did not see his youngest child for four days, since he would get in at night after the child had gone to bed and would be gone in the morning before the child awoke. . . .

. . . In addition, Mr. Blossom was the recipient of many threats against his physical safety and well being. Of the Board members, Mr. Upton, at least, was subjected to much personal harassment, mainly by telephone calls, and to such an extent that he had to take an unlisted number. . . .

[It] has been necessary to divert the time and talents of the trained administrative personnel from their normal duties in dealing with the many complex problems involved in the operation of a high school like Central to purely disciplinary matters; . . . the diversion of administrative skills and energies to discipline maintenance during the past year may have been one of the highest prices that the school district has had to pay. . . .

As stated, the evidence further showed that the school district has had to shoulder substantial financial burdens on account of integration, and that this has been at the expense of other school programs. Mr. Romine testified, for example, that it was necessary to employ five additional night watchmen at the high school and that the cost for this item alone was between nine and ten thousand dollars; further, when it became necessary to relieve Mr. Powell and Mrs. Huckaby of their teaching duties so that they could devote their energies to the administrative problems with which the school was confronted, substitutes had to be hired to take their places in the classrooms. Moreover, the Board had to spend money to repair the damages to the school property, and to replace locks which had to be cut off of lockers during bomb searches; on that point Mr. Romine said that at one time he saw a bushel basket full of cut locks, and that it cost the board $1.25 apiece to replace them. Mr. Romine further testified that the over-all maintenance budget for all the schools in the district for the fiscal year ending June 30 of the current year was $123,000, that by January of this year he saw that unless something was done that budget would be overrun by approximately $17,000. . . .

We further find that if the attendance of Negro students at Central High School is to be maintained during the next school year, the Board will have to have military assistance or its equivalent, and it is financially unable to bear the expense of hiring a sufficient number of guards to control the situation. It cannot be expected that the Little Rock Police Department will be in a position to detail enough men to afford the necessary protection. . . .

Now, while troops can disperse crowds, and can keep the Negro students physically within the school, and while it is possible that if troops were deployed in sufficient numbers all over the school vandalism could be checked, the presence of troops cannot reduce or eliminate racial tensions, or create a climate that is conducive to education; on the contrary, the presence of armed soldiers in a school is, as has been shown here, disrupting to the educational process. . . .

[The Board] has come here seeking relief only after it has been confronted with what is, from an educational standpoint, an intolerable situation, and it does not ask for an abandonment of its plan nor does it attempt to obtain an indefinite postponement. It is simply requesting a tactical delay. We are convinced that in seeking this delay the Board is still acting in good faith, and, upon the showing that has been made, we are satisfied that the Board needs more time to carry out its plan in an "effective manner," and that to grant the instant petition is in the public interest, . . .

The importance of maintaining educational standards today is certainly no less than it has been in prior years; in fact it is more urgent. And while the Negro students at Little Rock have a personal interest in being admitted to the public schools on a nondiscriminatory basis as soon as practicable, that interest is only one factor of the equation, and must be balanced against the public interest, including the interest of all students and potential students in the district, in having a smoothly functioning educational system capable of furnishing the type of education that is necessary not only for successful living but also for the very survival of our nation and its institutions. There is also another public interest involved, namely, that of eliminating, or at least ameliorating, the unfortunate racial strife and tension which existed in Little Rock during the past year and still exists there.

While we do not seek at this time to authoritatively define the term "all deliberate speed" employed by the Supreme Court in the Brown case, it does seems to us that the term is a relative one, dependent upon varying facts and circumstances in different localities, and that what might be "deliberate speed" under one set of circumstances could constitute headlong haste under another. . . .

The granting of the Board's petition does not in our estimation, constitute a yielding to unlawful force or violence, but is simply an exercise of our equitable discretion and good judgment so as to allow a breathing spell in Little Rock, while at the same time preserving educational standards at Central High School.

At one point in his testimony Mr. Blossom stated, and we agree with him, that a tactical delay is not the same as a surrender; and the delay here sought is not a vain thing or a mere frustration of the plaintiffs' rights. In the first place, the delay, in and of itself, may well be of material value to the Board in carrying out its announced purposes. In the two and one-half year period involved tempers will have a chance to cool down, emotions may subside to some extent, and there may also be changes in some of the personalities involved in the dispute. Of more significance, however, is the fact that the delay will afford time for the completion of the pending litigation in the state courts and for an appraisal of the results of that litigation. . . .

[There] has been a very radical change of situation since the former orders of this Court were entered, the occurrence and extent of which were not, to our mind, foreseeable at that time. . . .

While Dr. Rogers and Dr. Salten are doubtless well qualified to express opinions as to how school matters should be handled in areas of the country with which they are familiar and in which they have had experience, neither of those gentlemen has had any public school administrative experience in the South, or any personal familiarity with the Little Rock situation; nor has either of them ever had any experience with the problems involved in the transition from segregation to integration in a state where the former has been the accepted and traditional mode of life of the people and where its existence in the public schools has had the sanction of law for so long as those schools have existed. As regards Dr. Rogers in particular, his qualifications to speak on this subject were seriously impaired, in our eyes, by his suggestion that members of the student body at Central High School might have been used, in effect, as spies upon other students there. In view of these limitations upon the qualifications of the plaintiffs' witnesses, we cannot accept their opinions in preference to that of Mr. Blossom, who is also an expert, and who formed his opinion on the ground and has based it upon his own intimate experience with the problem.

It is true that the views of Vice-principal Powell coincide with the opinions of the plaintiffs' experts, as far as the situation inside the school is concerned; but it must be remembered that Mr. Powell had no ultimate disciplinary authority and no responsibility for any matters of over-all policy; he was a subordinate employee and it was not shown what qualifications, if any, he possesses as an expert in public school administration. He testified that he graduated from Central High School in 1940, that he was employed at the school in an undisclosed capacity in 1952, and that he has been vice-principal for boys for the past three years. His training and experience between 1940 and 1952 were not brought out in the evidence. It is also interesting to note in this connection that Mr. Powell's counterpart, Mrs. Huckaby, did not feel that the employment of stern disciplinary measures was the key to the problem. Actually, it occurs to us that Mr. Powell may well have been so close to the situation in all of its personally unpleasant aspects, that he has to some degree lost his sense of perspective in the matter.

In addition to all of the foregoing, it is well to keep in mind that the duty of maintaining discipline in the schools and of deciding what disciplinary steps would be taken is primarily the function of the school administration, and not that of the Court; and we would certainly be unwilling to substitute our judgment as to what should have been done for that of the Board in the absence of a showing that the Board had erred to such an extent as to indicate an absence of good faith on its part. There has been no such showing here.

Relative to interference from outside the school the plaintiffs urge that the Board should have either instituted criminal prosecutions against the persons responsible, or that it should have applied for injunctive relief, as was done in the Hoxie, Arkansas, and Clinton, Tennessee, cases. . . . In answer to that argument Mr. Blossom testified, and he was corroborated by Mr. Upton, that the Board had determined as a matter of judgment not to resort to criminal prosecutions or to seek injunctive relief; that it was not the function of the Board to prosecute people or to seek injunctions but to run a school system, and that it had already had all of the litigation that it wanted and was not anxious for any more. . . .

## "Governor Faubus' Stand on Forced Integration," July 1958*

MY POSITION on forcible integration of schools or other facilities has been publicly stated on numerous occasions. It is unnecessary now to elaborate. I stand now, and always, in opposition to integration by force,

---

* From *The Bulletin,* July 18, 1958, published by the Faubus Campaign Committee, p. 3, with the heading used here. For model documentation see p. 35.

and at bayonet point. This is a democracy—the people should have a voice in their affairs, and the constitutional provisions of this government should remain inviolate. Arkansas has a long record of friendly relations between the races, and these relations should not be disturbed by outside influences as has been the case in recent months.

I have taken my position in the protection and defense of the people of Arkansas, in your constitutional right to govern yourselves in state and local affairs. From this position, I shall not recede nor yield.

ORVAL E. FAUBUS

## Re-election of Governor Faubus, July 29, 1958*

GOVERNOR Orval E. Faubus won a third two-year term today [July 29] and overwhelming endorsement of his defiant stand against the Federal courts in the school integration controversy.

His overwhelming majority in today's Democratic preferential primary also was indicative of the resentment felt by Arkansans over President Eisenhower's use of Federal troops to enforce desegregation here at Central High last year. . . .

With 2,141 of the state's 2,321 precincts reported, the vote was:

| | |
|---|---|
| Faubus | 227,964 |
| Ward | 48,280 |
| Finkbeiner | 47,931 |

. . . . . . . . . . . . . . . . . . . . .

In a victory statement Mr. Faubus declared:

"The voting today was a condemnation by the people of illegal Federal intervention in the affairs of the state and the horrifying use of Federal bayonets in the streets of an American city and in the halls of a public school." . . .

Sentiment against a third term has been strong in this state. Only one Governor has been returned for a third time by the voters. . . .

Although Judge Ward described himself as a segregationist, he advocated that the South seek to ease the problem through legislative means. . . . [Mr. Finkbeiner], too, said he would seek to preserve segregation through legal means.

---

* *New York Times,* July 30, 1958, pp. 1, 14. For model documentation, see p. 12.

## Reversal of Integration Postponement, August 18, 1958*

. . . FROM the testimony of the superintendent, and voluminous exhibits, consisting mainly of newspaper articles and paid advertisements, it is demonstrated that pro-segregationists carried on a relentless and effective campaign during the summer of 1957. The Governor of Georgia, Marvin Griffin, and Roy V. Harris, publisher, of the same state, and Reverend J. A. Lovell, described as a "Texas radio minister," appeared in Little Rock and delivered speeches against integration to large audiences. . . .

. . . On July 9, 1957, what purports to be a full page paid statement appeared in the Arkansas Democrat, the first two paragraphs of which are typical, not only of the statement in its entirety, but of other articles appear[ing] from time to time in the same publication:

" 'PEOPLE OF ARKANSAS V. RACE-MIXING!

OFFICIAL POLICY OF THE STATE OF ARKANSAS

'The people of Arkansas assert that the power to operate public schools in the state on a racially separate but substantially equal basis was granted by the people of Arkansas to the government of the State of Arkansas; and that, by ratification of the Fourteenth Amendment, neither the State of Arkansas nor its people delegated to the federal government, expressly or by implication, the power to regulate or control the operation of the domestic institutions of Arkansas; *any and all decisions of the Federal Government to the contrary notwithstanding.'*

"WHOSE STATEMENT IS THE ABOVE?

"It is the statement of Gov. Orval E. Faubus of Arkansas. It is the core of the Resolution of Interposition which he personally fathered. Governor Faubus hired the solicitors who circulated the petitions to place this Resolution on the ballot. Governor Faubus filed Resolution and petitions with the Secretary of State on July 5, 1956, and the Resolution was submitted to the people in last November's general election. *The people of Arkansas by a tremendous, overwhelming majority gave it their thundering approval.*

"Sponsored by the Governor of Arkansas, adopted by a tre-

---

* From the opinion of the United States Circuit Court of Appeals, reversing the grant of 2½ years' postponement, August 18, 1958. Here reprinted from the *Race Relations Law Reporter*, August 1958, pp. 644-648. One of the judges dissented. At the School Board's request, the Appeals Court granted a stay of its order until the Supreme Court could rule on the case.

mendous majority of Arkansas voters, *the above statement is the will of the people of Arkansas.''*

. . . The events which occurred during the school year may be summarized as follows:

1) Although there were no unusual events in the classrooms, there were a number of incidents in the halls, corridors, cafeteria and rest rooms, consisting mainly of "slugging, pushing, tripping, catcalls, abusive language, destruction of lockers, and urinating on radiators."

2) Forty-three bomb threats necessitated searches of the school building, and particularly the lockers, some 2400 in number. These bomb threats were broadcast on the local radio and television stations, precipitating calls from parents and withdrawal of students for the day.

3) Numerous small fires occurred within the building, particularly in rest rooms where tissue paper and towels accumulated.

4) The destruction of school property throughout the school necessitated the expenditure of school funds, which might otherwise have been used for general maintenance purposes, to repair the damage.

5) Misconduct on the part of some students resulted in approximately 200 temporary suspensions for short periods of time, and two permanent expulsions.

6) The administrative staff in the school spent a great deal of time making reports of incidents, alleged and real, arising out of opposition to the presence of nine Negro students.

7) Teachers and administrative staff were subjected to physical and mental strain and telephone threats.

8) Inflammatory anti-integration speeches were made at public meetings by speakers from other states, and the local newspapers carried many anti-integration articles.

9) Vicious circulars were distributed condemning the District Court, the Supreme Court of the United States, and the school officials who recognized the supremacy of the federal law.

10) Vulgar cards, critical of the school officials, were given by adults to school children for distribution within the school building.

11) In general there was bedlam and turmoil in and upon the school premises, outside of the classrooms.

Careful and critical analysis of the relevant facts and circumstances in light of applicable legal principles, leads us to the inescapable conclusion that the order of the district court suspending the plan of integration can not stand.

In Brown v. Board of Education, 349 U.S. 294, the Supreme Court, in dealing with the manner in which integration should be effected, recognized that full implementation of the constitutional principles involved may require solution of varied local school problems—and that the school authorities have the primary responsibility for "elucidating, assessing, and solving the problems." . . .

The precise question at issue herein, *i.e.*, whether a plan of integration, once in operation, may lawfully be suspended because of popular opposition thereto, as manifested in overt acts of violence, has not received judicial consideration. But there is sound and convincing authority that a school board, "acting promptly and *completely uninfluenced by private and public opinion* as to the desirability of desegregation in the community," must proceed with deliberate speed, consistent with proper administration, to abolish segregation, Jackson v. Rawdon (5 Cir. 1956) 235 F.2d 93, 96, certiorari denied 352 U.S. 925; School Board of the City of Charlottesville, Va., v. Allen (4 Cir. 1956) 240 F.2d 59, certiorari denied, 353 U.S. 910; and while ". . . a good faith acceptance by the school board of the underlying principle of equality of education for all children with no classification by race might well warrant the allowance by the trial court of time for such reasonable steps in the process of desegregation as appears to be helpful in avoiding unseemly confusion . . . (n)evertheless, whether there is such acceptance by the board or not, the duty of the Court is plain. *The vindication of rights guaranteed by the constitution can not be conditioned upon the absence of practical difficulties.*" (Emphasis supplied). Orleans Parish School Board v. Bush (5 Cir. 1957) 242 F.2d 156 at p. 166, certiorari denied 354 U.S. 921. "The fact that the schools might be closed if the order were enforced is no reason for not enforcing it," Allen v. County School Board of Prince Edward County, Va. (4 Cir. 1957) 249 F.2d 462, 465, certiorari denied 355 U.S. 953, because, as the court there stated, at page 465: "A person may not be denied enforcement of rights to which he is entitled under the constitution of the United States because of action taken or threatened in defiance of such rights." . . .

An impossible situation could well develop if the district court's order were affirmed. Every school district in which integration is publicly opposed by overt acts would have "justifiable excuse" to petition the courts for delay and suspension in integration programs. An affirmance of "temporary delay" in Little Rock would amount to an open invitation to elements in other districts to overtly act out public opposition through violent and unlawful means. . . . This issue plainly comes down to the question of whether overt public resistance, including mob protest, constitutes sufficient cause to nullify an order of the Federal court directing the board to proceed with its integration plan. *We say the time has not yet come in these United States when an order of a federal court must be whittled away, watered down, or shamefully withdrawn in the face of violent and unlawful acts of individual citizens in opposition thereto....*

. . . Accordingly, the order of the district court is reversed, with directions to dismiss the appellees' petition.

## DOCUMENTATION SUITABLE FOR RESEARCH PAPERS

BIBLIOGRAPHY ENTRY

Aaron v. Cooper, Aug. 15, 1958, No. 16034, U.S. Ct. of Appeals, 8th Circuit. Excerpts reprinted from *Race Relations Law Reporter* in *LRUSA*.

FIRST FOOTNOTE

*Aaron v. Cooper*, Aug. 15, 1958, No. 16304, U.S. Ct. of Appeals, 8th Circuit, as reprinted from *Race Relations Law Reporter* in *LRUSA*, pp. 106-109.

SUBSEQUENT FOOTNOTE

*Aaron v. Cooper, LRUSA*, p. ■.

---

## From the School Board's Statement on the Appeals Court's Decision, August 18, 1958

THE Board of Directors of Little Rock School District used all resources at their command in their effort to secure a delay of two and one-half years in the program of integration. . . . The board will promptly pursue any and all legal remedies which it has, including an appeal to the United States Supreme Court, . . .

In any event we do not anticipate any significant change in the number of Negro students in our schools, . . .

. . . It is difficult to carry on a program of education in the present climate of public opinion. We would like to remind all people that the board of education is not a law enforcement agency and has no police powers. We sincerely urge the cooperation and understanding of students and adults of Little Rock, the state and federal governments in helping us to carry on our educational program, whatever the outcome may be. . . .
[*SSN* September 1958, p. 3]

*From Governor Faubus's Comments on the Appeals Court Decision, August 19, 1958*

THE reversal of the Lemley decision by the federal Court of Appeals is most alarming and dangerous.

The spotlight now has shifted to the school authorities, the officials of the NAACP and the parents of the Negro children. . . .

The school board now needs to take the people of the district into its confidence and let them know its intentions and its plans. Does the board intend to continue to promote the complete integration of the Little Rock schools while muttering insincere, half-hearted protestations or does it intend to fight in every legal way possible the integration by force, with such dire consequences for education in the affected school, and the peace of the community . . . ?

If the school board intends to continue to promote the complete integration of the Little Rock schools, the people are entitled to know. It is the people's business, because the schools belong to the people and not the School Board.

How many Negroes will be admitted to Central High School on opening day? If only those previously enrolled are readmitted, when will the number be raised to 90 or 900, the latter figure being the number eligible to attend Central High School under the board's complete integration plan? . . .

What other schools will be integrated on opening day? They are all in the plan of complete integration. When will white students be ordered to enter the Negro schools? Will that be on opening day this year, and if not, when will it be done? It is a part of the plan of complete integration, drawn up by the board and approved by the federal court. . . .

Why all the secrecy surrounding these developments? Why the secret board meetings? Aren't the people entitled to know about their own school affairs? . . .

Although [the Board] has been ordered to continue with the integration plan, it has every right to resist the order by any and every legal means.

1) The Board may use the school assignment law, now on the statute books, which was passed by the overwhelming vote of the people at the general election of 1956.

2) Meet with the parents of the Negro students, and the officials of the NAACP who have instigated and promoted the continued integration

efforts. Discuss frankly with them the situation as it now exists, with the dire consequences that may ensue as to the quality of education for the Negro students as well as others, and also the jeopardy to the peace and tranquility of the community. These Negro parents may rise above their desires for the attainment of their immediate objectives in this matter.

Their decision, the Negro parents and the NAACP, in the interest of harmony and greater good to the whole community, to allow a cooling off period, by sending their students to school with their own race during the coming year, would do much, if not more than anyone else could do, to resolve this whole unhappy situation.

3) Failing in both of the above, the school board could resign as previously suggested by Judge Pilkington and others, and allow the people to select a new board which would have the courage to act in conformity to their wishes. . . . [*SSN* September 1958, p. 3]

## From a Press Release of President Eisenhower, August 20, 1958

. . . EACH state owes to its inhabitants, to its sister states and to the Union the obligation to suppress unlawful forces. It cannot by action or deliberate failure to act permit violence to frustrate the preservation of individual rights as determined by a court decree.

It is my hope that each state will fulfill its own obligation with a full realization of the gravity of any other course.

Defiance of this duty would present the most serious problem, but there can be no equivocation as to the responsibility of the federal government in such an event. My feelings are exactly as they were a year ago.
. . .

. . . Every American must understand that if an individual, a community or a state is going successfully and continuously to defy the courts, then there is anarchy. . . . [*SSN* September 1958, p. 3]

## From Governor Faubus's Reply to President Eisenhower, August 20, 1958

THE free people of a democracy such as ours think of the 'law of the land' in terms of laws passed by their own votes at the ballot box, or in terms of laws passed by their elected representatives.

Time after time, the people of Arkansas and other states have voted overwhelmingly against forcible integration.

Furthermore, many, many eminent lawyers throughout the nation, regardless of their views on the segregation-integration question, have expressed the view that the United States Supreme Court decision of 1954 is without the basis of law. No law has ever been passed which says that all people of every section of the nation must be forced to integrate against their wishes, and regardless of the consequences, however bad they might be. . . .

Therefore, compliance cannot be obtained by invoking the sacred name of the Constitution, or by the use of the once-magic name of Eisenhower.

It is, then, inevitable that the integration of the races cannot be achieved without great discord, except by the process of evolution, which requires patience, tolerance and understanding, over a period of time. . . .

If it is the purpose of Mr. Eisenhower's statement to reaffirm his position of last fall, that it is my duty as Governor to use the military to enforce integration in any school district in this state, then I must say that my position of last fall is unchanged.

I do not interpret my constitutional duties to cover any such theory as that advanced by the President.

I do recognize my duty to preserve the peace of my state, and I shall continue to do so to the best of my ability. It is also elementary that I am bound under my oath of office to uphold the Constitution and to enforce the laws of my own state, within the framework of the Federal Constitution. [*SSN* September 1958, p. 3]

## Indecision of Negro Students about Registering, August 24, 1958*

WHETHER seven Negro students will attempt to register for classes at Central High School will be left up to them, several Negro leaders at Little Rock said yesterday.

Superintendent Virgil T. Blossom said Thursday that Central High would reopen September 2 as a segregated school. This was based on the latest legal action taken by the United States Eighth Circuit Court of Appeals [which stayed its ruling until the Supreme Court can decide the appeal].

If this action holds up until the start of the fall school term the Negro students will be transferred to the all-Negro Horace Mann High School.

---

* *Arkansas Gazette,* "Leaders Say Negro Students Must Decide for Themselves Whether to Ask CHS Return," August 24, 1958, p. 4A. For model documentation see p. 35.

The students haven't reached a decision or if they have they haven't said what it is.

They gathered at Washington this week end to receive scholarships from a National Negro Elks convention. Five of them went there from a summer camp in New York. Melba Pattilo flew to Washington from Little Rock with Minnijean Brown and Mrs. L. C. Bates, president of the Arkansas chapter of the National Association for the Advancement of Colored People, to join the others. Minnijean was expelled from Central High School last year for taking part in racial incidents. She also will receive a scholarship. . . .

## *Senator Fulbright's Brief Supporting Delay, August 27, 1958\**

. . . THE Arkansas senator, who is a lawyer and a former professor of constitutional law at George Washington University and the University of Arkansas, said the people of Arkansas were law-abiding, abhorred anarchy and disorder and until last year's school violence had not been troubled by any racial disorder for thirty years.

Fulbright suggested to the [Supreme] Court that the problem of school integration in Arkansas "is more likely—bearing in mind that flesh and blood is weak and frail—to yield to the slow conversion of the human heart than to the remedies of a more urgent nature."

"The meaningful realities of this situation are that due to unexpected developments of an unprecedented nature, this Court's original objective of procuring for Negro children education on an integrated basis cannot be provided under existing circumstances.

"Time is desperately needed to enable the authorities concerned to find an adjustment of this conflict.

"No decision which this Court can make will assure the rights of the Negro children more effectively than those decisions which it has heretofore rendered.

"In spite of the full force of the executive power of the federal government, even the use of the armed forces of the United States, the children did not and cannot enjoy a better, not even as good, an opportunity for education under the condition of turmoil and bedlam which results from such extreme measures.

"The education of all children, white and Negro, suffers from such disturbed abnormal conditions."

---

\* *Arkansas Gazette*, Gazette Press Service, from Washington, D.C., "Fulbright Asks to File Brief Seeking Delay," August 28, 1958, p. 1A. For model documentation see pp. 35 and 51.

## Provisions of New Schools Acts by Arkansas State Legislature

[THE legislature had been called into special session by Governor Faubus August 26 to deal with the school situation. It voted to:]

1) Shut down schools faced with integration and provide an election within 30 days to determine whether voters want them to stay closed or reopened on a desegregated basis.

2) Withhold state funds from integrated schools and turn over the money to either private or public schools which the students elect to attend.

3) Permit students to transfer to another school of their own race.

4) Assert that no student shall be denied the right to enroll or receive instruction because he refuses to attend integrated classes. This was interpreted to mean that classes could be segregated within an integrated school building.

5) Delay opening of Little Rock schools from the original date of Sept. 2 to Sept. 15.

6) Appropriate $100,000 for the governor to meet expenses connected with the bills. This includes $6,250 for a special assistant to the governor and $75,000 for the cost of holding school district elections.

7) Require a loyalty oath of school teachers and officials which would have them spell out the organizations to which they belong.

8) Provide certain changes in the school taxes which would give some assistance to school districts.

9) Allow recall of school board members if 15 percent of a district's voters petition for a recall election.

10) Withdraw the power of certain types of organizations to act as attorneys for individuals (aimed at the National Association for the Advancement of Colored People).

11) Prevent a so-called public sitdown in public schools by Negroes to avert the kind of campaign carried out in Oklahoma City during the past few days. It would prohibit unauthorized persons from entering school premises.

12) Require organizations aiming to interfere with state control of public schools to submit a list of members and other information to county clerks (aimed at the NAACP).

13) Make easier the legal processes required for search of the records of organizations by the attorney general's office (aimed at the NAACP).

14) Strengthen the state's anti-barratry laws—making it illegal to

solicit lawsuits or to cause acts of violence directed specifically toward causing a lawsuit (aimed at the NAACP).

15) Appropriate $19,200 for the attorney general's office for additional financial aid in integration suits.

16) Prevent any organization other than legal aid societies from representing a client in a lawsuit without cost to the individual (aimed at the NAACP). [*SSN* September 1958, p. 4]

## Faubus Charge about His Newport "Law of the Land" Statement, August 31, 1958*

GOVERNOR FAUBUS said yesterday that the White House had "required" him last fall to make his statement accepting the Supreme Court decision as the "law of the land."

The statement was "a requirement for further negotiations" with the president, Mr. Faubus said on the Columbia Broadcasting System telecast "Face the Nation" which originated at Little Rock.

The governor issued the statement about the Supreme Court decision last fall after conferring with President Eisenhower at Newport, R.I., on the school integration crisis.

He was asked yesterday why he had changed his mind since making the statement.

"I really haven't changed my mind," the governor said. "I was required to issue that statement as a basis for negotiations with the White House.

"Because I said it it didn't make it so."

"Did Ike insist on your making it?" a panel member asked.

The governor said Representative Brooks Hays (Dem., Ark.) and Presidential Assistant Sherman Adams insisted on the statement. Hays helped set up the Newport conference.

A panelist noted that Mr. Eisenhower announced at the time of the conference that Mr. Faubus would support the Supreme Court decision as the law.

"Only as the basis of negotiations," Mr. Faubus said.

He told reporters after the program that he was allowed to read the President's statement at the close of the Newport meeting, but he wasn't allowed to approve or disapprove the statement.

---

* *Arkansas Gazette,* "Faubus Says Law of Land Statement Forced on Him," September 1, 1958, pp. 1A, 4, 5. For model documentation see p. 35.

## *Faubus Warning about Federal Marshals, September 2, 1958\**

GOVERNOR FAUBUS warned yesterday that he would regard as force any attempt by the federal government to use marshals to enforce integration at Little Rock High School.

Under his self-imposed policy, he "is bound to offer opposition" to any such move. He said he would counter with the legislation handed to him by the General Assembly last week.

The keystone of this legislation is a bill under which Mr. Faubus could order the school closed. Mr. Faubus has not signed into law this and allied bills but he can do so at any time.

## *Dissension in White Citizens Council, June-September 1958†*

A SHARP division in the Capital Citizens Council was revealed yesterday when it was learned that three of its top leaders had been expelled.

The three men are:

Robert Ewing Brown, the immediate past president and a member of the Board of Directors; Will J. Smith, secretary and a Board Member, and Julian Miller, a Board Member.

Smith and Brown declined to comment. But Miller confirmed that all three had received notice of their expulsions after the monthly meeting in June.

Further confirmation of the expulsions was a Council letterhead which lists the officers and directors. In a letter dated in July and sent under the signature of Rev. Wesley Pruden, the Council president, the names of Smith, Brown and Miller were scratched through with ink.

Neither side of the controversy would give a reason for the expulsions.

Miller said he wasn't at the June meeting.

"I just got a notice through the mail that I was expelled," he said, "it didn't give the reason. I didn't even ask why and I didn't care."

Mr. Pruden would not confirm nor deny the expulsion reports.

"I am president of the Council and in this position I presided at the Board meeting," he said. "Business transacted in a Board meeting is

---

* *Arkansas Gazette*, September 3, 1958, p. 1A. For suitable documentation, see p. 35.

† *Arkansas Gazette*, "White Council Rift Bared; 3 Men Ousted," September 5, 1958, p. 1A. For model documentation see p. 35.

private and I couldn't reveal what took place. I have no authority to tell what took place."

## The U.S. Attorney General's Proposal, September 9, 1958*

ATTORNEY GENERAL William P. Rogers [who succeeded Herbert Brownell] called on Little Rock officials today to join the federal government in a double-barreled plan to prevent "disorder or violence" if the Supreme Court orders Negroes admitted to Central High School again Monday.

In a letter to City Manager Dean I. Dauley, Rogers said the Justice Department had arranged for a temporary expansion of the staff of the federal marshal's office and would "co-operate fully" with the Little Rock authorities in preserving peace.

In a companion letter to the Little Rock School Board, Rogers promised the full help of the federal government if the Board seeks injunctions against possible troublemakers. The Board did not seek such injunctions during last year's violence at the School.

In neither letter did Rogers mention the possible use of troops. Justice Department officials said this was not contemplated at the present. But they did not rule out such a move which, they said, would have to be taken at a higher level, presumably the White House.

It had been known for several days that the Justice Department had been recruiting deputy marshals for possible duty at Little Rock. Rogers' letters made it official that the marshal's office would be beefed up temporarily.

## Call for Stern Action by Two Clergymen, September 10, 1958†

TWO LEADERS of the United Presbyterian Church said today they favored enforcement of integration at the Little Rock, Ark., Central High School "with troops and tanks, if necessary."

The statement was made by Dr. Eugene Carson Blake of Philadelphia, chief administrative officer of the Church in this country, and Dr. Theophilus M. Taylor of Pittsburgh, presiding officer.

They said they drew up the statement in the hope of influencing any-

* *Arkansas Gazette,* United Press report dated September 9 from Washington, D.C., September 10, 1958, p. 1A. For suitable documentation see pp. 12 and 51.

† *Arkansas Gazette,* "Clerics Urge Stern Action in CHS Case," Associated Press report dated September 10 from New York, September 11, 1958, p. 1A. For model documentation see pp. 35 and 51.

one who has anything to do with the Little Rock situation—including the United States Supreme Court which holds hearings on the case tomorrow.

## *"Wall of Resistance" after a Year, September 1958\**

THE SITUATION at Little Rock looks infinitely more dangerous today than it did a year ago.

Sentiment has crystallized. Resistance to desegregating Central High School, scene of the 1957 riots, has become truly massive. The atmosphere in the city has changed radically.

A year ago, you found many shades of opinion at Little Rock . . . [e.g.] people who believed in segregation but not the use of force to achieve it.

A great many, without doubt, were honestly bewildered, torn by conflicting feelings, hardly knowing what to think.

Now, 12 months later, the feeling looks solid, a monolithic slab of resistance against desegregation. The evidence:

1. Governor Faubus' spectacular victory in the Democratic primary in July. He got 68 per cent of the total vote. Two respected and able opponents were unable to carry even their own counties.

2. The flurries of disturbance elsewhere in Arkansas. Last year, the high school at Van Buren admitted 24 Negro students: today, 13 have withdrawn because of opposition from white students. At Ozark the high school had Negroes in class during the spring term: today, they have been advised not to come back.

3. The change—this from a reporter's point of view—in the accessibility of key people. Last year, especially after the federal government moved into Little Rock, segregationist leaders were hard to reach, very guarded in what they said. Vice versa, representatives of the National Association for the Advancement of Colored People talked readily.

Today it is just the reverse.

4. The Little Rock School Board, which advanced the plan for integration in 1955 and set it in motion last year, now asks a 30-month delay. A federal district judge granted the request. It is this decision, and the reversal of it by the Eighth Circuit Court of Appeals which is now before the Supreme Court.

---

\* *Arkansas Gazette,* "Reporter Finds Wall of Resistance," Associated Press report from Little Rock by Relman Morin, September 12, 1958, p. 14A. Mr. Morin had covered the Little Rock crisis in 1957 and won a Pulitzer Prize for his work. He returned a year later to make this appraisal. For model documentation see p. 51.

These developments appear to have been inter-reacting—that is, they not only clearly revealed the temper of public opinion in Arkansas but hardened it.

In recognition of this, the *Arkansas Gazette* said recently:

"There is no way for the time being at least to obtain such compliance [with the Supreme Court order to de-segregate] without doing serious and perhaps irreparable harm to the system of public education upon which all our children, colored no less than white, are dependent."

So today, as the Supreme Court deliberates, the shadow darkens here.

The seven Negro children who attended Central High School last year say they will try to go back again—even in the face of potential physical opposition.

Mr. Faubus told a news conference yesterday, "I will not force my people to integrate against their will."

He has the power to close the High School. But he refused to say whether he would use it—although on several previous occasions he has said, flatly, that he would use this power.

This is a tense moment in the history of the South and the whole nation.

*The Supreme Court's Ruling, the Closing of the Public Schools, and the Chartering of the Private School Corporation, September 12-29, 1958*

THE U. S. Supreme Court ruled Sept. 12 that integration at Little Rock Central High School proceed without the two and one-half-year delay granted by District Judge Harry J. Lemley.

On Sept. 29 the high court followed up with a lengthy opinion setting forth the reasons behind its ruling and asserting that no "evasive schemes" could be used to avoid school integration. . . .

Gov. Orval Faubus signed the anti-integration bills approved by the special Legislature in August and under one of them he ordered the four Little Rock high schools closed. The same law requires a referendum in the school district "for" or "against" integration and he set the date for Sept. 27. . . .

Leading up to the Supreme Court decision Sept. 12 on Little Rock, the government got ready for any eventuality.

Three days before the decision Atty. Gen. William P. Rogers wrote letters to Little Rock City Manager Dean I. Dauley and to President Wayne

Upton of the school board promising "full co-operation" of the federal government to prevent disorder or to help the school board if it decided to seek injunctions. There has been no indication that the school board would do this.

Four Justice Department attorneys led by Malcolm R. Wilkey, head of the office of Legal Counsel, arrived two days before the decision. Wilkey said their mission was to assist District Attorney Osro Cobb and also the school board and the Little Rock city government in any matters that might arise after the decision. He said much planning already had been done and left the impression the government was prepared for any turn of events. Deputy marshals poured into town to join the staff of Marshal R. Beal Kidd. Some of them were regular marshals from other districts but many had been recruited in Arkansas for special duty at Little Rock. Kidd never would say how many he had but a reporter counted 137 coming out of a briefing session.

Advice from Washington was that the government would use marshals in the first attempt to enforce any integration order that might come, but Kidd said he would use the marshals as the court told him to and that he had not received any instructions from the court. At all levels on the government side, information was scarce. Wilkey said the attorneys were there to carry out the court ruling that admission to a public school could not be denied on the basis of race. As to when or how he declined to say. Then the court ruled and Gov. Faubus closed the schools and within a week the Washington attorneys and most of the marshals were gone—subject to recall if needed.

After the Little Rock Private School Corp. was chartered and Gov. Faubus in a television speech said the board should lease its closed schools to the corporation, the school board petitioned federal district court for advice. The board said it was willing to lease its property if that did not place it in contempt of the court whose last effective order in the suit was for integration to proceed. The NAACP intervened. It asked the court to rule the private school plan illegal or, if not, to order the private schools to admit Negro children in accordance with the previous court order. The Justice Department entered the case as "friend of the court" and argued on the NAACP side; its petition called the private school plan a "sham." The government move was taken as policy that the Justice Department would oppose any plan to let private school corporations use public money to get around integration orders. Federal Judge John E. Miller heard the petitions Sept. 25 at Fort Smith. He refused to advise the school board, and he dismissed the NAACP petition, saying that it involved passing on the validity of the state laws and that this required a three-judge court.

The NAACP immediately filed notice of appeal to the Eighth Circuit Court.

Two judges of the circuit court issued a temporary restraining order Sept. 29 to keep the school board from altering the integration or operational status of the high schools as of Sept. 25, pending a hearing set for Oct. 6 on an injunction against the school board. . . .

The Little Rock board started September in a state of suspense with its school opening delayed from Sept. 2 to Sept. 8. Then in anticipation of a Supreme Court ruling after the hearing set for Sept. 11, it delayed the high school opening to Sept. 15 and opened the elementary and junior high schools on Thursday Sept. 4.

When the court ruled on Sept. 12 the board met and drew up a statement that the high schools would open Sept. 15 and that qualified Negroes would be admitted. It released the statement at 3 p.m. An hour later, Henry V. Rath, accountant, resigned from the board in protest against the court ruling.

Gov. Faubus had declined to comment when the ruling came out during the morning, but he got into action in the late afternoon. Starting at 4:25 p.m. he signed into law all but one (the one delaying the Central High opening to Sept. 15) of the bills that had been approved late in August by the special session of the General Assembly. At 4:30 p.m. he signed the proclamation closing the four Little Rock high schools because "I have determined that domestic violence within the Little Rock School District is impending, and that a general, suitable, and efficient educational system cannot be maintained in the senior high schools of the Little Rock School District because of integration of the races." . . .

Supt. Virgil T. Blossom began getting a school-by-television program ready as a makeshift deal. It started Monday Sept. 22. Each of the three commercial television stations is giving two hours of time each day. One station handles 10th grade subjects, another the 11th and the third the 12th grade. Regular school teachers appear on television to teach. Only basic subjects are being taught. What credit, if any, students will get from this work was not known. Any work they do by TV is voluntary.

As the first week of no high school went by, some parents began sending their children to schools elsewhere. Some went to private schools, others went to relatives in other towns and enrolled in the public schools by paying tuition. By the end of the first week the number of these transfers was 395 out of the four-school total enrollment of 3,698. Among the transfers was Terrance Roberts, one of the seven Negroes registered at Central and a senior this year. His mother, Mrs. William R. Roberts, said he didn't want to wait and that she couldn't stand another year like the last one. Terrance is living with a grandmother at Los Angeles and going to school there.

On Sept. 17 six Little Rock residents received a charter from Pulaski County Circuit Court for a Little Rock Private School Corporation. Their plan was to lease the four high schools, if the election Sept. 27 went against integration, and operate them as private schools financed with tax money under the laws of the special session.

By the time the votes were counted election night, the school board and the corporation had begun negotiations on a lease. Both sides said it was going to be a "thorny" procedure because so many administrative and financial details were involved. The board's intention was to protect itself against possible court contempt by including some kind of escape clause in the proposed lease. . . .

[The governor's] school closing was unprecedented in Arkansas but it was followed by almost complete silence for a few days. Faubus announced that the next move was up to the federal government but the government didn't do or say anything, nor did anybody else for a while. Then it became apparent that the government wasn't going to do anything.

The school closing order came on a Friday before the schools were to open Monday. On that Monday, the governor noted there was no widespread opposition to the closing. He judged the attitude of the people to be one of "cold fury" toward the federal government.

Faubus closed the four high schools (not the elementary or junior high schools) because he had determined that "domestic violence is impending" if there was integration at Central High. . . .

On Sept. 18 the governor went on a statewide television network to explain his plan for the operation of the high schools at Little Rock on a private basis and to make what was taken to be an appeal for votes against integration in the Sept. 27 election.

The private school plan, he said, "is sound and workable. It is all legal. To this the advocates of the so-called 'law of the land' can have no objection." The plan is based on a provision in an 1875 state law which gives school boards permission to lease their buildings to private schools. State money would be provided to the private schools but Faubus said there was precedent for this.

On election eve the governor again went on television to assure the voters that his private school plan was legal and to remind them of the troubles that integration has brought elsewhere. Right after him on TV came four of the top clergymen of Little Rock pleading for votes to save the public school system.

Next day 19,470 votes were cast against integration, 7,561 for. Out of 32 polling places only five, in Negro neighborhoods, showed a majority for integration. The total vote of 27,031 was the second largest in history at Little Rock. . . .

[Faubus] said the court in 1954 had cited authorities who already had been cited for pro-Communist activity by the House Committee on un-American Activities and he raised the question of how high in the government the Communists had penetrated. He promised to continue to fight for "our constitutional rights and the basic precepts of democracy" but said no one could promise victory in this struggle. . . .

It was nearly a week after Gov. Faubus had closed the high schools at Little Rock that community forces began to be exerted toward influencing the voting on Sept. 27. In accord with the law, *Act 4* of the special session, the question on the ballot was "for" or "against" integration of all schools in the district. This was simple enough for the segregation side. But on the other side were those who saw a vote "for integration" as the only way that free public schools could be maintained at Little Rock, whether they approved of integration or not. This was the point they attempted to get across.

About 50 women, led by Mrs. D. D. Terry, wife of a former congressman, and Mrs. Joe R. Brewer, daughter of a former mayor, organized the Women's Emergency Committee to Open Our Schools. They called for votes "for integration" but explained that the Women's Emergency Committee was neither for nor against integration, that they considered such a vote the only way to get the schools open again. Sixty-three Little Rock lawyers signed a statement of their belief that the operation of private schools with public money was illegal and that they could see no alternative, distasteful though it might be, to "a limited integrated school system." They too urged votes "for integration."

The student body president at Hall High School, in a well-to-do section of Little Rock, said he and others had polled 501 students by telephone and reported 71 per cent of them favored reopening the schools, even with integration. Five per cent were undecided, the rest were against reopening with integration. Sixty-five Hall High students met at a church and 63 of them approved a statement that the school be opened, integrated or not. Four seniors polled Central High juniors and seniors by mail and said 71 per cent of 540 answers were against reopening the school with integration.

Two segregationist organizations, the Capital Citizens Council and the new States' Rights Council, denounced the lawyers who said the private school plan was illegal. The Rev. Wesley Pruden, Citizens Council president, said the lawyers were political enemies of Faubus and "are so desperate now they are coming out in the open." The States' Rights Council called the attorney's [*sic*] statement "preposterous." [*SSN* October 1958, pp. 5, 7]

## Presbyterian Ministers Deny Faubus Charges, September 16, 1958*

A GROUP of Presbyterian ministers and laymen, stung by Governor Faubus' charge that some of them had been "brainwashed by leftwingers and Communists," fired back yesterday with an angry denial and a demand for an apology.

The ministers and laymen acted at the semi-annual meeting of the Presbytery of Washburn at Central Presbyterian Church. The Presbytery embraces about one-third of the Presbyterian churches in Arkansas, stretching from Little Rock to Fort Smith.

Earlier in the meeting, the group adopted a resolution urging the governor to consider countermanding his proclamation closing the Little Rock high schools and to refrain from closing any other schools in the state.

A resolution also was adopted authorizing the moderator of the Presbytery to appoint a special committee on reconciliation to explore avenues of reconciliation in the school integration controversy with "other concerned groups or individuals."

Another proposed resolution to invite evangelist Billy Graham to Little Rock to try to mediate the integration controversy with Governor Faubus was withdrawn by its sponsors when it appeared headed for defeat. . . .

## Negro's Visit to White Church, September 28, 1958†

A NEGRO woman identified as Mrs. Pearl Lewis attended the morning service yesterday at the Pulaski Heights Methodist Church.

---

* *Arkansas Gazette,* "Presbyterians Deny Charge, Demand Apology of Governor," September 17, 1958, p. 1A. For model documentation, see p. 35.

† *Arkansas Gazette,* "Segregationist Brings Negro to Church," September 29, 1958, p. 2A. For model documentation see p. 35.

She was accompanied by Mrs. Roy T. Morrison of 714 North Tyler Street, who told reporters that she had brought the Negro woman to church because "I wanted to see if the members would practice what they preach."

Mrs. Morrison said she was a segregationist. The Church's pastor, Rev. J. Kenneth Shamblin, urged in his sermon last Sunday that his congregation vote for integration in the school election so public schools could be retained.

Mr. Shamblin said later that "it was a well advertised plan to embarrass me." Four photographers and reporters were in front of the Church as the Negro woman entered.

## Substitutes for the Public Schools, September-October 1958

LITTLE ROCK'S four public high schools remained closed under order of Gov. Orval Faubus while a private school sponsored by him got into operation financed by public donations. . . .

In one day at the end of September events occurred in the following order: The Little Rock school board leased its four high schools to the Little Rock Private School Corporation for use as private schools; two judges of the U.S. Eighth Circuit Court of Appeals issued a temporary restraining order to nullify the lease or any other action that would change the integration status of the public high schools; the U.S. Supreme Court issued a unanimous 17-page opinion backing up its decision of Sept. 12 that integration at Little Rock should proceed immediately. . . .

Copies of the temporary restraining order were served on about 190 individuals and organizations including Gov. Faubus, whose bodyguards prevented a federal marshal from serving it in person. . . .

The state Board of Education asked the attorney general whether in view of the restraining order it could comply with *Act 5* of the 1958 special session, the law that orders state aid withheld from any school closed because of integration and the money distributed to the locked out students according to a specified formula.

The board had determined that each Little Rock high school student had $172.66 coming for this school year, the money to be paid directly to whatever accredited school he might attend within the state.

The attorney general, Bruce Bennett, held that the board of education could proceed under *Act 5* and that this would not violate the restraining order.

Education Commissioner Arch W. Ford said the distribution of the money would begin soon but pointed out that the Little Rock Private School Corporation was not eligible to receive any money because it is not accredited. Normally a new school cannot be accredited until the end of one year of operation. . . .

Of the 3,698 students who registered at the four Little Rock high schools at the start of September, at least 2,532—and probably more—have arranged some other kind of schooling for themselves since the schools were closed Sept. 15 by Gov. Faubus to prevent integration. Some 212 of 717 Negro students and 2,320 of 2,981 whites are in some kind of learning situation. . . .

[A senior high school operated by the Little Rock Private School Corporation was opened in a former Methodist orphanage building originally erected about 1910.]

Most of the teachers came out of retirement to work for the private school, which makes a faculty somewhat older than would be normal in a public school. Supt. W. C. Brashears said he was hiring only persons with teaching certificates and that their pay would average about $400 a month.

Every student interviewed said "I like it." They were glad to be back in school, after the unexpected seven weeks of idleness, and said that's the way all the others felt. But they really couldn't tell much about the school yet because "it's all very confused." . . .

Several students want to take courses not offered. So many wanted typing and shorthand that these were added to the curriculum. No foreign language courses are available and this disappointed some students.

Their first impressions of their teachers were good ones. "They seem to be good," said one girl. "They know what they're talking about," another said. How strict are they? Just like in any school, the students replied, but the 11th graders interviewed said they had been told that the rules would be "very strict."

The senior class students were especially relieved to be getting the subjects they need for graduation but recognized that there are a lot of things the school doesn't have. Among the missing things: lockers for books, optional courses, social clubs, scholastic fraternities, athletics, student publications. . . .

Physical drawbacks at the school are considerable. The 48-year-old, two-story, 32-room former orphanage has only one restroom on each floor (with a total of three commodes). . . .

Some 766 white pupils are enrolled in this school. They had been without classes since Little Rock's high schools both white and Negro, were closed Sept. 15 in the state-federal impasse over school integration.

About twice as many more have made other arrangements to continue their education—either in the Pulaski County public schools outside Little Rock proper, in schools opened by their churches, or by moving to other places to live with relatives.

Of the 700-odd Negro pupils, about 200 transferred to the still-separate school operated by the Pulaski County School District. Two Negro colleges plan private schools. . . . [*SSN* November 1958, pp. 8-9]

## NAACP Conference, November 2, 1958

ROY WILKINS, executive secretary of the National Association for the Advancement of Colored People, was at Little Rock on Nov. 2 for the 14th annual meeting of the Arkansas State Conference of Branches of the NAACP. Several hundred persons at the meeting heard him declare the Negroes were winning their battle for equal rights, in the schools and elsewhere. . . .

Excerpts from his speech follow:

"The white South is fond of saying, 'Don't go too fast,' 'Don't push,' 'Don't flood us,' 'Give us time.' Last year at Central High proved they don't mean what they say. If they can't be sincere with nine out of 2,000 they don't intend to be sincere. Some of the great powerful, secure and superior white people of Little Rock and Arkansas apparently are afraid these youngsters and others like them may upset the doctrine of innate Negro inferiority. . . .

"Gov. Faubus is a valuable enemy. He has aided in many ways in clarifying the issue of segregation. . . .

"We must resist the temptation to backslide. Victory is near at hand, nearer than some of us think. The opposition is flopping about, but it knows that it doesn't have a leg to stand on. . . . Common sense will take over and Arkansas will rejoin the union. . . ."

The Arkansas NAACP by resolution set out a program including the following points: To encourage Negroes to pay their poll taxes and vote; to continue the effort to hasten compliance with Supreme Court rulings which outlaw racial segregation in public education, recreation and transportation; to press for the abolition of racial discrimination in employment; to encourage Negro participation in all worthy undertakings, to increase efforts to promote inter-cultural and inter-group understanding; to encourage the formation of youth councils; and to "urge schools, churches and other agencies concerned with the development of Negro children to counsel these children on the importance of developing and utilizing their talents to the fullest degree." [*SSN* December 1958, p. 12]

## Segregationist's Election to Congress in Political Upset, November 4, 1958

AN ARKANSAS congressman of 16 years standing was engulfed by the segregationist tide in Arkansas in November. Brooks Hays, renominated over vigorous opposition in the Democratic primary in July, failed to survive an eight-day write-in campaign by Dr. Dale Alford of Little Rock four months later and was unseated, 30,739 to 29,483. This might seem a surprising outcome: Hays is a veteran politician, well-established in Congress, nationally known, popular until now in his district, president of the Southern Baptist Convention, a signer of the Southern Manifesto and a moderate in approach to the racial situation.

Alford is an eye surgeon, has never been in politics, is serving his first term on the Little Rock school board (an unpaying job and normally not a political one). But Dr. Alford, Hays said and it is generally believed at Little Rock, had the support of Gov. Orval Faubus.

Alford campaigned against the Supreme Court and against Hays' attitude of moderation [Congressman Hays had tried to mediate the Faubus-Eisenhower impasse of early September, 1957] and promised to take action in Congress for the relief of Little Rock.

Hays defended his racial stand as the only route to a solution of the southern problem, called the Alford campaign a "sneak attack" on the Democratic primary system of nominating candidates.

Dr. Alford ran as an "independent Democrat." His campaign manager was Claude D. Carpenter Jr., one of Faubus' closest advisors and chairman of the Democratic state fund-raising campaign, a job he resigned temporarily. With an attorney general's ruling that it was legal, Dr. Alford used paste-on stickers to help write-in voters—the stickers had his name and a box with the "X" already marked in, the voter had only to stick them to the ballot. . . .

Hays later said he and Faubus had promised one another last spring not to interfere in each other's race, and that he didn't know why, as he claimed, Faubus violated the promise. Faubus denied taking any part in the campaign and said Hays himself was the main reason Hays was defeated.

Hays promised to continue his position of moderation and to keep trying to find a solution to the racial situation. . . .

Desegregation was the only issue in the campaign. Dr. Alford got his winning margin in Pulaski County and Little Rock where the four public high schools, closed by Gov. Faubus in September, are still closed. . . . [*SSN* December 1958, p. 12]

*Arkansas Education Association Resolution and Reaction,*
*November 6-7, 1958*

WITHOUT mentioning the word integration or the Little Rock crisis in which the public high schools are closed, the Arkansas Education Association in its annual convention [Nov. 6-7] took the stand "that the public school system is not expendable." It then adopted a plan of setting up local committees in the cities and counties to keep an eye on the 1959 Legislature for the purpose of preserving the school system. . . .

In its policy statement the AEA began, "We are deeply concerned over the continuing school crisis—for fear that long-sought and hard-won gains for public education may be lost" and then reviewed the legal and moral responsibility of the state for public education and the traditional principle of local autonomy over public schools. The final two paragraphs read: "There are sharp conflicts and often irreconcilable differences which go to the heart of our lives. Yet we solve our differences peacefully in this country, and we shall find answers to the complex problems emerging from the present crisis—answers which do not undermine the one institution upon which all we have and all we hope for rests, the public school system. . . ."

Meeting at Little Rock at the same time was the Arkansas Legislative Council, a body of 21 state senators and representatives which functions between legislative sessions.

They were outraged at what the AEA had done. They called the teachers stupid, said their reports were "reflections on our intelligence," suggested that they were innocent victims of subversive influence.

To a man they declared themselves supporters of the schools, that is, unless "circumstances" forced them into drastic action and five of them said they would close the schools rather than integrate them.

Then the Legislative Council ordered its committee on Subversion in Education to investigate the AEA reports, ordered a poll of AEA members to see if they agree with the reports and adopted a resolution implying that they could find some other use for the third penny of the sales tax, a new tax which produces about $14 million a year for the public schools. . . . [*SSN* December 1958, p. 12]

## School-Board Resignations, November 12, 1958

FIVE of the six members of the Little Rock school board resigned in a body Nov. 12, recognizing what they called "the utter hopelessness, helplessness and frustration of our present position." Dr. Dale Alford is the sixth board member. He objected to the resignations which came eight days after he had defeated Congressman Brooks Hays in a write-in campaign based on his opposition to school board policy.

Without being specific the five board members said they were resigning "in the light of recent events" and to give Little Rock voters the opportunity to select an entirely new board at the election Dec. 6.

On the night of their resignations the board members also voted, over Dr. Alford's objection, to buy up the contract of Supt. Virgil T. Blossom, which runs to June 30, 1960, at $1,100 a month. They voted to pay him $19,741.41 and to end his contract Nov. 30, 1958.

They did this, they said privately, because they were afraid that the new board to be elected in December would not treat Blossom fairly. . . . [*SSN* December 1958, pp. 12-13]

## Miscellaneous School Information, November 1958

THE state Education Department has received requests for state aid from 118 public school districts and three private schools for 1,199 high school students who have transferred from Little Rock. Such a transfer of state aid was provided for by special legislative session in August. . . .

The U.S. Appeals Court, Eighth Circuit, made permanent the injunction against the Little Rock school board to keep it from leasing its buildings or facilities to a private segregated school. It also ordered the school board to take affirmative steps, as directed by the district judge and on its own initiative, toward integration. . . .

Dr. T. J. Raney, president of the corporation which operates the white segregated school on public donations, announced donations totaled about $225,000 by Nov. 20. He had said earlier that it would take $500,000 to $600,000 for the school year. . . . [*SSN* December 1958, p. 12]

## New School Board, New Superintendent, December 1958

LITTLE ROCK, where the public high schools are closed by order of Gov. Orval E. Faubus, elected a new six-man school board. Three of the six were elected over the opposition of Gov. Faubus and the other three were endorsed by segregationist organizations at Little Rock. ...

Of the many problems awaiting the new board, one, getting a new superintendent, was quickly solved. Terrell E. Powell, principal of Hall High School, was promoted to replace Virgil T. Blossom. At the same meeting two important figures in the school system, Asst. Supt. Fred Graham and Business Manager Beall Hempstead, turned in their resignations: Hempstead because of ill health and Graham "to preserve my health, which has been impaired by the strain and tension of the past two years."

The only thing the board did during December about the court order that it must proceed with integration was to hire a new law firm, Mehaffey, Smith and Williams, of Little Rock. One partner, William J. Smith, is Gov. Faubus' personal attorney and political advisor. [*SSN* January 1959, p. 14]

## Court Action against NAACP, December 1958

THE ARKANSAS Supreme Court ruled against the National Association for the Advancement of Colored People in two appeals stemming from attacks made by state Atty. Gen. Bruce Bennett. In both cases the NAACP said it would carry its appeals to the U.S. Supreme Court.

The state supreme court upheld the contention of Bennett that the NAACP is liable for a $50 a year state tax on corporations and the validity of the "Bennett" ordinances adopted by Little Rock and North Little Rock.

Little Rock, North Little Rock, and several other cities adopted the "Bennett" ordinances in the fall of 1957, for the expressed purpose of giving themselves a way to determine whether certain organizations should be paying a municipal privilege tax. To make that determination the cities can demand that any organization file a list of its members, contributors, expenditures and other information. ... [*SSN* January 1959, p. 14]

## Women's Emergency Committee Proposal, December 1958

THE Women's Emergency Committee to Open Our Schools asked the Little Rock City Manager Board late in December to establish an inter-denominational inter-racial "City Commission on Civic Unity" to promote better community relations, to cultivate better understanding among the segments of the population and to foster the good name of Little Rock. There was no immediate reaction from the city government. ... [*SSN* January 1959, p. 14]

## Arrangements for Students, December 1958

WHAT has happened—as far as formal education is concerned—to the 3,698 white and Negro students displaced when four Little Rock high schools closed last September because of court-ordered desegregation of one of them? . . .

1,299 of the total of 3,698 white and Negro pupils are in private schools full-time. These private schools are operated by the Little Rock Private School Corp., and by various churches and church related colleges.

527 pupils are getting part-time education by correspondence or in private schools.

1,168 are enrolled in public schools in other parts of the state.

100 (estimated) are enrolled in public schools outside the state.

604 apparently are getting no formal education.

Of the 177 teachers and four principals at the closed schools, one has resigned to enter business; all the rest still are on the school district payroll. None is teaching in private schools or other public schools, though some have been called on to do substitute teaching in the city's still open, still segregated public elementary schools. [*SSN* January 1959, p. 14]

## New School Proposals and Discussions by Governor Faubus and Others, January 1959

GOV. ORVAL E. FAUBUS, second man in Arkansas history to get a third term, offered a new plan for withstanding school desegregation, said by his advisors to be beyond the reach of the federal courts.

It's a constitutional amendment to relieve the state of its duty to provide free public schools and to leave this function up to local school districts. It also empowers the school districts, if they wish, to abolish their public school systems, then distribute school money equally among the pupils. It would be up to the pupils individually to get an education.

This was the keystone of a three-point program given by the governor to the Legislature that convened in January. . . .

The Rev. Charles A. Higgins, dean of Trinity Episcopal Cathedral at Little Rock, offered his own personal solution to the segregation-desegregation problem: Strip the schools of all but the basic courses of learning and eliminate all their social and extra-curricular activities, then open them desegregated as to race but segregated as to sex.

A committee of the American Association of University Women, Little Rock branch, interviewed 85 Little Rock businessmen during November, December and January, asking one question: "Has the Little Rock school situation affected your business?" Forty-four said there had been an adverse effect, six a favorable effect and 35 no effect. The AAUW concluded that business had suffered.

The Little Rock City Manager Board declined to consider, officially, the request made by the Women's Emergency Committee to Open Our Schools that the board appoint an inter-racial commission on civic unity. . . .

The new president of the Little Rock Chamber of Commerce, E. Grainger Williams, in his first speech urged that Little Rock reconsider "the cost of public education and the cost of *lack* of education."

That week the Chamber of Commerce officially recognized the school situation for the first time. It adopted a resolution of support for the new school board's plan to reopen the high schools segregated while working on a new integration plan. And in its program of work for 1959 the Chamber said it would encourage a climate of opinion in which communication among citizens could be restored. . . . [*SSN* February 1959, p. 14]

## Accreditation of Private Schools, January 1959

IN JANUARY the T. J. Raney High School at Little Rock held a Sunday afternoon open house for the public, was accredited by the state with a Class A rating and applied to the state for financial aid for the former Little Rock public high school students it is educating. Raney is the school started last October by the Little Rock Private School Corp., which was created with the help of Gov. Faubus after he had closed the public high schools. It operates on public donations which at mid-January had gone over $300,000.

Raney High received its state accreditation Jan. 14 and this made it eligible to apply for state aid. . . .

Baptist High School, founded at Little Rock last October by Ouachita Baptist College of Arkadelphia and Southern Baptist churches of Little Rock, was accredited by the state and received a Class A rating. Since it is church-sponsored it is not expected to apply for state aid. . . . [*SSN* February 1959, p. 14]

## Further Court Action, January-February 1959

ALL DURING January there were filings, arguments and hearings in the
Little Rock school desegregation case, but at the end of the month the four
public high schools still were closed.

When the year opened the U.S. Appeals Court, Eighth Circuit, had
sent down its mandate to District Judge John E. Miller of Ft. Smith telling
him to prevent the use of Little Rock public schools as private segregated
schools and ordering both him and the school board to take "affirmative
steps" toward carrying out the court-approved plan of integration.

Judge Miller held a hearing Jan. 6 on this mandate and heard the
suggestions of the new school board, the U.S. Justice Department and the
Negro plaintiffs as to what the appeals court meant by "affirmative steps."
Judge Miller commented, "This type of litigation can't go on and on" and
said it was time to settle the case. . . .

Later that week Judge Miller issued his order. He did not tell the
board to reopen the high schools but said that if public schools were operated there was no alternative but to integrate them. He told the school
board to "move forward within their official powers" to carry out the integration plan and to report back to him within 30 days on what they had
done and were planning to do. . . .

Eleven days later the school board was back in court to present this
proposition: With the court's permission it would open the four high
schools immediately (Monday, Jan. 26) as segregated schools and would
offer to the court by Aug. 15 a new integration plan that it said would
satisfy both the federal courts and the residents of the school district. The
board asked for this as a way of restoring dignity and calm to the local
situation. [Board President] McKinley explained he had already discussed
it with Faubus and that he believed the governor would give the board
permission to open the schools if the court approved.

What kind of plan the board could produce that would meet the requirements of the court to integrate and would also satisfy Little Rock
residents, favoring segregation, the board did not explain. McKinley said
the board was already in touch with outside education experts about
helping.

The Negro plaintiffs objected to the new proposition and said the
school board was trying "to move backward, rather than forward, in carrying out the integration plan." Judge Miller called a hearing on it for
Feb. 3 at Little Rock.

The Justice Department also objected. In a motion signed by Atty. Gen. William P. Rogers and others, the government said the school board plan was offered "in bad faith to avoid compliance" with previous court orders and the board should be held in contempt unless it tried to proceed with the approved plan of gradual integration.

On Feb. 3 Judge Miller rejected this proposal by the board.

In another phase of the Little Rock case, the Negro plaintiffs asked the district court on Jan. 12 to nullify *Acts 4* and *5* of the 1958 special legislative session and then to order the high schools reopened and desegregated immediately. *Act 4* is the law under which Faubus closed the four schools, and *Act 5* is the one under which state aid is withheld from the closed schools and given to the schools attended by the former Little Rock students. As part of this motion, the Negro plaintiffs asked that 15 stated officials, listed by name and office, be enjoined from enforcing the acts.

A three-judge court will be convened to consider this request. *Acts 4* and *5* are already being challenged in the state courts, and Atty. Gen. Bruce Bennett will ask the federal court not to act until the state courts have completed their adjudication. . . . [*SSN* February 1959, p. 14]

## Alternative Schooling Costs Taxable, January 1959

THE Women's Emergency Committee to Open Our Schools, of Little Rock, asked the state Revenue Department and the Internal Revenue Service if the cost of sending high school students off to school, because the Little Rock high schools are closed, would be deductible for income tax purposes. Both ruled it would not. . . . [*SSN* February 1959, p. 14]

## Student Opinion in the Private High School*

EVEN to me, a teenager, it has become evident that in order to keep the freedom we inherited we must not become complacent, but, strive, work, and sacrifice to keep the blessings of liberty alive.

I sometimes believe the present generation is too unconcerned about our government which decides whether the people shall live under freedom

---

* An editorial from the first issue of the *Rebel Rouser*, official paper of the Raney private high school in Little Rock, as reprinted in *Common Sense*, a publication which bills itself as "The Nation's Anti-Communist Newspaper." In its issue of February 15, 1959, *Common Sense* headlined this editorial, "A Teenager Speaks Out for Liberty."

of speech and religion or under the socialistic or communistic way that is slowly overcoming our constitution and American beliefs.

As I look under the surface I find our country's freedom is being overcome by the Supreme Court and powerful bureaus, through usurpation of power granted by our Constitution to Congress.

We should all take the time and interest to learn the character and principles of men we send to Congress, for therein lies our hope for a return to a conservative Constitutional government.—Bobbalu Cook

### DOCUMENTATION SUITABLE FOR RESEARCH PAPERS

BIBLIOGRAPHY ENTRY

Cook, Bobbalu. Editorial from *Rebel Rouser. Common Sense,* February 15, 1959. Reprinted in *LRUSA.*

FIRST FOOTNOTE

*Bobbalu Cook, editorial from *Rebel Rouser, Common Sense,* February 15, 1959, reprinted in *LRUSA,* p. 135.

SUBSEQUENT FOOTNOTES

*Cook, *op. cit., LRUSA,* p. ■.
*Cook, editorial, *LRUSA,* p. ■.
*Cook, *LRUSA,* p. ■.

*Federal Judge's View on Responsibility of the Courts, February 12, 1959*

[DISTRICT JUDGE John E.] Miller made a speech Feb. 12 to the Sebastian County (Ft. Smith) Bar Association on the responsibility of the bar for keeping the courts "always mindful of the customs and traditions of our people." He said, "Judges must speak for the will of the people. . . . Our greatest problem is the inclination of some of the appellate courts of the land to arrogate unto themselves the power to declare for us certain standards contrary to the mores and conditions which have existed for centuries in this country." He didn't mention desegregation but the Associated Press said his remarks obviously were concerned with that. . . . [*SSN* March 1959, p. 2]

## *Public-School Finances, February 1959*

THE Little Rock School District was $139,844.59 short of having enough money to pay its bill for February, Supt. Terrell E. Powell said in a financial report distributed to board members in advance of the board meeting Feb. 26. He said the district was in trouble because of the money being withheld by the state to pay for the education at other schools of the students who would have attended the four high schools closed by Gov. Faubus. . . .

The school district ended the previous year—and started this one—with a cash balance of $551,656.

State money withheld will total about $610,000 by the end of the year.

The school board—all new members after the Dec. 6 election—found out right at the start that it was going to have money trouble and began economizing immediately. For example, no teacher who leaves the system is replaced with a new one. Instead one of the idle high school teachers is moved into the vacancy. Supplies and equipment unless essential are not being replaced when used up. [*SSN* March 1959, p. 2]

## *Conflict within the New School Board, February 1959*

ROBERT W. LASTER, traffic judge and board member, produced the simplest plan of all for getting the high schools open again: Ignore the courts, open all four as segregated schools and, as far as the federal government is concerned, "let the devil take the hindmost." The government, he said, could send the troops again, which he didn't think it would, or it could throw the board members in jail for contempt of court. Other board members were reserved on the Laster plan, and one, Ted Lamb, said Laster was just trying to set himself up to run for governor in 1960, an ambition Laster does not conceal.

Then Laster came out with a second plan: Add to the teacher contracts a clause that the contracts are automatically cancelled if the schools are desegregated. The effect would be that a school desegregated by court order would find itself without a faculty, he said, and that would be the federal court's problem. . . .

Saturday night, Feb. 28 [Everett Tucker, Jr., Ted Lamb, and Russell H. Matson—the three moderates], issued a long statement giving an explicit description of their view of the board's situation. It was that legally the only courses available are non-segregated public schools or no public schools. They prefer public schools and said the board should start immediately to work on a plan of "controlled integration" to have ready for the moment, soon to come they thought, when the courts again would order them to open the schools with desegregation. . . .

At the request of Faubus and Little Rock School Board President Ed I. McKinley Jr., [State Legislative] Rep. T. E. Tyler of Little Rock introduced *House Bill 546* on Feb. 26 to let the governor appoint three more members to the six-member School Board. Tyler candidly explained that the Board was split 3-3 and couldn't do anything. "I know it's a little on the dictatorship side but we have no choice," Tyler said. "The people voted the man [Faubus] back to do whatever he can to preserve their way of life. This is part of meeting that demand." . . . [SSN March 1959, p. 2]

## Proposal to Dismiss Teachers and Administrators, February 1959

A TEACHER purge report was published in the *Arkansas Gazette* of Feb. 8. The newspaper said it had learned that a proposition calling for the payment of its withheld state aid to the Little Rock district in return for the firing of four school administrators and other teachers had been presented by Supt. Powell, acting as messenger, to Lamb, Matson and Tucker, the three board members who do not endorse the Faubus policies. It did not say who had sent Powell to them. Lamb confirmed the information. Matson and Tucker would neither confirm nor deny it. Board President Ed I. McKinley Jr. called it a "ridiculous falsehood."

The *Gazette* listed the four administrators as Jess W. Matthews, Central High principal; J. O. Powell and Mrs. Elizabeth Huckaby, assistant principals, and L. M. Christopher, Negro, principal of Mann High School for Negroes.

Next day Gov. Faubus denied knowing of any purge but added that he would like to see three school people fired. He named Matthews, J. O. Powell and Mrs. Huckaby, because "they did everything they could to discriminate against white students" during 1957-58. . . . [SSN February 1959, p. 2]

## Negroes' Conduct during Integration Crisis

THE conduct of Negroes during the Little Rock crisis was praised by the Rev. Z. Z. Dryver in a speech at a public meeting of the NAACP Feb. 8. He is pastor of the Union African Methodist Episcopal Church where the meeting was held. Negroes have committed no violence and have kept their conduct on a high plane, the Rev. Dryver said. "The white people themselves have admitted that the Negroes are much more decent about this integration fight than whites. Let's keep it that way." [*SSN* March 1959, p. 2]

## *Charges of Communist Influence, February 1959*

REP. Dale Alford of Little Rock (D-Ark.) told the U.S. House of Representatives in a speech Feb. 17 that Communists and their dupes had flitted in and out of Arkansas for years and were responsible for the racial trouble in the state. He said this was part of the Communist plan to create unrest and finally to divide the country. He expressed alarm at the "complacency of some officials" toward this development and concern that the Justice Department "yields" to an organization such as the NAACP. . . .

Without calling anyone a Communist, state Atty. Gen. Bruce Bennett in a speech Feb. 16 implied that the NAACP and the *Arkansas Gazette* were acting as agents of a Communist conspiracy to set up a "Black Republic" in the South. He also said the 15 bills he had submitted to the current Legislature were "designed to harass, to keep the enemies of America busy." Most of them were aimed at restricting the activity of the NAACP. [*SSN* March 1959, p. 2]

## *Position of Little Rock Chamber of Commerce, March 23, 1959*\*

TO DATE: This is the position of the Little Rock Chamber of Commerce on the Little Rock School Crisis.

No More—No Less!

I. On January 26, 1959, the Board of Directors of the Little Rock Chamber of Commerce, by unanimous action, approved as a major project the following statement:

> To the end that the solution to Little Rock's Public School problem may be found at the earliest possible time:
>
> 1. Encourage a climate of communication through which all citizens can discuss the problem with understanding and respect for one another;
> 2. Press for the culmination of whatever legal and/or legislative

---

\* From a printed resolution. Typography modified for convenience in printing in this collection.

matters that have to be resolved by the responsible local, state and Federal bodies.

II. On January 26, 1959, the Board of Directors of the Little Rock Chamber of Commerce, by unanimous action, voted to support the Little Rock School Board's request to the Federal Courts that the School Board be allowed to reopen the Little Rock High Schools on a *segregated basis* for the remainder of the school year; and in turn, the School Board would submit a new plan by August 15th.

This request was rejected by the Federal Courts.

III. On February 23, 1959, the Board of Directors of the Little Rock Chamber of Commerce, by unanimous action, voted to ask the general membership of the Chamber of Commerce to vote on two (2) questions.

The questions were:

1. Do you favor Little Rock's continuing with closed public high schools?
2. Do you now favor the reopening the Little Rock public high schools on a controlled minimum plan of integration acceptable to the Federal Courts?

The vote on question number 1 was: Yes—230; No—632; Not voting—285.

The vote on question number 2 was: Yes—819; No—245; Not voting—83.

IV. On March 2, 1959, the Board of Directors of the Little Rock Chamber of Commerce, by unanimous action, voted to request the Arkansas State Supreme Court to rule on the validity of *Acts 4* and *5* at the earliest practicable date, because:

A. Until decisions were handed down the Little Rock School Board could not plan for the future use of the School properties.
B. The School Board could possibly not be able to renew teacher contracts; and the high schools faced the loss of the teachers, which would severely harm the academic level of the schools.
C. Funds were being drained rapidly, to the point that standby operation and custody of the high schools was jeopardized; and reasonable recovery was not foreseen until the legality of the school closing laws was determined.

Now: This We Believe To Be True!

The two major responsibilities of a Chamber of Commerce to its membership and the people in the area it serves are: (1) Economic Development, (2) Cultural Development. Education is a primary part of the cultural development of any city, and therefore, is a responsibility of a Chamber of Commerce.

These facts lead us to believe the following outlined policy is in the best interest of the City of Little Rock.

Before outlining the policy, certain actions and opinions should be reviewed in order to define the Board's opinion.

In our opinion, the State of Virginia has exhausted every possible legal method a state can attempt to get around United States Supreme Court decision and maintain a state-wide public school system. Also, this same Supreme Court clearly points out that no state can use evasion to avoid complying with the decision.

Unfortunately, Little Rock's choice narrows down to public schools operating under a pupil assignment system or, no public schools at all. The pupil assignment system has been upheld by the United States Supreme Court.

North Carolina's pupil assignment system has worked in controlling integration. At one time there were 14 Negroes in the white schools of North Carolina while only 11 are enrolled now. September will mark the third year of pupil assignment in North Carolina.

The State of Arkansas has a similar pupil assignment law that can be used by the Little Rock School Board.

It is impossible for all the people of Little Rock to agree on any one suggestion for ending the problem.

THEREFORE, We Recommend:

Based solely on the reason that we desire to seek a solution acceptable to a large majority of the people of Little Rock, the Board of Directors of the Little Rock Chamber of Commerce favor:

1. The continuation and community support of high schools in Little Rock operating with private funds.

2. The reopening of the Little Rock Public High Schools by using a pupil assignment system acceptable to the School Board and the Federal Courts.

3. The School Board assuring all teachers that their contracts will be promptly renewed; in order that we do not lose our valuable and loyal staff.

4. Accepting the responsibility to seek new laws in Congress that would return the operation of public schools to each individual school district; regardless of the outcome of our present school crisis.

Each of us, in reaching our personal decision, should remember that our country was founded, operates and receives its strength by living within the law. The decision of the Supreme Court of the United States, however much we dislike it, is the declared law and is binding upon us. We think that the decision was erroneous and that it was a reversal of established law upon an unprecedented base of psychology and sociology. But we must in honesty recognize that, because the Supreme Court is the court of last resort in this country, what it has said must stand until there is a correcting constitutional amendment or until the Court corrects its own error. We must live and act now under the decision of that Court. We should not delude ourselves about that.

## DOCUMENTATION SUITABLE FOR RESEARCH PAPERS

BIBLIOGRAPHY ENTRY

Little Rock Chamber of Commerce. Statement of position in school crisis, March 23, 1959. Reprinted in *LRUSA*.

FIRST FOOTNOTE

*Little Rock Chamber of Commerce, statement of position in school crisis, March 23, 1959, reprinted in *LRUSA*, pp. 141-142.

SUBSEQUENT FOOTNOTE

*Little Rock Chamber of Commerce, statement, *LRUSA*, p. ▨.

## New Racial Bills in Arkansas Legislature, February-March 1959

COMPLETING its biennial 60-day session the Arkansas General Assembly could count 32 measures on or related to desegregation approved and sent to the governor, including the four offered by Gov. Faubus. The governor has until April 4 to sign or veto the others.

Only two of the bills caused a ruckus—one to require the labeling by race of blood for transfusions, which was approved, and the other [by Representative Tyler of Little Rock] to let the governor appoint three extra members to the Little Rock school board, which was defeated. . . .

The Little Rock PTA Council opposed the Tyler bill and so did the Little Rock Chamber of Commerce and the Women's Emergency Committee to Open Our Schools, of Little Rock. Many newspapers in the state objected to it. All the objections dealt with state interference in a local district's affairs. [The other 11 Little Rock legislators voted against it.] . . . [*SSN* April 1959, p. 10]

## Federal District Court to Rule on State School Laws, March 7, 1959

AT A HEARING March 7 at Little Rock three judges in federal district court made these decisions: (1) to proceed with a hearing set for May 4 on the validity of the 1958 school closing laws, without waiting for the state courts to rule first; (2) to enjoin the state from distributing to other schools any more of the state money being withheld from the closed Little Rock high schools pending the outcome of the hearing on May 4.

This was the first time in the long history of the Little Rock litigation that the federal courts had not stood aside to let the state courts rule first on state laws. Apparently the three judges were convinced by attorneys for the Negro children, the plaintiffs in the original Little Rock desegregation case, that time was of the essence. . . . [*SSN* April 1959, p. 10]

## Community Reaction, March 1959

THE Little Rock Chamber of Commerce polled its 2,014 members on the school situation and released the following questions asked and answers received:

Do you favor Little Rock's continuing with closed public high schools? Yes 230, No 632, no response 285.

Do you now favor the reopening of the Little Rock public high schools on a controlled minimum plan of integration acceptable to the federal courts? Yes 819, No 245, no response 83.

The chamber board immediately adopted a resolution asking the state supreme court to rule as soon as possible on the school closing laws. E. Grainger Williams, said the chamber was not taking sides but did want to get the schools open again. The segregationist Capital Citizens Council then published newspaper advertisements calling on chamber members who were against integration to send in their names and addresses and promising to publish those names. Segregationists will hold chamber members "accountable for promoting integration," the ads said, unless they sign a statement that they do not favor it.

Three weeks later the Chamber of Commerce took another step in a resolution recommending the following: (1) Continuation of the private segregated high schools at Little Rock and with community support; (2) Reopening the public high schools by using a pupil assignment law acceptable both to the school board and the federal courts; (3) Assurance to all teachers that their contracts will be renewed; (4) Acceptance of responsibility for seeking new laws in Congress to return the operation of schools to local school districts. . . .

The board of the Little Rock League of Women Voters has recommended action to "promote the opening and continued operation of the Little Rock public high schools."

The Arkansas Society of Sons of the American Revolution adopted a resolution censuring the U.S. Supreme Court for its decisions on desegregation and other matters. . . .

*The Arkansas State Press,* weekly [Negro] newspaper at Little Rock, said Gov. Faubus has as many headaches after the 1959 Legislature as he had before it met. It gave two reasons: The Negroes who want to attend Central High are still on hand, and "for once, the Negro has the federal government on his side, and it is his intention to keep those squirming who would deny him of that protection." . . . [SSN April 1959, pp. 10, 12]

## Governor Faubus's Action on New Racial Bills, April 1959

AMONG the last legislative bills for Gov. Faubus to sign or veto before the April 4 deadline for him to act were four related to desegregation. One of them he vetoed, to considerable surprise. It was *Senate Bill 346* and provided that a school closed by the governor was to be reopened in the normal way after one school year. Faubus had raised no objection to his bill when it was before the Legislature and in fact seemed to approve it.

He gave three reasons for vetoing it. First, he said, it would prevent his reopening a closed school before the end of a school year, if he wanted to do that. Under the school closing law, he said, he can reopen a closed school by proclamation any time. (Before this, his position had been that he wasn't sure whether he could reopen a closed school unless there had been another special election in the school district. This also is the Justice Department's interpretation of the law.) His second reason was that SB 346 did not specifically reserve to the governor the right to reopen closed schools. The third was that the school closing law was still being tested in court. . . . [SSN May 1959, p. 6]

## *Faubus Hint at "Compromise," April 6, 1959*

[FAUBUS] said there was a possibility the closed Little Rock high schools could be reopened next fall with limited desegregation; first, though, the opposing sides would have to get together on a compromise. His use of the word "compromise" and seeming acceptance of "limited desegregation" raised a two-day splurge of headlines.

The reaction was mostly negative. The Capital Citizens Council, segregationist and normally strong for the governor, declared token or limited integration would never be allowed. Segregationist members of the Little Rock School Board took the same position, but one board member found the governor's remarks encouraging.

On the following Sunday, the *Arkansas Democrat* of Little Rock, which endorses the Faubus policies, analyzed Faubus' comments and said they meant this: If the NAACP would let stand the state laws for tuition grants to students so they could attend segregated schools, and if the school board and Little Rock residents would allow token desegregation, then something might be worked out, and the result would be desegregated public schools and segregated private schools subsisting on student tuition paid by the state. . . . [SSN May 1959, p. 6]

## *Criticism of Negro Ministers, April 1959*

THE *Arkansas State Press,* weekly Negro newspaper published at Little Rock by L. C. Bates, whose wife is the state NAACP president, is the only publication in the state openly and militantly pressing for desegregation and other Negro causes. In April it voiced disappointment, first, that not all Negro ministers hold the same attitude as the paper and, secondly, that not all Negro residents do either.

An editorial in the April 10 issue took up the Negro ministers. They are the leaders of their community, they are successful in their field and, the *State Press* said, it is convinced they do not endorse segregation. Why then, it wondered, don't they help Negroes to a better role as American citizens. The *State Press* had discussed this with the ministers and it gave what it called the "alibis" of two of them. One said most of his congregation worked as servants for wealthy white families and he did not want to hurt them. The other said he was staying out of the desegregation controversy because he didn't want the windows of his home broken.

A week later the *State Press* apologized. On reflection it had decided the ministers are the way they are because too many Negroes themselves are apathetic, satisfied with "the master-slave relationship which the whites call good race relations," and lack determination to fight for their constitutional rights. . . . [*SSN* May 1959, p. 6]

## School Operation and Disaccreditation, April 1959

IN EFFECT this year for the first time as the school districts begin offering teacher contracts for 1959-60 are two new laws: *Act 10* of 1958 requiring teachers before being employed to list under oath all the organizations to which they have contributed or belonged in the last five years, and *Act 115* of 1959 barring public employment to any member of the NAACP.

A Little Rock Negro teacher and NAACP member filed suit in federal court against both laws.

Teachers generally resent *Act 10* but protests against it were scattered. Two Little Rock teachers have refused to sign *Act 10* affidavits; one filed suit, the other gave the newspapers the list of his organizations. One North Little Rock teacher refused to sign. A faculty group at the University of Arkansas met to discuss whether to fight the law and the university chapter of the American Association of University Professors announced it would support "any reasonable legal action" against *Act 10*. Several university professors made public statements against the law, including the law school dean, but the president, John T. Caldwell, announced he would sign an affidavit even though not required to.

A survey of seven other state-supported colleges brought reports that the faculty members were grumbling but signing. Public school administrators generally spoke of it as distasteful but, still, the law.

The segregationist Capital Citizens Council at Little Rock called it a good law and voiced suspicion that teachers at two colleges and five high schools were committing perjury by not listing all their memberships and said it would inspect their affidavits to be sure. Both Little Rock and Van Buren then asked the state attorney general if the affidavits were public records, and he ruled they were personnel records, and thus private but a school board could make them public.

Three of the four closed Little Rock high schools were accredited (Tech High was not) with the North Central Association of Secondary Schools and Colleges. All three of them lost that accreditation at the annual NCA meeting in April at Chicago. . . . [*SSN*, May 1959, p. 7]

## *More Conflict Within School Board, April 1959*

THREE of the Little Rock board members—Ted Lamb, Everett Tucker, Jr. and Russell H. Matson Jr.—disclosed that they had been visiting various schools for lunch with the teachers. They said they found teacher morale low and the teachers worried about the proposed purge of high school teachers (SSN for March and April), their job prospects for next year and the racial situation. They reassured them as best they could about the purge and job prospects. As for the racial situation, they said they told the teachers they thought the high schools would be open next fall with limited desegregation under the pupil placement laws. [Early in April Governor Faubus had vetoed a state legislative act providing for the automatic re-opening of the schools in the fall of 1959.]

That last statement provoked the wrath of other board members, who oppose desegregation at any cost and who were not invited to the luncheons with the teachers. Board President Ed I. McKinley Jr. condemned the meetings as an effort to intimidate the teachers and "soften them for integration." Said McKinley, "I condemn the use of the words 'token,' 'controlled' and/or 'limited' integration. There can be no such thing, and the integrationists know it."

A lawsuit to prevent the Little Rock School District from paying $19,741.41 to former Supt. Virgil T. Blossom—the full amount for the remainder of his contract after his discharge last Nov. 12—was dismissed when Blossom filed a response rejecting that offer. His attorney said that since Blossom had a new job starting July 1, he would file a claim only for time between Nov. 12 and July 1, or about $7,700. [*SSN* May 1959, p. 7]

## *School-Board Recall Election after Teacher-Purge Attempt, May 1959*

THREE members of the Little Rock school board tried to fire 44 teachers and school employes May 5 because they had shown what the board called "integrationist" tendencies. Twenty days later all six board members faced a recall election. After a very heavy voter turnout and by narrow margins, the three purgers were voted off the board and the other three, opponents of the attempted firings, were retained.

The three board members who attempted the firings were the pro-Faubus half of the board. Gov. Orval E. Faubus went on television to give them full support. So for the first time since September 1957 there was widespread opposition to Faubus at Little Rock on a school matter. . . .

The total vote of 25,457, out of about 42,000 eligible, was nearly twice the number cast in the regular school election in December and only 2,000 short of the total in the school closing referendum of September 1958. From the day of the attemped dismissal of the teachers to the election, the whole episode took only 20 days.

When the board met May 5 it was time to consider teacher contracts for 1959-60. That a purge of the faculty might be attempted was known (SSN for March, April and May) from previous statements by Gov. Faubus and the three board members on his side.

The other three board members held that the faculty ought to be maintained intact and relied on school board policy of years standing that a teacher to be dismissed had to be notified by Jan. 15. . . . [These three members] oppose integration but are not willing to do away with the school system. . . .

. . . After a two-hour recess for lunch, the board reconvened and Tucker restated his side's position, then announced that he, Lamb and Matson were withdrawing and that this would leave no quorum. They left.

McKinley ruled that since the meeting had opened with a quorum, a quorum still existed. He also pointed out that the current board membership, elected in December, had never voted to adopt the old board's rules and policies so that it was not bound to notify teachers in advance of the intention to dismiss them.

Then from 1:30 to 6:30 p.m., McKinley, Rowland and Laster made decisions. They voted to hire T. H. Alford, father of Congressman Dale Alford, as superintendent (T. H. Alford is principal of the Jacksonville, Ark., schools, a part of the Pulaski County Rural School District); they voted to recommend a three-mill reduction in the school tax rate, from 40 to 37 mills, at the next regular school election; and they voted to raise the pay of all teachers by five per cent in 1959-60, if there was money for it.

And they took up the teacher contracts, by schools in some cases and teacher by teacher in others. They approved 764 teacher contracts, did not approve 44 and did not act on one of the six non-signers of *Act 10*. . . .

Among the 44 were J. W. Mathews, Central High principal and his two vice-principals, J. O. Powell and Mrs. Elizabeth Huckaby, and L. M. Christopher, principal of Horace Mann (Negro) High, all four of whom were mentioned last February by the McKinley group and Faubus as ones they'd like to fire. . . .

That night, by coincidence, a new elementary school was dedicated with Tucker as the speaker. The hall overflowed and Tucker, Lamb and Matson received standing ovations from the crowd.

Next day the Little Rock PTA Council, composed of representatives of all white PTAs, adopted a three-paragraph statement of which the first two paragraphs expressed a desire to "protest vigorously" and the third paragraph said: "We feel that board members who attempt such high-handed tactics are not qualified to hold offices of such great responsibility. It is our feeling that Little Rock voters should carefully consider all legal measures allowed by Arkansas law to achieve recall of officials who use their positions to jeopardize our public school system."

From there the recall movement against McKinley, Rowland and Laster spread. Every night that week there was a PTA protest rally at one school or another with crowds ranging from 200 to 800. Within a week 17 school PTAs had endorsed the PTA council statement, one had endorsed the first two paragraphs but not the third, four had rejected the whole statement and three had taken no action.

On Friday afternoon, three days after the school board meeting and after some PTAs had already started recall petitions, 179 downtown business and civic leaders organized a Committee to Stop This Outrageous Purge (STOP). All 179 signed the following statement:

"In these principles we stand united. 1) We oppose the action taken by three members of the Little Rock school board in attempting to discharge teachers without giving them notice or a fair and impartial hearing. 2) We believe the action of these three men constitutes a denial of basic rights to employes of our schools and will cause irreparable damage to our public school system by destroying academic freedom and the faith of our teachers in themselves as free citizens. 3) We characterize the action taken by these three men as a purge which was cynical and designed to create a fear that stalks the classrooms. 4) The actions taken by Ben D. Rowland, Ed I. McKinley Jr., and Robert W. (Bob) Laster are a breach of public trust and justify their recall as members of the Little Rock school board."

Others signed the pledge later. STOP limited itself to the recall and specifically avoided taking any stand on desegregation.

Both the Mothers League of Central High and the Capital Citizens Council had endorsed the McKinley group's actions on teacher contracts and the day after STOP was organized they began circulating recall petitions against the other three board members, with aid from the States' Rights Council. . . .

None of the 44 teachers ever were told by the McKinley group why their contracts had not been renewed, and it developed that the board members were waiting for the teachers to ask. During the recall campaign, McKinley, Rowland and Laster all mentioned that most of the 44 contracts had not been renewed because the teachers either were "integrationists" or cooperated with "integrationists." And McKinley said that any of them who volunteered to abide by the public policy of segregation could have their jobs back.

After their own investigation the Classroom Teachers Association and the Arkansas Educational Association said they had found that the reasons for the contract actions included such things as trying to maintain classroom discipline, letting a Negro student take a regular turn at Bible reading in class and failing to give good grades as demanded by "members of the purge faction."

One night during the campaign STOP put on a public rally at a downtown auditorium as a tribute to all white teachers. It was for whites only; a Negro group was having a similar rally the same night for Negro teachers at another place. During the afternoon bogus mimeographed invitations with the typed signature of the STOP chairman were circulated in Negro neighborhoods, inviting Negroes to the STOP rally. Dr. Drew F. Agar, STOP chairman, went immediately to Prosecuting Attorney J. Frank Holt and with [in] an hour two Negro men who had been handing out the letters were under arrest. Next day Holt questioned three more persons, one of whom was Laster, a school board member. Then Holt said the matter would be taken up by the Pulaski County Grand Jury.

During the campaign, CROSS [the Committee to Retain Our Segregated Schools] published an advertisement in the *Arkansas Democrat* saying that McKinley, Rowland and Laster had not renewed the 44 teacher contracts for one or more of the following reasons: "Teaching alien doctrines, incompetency, breaking and entering, trespassing on private property, invasion of privacy, improper punishment, intimidation of students, immorality." It was signed by Rev. M. L. Moser Jr., CROSS chairman, who when asked by reporters where he got the information said it came from McKinley. Within 48 hours the 39 white teachers among the 44 had filed a $3,900,000 libel suit against McKinley and Moser, asking $100,000 each.

A week before the May 5 school board meeting, Supt. Terrell E. Powell said it looked like 176 of Little Rock's normal 828 teachers would not return for the 1959-60 school year. Of these 98 were going to resign, 56 probably would resign, 14 were retiring and eight were taking leaves of absence. The figures were obtained in a poll by school officials to determine teacher intentions.

A few weeks later Powell reported on the number of applications for teaching jobs and said they were about a third as many as usual. There had been 63 applications by May 21. At that rate, he said, it was going to be a problem to get enough teachers for all 36 schools.

In Federal District Court May 4, Powell testified that 266 white and 376 Negro students, of the 3,665 who would have attended the four closed high schools this year at Little Rock, were not in any school. The comparative figures he gave on Feb. 3 were 643 white and 442 Negro students. . . .

Gov. Faubus in commenting on the Little Rock School Board recall election, first recalled that he too had been fired as a teacher one time but didn't get mad about it, just went out and got another job. Then he said if they were going to recall three board members, they might as well recall all six. After two weeks he said the tension was getting so strong in Little Rock that he was worried. Finally he took to television three nights before the voting and came out against the recall of Ed I. McKinley Jr., Ben D. Rowland Sr. and Robert W. Laster, who had tried to fire the 44 teachers.

The governor said the issue was segregation-desegregation and that all the rest was just a smokescreen thrown up by "integrationists" in STOP. He addressed his remarks to the "good honest hard-working people of the lower and middle classes" and warned them to look out for a "charge of the Cadillac brigade of wealthy and prominent leaders." . . .

W. S. (Will) Mitchell, campaign chairman for STOP, commented that the governor had been misinformed about what the election was about, that the issue was "the firing of 44 teachers without reason, without notice, without hearing"and that integration had nothing to do with it. On television himself the following night, Mitchell pleaded with the governor "to leave us alone at Little Rock and let us return to the rule of reason."

In a speech during the recall campaign McKinley, president of the school board, discussed the reasons for the failure to renew some of the 44 contracts. The reasons he gave were direct quotes relating to the desegregation of Central High in 1957. He attributed them to some of the 44 teachers and afterward told reporters the teachers had made the statements to the state police during their investigation of the Central High crisis last year.

That investigation was made at the request of the Legislative Council and with Faubus' approval; so far as known it consisted solely of interviews with Central High teachers; no public report on it has been made. How did McKinley get possession of the statements? State Police Director Herman E. Lindsey, Faubus and Rep. Paul Van Dalsem of Perry County, Legislative Council chairman, all said they had not given them to McKinley. But they mentioned that others—Council members and staff, attorney general and his staff—had access to the State Police reports. McKinley himself declined to say how he got the information. . . . [*SSN* June 1959, p. 2]

## Religious Leaders' Attitudes, May 1959

At Fort Smith the Baptist Ministers Fellowship, composed of 18 North American and Southern Baptist ministers, went on record favoring the requirements of Act 10 of 1958.

At Batesville the Presbyterian Synod of Arkansas adopted a position opposing the destruction of the public schools and calling on each local church session to support the public schools. . . .

The Rev. F. L. Shuttlesworth, Negro leader at Birmingham, Ala., spoke at an NAACP Decision Day meeting at Little Rock on the fifth anniversary of the 1954 Supreme Court ruling on desegregation. He said:

"In a very large sense Little Rock has become the 'biggest rock' in human affairs. . . . From darkest Africa to sunny South America, from pious England and aristocratic France to the sprawling land of Manchuria in China and the islands of the sea, the name of Little Rock is fully known. The thought of Little Rock's incorrigibility is abhorred. The dream of Little Rock brings nightmares, as civilized people the word over wonder how low can ideals sink, how beastly can some men be, and how hard can the human heart become, how silly, stupid, and sickening can some officials act.

"Here a thought-to-be intelligent and progressive American city turned upside down simply because a decision was made and followed by families of nine Negro children that they just wanted and intended to be free! . . ." [*SSN*, June 1959, pp. 2-3]

## Closing of Schools Ruled Unconstitutional, June 18, 1959

THREE federal judges ruled unanimously June 18 that *Acts 4* and *5* of 1958 were unconstitutional *(Aaron v. McKinley)*. The two laws, produced by a special legislature at the request of Gov. Faubus, gave him power under *Act 4* to close a school about to be integrated and under *Act 5* to withhold state aid from a closed school and transfer it to whatever schools the displaced students went to. Faubus used the laws, once, to close the four public high schools at Little Rock last September. Both laws had been upheld by the state Supreme Court which based its *Act 4* ruling on the theory that the law was a proper use of the state's police power.

The federal judges—John B. Sanborn of St. Paul, Minn.; John E. Miller of Fort Smith, Ark. and Axel J. Beck of Elk Point, S.D.—took note of the state court's holding but rejected it. For one thing, they said, the U. S. Supreme Court has already ruled that violence or threat of violence cannot justify a state's using its police power to deprive a citizen of his constitutional rights. They also remembered the finding by District Judge Harry J. Lemley a year ago that conditions had been "deplorable" inside integrated Central High, and that his order for a two and one-half-year delay in integration because of that had been knocked down by both the Appeals Court and Supreme Court. From that, the judges wrote, "we can see no basis whatever for a ruling by us that Act 4 constitutes a valid and reasonable exercise of the police power of Arkansas to meet an emergency."

The ruling renewed the order to the Little Rock School Board to proceed with the plan of gradual integration originally approved by the Court in 1956.

Faubus said he was disappointed, especially about *Act 5,* and indicated that he would appeal.

A few days earlier another three-judge court—Sanborn, Miller and J. Smith Lemley of Harrison, Ark.—had ruled on two other state laws. They upheld *Act 10* of 1958 but ruled out *Act 115* of 1959. *Act 10* requires teachers to list their memberships and contributions for the last five years; *Act 115* barred public employment to members of the NAACP. . . . [*SSN* July 1959, p. 8]

## *School Board Activity with New Members, June 1959*

SEVENTEEN days after the election in which three men, or half the membership, of the Little Rock School Board were recalled, three replacements were appointed by the Pulaski County Board of Education. Two of them— J. H. Cottrell Jr., loan executive and a state representative, and B. Frank Mackey, insurance salesman and former detective—joined the holdover board members in declaring their intention to keep the schools open if possible. The third, Henry Lee Hubbard, building contractor, never gave a clue to his views on the racial situation and resigned four days after being appointed, saying he had realized that he was ineligible to serve. . . .

The five-man Board at its first meeting expunged from the record the purge of 44 teachers and everything else done by a three-man session of the board on May 5, the meeting that led to the recall of the three members. The board talked of plans to reopen the four closed high schools in September, in a way acceptable to the federal courts, but did nothing definite.

At its next meeting the board announced officially that it intended to reopen the four closed high schools in September and, without violating the federal court order, would use the state's two pupil assignment laws.

Three days later the federal court invalidated Gov. Faubus' school closing laws, thus returning the closed schools to the jurisdiction of the school board and again placing the board under orders to integrate under the plan previously approved by the court. . . .

A few days after the Little Rock School Board recall election in which Gov. Faubus campaigned for three board members who were recalled, Faubus gave his view of the outcome: He did not see it as a hands-off notice to him from Little Rock voters; he could not see any shift in sentiment toward the basic desegregation issue; his position on forced integration was unchanged and only time and events would tell whether the election was a political setback for him. [*SSN* July 1959, p. 8]

### Private High-School Commencement, June 1959

THE Little Rock Private School Corp. announced that it would charge tuition of $15 a month at T. J. Raney High School next year. It did not charge any tuition this year.

Raney High with 827 students is the largest of the private schools formed last fall after Gov. Faubus closed the four public high schools at Little Rock. It operated on donations, solicited with the help of Faubus, and about $78,000 in state aid.

With Faubus as commencement speaker, it graduated 190 seniors at the end of June. The governor said they had played a historic role in the history of education and that the name of their school might become as significant to Americans as those of Valley Forge, Gettysburg and Omaha Beach. . . . [*SSN* July 1959, p. 8]

### Negroes' Policy in School-Board Recall Election

A NEGRO organization, Save The Education Program (STEP), formed during the Little Rock School Board recall election, decided to continue as a permanent organization. . . .

The [*Arkansas State*] *Press* also undertook to explain to Gov. Faubus why Little Rock Negroes voted with STOP in the school board recall election, even though STOP made a point of avoiding the integration issue. It was because STOP wanted to preserve the public schools and keep them open, the *Press* said to the governor, whereas "Under your program, the Negro has no chance—not even in the courts." . . . [*SSN* July 1959, p. 8]

## Moves to Reopen Schools, July 1959

THE Little Rock school board, completely reconstituted in the last seven months, moved ahead in July with its plan to reopen the high schools under a three-year-old federal court order. It intends to use for the first time a state pupil assignment law.

In preparation the board sent its president, Everett Tucker Jr., Supt. Terrell E. Powell, and attorney Herschel H. Friday Jr., to Charlotte, N. C., and Norfolk, Va., to see how their desegregation was done under pupil assignments. On their return the board ordered that high school students register a month earlier than normal, on July 21-24, so as to leave time for the board to make assignments.

The board also made a change in the high school attendance areas by taking a 156-block area from Central High and adding it to Hall High. There are about 26 Negro high school students in this area. The board gave no explanation; but one of the main criticisms of the Little Rock desegregation plan has been that it meant desegregation for Central High, which serves most of the middle class families, but not for Hall High, which serves well-to-do Pulaski Heights.

Registration went off without a hitch, to the expressed satisfaction of the school board and the authorities. Enrollment in the city's four high schools is as follows, with comparisons for the previous year:

|         | 1958 | | 1959 | |
|---------|------|------|------|------|
|         | W | N | W | N |
| Central | 2063 | 8 | 803 | 49 |
| Hall | 731 | 0 | 679 | 5 |
| Tech | 179 | 0 | 108 | 1 |
| Mann | 0 | 717 | 0 | 591 |
|         | 2973 | 725 | 1590 | 646 |

The Negro applicant at Tech High was the first at that white high school. One Negro had applied to Hall High last year but was not accepted.

Compared to registration a year ago this left 1,462 students not accounted for. But T. J. Raney High, a private school for whites, now exists, and it has registered 1,208. That leaves 254 students, mostly white, not accounted for. However both the public schools and Raney expect further registrations during August.

At the same meeting at which the school board took its first steps toward reopening the high schools, it addressed a statement to Gov. Orval Faubus inviting him to come forward if he knows how the schools can be legally operated with segregation. It stated that each member of the board personally prefers segregation but "if no choice is offered, we will not abandon free public education in order to avoid desegregation."

This statement by the board apparently was in response to a press conference comment by the governor five days before. He had said, "I think there is something the Legislature can do to delay any integration," but would say no more.

The board plans to use *Act 461* of 1959, the second Arkansas pupil placement law. *Act 461* was adopted by a legislature dominated by Faubus and the law was signed by the governor, a fact the school board has called to his attention.

Attorneys here have these views on the placement law: If the desegregation decisions allow white students the preference of attending white schools and Negro students the preference of attending Negro schools, then the law provides for procedural and judicial appeal by students who prefer other schools. On this basis the law permits "voluntary segregation" but not discrimination.

Practically, the law does not lend itself to use in class lawsuits as all Arkansas desegregation suits are now (in which one or a few plaintiffs sue for all persons situated as they are). Instead each student who thought himself aggrieved under it would have to sue for himself alone. In addition it establishes a number of administrative steps that must be completed before a lawsuit can be filed.

These attorneys do not consider the law a part of a scheme by the state to avoid giving Negro students their constitutional rights as granted by the Supreme Court. The NAACP holds the opposite view on this point and is attacking the placement law in the Dollarway School District suit.

The Little Rock school board got its sixth and final member early in July when both the board and the Pulaski County Board of Education agreed on the same apointment to avoid any legal question as to which board was entitled to make the appointment. They agreed on William C. McDonald, 44, manager of a newspaper supply house. He immediately joined the other five members in taking a stand for free public education and keeping the schools open "in spite of our feelings about integration and segregation." . . .

Gov. Faubus produced his own plans for the integration of Little Rock schools late in July, responding to a challenge from the school board to speak out if he knew how segregation could be maintained legally. His plan is for voluntary integration in two high schools and voluntary segregation in two others, with the same system to be applied later to the junior high and elementary grades. It also calls for segregation by [sex], with boys going to one integrated high school and girls to the other. These two schools would be Horace Mann, now the all-Negro school, and Hall, in the upper-class Pulaski Heights section of town. Central and Tech would remain segregated and co-educational.

The school board announced it was taking Faubus' plan under advisement while waiting for its lawyers to say whether the use of it would subject the board to contempt of federal court. The board is still under court order to desegregate, a fact that Faubus omitted from his plan.

Organized segregationists were nearly silent. The Capital Citizens Council, whose position is and has been that Little Rock will never stand for any integration, declined to comment until further study of the 2,200-word letter in which Faubus outlined his plan. Mrs. Margaret C. Jackson, president of the Central High Mothers League, said she didn't like it very well but that she would take it to keep Central from being desegregated.

The governor made it clear his basic position had not changed. That is opposition to what he calls "forcible integration." Three weeks before he had said again that he did not believe Little Rock was ready for desegregation and that if Little Rock schools were desegregated this year, it would be done with federal force using "live ammunition." There would be "bomb scares, trouble at the schools, incidents of various kinds and even friction outside the schools," he predicted early in July.

"We are no nearer to being integrated now than we were in 1957," he said.

Faubus hasn't given up on two of his laws, *Acts 4* and *5* of 1958, the ones he used to close the schools. A federal court overruled them June 18, and Faubus said in July that he would appeal to the Supreme Court. . . . [*SSN* August 1959, p. 6]

## Public Support for Public Schools, July 1959

A CAMPAIGN to support the idea that the public school system must be maintained and peacefully operated, whether with integration or not, was under way at Little Rock in July.

Items: (1) More than 100 persons including prominent civic leaders met at a downtown hotel and organized the "Committee for the Peaceful Operation of Free Public Schools." (2) More than 70 persons attended a meeting called by labor union leaders and, over some protest, organized the "Committee With Members of Organized Labor to Maintain Our Free Public Schools." (3) The City Manager Board revised its policy toward possible violence at the schools and made it slightly more direct and affirmative.

They joined the ranks of the Women's Emergency Committee to Open Our Schools, formed in September 1958; the Little Rock Chamber of Commerce, which adopted a reopen-the-schools policy in March this year; and the *Arkansas Gazette,* in support of the school board. . . .

Amis Guthridge, attorney for the Capital Citizens Council, was quoted by the Associated Press as saying Little Rock would never accept integration in any form. Guthridge promised the Citizens Council would take "action," legally but not in the courts, to prevent integration. He refused to explain.

Since September 1958 the City Manager Board's policy has been that it would protect life and property but that any enforcement of integration court orders was up to the federal government. It revised this slightly on July 17 as follows: "The Little Rock school board has announced the opening of schools this fall. The board of directors of the city of Little Rock, knowing that this is a law-abiding community and conscious of their responsibilities to the citizens of Little Rock, has instructed the Police Department to deal firmly and quickly in the protection of life and property should the need arise."

Police Chief Eugene G. Smith, who was in charge of the local police when they fought the mob at Central High in 1957, took those words "firmly and quickly" at face value. Four days later came the first day of registration at the high schools; no spectators showed up but there were plenty of reporters and photographers on hand. All during the four-day registration Smith and police patrol cars kept a constant eye on the proceedings.

By coincidence, the City Manager Board issued its policy statement on the same day that the Committee for Peaceful Operation of Free Public Schools was formed. Forrest Rozzell, executive secretary of the Arkansas Education Association, read a brief statement at the meeting to tell what it was for. He said its purpose was to start a movement through which the issues facing Little Rock could be resolved.

What kind of movement is needed? Rozzell asked, and answered himself, "We need a systematically planned and aggressively executed movement for the peaceful operation of our public schools which contemplates the active involvement of every interested citizen." . . .

Earlier in the month the labor union group had met without as much success. About 70 persons attended and about 20 of them opposed the formation of the committee. They were able to agree, after some haggling, on the following resolution adopted without dissent:

"We are united in these beliefs: The children of all people must be given the same educational opportunities. Weakening or destroying tax-supported public schools in favor of private tuition-supported schools would limit educational opportunities for the children of all people. Our public school system must be maintained and improved at all levels. We as individuals should support these beliefs with community action."

Odell Smith of Little Rock, president of Teamster Local 878 and former president of the state AFL-CIO council, presided.

Just before that, the *Union Labor Bulletin,* official publication of the state AFL-CIO organization, had published a questionnaire on schools and invited its readers to mail them in. On the key question, "Do you think public schools should be abandoned and a private segregated system established?" the final vote was 93 no and 90 yes. Replies postmarked at Little Rock were 71 to 42 against abandoning public schools.

As soon as Gov. Faubus and Amis Guthridge had spoken out about Little Rock not accepting integration peacefully, the Women's Emergency Committee stepped forward. Mrs. Joe R. Brewer, chairman, issued a statement saying, "We have utmost confidence that Little Rock is a law-abiding city and that adequate protection for the peaceful opening of our schools will be provided." [SSN August 1959, p. 6]

## Continued Operation of One Private High School, July 1959

ALL BUT one of the private high schools set up last fall when the public schools were closed have now shut up shop. The exception is T. J. Raney High School, created and supported with the aid of Gov. Faubus. It is adding 28 new classrooms and laboratories to its present building in preparation for permanent status. W. C. Middleton, principal, said the registration at Raney for 1959-60 had reached 1,200 pupils by July 24. . . . [SSN August 1959, p. 6]

## Effect of School Crisis on Industrial-Development Program

THE Associated Press started an article with the question, "What killed Little Rock's ambitious industrial development program?", then gave the answers it got from the Little Rock Chamber of Commerce, Gov. Faubus and the Arkansas Industrial Development Commission, a state agency.

The school crisis and the closed schools was the chamber's answer.

"Not necessarily so," said Faubus. "I sympathize with Little Rock's industrial problems, but I would have to disagree with those who want to place the blame on the school situation. All areas have periods when they have no industrial expansion. Little Rock's decline might have occurred even if there had been no integration crisis."

"Let the figures speak for themselves," said the AIDC.

The AP article continued: "The figures show that 10 industries, five of them considered major ones, located in the Little Rock Industrial District in the two years prior to September 1957. Not one single commitment has been signed since the day Faubus ordered the National Guard troops to block the entry of nine Negroes to Central High, touching off Little Rock's integration dispute." [*SSN* August 1959, pp. 6, 12]

## Ku Klux Klan Recruiting

A. C. HIGHTOWER of Little Rock, grand dragon for Arkansas of the U. S. Klans, Knights of the Ku Klux Klan, said the KKK was conducting a statewide membership drive but he wouldn't say how it was doing. [*SSN*, August 1959, p. 12]

## Bombing of Home of NAACP Leader, July 7, 1959

ANOTHER bomb was exploded the night of July 7 at the Little Rock home of L. C. Bates whose wife is the state president of the NAACP. It was thrown from a car passing by, fell into the yard and blew a hole about 16 inches in diameter, doing no damage to the house. Police said it was home-made, a can stuffed with black powder and shredded newspaper.

Bates said this kind of thing had been going on since the early 1940s when he and his wife established a newspaper, the *Arkansas State Press,* and had become intensified since the Little Rock desegregation suit was filed in 1956.

Since Oct. 11, 1956, Bates said, the score is: Three crosses burned in the yard, five bombs thrown at the house, a burning flare thrown on the roof and 13 bricks, rocks and other objects thrown through the picture window in the living room, a few yards from the street. The Bateses first taped the picture window together; in the fall of 1957 they put up a heavy metal lattice to protect it. Both tape and lattice are still there. [*SSN* August 1959, p. 12]

## NAACP Challenge to Use of Pupil-Placement Law, August 8, 1959*

A NEGRO attorney yesterday asked the federal District Court to deny the Little Rock School Board the right to limit high school integration through use of the pupil placement laws.

Wiley A. Branton of Pine Bluff asked that the right of Negro students to attend Central, Hall and Technical High Schools be limited only by the areas in which they lived. Court approval of his request would open the way for greatly increased integration of the high schools.

Federal Judge John E. Miller said at Fort Smith that Branton had raised a legal question which hadn't been before the Court previously in the Little Rock desegregation case.

Attorneys for the Little Rock School Board had no comment.

The Negro lawyer argued in papers filed at the Federal Building that the School Board could not use the placement laws to frustrate federal court orders and the "Blossom Plan" of gradual desegregation. He charged that the Board had used the pupil placement laws to do this.

Should the Court grant Branton's request, the School Board apparently would be forced to admit all Negro students who want to attend Central, Hall or Tech and can qualify for attendance under the Board's school zone regulations. These regulations set up attendance areas for Central, Hall and the all-Negro Horace Mann High School. They provide that any student in the District can ask admission to Tech.

Branton's new action on the legal front came just four days before the Little Rock high schools are scheduled to open with token integration.

Using the state's pupil assignment laws, the School Board trimmed the 55 Negro students who asked entrance to Hall, Central and Tech to six. Three of these were assigned to Hall and three to Central.

Nine Negroes attended Central High School in 1957-58. Central is the only Little Rock public school which so far has been integrated.

Everett Tucker Jr., president of the School Board, was surprised by the court action.

He said the Board had been advised by its attorneys that the course now being followed "is proper under the existing situation." He also said

* *Arkansas Gazette,* "Negroes Challenge School Board Use of Placement Laws," August 9, 1959, p. 1. For model documentation see p. 35.

it seemed to him that the Negroes, "who were the principal victims of the school closings, should be gratified that the School Board is making it possible for Negro children to resume their interrupted education.

"However," he added, "they elect to attack us in court."

Asked whether the Board would fight the motion, Tucker replied, "I don't guess we have any choice."

In the papers filed yesterday, Branton did not attack the pupil placement laws as such. He argued instead that they couldn't be used to alter the original Little Rock integration plan and the Court orders which have directed that the plan be put into effect. . . .

## Reopening of the Public Schools, August 1959

AFTER getting its high school students registered in July, to leave time for the use of pupil assignment laws, the Little Rock School Board pulled its biggest surprise Aug. 4 by deciding to reopen the high schools Aug. 12, nearly a month early. It said the earlier date, providing 19 extra class days, was needed for "orientation" because the schools had been closed for a year. It seemed clear that the early date was a maneuver to foil any plans Gov. Faubus might have had for a special legislative session such as he called the last week of August 1958. Board Secretary Ted Lamb later confirmed this motive on a national television show where he seized the opportunity to label the governor a "demagogue."

This was only three days after the Board had made its pupil assignments—three Negroes each to Central and Hall, once all-white schools. Central got Jefferson Thomas, Carlotta Walls and Elizabeth Eckford, who had attended Central in 1957-58, and Hall got Effie Jones, Elsie Robinson and Estella Thompson. The Board had received 60 requests from Negro students for admission to white schools. Of the 54 denied admission, 19 filed protests with the Board and 18 of them decided to stay out of school until they were admitted to Central or Hall. Among the 54 are two who had already spent a year at Central—Thelma Mothershed and Melba Pattillo; the other four of the Little Rock nine of 1957-58 have either finished high school or moved away. In addition one of the three assigned this year, Elizabeth Eckford, found that she had enough credits for graduation and actually went to Central only one day this year. Another of the Central three, Carlotta Walls, was in summer school in Chicago and not present for the early school reopening.

Faubus objected to the board's action because, "As long as integration is compulsory, I'm against it." He also doubted that token integration could be maintained. "Six this year, 60 next year and 600 the next—it could go something like that," he said.

Amis Guthridge, attorney for the Capital Citizens Council, issued a long statement mentioning "communists," "war," "cowardly yellow quitters" and ending with "Our answer to the leaders of this diabolical race-mixing plot is NEVER."

Mrs. L. C. Bates, state NAACP president, was disappointed at the small number of Negro students assigned to Central and Hall and expressed doubt that the school board was acting in good faith. Three of the Negro students filed in federal court, for themselves and others, to have their assignments to the Negro school revoked.

Mrs. Joe R. Brewer, chairman of the Women's Emergency Committee to Open Our Schools, said, "We approve of every definite move" toward getting the schools reopened and operating peacefully. "All the world is watching us," she said.

The Little Rock School Board rejected Gov. Faubus' own plan for integration. It released an opinion by its attorney which said the governor's plan was certain to fail in the courts simply because it would require the voluntary co-operation of the NAACP which he said had never been forthcoming at Little Rock. The governor's plan was for two integrated and two segregated high schools, on a voluntary basis, with the integrated schools to have segregation by sex.

The school board ordered Hall, in well-to-do Pulaski Heights, and Horace Mann High Schools reopened at 9:30 a.m. Aug. 12, leaving Central and Tech to reopen at 1 p.m. At Hall, nothing happened. Three Negro students entered and left through a heavy police guard and before a crowd of newsmen and a few spectators. The only difficulty was at Central and only on the first day when 200 segregationists marched toward the school after a protest rally on the state capitol steps. [See "Segregationist Demonstration," p. 165.] Little Rock police broke up the march a block from Central and 20 minutes later Jefferson Thomas and Elizabeth Eckford walked into the school. Thereafter Thomas attended alone and no further trouble was reported either inside or outside the school. . . .

A Little Rock attorney, John A. McLeod Jr, whose daughter attends Hall High, invoked *Act* 7 of 1958 with a request that his daughter not be assigned to any class in which there is a Negro student. The school board said it would abide by his request and by *Act* 7. Wide publicity followed this and later nine other white students made similar requests. The law says that no student is required to attend a class with a student of another race. . . . [*SSN* September 1959, pp. 1-2]

*Public Expressions of Governor Faubus and Senator Fulbright,
August 1959*

As THE reopening date of the Little Rock high school approached nearly
all attention turned toward Gov. Faubus. Two years ago he used the National Guard to bar Negro students for three weeks from Central High; a
year ago he simply closed all four high schools; what, this time? He never
would say. In the end, he made some speeches and, after the schools were
reopened, announced he had had both the National Guard and State Police
alerted to move in if the Little Rock police couldn't control the crowds.

On the night before the school opening, with barely an hour's notice,
he went on television. His 15-minute speech was mostly a review of the
crisis in which he criticized the "integrationists" and "federal puppets,"
from the Supreme Court down through the Little Rock Police Department.

At the end he introduced two new elements, both addressed to segregationists: (1) "The battle to retain control of your own schools was
largely lost in last December's school election and in the recall election of
this spring. The battle to retain control must be fought in this arena also."
(2) Since the local police were going to be at the schools with "armed
might," he concluded, "I see nothing to be gained tomorrow by disorder
and violence."

Next morning, three hours before Central High was to reopen, segregationists rallied on the capitol steps and the governor came to talk to
them. "We are fighting for democracy," he said. "We must not violate
the struggle as free, honest and law-abiding people." He suggested the
way to do this was "the wise use of your vote." He went on, "I see no
reason for you to be beaten over the head today by the forces in the field,
or to be jailed. That should be faced only as a last resort, and when there is
much to be gained. Honestly, I do not think that should be faced today."

That night, after the Little Rock police had broken up segregationist
demonstrators at Central High, Faubus spoke again, at a chicken fry near
Dardenelle in the Arkansas River Valley northwest of Little Rock. He was
caustic and scornful of the "integrationists, puppets, hypocrites" and especially of Little Rock Police Chief Eugene G. Smith and School Board
President Everett Tucker Jr. He compared Smith to Janos Kadar, Hun-
garian puppet of the Russians. As to Tucker, the governor said he used to
credit him with having "some of the marks of a gentleman" but would
never do that again. Several hundred persons cheered the governor. . . .

Sen. J. William Fulbright (D-Ark.) said on a national television show he thought "there's no doubt" that Gov. Faubus had handled the Little Rock school crisis wrong. "There are very few people who don't think so that I am aware of in Little Rock," he said. This was the first open criticism of the governor by Fulbright—or any other member of the Arkansas congressional delegation—since the crisis began two years ago. In that time Fulbright has several times criticized the Supreme Court for its desegregation rulings and he did again on the same program where he said Faubus had handled the situation wrong.

"I think there is very bitter resentment about this matter but I think, as people must do in our system, they are trying to adapt themselves to this decision and they are proceeding to do it, I think, in a dignified and intelligent way," he said. . . . [*SSN* September 1959, p. 2]

## Segregationist Demonstration, August 1959

THE DAY before the school reopening, the Capital Citizens Council called for a "buyers strike" against the downtown merchants because they were supposed to be promoting school integration. There was no evidence that the strike had any effect. The Federal Reserve Bank later reported that department store sales at Little Rock rose by one per cent that week.

School opening preparations seemed not to daunt the segregationists. Police Chief Eugene G. Smith without saying exactly what his plans were announced ahead of time he would put up with no foolishness around the schools. The entire responsibility for preserving law and order was on his shoulders this time with orders from the City Manager Board to deal "firmly and quickly" to protect life and property. Eighteen lawyers on the Legal Committee of the Committee for the Peaceful Operation of Our Free Public Schools announced they were standing by [to] move for court injunctions if needed to curb agitators.

Despite all this and the governor's advice that they should turn to the ballot box, the segregationists went on with their plans for a giant rally at the state capitol at 10 a.m. on school opening day. About 1,000 persons were there, most of them from out of town, according to a state policeman. They carried American and Confederate flags and various signs. There were more women than men and more teenagers than adults.

It was a noisy crowd and responsive to the speakers. One of these was Timothy Canada, Negro employee at the capitol, who declared that Faubus was the best governor Arkansas had ever had and that Negroes should "stay in our place." White men came up to him and patted him on the back and shook his hand. Three Negro reporters on the edge of the crowd were ordered away by white men and left.

City police arrested three white men at a car containing nine sticks of dynamite but it was on the capitol grounds so they turned them over to the state police; the state police released the suspects and nothing more was heard of this incident. A sound truck played records of the "King Cotton March" by John Phillip Sousa and a parody of "Dixie." The crowd milled around in the hot sun and cheered and listened to speeches for 50 minutes before Gov. Faubus came out, received an ovation and delivered a seven-minute talk. The last speaker was Robert J. Norwood of Little Rock, president of the States' Rights Council, who urged the crowd to march through the streets to Central High School, 15 blocks away, and hold a "peaceful assembly" at the school.

About 200 took that suggestion. Through the streets they walked with the sound truck blaring while the crowd chanted "Two four six eight, We don't want to integrate" or sang along with the "Dixie" parody, "In Arkansas in the state of cotton, The federal courts are good and rotten, look away, look away, look away, Dixieland." They carried signs with such messages as "Race-mixing is Communism," "Save Our Constitution, Follow Faubus" and "Follow Faubus for Freedom." At the head of the crowd were five men carrying American flags and a sixth carrying an Arkansas flag. There was a bugler in the crowd playing Confederate songs.

It was nearly 12:30 p.m. when the marchers came in sight of the police line, placed by Chief Smith across Fourteenth Street at Schiller Avenue, one block east of Central High. As they approached members of the crowd cursed the police and called them Communists and cowards. The marchers came up to within arm's length of the police line. Chief Smith through a portable electric megaphone called out "Your behavior is a disgraceful matter . . . let's get out of the street."

After a tense moment or two, four men at the front of the crowd tried to push through the police line. The police grabbed them by the arms and hustled them off to a paddy wagon waiting behind the police line. At the same time the police line began moving forward in a kind of V-shape, point first, splitting the crowd and moving it back out of the street. They met some resistance and used their billy clubs on at least three men. One elderly woman in the crowd was pushed or fell down. The police called up a fire truck and firemen sprayed the stragglers out of the street.

That was the end of it. The police had arrested 21 members of the crowd, including one woman, two teenage girls, eight men and 10 teenage boys. One of the men was Robert J. Norwood, the States' Rights Council president. The charges included loitering, disturbing the peace, resisting arrest and assaulting an officer. A few days later the group of suspects appeared in Little Rock Municipal Court with their attorneys, Amis Guthridge, who is attorney for the Capital Citizens Council, and Robert W. Laster, city traffic judge and a strong segregationist who was voted off the school board in the recall election in May.

Municipal Judge Quinn Glover passed their cases until September but first he gave them a stern lecture about behaving themselves and warned them specifically about getting into any more trouble before he disposes of the current charges. Judge Glover is a high-ranking officer in the Shrine, which has a regional "Shrinerama" scheduled at Little Rock for mid-September, and he told the defendants that their conduct was causing much concern among Shriners about whether they should come to Little Rock. . . .

Mrs. Margaret C. Jackson, president of the Mothers League of Central High, sent a telegram to Mayor Werner C. Knoop demanding a public meeting with the City Manager Board and Chief Smith. "We want to ask who gave Smith the right to use such brutal force against such unarmed people who were peaceably assembled in protest of the integration of Central High. . . ." [*SSN* September 1959, p. 2]

## *Postscript by the Editors*

THOUGH the relatively undramatic opening of Little Rock schools in August 1959 is a good point at which to end our documentary presentation, the Little Rock story goes on and on. During the school year of 1959-1960 occurred a number of events worth summarizing to help round out the story.

A series of bombings, beginning with a dynamiting of the School Board building on Labor Day, evoked the censure of community leaders. The Chamber of Commerce raised $25,000 as a reward for information, and several convictions were made. Though the NAACP and individual parents protested the acceptance of only eight out of 59 Negro applicants for Central and Hall Highs, the Federal District Court in October upheld the state pupil-placement laws of 1956 and 1959. An initiative by the people of Arkansas had produced the 1956 statute, a rather simple one; the 1959 act was more detailed, being a virtual replica of the Alabama law which, a Federal District Court had previously found, did not on its face contravene the Supreme Court's decisions of 1954 and 1955, since none of the sixteen criteria for assignment of individual pupils was race-based.

In November, the *Arkansas State Press,* published by L. C. Bates, husband of NAACP leader Daisy Bates, suspended operations because of failing advertising and circulation. A School Board member explained that two of the original nine Negroes at Central had been transferred back to Horace Mann because one was a cripple (Mann is a one-story school) and because the other, though not a trouble-maker herself, seemed to "attract trouble." The Board member called pupil-placement laws "the salvation of Little Rock schools" but warned that some integration in junior high schools and in the lower grades was inevitable. The Arkansas NAACP pledged itself to help any dissatisfied Negro parents to appeal placement decisions.

In December, a School Board survey revealed that more than a fourth of the Little Rock boys and girls who should have been in the local high schools were not there. A Negro Congressman from Michigan, after a week in Little Rock, declared that the eight colored students at Central and Hall were being mistreated. This charge was emphatically denied by school officials. A group of local ministers found things "almost normal" at Hall and much improved (over 1957) at Central. In January, the School Board announced that the rate of teacher retirement had climbed precipitately.

During February, the Board asked its attorneys to try to recover the $510,220 in state funds withheld from Little Rock schools in 1958-59 under Acts 4 and 5, subsequently declared unconstitutional; only $187,768 of these funds had been paid out to Raney and other schools before an injunction halted the drafts. Spring brought a hearing, in Federal District Court, on the pleas of Negro students whose applications to Central and Hall had been rejected. Judge Miller declared that in future such complaints must be filed in individual litigations rather than under Aaron v. Cooper. The NAACP claimed that by using the 1959 pupil-placement law in the 1959-1960 school assignments, the School Board had departed from the original Court-approved plan, shifting "the burden of the initiative for ending segregation to the Negro pupils and their parents."

In April, Little Rock high schools regained accreditation by the North Central Association of Secondary Schools and Colleges. The graduating class of 415 at Central included Jefferson Thomas and Carlotta Walls, two of the "original nine." Hall graduated one Negro girl in a class of 215.

All ninth-graders, including 326 Negroes, were given a battery of tests in the spring; of the 35 Negroes who were judged capable of adjusting to predominantly white schools, eight were assigned to Central and Hall (five and three, respectively). No white students were assigned to Horace Mann. By June 13, the final day for protesting a school placement, 73 Negroes had asked for reassignment to desegregated schools. Thirty-nine of these were at the junior-high level, where, the Board had reaffirmed in March, there would be no integration in 1960.

Governor Faubus, running for an unprecedented fourth term, won an overwhelming victory in the July primary. Congressman Alford won renomination in a close race. When school opened for the fall term, there were 8 Negroes at Central, 5 Negroes at Hall, and no whites at Horace Mann.

The June-July issue of the NAACP *Crisis* told where the "original nine" were. Ernest Green had completed his sophomore year at Michigan State University. Elizabeth Eckford (who appears on our cover) and Thelma Mothershed, who took enough correspondence courses from the University of Arkansas during 1958-59 to receive certificates of graduation from Central in the fall of 1959, were enrolled respectively at Knox College (Galesburg, Illinois) and Southern Illinois University (Carbondale). Minnijean Brown, who was expelled from Central, went on to Lincoln High in New York City and had just completed her second year at Mount Sinai College of Nursing. Melba Patillo, after finishing high school at Santa Rosa, California, was enrolled at San Francisco State College. As was indicated previously, two had just graduated from Central and the remaining two had just completed a year at Horace Mann after being transferred back there.

# The Meanings of Little Rock:
# A Spectrum of Opinion

## *Letters to the Editor of the* Arkansas Gazette*

. . . GRADUATION from a mixed school will guarantee no one a job, and the progress of the Negro to acceptability by the whites depends upon factors not taught in the class room, i.e., their own personal behavior.

Prejudice that affects us all is not confined to the Negro, but is common amongst the whites—even wealthy whites. Not long ago Tommy Manville, of the asbestos millions, was told by the residents of Westchester to move out of their community—his notoriety could no longer be tolerated.

A Negro or a white student can only progress through understanding and respectable behavior in both private and public life. Only in this way can he be absorbed into society as a whole.

Laws and edicts from Washington forcing children together is not the answer at all and will have no meaning in the matter of earning a living, unless, of course, the government transforms itself into a dictatorship to enforce its edicts upon society beyond the schoolroom and sets up a police state in a totalitarian fashion. That could happen here, and still would not answer the questions or solve the problems.

VICTOR CAMPBELL
*Cave City, Arkansas*                                        August 19, 1957

### DOCUMENTATION SUITABLE FOR RESEARCH PAPERS

BIBLIOGRAPHY ENTRY

Campbell, Victor. Letter to the editor, *Arkansas Gazette,* August 19, 1957. Reprinted in *LRUSA.*

FIRST FOOTNOTE

*Victor Campbell, letter to the editor, *Arkansas Gazette,* reprinted in *LRUSA,* p. 172.

SUBSEQUENT FOOTNOTES

*Campbell, letter, *LRUSA,* p. ■.

---

* Printed by the *Gazette* as submitted, without revision for errors of fact, spelling, or the like; here reprinted as they appeared in the *Gazette,* with the senders' localities and the dates of publication supplied. Letters were selected by the Records to present the widest possible range of opinion, without respect to the relative numerical strength of the different views.

These examples are models for other letters to editors of newspapers and magazines in this collection.

‖‖‖‖‖‖‖‖‖‖‖‖‖‖‖‖‖‖‖‖‖‖‖‖‖‖‖‖‖‖‖‖‖‖‖‖‖‖‖‖‖‖‖‖‖‖‖‖‖‖‖‖‖‖‖‖‖‖‖‖‖‖‖‖‖‖‖‖‖‖‖‖‖‖‖‖‖‖‖‖‖‖‖‖‖‖‖‖‖‖

. . . IN THE "Uniform Crime Reports for the United States," issued by the FBI, Department of Justice, Vol. XXV, No. 2, Annual Report 1954, and published by the Government Printing Office are reported arrests in 1,389 cities with a total population of 38,643,183 during that year of 1954. Bear in mind that the 1950 census reported Negroes as 10 per cent of the total population:

63 per cent arrested for murder were Negroes;
63 per cent arrested for dope violations;
63 per cent arrested for aggravated assault;
62 per cent arrested for prostitution;
55 per cent arrested for possession of deadly weapons;
53 per cent arrested for robbery;
43 per cent arrested for all other assaults;
41 per cent arrested for liquor violations;
40 per cent arrested for rape.

Here are some more statistics, from *Mississippi.*

A total of 28,045 white babies and 28,679 Negro babies were born in 1953.

Of that total, 7,327 were born out of wedlock—7,070 Negroes, 257 whites.

T. JONES
*Little Rock*                                                  August 19, 1957


A GOOD illustration of some of the goofy attempts to think is demonstrated in the letter of "Reader" from Wilkes-Barre, Pa. Admitting that he is not a resident of the South he then goes on to explain in detail how the South should conduct its affairs and solve her problems.

"Reader" can love the Negro as much as he claims, but why should he try and enforce his decadent theories on a people, who have forgotten more about the Negro problem than all the peanut brains in the North will ever know!

In the same issue that the letter of "Reader" appeared, there was also printed a news item from Levittown, Pa., which stated that the authorities there had threatened to "load up the white residents in buses and arrest them if they protested against the moving in of a Negro family.

. . . Since the exodus of the Negro from the South to the North in the last 10 years or more, the South has advanced more than in the last 300 years. And the North has deteriorated at the same rate.

The Negro has never been an asset to any intelligent community, nor can any intelligent being conceive of any opinion that will fill that thousands of years civilization gap that separates the Caucasian and Negro races.

The North can have 'em, we don't want 'em, and they love 'em up in Pennsy anyway.

JOHN S. THOMPSON
*Malvern, Arkansas*　　　　　　　　　　　　　　　　　August 24, 1957


THE MAN who signed himself as "Golden Ruler" in your letters column August 23 certainly lives up to his name. His letter was an answer to T. Jones' "statistics" on Negro Crime, and showed racial discrimination in employment as one of the contributing factors. This type of discrimination operates in the South to a degree that makes life virtually a dead-end street for any ambitious and intelligent Negro. It also exists in the North, but he can fight it because racial prejudice in the North is not backed up by politics and public opinion. It is a tough fight and a disillusioning one. A superman can win it.

There are two other factors which may play an important part in this conditioning for crime. One is the double standard of morality which has been traditional in the South. I refer to the different types of justice for Negro crimes against Negroes and Negro crimes against whites. Another, and possibly the most important of all, is the day-by-day assault on dignity, nerves and emotions almost any American Negro must undergo—North and South.

Many white people who would not "harm a fly" think nothing of cruelly bruising the emotions of a Negro. The community of Levittown, Pa., is a good example of this. The Negro who moved into this community is apparently well-educated and well-mannered (more so than some of the whites there), yet they have branded him as untouchable. Such incidents make news in the North (and they should), but equally and more painful insults are delivered daily on a smaller scale and little noted (except by the Negroes involved).

Negro crime statistics do not amaze me. What amazes me is that most

Negroes are decent peace-loving citizens. The way is clear for us to increase the size of this group. Or we can increase the criminal group— by continuing to deny Negro citizens the rights the rest of us take for granted.

MARGARET HUNCKE
*Mountainburg, Arkansas*                                    August 27, 1957

THE PEOPLE of Little Rock and North Little Rock, Arkansas, in one week of thoughtless action against a minority group, have destroyed the faith that our diplomats have been working so hard to build up in the orient and Middle East. How can the people of these countries have faith in our government when we so openly show hate for anyone outside the white race?

We are living in a world that can come to an end in less than one hour. The people of this community could conceivably be saved from destruction by colored officers flying our latest inter-continental bombers. While you of Little Rock are showing your hate for the children of a minority group, the same group is ready to lay down their lives for you!

WHITE AIR FORCE CAPTAIN
*Little Rock Air Force Base*                                September 14, 1958

THE "conscience of the South" expressed in a crescendo of power purpose and dedicated resolve by the voters of Arkansas has condemned the Left-wing "termites" of this nation, who would overthrow the Constitution of the United States and/or twist its hallowed meaning into "laws" to suit their own devious purpose, destroy these free and independent states, advocate federal dictatorship, Gestapo force, and the unholy philosophy of racial "melting-pot-ism" (such "melting" of the Negro and Caucasian races an affront to human and divine Nature itself), with all the human bondage and moral deterioration these evils would bring upon us.

As one in whom this "conscience" dwells pure and absolute, wholly free of fear, fanaticism or any shadow of a "guilt complex" (an affliction of the "liberals" and "moderates" I shall avoid like the plague) to mar the clarity of my thinking and correct sense of Divine Justice, Love, Law, Truth and Unity and the demonstration of these attributes toward, and within, all races, creeds, colors and nations, I can say unhesitatingly that the South neither now nor in generations to come, will never write an "epitaph" to this good conscience which issues not from "hate" and "prejudice" (unless prejudice be the wise and good use of sound judgment and discrimination in discerning and preserving the higher values), but from deep moral and spiritual convictions, tempered with justice for all and malice toward none.

This stand will not win us the Pulitzer Prize in this age of confused values with its accompanying "confusion of tongues"—but it will win us brillant and imperishable stars in the eternal Crown of Liberty.

MRS. MARION LEATH
*Eureka Springs, Arkansas*                                   August 15, 1958

. . . THREE years ago I graduated from Henderson State Teachers College with high hopes and ambitions of going to Texas or California to teach school. However, during our last session of the education bloc, something happened to make me change my mind. One of the instructors reminded us that we were, first of all, Arkansans. She readily admitted that we could go to almost any other state and make higher salaries, and perhaps the classrooms would have better equipment and be less crowded, but she also pointed out the fact that someone is going to have to stay at home and help to continue the fight for better schools.

This fight has been going on for years and will continue as long as there are people in the state who want their children to have the same opportunities, the same educational prestige as children of other states. She presented us with a challenge, stating that it wouldn't be easy, that at times we would feel as if we were beating our heads against a stone wall. She was right about that, but she was also right about something else.

She told us that we could feel the pride that comes from facing a challenge and doing your best, not just for yourself, but for the future generations.

I am glad I stayed in Arkansas. I am glad that we have teachers who can instill the will to fight for and work for a worthy cause. I am not proud of the fact that our people find it so important to carry the torch of political differences with them until it blinds them to the real problems of the day.

Maybe we didn't all want to re-elect Faubus. Maybe a lot of us thought that he wasn't the man for the job. The fact remains that he WAS elected by a great majority of the people of the state of Arkansas, and it is up to the entire population of the state to work together in this "Land of Opportunity."

Things never get so bad that they couldn't be worse. Why can't we shed the disappointments and hurts of the last election and go to work for some of the things we believe in.

Personally, I carry a lot of racial prejudices that most people of the South have built up over the years. I wouldn't be just tickled pink to have Negroes in my classroom, but if they were there I would try to uphold my duties and obligations as an American citizen and teach them, along with the white students, to the best of my ability.

Let's not forget nor ignore the law of the land, the Constitution of the United States. Can't we remember, too, that whatever the color of the skin, the children in the classroom today are the hope of America. Let's give them a fair chance!

TEACHER
*Fayetteville, Arkansas*                                         August 17, 1958


IT HAS happened again. Two years ago Jim Johnson ran for governor on a strong segregation ticket and was soundly thrashed by Governor Faubus, and again last month Amis Guthridge, Lee Ward and Chris Finkbeiner also ran on a segregation ticket and they were also buried in the landslide.

Governor Faubus' opposition tried to force him to state publicly his stand on the segregation issue but a man with a public record does not have to state his stand on public issues; in that case action speaks louder than words.

He has done more for the Negroes in Arkansas than all the other governors combined. He has put several Negroes on the state Democratic Committee, he has given them state jobs, aided them with free food by the thousands and given welfare aid, with increases to other thousands.

In addition to this, buses and schools have been integrated in Arkansas, all of these good things he has done for Negroes and peacefully, too, with the exception of Central High School. And it, too, would have been integrated without trouble if it had not been for those rabble-rousers. I don't blame the governor for calling out the soldiers: he had to do something to protect the little children from that mob.

In the future I fully believe that Governor Faubus will continue to give equal rights to all, regardless of what color their skin may be. I am glad that Amis Guthridge was defeated, and maybe now he will quit sticking his nose in Governor Faubus' business. Congressman Hays and Governor Faubus will make a great team if left alone by those rabble-rousers.

TRUE AMERICAN
*Paragould, Arksansas*　　　　　　　　　　　　　　August 17, 1958


THIS IS a copy of a letter to Mr. Virgil Blossom, superintendent of Little Rock Public Schools.

"Dear Mr. Blossom:

"The Council of the Little Rock Parent-Teacher Associations feels the necessity for expressing its appreciation to you and to the members of your Board for your firm leadership in the tumultuous school session of 1957-1958.

"It was only through your complete faithfulness to civic responsibility that you were able to maintain such firm leadership so imperatively demanded by this situation."

MRS. LEON S. HOFFMAN
President, Little Rock Council
Parent-Teacher Association
*Little Rock*　　　　　　　　　　　　　　　　　　August 22, 1958


TIMOTHY PECKWORTHY sat in his feed store and gave one more irritated look at the opinion of the Circuit Court of Appeals.

"The fat's in the fire," he said. "There'll be the devil to pay when school opens in September."

"Why?" I asked.

"Because parents of the white kids won't stand for it," he replied. "There'll be the same hooting and hollering we had last year."

"I wouldn't get upset about it," I told him. "As a matter of fact, it's very wholesome for parents to take such an interest in the schools. Of course, right now they're preoccupied with the color scheme that will be produced when seven black students are scattered amongst about 2,000 white ones. But this lively concern about interior decorating might lead the parents into other and more important interests. They might begin to wonder what the teachers are teaching and whether the students are learning."

"You don't understand," Timothy declared, "the crisis will soon be upon us. Something will have to be done."

"We could make the black students put flour on their faces," I suggested, "or maybe the white ones could be persuaded to black up."

"This is no time to crack jokes, or whatever you're doing," Timothy warned. "We are going to be in serious trouble unless somebody comes up with the right answer."

"Of course it's serious," I agreed. "We've got some characters in this state who like to stir up the people on this subject, and we've got more than enough people willing to be stirred up. It's going to take quite a bit of time to rig up a legal and effective scheme to violate the Supreme Court's decisions. Even if the legislature should meet tomorrow and aim all its brains squarely at the problem, there wouldn't be time to solve it before September. What we need is a temporary, makeshift solution that will cool off the hotheads, and I think I've found it.

"Those of us who don't like violence and who recoil with horror at the sight of innocent, blustering, inoffensive, loud-mouthed Arkansas citizens being pinked by federal bayonets should get together and appeal to our governor. 'Dear Governor,' we should say. 'We know the primaries are over and that your interests in local districts will subside for awhile, but we need your help. Please go out to Central High—go yourself this time; don't send a pack of nervous youngsters in uniforms—and look at all the students. Pay especial attention to the seven who are said to be Negroes. Then announce to the people of this state, by radio, television, newspaper interviews, carrier pigeons, and other appropriate ways, that all these students at Central High are white. This will allay excitement and will stave off the crisis that Timothy Peckworthy keeps yapping about.' "

"That's silly," Timothy said. "It'll never work."

"It'll work like a charm," I insisted. "For nearly a year, the governor has been saying that black is white, and a quarter of a million of his fellow citizens believed him."

HARDSCRABBLE
*Conway, Arkansas*                                                  August 22, 1958

. . . [Now] in Arkansas a democratic tragedy has occurred, as Mr. Faubus and Mr. Johnson became the masters of practical politics and gave Southerners the old appeal: Defiance to the "Federals," confusion to the rich Yankee "outsiders," and shame to the local "Left-wingers."

The voters swallowed it all, felt that old feeling, and voted accordingly. Thus, with the real issues hidden, intelligence was scorned and democracy failed to work well.

Given the social fears and prejudices that spring from the advent of racial integration in the South, and knowledge of history, the result, no doubt how bad it may be, should not shock anyone into apathy; all that happened was definitely to be expected. The only fear that responsible citizens can have is that a greater tragedy will be the falling silent of men and women of leadership, true liberality, and intelligence. The old rationalization that everything will turn out all right is nonsense. It won't unless someone makes it.

Even the most embittered member of the minority owes Mr. Faubus and Mr. Johnson some degree of obedience during their terms of office; they will almost certainly be the duly elected officials of this community. But when these men fail themselves to obey higher constitutional authority, it is the duty of all men of intelligence to speak loudly and clearly. . . .

In closing my warmest congratulations to the *Arkansas Gazette* for stating that it will continue its devotion to due process of law. It's courage that counts.

And there is nothing that hurts like the truth.

JOHN A. THOMPSON
*Little Rock*                                                                  August 24, 1958


I AM heading for Siberian salt mines (via the Sovereignty Commission, "States Rights" route) by writing this letter and signing it with my honest-to-goodness name. But this madness that has befallen the state of Arkansas and its leadership astounds me.

For the last two years ('56-'58), I have served as the state president of the National League of American Penwomen. (My successor is Iris Moore Clark of Little Rock.) I have loved this state as no other, having been born in Madison County and educated (?) in Washington County. My roots are deep, and I have represented the writers of this state at National Conferences in Washington, D.C., on various occasions. (Also composers and artists.) When I received awards I have felt I was promoting the literary standards of the state and never failed to mention the fact at the Conferences.

But it was not true last year. Members of Panama, Alaska, and every state in the Union confronted me with the question of our madness. I was humiliated and heartbroken. . . .

Things that are happening in this state will come home to each of you in time. We, a writer friend and I, were discussing the calling of the special session of the legislature and how much it was to cost us, (fifth bill) over long distance and we were abruptly cut off. A minister of the gospel was bringing a devotional expressing the loss of our freedoms to the States Rights Amendment (?) and he was cut off the air without explanation. Before the last primary, the state highway trucks and the welfare agencies in sections of the state, carried stickers and sponsored candidates. I saw the trucks myself. This is no hearsay. . . .

Please, please, friends and fellow Arkansans read your Constitution. The great, great literary masterpiece. Then read your Bible; how God sent His Son to save the world. The World. Then pray for guidance. You will help your own children and maybe, somehow, even at this late date, save our state's dignity and honor.

I am going to enroll in the University at once and take a course in Arkansas government. I am going to attempt to learn why we pay more taxes than almost any other of the states in the Union. I am going to work for allowing 18-year-olds to vote. I believe, like the Hebrew nation that wandered in the wilderness until the doubters fell by the way side, that our young people can lead us out of this dilemma of prejudice and hate.

I would get out of the state, but who would pay the $250,000 to support the Commission, and who would pay the $1,000 assessment taxes I have to pay, and the salaries for the legislative session.

MARIE MORRIS RUSHING
*Fayetteville, Arkansas*                                        August 31, 1958

THIS IS a copy of a letter to President Eisenhower:

I notice by the press that you are trying to soften up a little on the Negro proposition. The only reason you will stay with your former plan is to show the people throughout the country how powerful and mighty you are: it could not be because you are right in any sense of the word.

If you and your crowd would let the Negroes alone, we would not have any trouble with them whatever, and you are bound to admit the white people have not had any trouble with the Negroes in the South for the last 100 years or more, and if you and your crowd would let the Negroes alone we would not have any trouble with them now.

I think your crowd realizes you overstepped your bounds in taking charge of our public schools in Arkansas and you would like to get out of that if you could without admitting you are in the wrong. I do not think you would admit you were wrong for any purpose in the world.

I think if you would play golf all the time and stay out of the White House until your time expires, the whole country would be better off. I sincerely hope that we will never have another military man for any high office in this country.

G. W. Botts
*De Witt, Arkansas*                                           September 3, 1958

I AM amazed at the parents who stand by and let their children (even encourage them) to strike and jeer at others, regardless of skin color.

The fact that these children are allowed to sneer and post ugly signs at innocent victims shows what little control these parents have over their children.

There is no doubt that these parents are encouraging their children in wrongdoing. In years to come, when these children are older, looking for excitement and publicity, these parents may look back and wish they had never encouraged their children to be demonstrators.

Incidents of this sort start out small and end up sometimes in mob violence—in later years, after getting a taste of being in the limelight (regardless of how), some of these children may end up behind bars.

Besides, these colored children, being innocent, it seems that to keep peace has no meaning to some people. All over the world people are begging for peace . They HAD looked to America to help find it, yet how can we help, when in a few of our states we resort to unpeaceful methods to settle a little question like the color of one's skin going to school with another color.

Mrs. B. J. Rupert
*Jacksonville, Arkansas*                                      September 9, 1958

I WANT to reaffirm my faith in the good people of Arkansas.

I believe this faith is justified by the experiences of our family with as fine a group of neighbors as any family ever had. My personal religious convictions differ in some respects from theirs. The religious group to which I belong includes Negro members. We are too few to own or rent a church building so we hold our study classes at our private homes. The study classes are open to any and all who have an interest in our work.

My home has served for these classes no more often than one Sunday afternoon each month. Just a few days ago our family learned that most of our neighbors do not consider this proper conduct. Because I like to teach and because I thought I was being of service to the community I have given one evening a week of my time to one of the local Negro colleges. I have been surprised to learn that this also is considered improper. Apparently this educational and religious association with a few Negro friends led to much speculation and rumor in our neighborhood for months before we became aware of it.

This state of affairs was a source of great embarassment to our closer neighbor friends. Nevertheless most of them tried to find excuses for us and defended us with the assertion that we had always been good neighbors to them. And they never once breathed a word of their discomfort to us.

When threats informed us of the situation, we apologized to those friends and most of them have said "of course we would never do anything like that ourselves and we do not approve of your doing it. Nevertheless it is your house and it is none of our business who you have in it." We deeply appreciate this attitude and believe that we should consider the feelings of our neighbors in deciding upon the things we shall or shall not do. Out of consideration for their feelings, we plan for the present to have no more of these meetings at our homes.

And to those few people who have threatened to kill our sons and burn our homes and other acts of physical violence we say, "we are very sorry that acts of ours may have been in part responsible for bringing this hatred into your hearts. Truly we would like to make amends and do something to help you replace it with love. We are not big enough to say we love you, as Jesus asked us to do when he said, 'love your enemies.' But we do know that God's great love enfolds you too, and that if He so wills it, His love can come to you through our hearts as well'."

ELDON DENNIS
*North Little Rock, Arkansas*                        September 30, 1958

## *A Carolina Humorist: A Quick Solution**

THOSE who love North Carolina will jump at the chance to share in the great responsibility confronting our Governor and the State Legislature. A special session of the Legislature (July 25-28, 1956) passed a series of

---

* "The Vertical Negro Plan," by Harry Golden, editor of *The Carolina Israelite,* in which this essay was first published; reprinted in Mr. Golden's book *Only in America* (New York and Cleveland, World Publishing Company, 1958; copyright), pp. 121-123, from which this selection is taken.

amendments to the State Constitution. These proposals submitted by the Governor and his Advisory Education Committee included the following:

(A) The elimination of the compulsory attendance law, "to prevent any child from being forced to attend a school with a child of another race."

(B) The establishment of "Education Expense Grants" for education in a private school, "in the case of a child assigned to a public school attended by a child of another race."

(C) A "uniform system of local option" whereby a majority of the folks in a school district may suspend or close a school if the situation becomes "intolerable."

But suppose a Negro child applies for this "Education Expense Grant" and says he wants to go to the private school too? There are fourteen Supreme Court decisions involving the use of public funds; there are only two "decisions" involving the elimination of racial discrimination in the public schools.

The Governor has said that critics of these proposals have not offered any constructive advice or alternatives. Permit me, therefore, to offer an idea for the consideration of the members of the regular sessions. A careful study of my plan, I believe, will show that it will save millions of dollars in tax funds and eliminate forever the danger to our public education system. Before I outline my plan, I would like to give you a little background.

One of the factors involved in our tremendous industrial growth and economic prosperity is the fact that the South, voluntarily, has all but eliminated VERTICAL SEGREGATION. The tremendous buying power of the twelve million Negroes in the South has been based wholly on the absence of racial segregation. The white and Negro stand at the same grocery and supermarket counters; deposit money at the same bank teller's window; pay phone and light bills to the same clerk; walk through the same dime and department stores, and stand at the same drugstore counters.

It is only when the Negro "sets" that the fur begins to fly.

Now, since we are not even thinking about restoring VERTICAL SEGREGATION, I think my plan would not only comply with the Supreme Court decisions, but would maintain "sitting-down" segregation. Now here is the GOLDEN VERTICAL NEGRO PLAN. Instead of all those complicated proposals, all the next session needs to do is pass one small amendment which would provide *only* desks in all the public schools of our state—*no seats*.

The desks should be those standing-up jobs, like the old-fashioned bookkeeping desk. Since no one in the South pays the slightest attention to a VERTICAL NEGRO, this will completely solve our problem. And it is not such a terrible inconvenience for young people to stand up during their classroom studies. In fact, this may be a blessing in disguise. They are not learning to read sitting down, anyway; maybe standing up will help. This will save more millions of dollars in the cost of our remedial English course when the kids enter college. In whatever direction you look with the GOLDEN VERTICAL NEGRO PLAN, you save millions of dollars, to say nothing of eliminating forever any danger to our public education system upon which rests the destiny, hopes and happiness of this society. . . .

### DOCUMENTATION SUITABLE FOR RESEARCH PAPERS

BIBLIOGRAPHY ENTRY

Golden, Harry. "The Vertical Negro Plan." Reprinted from his *Only in America.* In *LRUSA.*

FIRST FOOTNOTE

*Harry Golden, "The Vertical Negro Plan," reprinted from his *Only in America* in *LRUSA,* pp. 184-185.

SUBSEQUENT FOOTNOTES

*Golden, *op. cit., LRUSA,* p. ▧.
*Golden, "Vertical," *LRUSA,* p. ▧.
*Golden, *LRUSA,* p. ▧.

---

## A Carolina Reporter: Emergence of the NAACP*

. . . AT THE turn of this century Booker T. Washington was the most influential spokesman for the Negro people. He generally accepted things as they were, saying that the Negro must earn a place for himself in society through self-improvement. But that placid philosophy of gradual, firmly-footed change, while it was largely approved by Southern whites and Negroes, was challenged by a small but very articulate group of angry young colored men.

As a result of the Civil War and the Reconstruction era, the Negro was freed from slavery by the 13th amendment to the Constitution. The

* From an article on the NAACP by Chester Davis in the Winston-Salem *Journal and Sentinel,* February 26, 1956, distributed by the NAACP in a reprint from which this selection is taken.

14th amendment granted him full and equal citizenship. The 15th amendment gave him the right to vote.

In the years between 1870 and 1910 these rights were largely lost. They were lost because of the threats and force used by organizations like the Ku Klux Klan. They also were lost because of legal devices such as the "Grandfather clause." During this same period the Supreme Court, in the case of Plessy vs. Ferguson, laid the foundations for segregation based on law.

Those changes saddened Booker T. Washington. But he accepted them. He told his people that, if they were to regain their rights, they must earn them.

"Let us," he said, "spend less time talking about the part of the city that we cannot live in, and more time in making that part of the city that we live in beautiful and attractive."

This policy of self-improvement did not satisfy militant young Negro intellectuals like W. E. B. DuBois, then a teacher in a Negro school in Atlanta.

DuBois openly broke with Booker T. Washington in 1903. He challenged the older man's philosophy of compromise and self improvement, saying that the Negro must fight for certain fundamental civil rights before self improvement was really possible.

In 1905 DuBois called his followers, then a very small group, to a secret meeting at Niagara Falls. There he preached his doctrine of organization, and militant—although legal—agitation.

This group, now known as the Niagara movement, met again in 1906 at Storer College in Harpers Ferry, West Va. There, in the shadow of the tradition of abolitionist John Brown, DuBois stated his creed:

> "We should not be satisfied with less than our full manhood rights . . . We claim for ourselves every right that belongs to freeborn Americans—political, civil and social—and until we get these rights, we shall never cease to protest and to assail the ears of America with the story of its shameful deeds toward us."

But, despite its militancy, the Niagara movement accomplished little. Booker T. Washington's opposition cost it support—both white and Negro —and the movement's own leadership was inexperienced and fumbling.

In the summer of 1908, while the all-Negro Niagara movement floundered, a race riot occurred in Springfield, Ill., the home of Abraham Lincoln. William English Walling, a New York journalist, visited Springfield and wrote a heated story entitled "Race War in the North." This article was published in "The Independent," a crusading magazine in the Civil Rights field.

Walling's thesis, based largely on the Springfield riot, was that, unless the old abolitionist spirit "of Lincoln and Lovejoy" was revived, the war of the white on the Negro would be transferred from the South to the North.

Mary White Ovington, a New York journalist and social worker, read Walling's story. Early in 1909, Miss Ovington and Dr. Henry Moskowitz, a man keenly interested in the problems of European immigrants, met at Walling's home in New York City.

These three—all of them white—decided to call a meeting to discuss the race problems. "The Call" to this meeting was written by Oswald Garrison Villard, publisher of the New York Evening Post and the grandson of the abolitionist, William Lloyd Garrison; it was signed by 53 prominent Northerners.

The meeting was held Feb. 12-13, 1909. Out of it came a group—most of them white—known as the National Negro Commission. The commission's purposes were:

1. The abolition of all forced segregation,
2. Equality in education for Negro and white,
3. Obtaining the vote for the Negro,
4. Enforcing the 14th and 15th amendments.

In 1910 the commission absorbed the Niagara movement and this blending of abolitionist white and militant black became the National Association for the Advancement of Colored People. . . .

Because it has had a part in bringing about the crisis we face today there has been a tendency to heap extravagant amounts of both blame and praise on the head of the NAACP. Yet, to a considerable degree, the changes which have occurred over the past 40 years have occurred for reasons more fundamental than anything the NAACP has done or failed to do.

It is important to recognize that the work of the NAACP has coincided with a period in which the basic building blocks of sound race relations have undergone substantial change.

Man's outlook on race relations has undergone more extensive changes than we tend to recognize. The collapse of colonialism and the rise of communism (with its special propaganda appeal for colored peoples) have helped to alter our point of view. The rising literacy and the enlarged accomplishments of the Negro people themselves also have paved the way for change. And there has been an increasing interest on the part of white people in the general welfare of the Negro and in his rights as a citizen.

Many organizations—white, Negro and interracial—have contributed to this change. The National Urban League, an interracial organization that also was established in 1910, is an excellent example of the fact.

Even so, the NAACP has been in the forefront of the struggles over lynching, legal redress, voting, employment and segregation in schools, transportation, housing and in public accommodations. . . .

A good many Southerners feel that the association is little more than a mouthpiece for white Northerners with abolitionist leanings.

The NAACP was organized by white men and women who sought to revive the spirit of the old abolitionists. But, over the years, the NAACP has become more and more a Negro organization.

Since World War I there has been a massive migration of Negroes out of the South and into the North and West.

These migrating Negroes supply the NAACP with much of its driving force. NAACP branches in the Northern states often have full time professional secretaries. They have some white members (which is uncommon in the South) but the vast majority of the membership is colored.

It is, in the opinion of this reporter, an over-simplification to blame the militancy of the NAACP on mischief-minded white Yankees.

If the South is going to continue to oppose the work of the NAACP —and, again in the opinion of this reporter, the white South is going to do just that—it is essential that this opposition be based on legitimate criticism. And the NAACP is open to legitimate criticism.

Many people of both races are convinced that the NAACP is pushing too hard and too fast. They believe that this militancy will cause reaction and invite trouble.

Many Negroes who support the NAACP on matters of broad strategy sometimes differ with the association when it comes to matters of tactics. In this group you also find men who wish that the NAACP would be more moderate.

The disturbing question is whether the association is in a position where it can follow a moderate course.

Up until the end of World War II the NAACP was moderate. In establishing the legal foundations for its all-out push against segregation the association's attorneys carefully selected their test cases. They avoided mass legal actions, partly because they could not afford that course but mainly because they feared the reaction such mass actions might touch off in the South.

But now the legal basis for the all-out push against segregation exists. The NAACP's next job is necessarily that of translating abstract legal principles into action at the local level.

That means the NAACP now must turn to mass legal actions, going to court everytime a Southern community fails to abide by a Supreme Court ruling. Doing that forces the association—whether it likes it or not—into the position of a "pushy" militant agitator.

This role already has caused a reaction among white leaders who ordinarily are sympathetic to the Negro's aspirations.

President Eisenhower, for example, lashed out at the NAACP on June 8, 1955, saying that by insisting on anti-segregation amendments to important legislation the NAACP was holding up laws vital to the national security.

More recently the President has warned that attempts to tack an anti-segregation rider on to the Federal aid to schools program may result in the defeat of this legislation.

Here in North Carolina Governor Luther Hodges has warned the NAACP that over-militancy on its part may well cause this state to close its public schools.

In other Southern states the machinery for closing out the public school system already exists. It is highly possible that machinery will be put into action if the NAACP pushes too hard for prompt desegregation.

Throughout the South, white groups have organized in reaction to the NAACP program. Yet, in talking with leaders of the NAACP, this reporter gathered the impression that these signs are not taken too seriously. But in talking with white leaders you get the impression that they are signs not to be disregarded. That fact points to a lack of adequate communications between the leadership of the two races.

The terrible difficulty is that the NAACP has reached a place in its program where it must either risk mass action to break down segregation or accept the risks involved in letting well enough alone.

NAACP leaders don't believe that they dare stand still. Thurgood Marshall, the man who has spearheaded the association's legal fight since 1938 says:

> "We can't stop now. If we stop now we're lost. They're going to try everything in the book to get out from under. Our job is to stay ahead of them."

And there you have it. Someone has a bear by the tail.

Whether it's the white man or the Negro who has the tailhold is a matter which you and I are likely to answer largely on the basis of whether we sit in the front or the back of the bus.

### DOCUMENTATION SUITABLE FOR RESEARCH PAPERS

BIBLIOGRAPHY ENTRY

Davis, Chester. Feature story on NAACP, Winston-Salem *Journal and Sentinel*, February 26, 1956. Reprinted in *LRUSA* from a reprint distributed by the NAACP.

FIRST FOOTNOTE

*Chester Davis, feature story on NAACP, Winston Salem *Journal and Sentinel*, February 26, 1956, reprinted in *LRUSA*, pp. 185-190, from a reprint distributed by the NAACP.

SUBSEQUENT FOOTNOTES

*Davis, *op. cit.*, *LRUSA*, p. ■.
*Davis, *LRUSA*, p. ■.

---

## A New York Journalist: The Organization and Aims of the NAACP

### FIRST PART*

. . . TODAY, after 47 years, [the NAACP] has become the largest—and oldest—civil rights organization in the country. Its national office, two floors of Freedom House, 20 W. 40th St., serves as a watchdog over Negro rights throughout the nation.

It has 310,000 members, who pay dues from $2 for straight membership to $500 for life membership. There are 1300 branches—at least one in every state but New Hampshire, Vermont, North Dakota, Wyoming and Maine.

Although no color records are kept, 10 to 15 percent of the 310,000 are white. Sixty percent of the total live in the South.

---

* From "What's Behind the NAACP?" by Frederick Woltman, *New York World-Telegram and Sun Saturday Magazine*, May 12, 1956, distributed by the NAACP in a reprint from which this selection is taken. Mr. Woltman is perhaps best known for his articles on Communism in the United States. For model documentation see above, on this page.

Since 1909, there have been three presidents, all whites. The first, Moorfield Storey, had been secretary to Massachusetts' abolitionist Senator, Charles Sumner. Later he became president of the American Bar Assn. A Columbia University literature professor, Joel E. Spingarn, was second. The third is his brother, Arthur B. Spingarn, a New York lawyer.

NAACP's operating heads, on the other hand, have mostly been Negroes. Such as James Weldon Johnson; Walter White, who until his death on March 21, 1955 had for years been its moving spirit; and Roy Wilkins, its present executive secretary.

Its top executive board is strictly interracial, with the 48 directors divided about 50-50 between Negroes and whites.

The directors today include Eric Johnston, Oscar Hammerstein II, Sens. Herbert H. Lehman and Wayne Morse, Walter Reuther, Dr. Ralph C. Bunche, Judge William H. Hastie, Rabbi Judah Cahn and George K. Hunton, secretary of the Catholic Interracial Council.

Recently, Alabama's legislature ordered an investigation into whether the NAACP is Communist-dominated. And Georgia's attorney general charged it with "subversion" in the NAACP's antisegregation crusade.

But J. Edgar Hoover, FBI director, had this to say about it:

"Equality, freedom and tolerance are essential in a democratic government. The NAACP has done much to preserve these principles and to perpetuate the desires of our founding fathers."

And Francis Cardinal Spellman declared:

"Despite many misunderstandings and difficulties and much opposition, the NAACP has made tremendous progress in the struggle to secure for the colored citizens of the United States that place in our civic life to which they are entitled in accordance with the rights that proceed from our common Creator and are proclaimed in the American Constitution."

Militant and highly-articulate, the NAACP registers as a lobby, hence is non-tax exempt. It frankly tries to influence civil rights legislation in Washington as well as the state capitals. It works hard at it. . . .

Publicity and education are its principal tools. Besides a monthly magazine, The Crisis (50,000 circulation), and the NAACP Bulletin, its national office got out 14 pamphlets and brochures last year—altogether about a million and a half pieces of literature.

One pamphlet by Roy Wilkins takes up the Southern states which are defying the Supreme Court order to integrate white and Negro pupils in the public schools. Its title: "The War Against the United States." While challenging and provocative in tone, NAACP's printed output is generally held to be scrupulously accurate as to facts. . . .

All told, the NAACP has poured millions into its educational program over the years. Last year's national budget came to over $600,000, with but a handful of the gifts falling into the $1000 category. The total income, including branches and other activities, reached $1.2 million.

Included was $311,000 for NAACP's Legal Defense and Educational Fund, Inc., a separate unit, which is tax exempt. These contributions ranged from $1 to $50,000.

Headed by Thurgood Marshall, NAACP's chief counsel, the Fund has a staff of six full-time paid attorneys; and a reservoir of at least 40 volunteer lawyers around the country, many of them eminent members of the bar.

About 500 requests for legal support passed through the Fund's office for screening in 1955. A large percentage originated locally, either from branches or from individuals and Negro groups with no NAACP affiliation. One such was the Montgomery, Ala., bus boycott.

Often, in the South, the NAACP is accused of moving into an otherwise contented Negro community and stirring up trouble. Often, according to [Public Relations Director Henry Lee] Moon, the discontent is indigenous as in Montgomery where the NAACP was unaware of the brewing resentment—and it had no hand whatsoever in the boycott which was as peaceful as it was successful.

Only after the city indicted 100 of the Negro leaders on a conspiracy charge, did the Fund step in with legal defense.

"Great progress" has been made in breaking down racial barriers since NAACP was founded in 1909, its leaders say. That year, for instance, 75 Negroes were lynched. The public almost overwhelmingly took lynchings as a matter of course, as punishment for the rape of white women. The NAACP made a survey and found that less than one-sixth of 5000 lynchings over a 30-year period involved sex crime accusations even by the lynch mobs themselves. It hammered away at the national conscience. Gradually opinion turned.

In 1955 the nation had three lynchings, all in Mississippi, according to the NAACP's own count. (NAACP excludes "race-hate" killings unless three or more persons act in concert.) Progress came in other directions, too.

"Segregation in public places and recreation has been banned," the NAACP says. "Negroes are voting freely in most states except Mississippi. The Jim Crow car in interstate travel has been derailed."

Over 2000 Negro students now attend a score or more of Southern colleges which excluded them as recently as 1950. A quarter of a million colored boys and girls attend public schools with white boys and girls in states that separated them less than two years ago. Fifteen states have job equality laws. Segregation in the armed services has been eliminated.

For all of this, the NAACP takes a large share of the credit. The fact is that since 1909 it has pressed literally hundreds of cases in the courts as well as the law-making bodies to help establish equal treatment under the law.

Its greatest victory came on May 17, 1954, when the Supreme Court unanimously declared public school segregation to be a violation of the Constitution. No court since the famous Dred Scott decision of 1857 had ruled on so vital an issue in the field of racial relations.

More than any other person, Thurgood Marshall was responsible for pushing the historic school-segregation case through to a final triumph for the NAACP. Now 47, Mr. Marshall joined its legal staff in 1938 as a special counsel. His salary was $2400.

Since then, he has spent much of his time pleading civil rights cases before the higher courts and is now regarded in his profession as one of the finest constitutional lawyers in the country. Out of 16 cases he has argued before the United States Supreme Court, Mr. Marshall has won 14.

This is a remarkable score in itself. It becomes considerably more so in light of the fact that all 16 were appeals from lower court decisions, the toughest of all to win. In private practice, he could easily quadruple his present salary of $14,000. . . .

SECOND PART*

. . . How DOES the NAACP stand, [Mr. Wilkins] was asked, on the big problem of the future—public school integration? How fast should it be, particularly in light of the Supreme Court order that "a prompt and reasonable start" be made "in good faith . . . toward full compliance?"

"We don't regard that as a fixed, overall formula," he declared. We recognize many difficulties are involved. Where they can desegregate next month, they ought to; if by next fall, they should then.

---

* From "The NAACP: What Is Its Ultimate Goal?" by Frederick Woltman, *New York World-Telegram and Sun Saturday Magazine*, May 19, 1956, distributed by the NAACP in a reprint from which this selection is taken. For model documentation see p. 190.

"Where honestly, for legitimate, discernable factors, they can't until a year from now, it ought to be a year from now. We believe this has to be worked out on the local level. But we have no patience with those who say it's never going to happen and they won't start it; or with those who stall."

The trouble now, the NAACP feels, is that Southern whites have no way of communicating with Negro groups to learn their areas of disagreement. Throughout the South, the NAACP says, its local branches have offered to sit down with local school boards to resolve their differences. The NAACP itself would like to send speakers to talk with local Chambers of Commerce and Rotary Clubs.

"But all of that's impossible," according to its executive secretary, "so long as the Negroes are still considered wards of the white people."

As a model solution, he mentioned St. Louis. "Everything but transportation was segregated there—schools, theaters, hotels and restaurants," he went on. "Several years before the public school decision, the community itself mapped out a program of education.

"Committees were formed, including Negroes. There were many discussions and public forums. As a result, the public was educated and today the St. Louis school system is completely desegregated."

In contrast, he pointed to the White Citizens Councils, which claim 50,000 members in Mississippi and are spreading in the South.

"They—and the ideas they stand for—are the extremists," said Mr. Wilkins. "They're the ones who give the green light to the hoodlums. While they claim to use non-violent methods, they say openly any Negro who seeks his civil rights will find it impossible to get a job, get credit, maintain a business or have a home. It was in this reign-of-terror atmosphere that three Negroes were murdered in cold blood last year in Mississippi. Yet, in the Montgomery, Ala., bus protest, not a rock was thrown by a Negro. It was restrained, orderly and reasonable throughout. Who are the moderates now?"

Meanwhile, ghosts of the Ku Klux Klan have materialized here and there in the South to capitalize on the segregation issue. From Waco, Tex., recently, a rabble-rousing leaflet went through the mails to Southern states.

"Wouldn't you join the KKK," it said, "to protect your home and womanhood from the disease-ridden NAACP Mau Mau hordes? The National Assn. for the Advancement of Communist People Mau Mau are the tool of Talmudic Communism. The Aryan Knights of the Ku Klux Kreed shall never exchange their birthright for a mess of mixed-up, diseased, Talmudic Communism or Romish Popedom. Because that's the Semitic way of Mau Mau life."

Such wild incitements the NAACP properly attributes to isolated crackpots. But they raise two accusations used widely in the South by the Citizens Councils and its more respectable enemies to stigmatize NAACP activities against segregation. And these accusations do carry weight. Namely, that the NAACP is communistic. And that it, basically, wants to force intermarriage on the South. Both, of course, the NAACP stoutly denies. In the states that do not outlaw intermarriage, Mr. Wilkins points out, its incidence is "infinitesimally small."

"Our accusers make a basic assumption that's fantastically wrong and insulting," he says. "They assume that white people are ready and waiting to marry Negroes; that Negroes are ready and waiting to marry whites; that only the law restrains them.

"The NAACP regards marriage as an intimate personal affair between two people who should have freedom of choice. We are neither for nor against intermarriage. One basic reason we oppose laws against intermarriage is that in the South they deprive Negro women of protection in maternity cases. We seek social equality only in its broadest sense. Freedom includes the right to individual prejudices. Our sole program is against making individual prejudices into law."

On the charge of communism, this writer, who was awarded the Pulitzer Prize in journalism for exposing Red infiltration in this country during 1946, has first-hand knowledge. It goes back more than a decade and a half.

Over those years, the NAACP was one of hundreds of church, labor, civic and other groups the Communist party tried desperately to infiltrate. Of them all, the NAACP was one of the least receptive.

Negroes make notoriously unreliable Communists. At no one time could the party claim more than a few thousand members. The turnover is enormous.

Yet, as a permanent tactic, the Communist party always makes a heavy pitch for the support of Negroes. And, in order to exploit their grievances, it tries to latch on to individual civil rights causes of the NAACP.

Just as persistently, the NAACP's top leaders have sternly resisted Communist inroads. Not only are they opposed to the philosophy and strategy of communism, but they realize the Communists' first allegiance goes to Russia and world revolution. And that the Red tag could mean the kiss of death to their entire movement.

Consequently, the Communists have waged intermittent war on Roy

Wilkins, the late Walter White and other NAACP officers. As the NAACP says, "We have been smeared and vilified as much in the Communist Daily Worker as in the Jackson (Miss.) Daily News."

Politically, the NAACP insists it's strictly nonpartisan. "Our business is civil rights," says Mr. Wilkins. "Our aim is civil rights legislation and we don't care whether we get it from the Republicans or the Democrats. We seek friends in both parties."

Although it criticized the late President Franklin D. Roosevelt in specific instances, the NAACP generally backed the New Deal.

It was FDR's successor Harry Truman, the NAACP believes, who did more to restore the Negro to the status of a first-class citizen than any other President—and showed greater courage in doing it.

President Eisenhower, the NAACP's leaders would probably agree, is sympathetic to its objectives and, as one of them put it, "has done some very good things." There is a feeling, however, that the President might have exerted a more positive influence in the segregation crisis. . . .

The NAACP has set Jan. 1, 1963, as its "target" for "the complete elimination of all vestiges of second-class citizenship under which Negro Americans still suffer." That will be the 100th anniversary of Abraham Lincoln's Emancipation Proclamation.

By then, the NAACP hopes to achieve equal rights in employment, housing, voting, education, transportation and public accommodations. . . .

## *An Arkansas Legislative Committee: Communist Influence in the School Crisis?** 

THE BASIC question presented for determination by this Committee is: "Has there been subversion present in Arkansas which has encouraged racial unrest?"

It is a matter of common knowledge that communism thrives where strife, tension, turmoil and chaos is present. Arkansas became a State of the Union in 1836; peace, progress and tranquility marked the attitude of *all* our people for the next 122 years. This Committee has found that the incident which occurred at Little Rock on September 2, 1957, was not something that just happened overnight. It was planned, schemed, calculated, and had as its motiv[at]ing factor the international communist con-

---

* From the conclusion of a report by the Special Education Committee of the Arkansas Legislative Council (an interim committee of the State Legislature), after hearings in December 1958 (mimeographed), pp. 29-32.

spiracy of world domination squarely behind the entire shocking episode.

The people of Arkansas are basically men of good will. Communism, heretofore, has always been something that happened elsewhere; but the record reflects that for a number of years an almost incredible number of communists, pro-communists, fellow travelers, dupes and those who make a career out of being duped, have flitted in and out of Arkansas, and while here, they sowed the seeds of dissension and discord. . . .

The Committee is convinced that the racial unrest in Arkansas was deliberately planned by the Communist Party as part of the directive handed down by Moscow in 1928. The communist apparatus has used many organizations in our State. Some of them have been found subversive by appropriate governmental instrumentalities; others include in their officers and directors those individuals who have been cited as aiding and supporting communist or communist front organizations. We find it noteworthy that these organizations, infiltrated with communists and pro-communists, have actively supported racial unrest in Arkansas. They tried, and were successful, in making Little Rock a world-wide incident. From the evidence introduced at the hearings it is quite apparent, when once perceiving the goals and operations of the Communist Party, that the Little Rock incident was certainly another link in its chain of created incidents designed for its benefit alone, which was mapped out four decades ago.

The Committee further finds—based on credible evidence from the files of the House Un-American Activities Committee, the United States Attorney General's Subversive List, the Senate Internal Security Sub-Committee and others—that many of the top officers of the national NAACP have been cited numerous times for aiding and abetting communist or communist front organizations. These top officials have sent individuals of very questionable loyalty to our government to Arkansas as their paid employees. In turn they met with local officials of the NAACP and planned the events which culminated in the so-called Little Rock incident. We believe that the NAACP is and has been sympathetic toward communist causes, and that the goal of the communist is not to help the Negro as such, but merely to use him. In that desire to use the Negro, we find that the communists have always tried to infiltrate organizations attractive to the Negro race.

The Committee feels that it would be amiss of its duty should it not report its findings in regard to various corporations that worked in Arkansas. We have been unable to learn of any public or private good that the Arkansas Council on Human Relations has ever rendered, and the same may be said of the Southern Regional Council. Both of these organizations have been subsidized by the Fund for the Republic. The NAACP appears to have been heavily infiltrated with subversives and, wittingly or unwittingly, is now a captive of the communist apparatus. The Fund for the Republic, with Harry Ashmore of Arkansas on the national board of directors, has given considerable money to the NAACP. It has also given about one-half million dollars to the Southern Regional Council—with Daisy Bates on the board of directors, who in turn channeled part of the money to the Arkansas Council on Human Relations, which had the same Ashmore and Bates as incorporators. A former F.B.I. agent of 20 years service, when questioned at the hearings about the activities of these three organizations, summed up his disgust at their nefarious schemes by simply answering, "to create mischief."

The Committee has become aghast at the viciousness with which some segments of the press have attacked the purposes of the hearings. We feel that the people of the world are entitled to know that a peaceful people have been torn asunder by the communist conspiracy. But some members of the press seem determined to becloud the issue, smear the purposes of the hearings, and reach any conclusion other than the fact that there was subversion present in our difficulties here. This the Committee deplores.

It is the conclusion of this Committee that from the evidence presented before it, and from the findings of fact which this Committee has made, that subversion was present in the racial unrest in our State. We further conclude that had it not been for the communists, pro-communists, fellow travelers and dupes—along with the organizations above listed—that the harmony and peace existent between the races for over 100 years would not have been interrupted. We pray for a restoration of that peace and harmony so that all the people of Arkansas may march forward to a more abundant and proud life under our Creator, Almighty God.

## DOCUMENTATION SUITABLE FOR RESEARCH PAPERS

BIBLIOGRAPHY ENTRY

> Special Education Committee, Arkansas Legislative Council. Report after hearings on the Little Rock school crisis in December 1958. Reprinted in *LRUSA* from mimeographed release.

FIRST FOOTNOTE

> *Special Education Committee, Arkansas Legislative Council, report after hearings on the Little Rock school crisis in December 1958, reprinted in *LRUSA*, pp. 196-198, from mimeographed release.

SUBSEQUENT FOOTNOTES
     *Special Education Committee, *op. cit., LRUSA,* p. ■.
     *Special Education Committee, report, *LRUSA,* p. ■.

---

## An NAACP Editor on Charges of Extremism*

ENEMIES of the NAACP, and even some of our best friends and well-wishers, are charging the Association with immoderate and unreasonable haste, of intransigence and extremism, not only in our procedures in public school desegregation, but in other related aspects of our fight for full citizenship. According to these critics, there is no middle group—only the White Council extremists on the one hand and the NAACP radicals on the other. Newspapers in the Deep South are filled daily with the wildest lies of hatred and fear, smears and innuendoes, unfounded assumptions and groundless charges that the Association is stirring up racial tension, is made up of Communists, etc., etc.

Actually, however, our fulminators and defamers are the real extremists, the most stubborn upholders of segregation and racial inequality to be found in the United States. Some of them, including some Congressmen, are even trying, it seems, to organize a New Confederacy, not only to fight the NAACP, but also the United States Supreme Court and all constituted authority. These are the people who are openly boasting that they will not obey the law of the land, the people who plan to keep the Federal Courts busy on "nonracial excuses" for continued segregation, the people who rant about the nine Supreme Court justices as the "nine ninnies." These are the real extremists—not the NAACP.

These white Southern extremist groups accuse the Association of being precipitous and thoughtless in action, and guilty of irresponsible rabble rousing.

However, the charge currently being made (and echoed in sections outside the South) is that the Association is "forcing" the issue, "going too fast" and "pushing too hard." The Southern wail now is "go slow!"

Let us examine this "gradualism" warning to see what it means to most Southerners and what it means to Negroes and the NAACP. To most Americans the word has its simple dictionary definition of "changing or moving by degrees." To the defiant Southerner, however, the word, as he

---

* From an editorial in *The Crisis,* NAACP monthly magazine, April 1956, pp. 226-227. For suitable documentation see p. 47.

uses it, always means "never." What the Southerner wants, it seems, is a gradual improvement of the Negro's status *within* the segregated pattern. He wants the Negro to advance over on the "Negro's side" of the racial fence as a Negro, but he wants no breaches made in the wall of racial separation. Even the slightest change arouses his fears and he begins to rant about "outside pressures," "gradualism," "our Negroes want segregation," and all sorts of twaddle which has not even the remotest connection with the issue under discussion.

Take the case of Autherine Juanita Lucy which provoked the mob action at the University of Alabama. Did the NAACP act precipitously in her case, since many of our friends, as well as our enemies, have accused us of pushing her entry into the University? Miss Lucy applied for admission to the University of Alabama, not under the recent United States Supreme Court rulings of May 17, 1954, and May 31, 1955, but under the Court's ruling on the admission of Negro students to southern graduate schools, a decision handed down in June 1950. It was not until two years later, in 1953, that Miss Lucy applied for admission to the University of Alabama. And she spent two years in the courts seeking admission. No court action is ever hurried or precipitous and neither Miss Lucy nor the NAACP can be accused of unreasonable haste in her case. Miss Lucy was patient. The NAACP was patient. NAACP lawyers were patient. Surely this was gradualism to suit the most technical interpretation, but what happened when the Court, on February 1, 1956, ordered Miss Lucy's admission to the University of Alabama?

The whole world knows of the rioting, the mob rule on a university campus, and the threats of lynching when she applied at the beginning of the semester in February. We ask, who were the gradualists in this case? Who were the unreasonable, precipitous groups? . . .

Negroes worked for thirty years to be allowed to purchase Pullman accommodations in the South, to be permitted to eat in dining cars without being hidden, like lepers, behind a curtain. . . .

Segregation, "the Southern way of life," is doomed. It is doomed legally; it is doomed morally. The Negro masses are in revolt against it. They know from bitter experience that separation always means inequality. They know that Southerners have never done anything effectual to bring them equality, that outside pressures and the courts—perfectly legal procedures—are always needed to achieve even the modest gains we have made. And these the NAACP and Negroes shall continue to use. No time is gained by settling a great question wrong. And the NAACP and Southern Negroes are resolved to settle it right—by legal and constitutional means.

## A Southern Author: Where Is the NAACP Going?*

. . . WHY did [Mr. White] fail to give credit to others? There are two reasons. One is far less significant than the other, but let's deal with it first: Mr. White was a super salesman. He was selling to the American public a package called "the Negro group;" he wanted to make big sales for his product and he wanted his firm (the NAACP) to get the credit for the sales. Any organization that sold "the Negro group" wrapped up in a slightly different package hurt his firm's sales and was a competitor. Any writer, poet, artist (colored or white) who poked around in that package and spilled out the human beings in it, showing them with their virtues and faults, their aches and pains, their dreams and their nightmares, their meanness and their sweetness, spoiled the nice clean package—that's all.

The second and far more important reason was this: a few of us were working for something much bigger than "the Negro problem"—and Mr. White knew it and feared it. He was fighting a battle for the Negro group's civil rights; we were, and still are, engaged in a never-ending war for an open society for all people everywhere. This open society requires that barriers in minds and imaginations and hearts be leveled as well as barriers in the external world. Because we believe this we are as concerned about the segregation of an idea, of a crippled or blind child, of a new dream, or an old or new poem, as we are about segregation of people who are different in color. We think the act of withdrawal injures the segregator as much as it does the segregated. We value as much as Mr. White ever did that idea we call "human dignity" but we know that the real barriers that cramp its growth are largely inside a man's own mind and soul and that dignity lives or dies because of what it feeds on there.

This concern with the inner man, with the quality of human beings, and with the complexities of the human mind puzzled and frightened Mr. White. He wanted "sensible things": he wanted for the Negro group the right to be "normal Americans," he wanted for them freedom to conform, and especially did he want for them a big role in the great American success story. The urgent question in Mr. White's mind was, "How soon can

---

* From "Negroes in Gray Flannel Suits," a review-essay by Lillian Smith, southern author, discussing Walter White's book *How Far the Promised Land,* in *The Progressive,* February 1956, pp. 33-35. Miss Smith criticizes Mr. White, long-time executive secretary of the NAACP, for not giving enough credit, in his book, to the many individuals and groups outside the NAACP who contributed to the racial progress of recent decades. For model documentation see p. 47.

we get every Negro into a gray flannel suit and traveling down the middle of the road shoulder to shoulder with all the other gray flannel suits?"

Traveling where? To the Promised Land? Or to the point of no return? Mr. White never asked himself these quetions. He took it for granted that it was the road to the Promised Land, of course. No wonder he was restive around those who kept talking about the problem of the individual versus mass-conformity, the profound right, indeed the necessity, to protect men's differences since mankind's progress comes out of the great deviations—not of color, which is no real difference at all, but of ideas. He could feel no more sympathy with such talk than would a Communist or a middle-of-the-road Republican or a gradualist Democrat. And, being a practical man, he probably thought such talk could do the Negro's cause no immediate good and would only keep needed dollars for "the work" away.

I don't know why this saddens me, but it does. Perhaps, because long ago when I first met Walter White I thought he had fine potentialities as a person and a leader. He had something that set him far above many others: courage. And he *believed*. He believed enough in a dream to risk his life for it, not once but many times. And I don't think that dream when he was young was dressed in a gray flannel suit. He held on to his physical courage throughout his life and to his capacity for hard, persistent work; and he carried with him always a "good fellow" flavor that made him most likable. If only he had not let his young dream die. . . Did he kill it? Did the pressures of racial discrimination kill it? Or did the false values of American culture with which he identified himself so ardently do the job for him?

It is a tragic question. Let us push it back now and look once more at the NAACP which his efforts helped build into a strong organization. At this moment, when the walls of race segregation are falling—for which every decent person is glad—at this triumphant moment when the Negro group (through valiant efforts of NAACP and the equally valiant efforts of uncounted others) has gained many of its civil rights, I would like to ask a few qeustions:

Does the NAACP have a new leadership wise enough, disciplined and generous enough to survive success? Can it endure unless it extends the dimensions of its cause to include those spiritual goals which can never be attained but must always be tried for? Can it stay alive unless it begins soon to work for human excellence as well as for human rights? Can it work only for itself or will it, to survive, have to include all people's rights in its agenda? Do its leaders have the vision to make the choice at the crossroads that lie just ahead?

These are questions not for them only, of course, but for this reviewer and every American to answer. For when the crossroads are reached, we shall all be there together.

## A South Carolina Governor: The Supreme Court and the Constitution*

TWO YEARS ago, on May 17, 1954, the Supreme Court of the United States reversed what had been the law of the land for 75 years, and declared unconstitutional the laws of 17 States under which segregated public-school systems were established.

The Court did not interpret the Constitution—the Court amended it.

We have had a written Constitution. Under that Constitution the people of the United States have enjoyed great progress and freedom. The usurpation by the Court of the power to amend the Constitution and destroy State Governments may impair our progress and take our freedom.

An immediate consequence of the segregation decision is that much of the progress made in the last half century of steadily advancing racial amity has been undone. Confidence and trust have been supplanted by suspicion and distrust. The races are divided and the breach is widening. The truth is, there has not been such tension between the races in the South since the days of Reconstruction. . . .

In 1896 in a case known as Plessy v. Ferguson, involving a statute providing for segregation of the races on railroad trains, the United States Supreme Court held that a statute providing for separate but equal facilities was not in violation of the Fourteenth Amendment to the Constitution. Thereafter, the Supreme Court in several cases involving schools upheld this doctrine.

Later, the Court, when it included such great judges as Chief Justice Taft and Justices Holmes, Brandeis and Stone, unanimously said that segregation in public schools had been "many times decided to be within the constitutional power of the State legislatures to settle without interference of the federal courts under the Federal Constitution." . . .

* From *The Supreme Court Must Be Curbed,* by James F. Byrnes, former United States Senator, Supreme Court Justice, and Governor of South Carolina, in *U.S. News & World Report,* an independent weekly news magazine published at Washington, May 18, 1956, reprinted as a pamphlet by the Association of Citizens' Councils, Greenwood, Mississippi, from which this selection is taken. Copyright 1956 by United States News Publishing Corporation.

The facilities for negro students in many States were not equal to the facilities provided for white students. The degree of equality differed not only in States, but in counties within a State. The situation in South Carolina was typical of the South. As a rule, the facilities for negro students in the urban centers were superior to the facilities provided in rural areas. The same was true of facilities for white students. Schools were dependent upon local taxation, and much of the inequality was due to the greater value of industrial property and higher income of the city dweller.

A realization of the inequality that existed between rural schools and urban schools, as well as between the races, influenced me greatly to become a candidate for Governor of South Carolina in 1950.

In my inaugural address I advocated a bond issue of 75 million dollars and the levying of a sales tax of 3 per cent for the purpose of equalizing the school facilities. In presenting this, I said:

> "It is our duty to provide for the races substantial equality in school facilities. We should do it because it is right. For me, that is sufficient reason."

Of the 75 million dollars authorized, 70 per cent was allocated to negro schools even though the negro school enrollment constitutes but 39 per cent of the total school enrollment. . . .

About the time the educational program was inaugurated in South Carolina, there was pending in the United States court a case from Clarendon County, asking equal facilities for negro schools. Later, that suit was withdrawn, and a suit was brought by the same complainants, asking the court to declare unconstitutional all segregation laws.

The three-judge court, presided over by Judge Parker, senior judge of the Fourth Circuit, held that under the decisions of the United States Supreme Court from 1896 to that date, the segregation provisions of the Constitution and statues of South Carolina were not in violation of the Fourteenth Amendment. The lawyers for the National Association for the Advancement of Colored People appealed the case to the United States Supreme Court.

In that Court, the case for Clarendon County was argued by the late Hon. John W. Davis. He was so convinced of the soundness of the decision of the three-judge court that he agreed to argue the case and declined to accept compensation for his services.

Had the Court been unanimous in the view that segregation statutes were in violation of the Fourteenth Amendment, such an opinion would have been written within a few months.

Instead, after many months, the Court announced that the cases should be re-argued, and counsel should direct their arguments to certain questions.

The first question was:

> "What evidence is there that the Congress which submitted and the State legislatures and conventions which ratified the Fourteenth Amendment, contemplated, or did not contemplate, understood, or did not understand, that it would abolish segregation in public schools?"

Such a question would not have been asked if a majority of the Court was already satisfied that Congress and the State legislatures DID contemplate that the amendment would prohibit segregation in public schools.

Attorneys representing the parties involved and the attorneys general of many States having segregation statutes filed briefs. The overwhelming preponderance of the legislative history demonstrated that abolishing segregation in schools was not contemplated by the framers of the Fourteenth Amendment, or by the States.

We can only speculate as to how the Court reached its decision. In that speculation, it is interesting to read in the "Harvard Law Review" of November, 1955, an article entitled, "The Original Understanding and the Segregation Decision," written by Alexander M. Bickel, who, according to the "Review," was the law clerk to Mr. Justice Frankfurter during the October term, 1952, when the case was first argued. After a lengthy resume of the evidence, the writer states:

> "The obvious conclusion to which the evidence, thus summarized, easily leads is that Section 1 of the Fourteenth Amendment, like Section 1 of the Civil Rights Act of 1866, carried out the relatively narrow objectives of the moderates, and hence, as originally understood, was meant to apply neither to jury service, nor suffrage, nor antimiscegenation statutes, nor segregation. This conclusion is supported by the blunt expression of disappointment to which Thaddeus Stevens gave vent in the House."

The Court, in its opinion, did not admit, as did Mr. Bickel, the conclusiveness of the evidence that the Fourteenth Amendment did not apply to school segregation. The Court said the evidence was "inconclusive."

Our Constitution is a written instrument. The Fourteenth Amendment does not specifically mention public schools. Having decided unanimously that the legislative history was not "conclusive" that the Congress or the States intended it should apply to schools, one would think the Court would have stopped there and upheld the previous decisions of the Court. Instead, it proceeded to reverse those decisions and legislate a policy for schools.

An explanation of this extraordinary decision is offered by Mr. Bickel in his "Harvard Review" article on page 64, where he said:

> "It [the Court] could have deemed itself bound by the legislative history showing the immediate objectives to which Section 1 of the Fourteenth Amendment was addressed, and rather clearly demonstrating that it was not expected in 1866 to apply to segregation. The Court would in that event also have repudiated much of the provision's 'line of growth.' For it is as clear that Section 1 was not deemed in 1866 to deal with jury service and other matters 'implicit in . . . ordered liberty . . .' to which the Court has since applied it."

If this law clerk is correct (and I can assure you the law clerks in the Supreme Court are well informed), it means that the Court, having previously interpreted the Fourteenth Amendment to apply to jury service and other matters not specifically delegated by the Constitution to the Federal Government, felt that the soundness of those decisions would be questioned unless the Court held the Fourteenth Amendment to apply to schools.

But there was a distinction. Previously the Court had held that State laws providing separate but equal school facilities did not deny a constitutional right. The control of schools had been proposed by some framers of the Fourteenth Amendment and rejected. There was no legislation by Congress prohibiting segregated schools. The only change in conditions was that several million negroes had migrated to the big cities in Northern States and constituted the balance of political power in several States.

Once the Court becomes committed to a course of expanding the Constitution in order to justify previous expansions, there is no turning back. When next the Court is called upon to "read into" the Constitution something which was never there, another segment of the people may be the victim. It may be YOU.

The Constitution provides that any amendment submitted to the States must be ratified by three-fourths of the States.

Change was purposely made difficult by the framers, who jealously guarded their liberties. They knew "the history of liberty is the history of limitations on government." . . .

In 23 of the States that ratified the Fourteenth Amendment, the courts of last resort held it did not abolish segregation. The Supreme Court itself, in six cases decided over a period of 75 years, upheld the doctrine of equal but separate facilities.

The Court ignored all of these legal precedents and the Constitution and said, "We cannot turn the clock back to 1868 when the amendment was adopted, or even to 1896 when Plessy v. Ferguson was written."

Why not? The function of the Court is to interpret the Constitution, not amend it. Heretofore, whenever in doubt about the proper interpretation of the Constitution or a statute, the Court has turned the clock back to the time of adoption to ascertain the intent of the draftsmen. When the Court states, "We cannot turn the clock back to 1868," will it ever consider the intent of the framers of the Constitution in 1787? . . .

The Court made a terrible indictment of the negro race. Because— whether a person be black, brown or yellow—whenever the Supreme Court says he cannot develop unless while in school he is permitted to sit by the side of white students, the Court brands that person an inferior human being.

Now mark this well! The Court not only ignored the Constitution and its own decisions, but, in establishing a policy for schools, ignored the record in the case.

In support of its decision, after citing K. B. Clark, who was employed by the National Association for the Advancement of Colored People, it cited the writings of a group of psychologists who had not testified in the trial court. Counsel for the States had no opportunity to rebut the opinions of these psychologists. In such procedure there lies danger for all of us!

And the Court was guilty of what it has frequently condemned. As late as 1952 in the case of Beauharnais v. Illinois (343 U. S. 250) the Court said:

> "It is not within our competence to confirm or deny claims
> of social scientists as to the dependence of the individual on the
> position of his racial or religious group in the community."

. . . And loyal Americans should stop and think when the executive branch of the Federal Government brands as subversive organizations whose membership includes certain psychologists, and the Supreme Court cites those psychologists as authority for invalidating the constitutions of 17 States of the union. . . .

The fifth section of the Fourteenth Amendment authorizes Congress to enforce *that* amendment. Congress never legislated to require integrated schools because the Fourteenth Amendment did not embrace schools. On the contrary, Congress specifically appropriated for segregated schools in the District of Columbia. Now that the Supreme Court has amended the Constitution to embrace schools, Congress could legislate on the subject but the Supreme Court knows the representatives of the people will not legislate. Therefore, it calls upon the States of the South to enforce its new policy for schools.

The people of the South are law-abiding. They do not talk or even think of armed resistance. They realize the United States Government has the power to enforce a decision of the Supreme Court. But they believe the decision will close many schools, and think that the Court that ignored the Constitution and rendered the decision should assume the responsibility for its enforcement.

It is unrealistic to expect local school officials to destroy the public schools. With few exceptions, school trustees in the South are white men. They are highly respected in their communities. They serve without compensation. Do you think they will force the children of their neighbors into mixed schools? Many trustees will resign. Negroes will not be selected to succeed them. The schools will be closed.

When Northern newspapers criticize local officials who will not cooperate in the enforcement of this decision, they should recall the prohibition era. There were few Northern newspapers clamoring for the enforcement of that law by local authorities.

The so-called "best people" of many States did not hide their violations of the prohibition law. They regarded it as "smart" to boast of making gin in the bathtub and carrying whisky in a silver flask to public places. They fought the law until it was repealed.

However, there was this difference: The prohibition law was enacted as a result of an amendment to the Constitution which was adopted in the manner provided by the Constitution. It was not, as in this case, a decision of nine men on the Supreme Court—in effect—amending the Constitution.

The National Association for the Advancement of Colored People, financed by tax-exempt organizations and some well-intentioned but misguided people, for years demanded the reversal of the "separate but equal" decisions of the Supreme Court, even though 40 years ago Justice Charles Evans Hughes, speaking for the Court, said the question could "no longer be considered an open one." Now these same people would deny to the people of the South even the right to criticize the recent decision in the school case.

A statement of some of the practical difficulties certain to follow enforcement of the segregation decision demonstrates the seriousness of the problem.

The case from South Carolina originated in a school district in Clarendon County where there were approximately 2,900 negro students and 290 white students. The goal of educators is to limit a class to 30 students. In the Clarendon District, all classrooms have more than the standard.

No white student will ask to go to a negro school. But suppose some negroes in the tenth grade of a negro school ask for a transfer to the tenth grade of a crowded white school and the trustees decide it is unwise to further increase the enrollment in that school. Will the Court decide the rejection was on account of race, instead of efficiency, and cite the trustees for contempt?

Suppose the negroes are admitted: It is agreed that the average negro child, having had little training at home, does not possess the training of the average white child in the same grade and age group. Shall the white children be held back to help the negroes progress?

The white parents in the District of Columbia can answer that question. They have had some sad experiences in the last year. As a result, approximately 60 per cent of the students in the public schools of the capital of this nation are negroes. Many white families have moved to Virginia; many, though they can ill afford it, have placed their children in private schools.

If the negro students are not able to do the work of the white students, can the races be segregated in the classroom and assigned different class work? Would not the scars inflicted upon the negro child by such segregation be far deeper than the harm done him by associating with only negro students in segregated schools?

Should the races be mixed in a school, will a board of trustees composed of white men in a Southern State employ negro teachers? If not, what will happen to the negro teachers now employed in the South?

Today, high schools in the South are more social institutions than in the past. There is a cafeteria where all students lunch together. There is a gymnasium where students of both sexes engage in various sports.

Athletic contests, as a rule, are held at night. Students, following the team, travel in school buses. When the races have been accustomed to separation in buses, who can assure there will not be serious consequences?

These are only a few of the problems. . . .

The hope is for voluntary segregation. As the negro has progressed educationally and economically, a constantly increasing percentage of them have developed a pride of race. That negro does not want his children forced into schools where they will not be welcomed. He prefers to have them attend schools for negroes, taught by negroes. However, recent events indicate such men will be coerced by the National Association for the Advancement of Colored People and Northern negroes to demand admission to white schools. Therefore, there is fear for the future.

Plans vary. In some States, the legislature has repealed the statute requiring children to attend schools. When the overwhelming majority of the people of a State are opposed to integrated schools, they could not be expected to enforce laws requiring children to attend mixed schools.

In most States, the law now requires trustees or other school officials to assign children to schools. In the cities where the negro population is usually concentrated in two or three areas, schools have been placed in those areas. It is reasonable that negroes should be assigned to schools nearest their homes. In the rural districts there is no such segregation of homes. There the problem will be more difficult, and—more dangerous.

In South Carolina and in some other States, laws have been enacted providing that if—by order of any court, State or federal—a student is assigned to a school different from that to which he is assigned by school officials, all appropriations for the school to which that student is assigned and all appropriations for the school from which he comes shall immediately cease. Similarly, it is provided that funds appropriated for operation of school buses shall be available only for segregated buses.

The theory of this legislation is that under the Constitution there are three branches of Government *which shall forever be kept separate.* It is the function of the legislative and executive branches of State governments to appropriate for and administer school funds. If a State or federal court shall arrogate to itself the right to assign children to schools different from the assignment made by the officials designated by the legislative and executive branches of the State Government, no funds shall be available for such schools. . . .

The present trend brings joy to Communists and their fellow travelers who want to see all power centered in the Federal Government because they can more easily influence one Government in Washington than the 48 governments in 48 States.

But the trend of the Court is disturbing to millions of Americans who respect the Constitution and believe that in order to preserve the republic we must preserve what is left of the powers of the States. . . .

DOCUMENTATION SUITABLE FOR RESEARCH PAPERS

BIBLIOGRAPHY ENTRY

Byrnes, James F. *The Supreme Court Must Be Curbed.* Greenwood, Mississippi, n.d. Pamphlet reprinted in *LRUSA.*

FIRST FOOTNOTE

\*James F. Byrnes, *The Supreme Court Must Be Curbed,* pamphlet (Greenwood, Mississippi, n.d.), reprinted in *LRUSA,* pp. 203-210.

SUBSEQUENT FOOTNOTES

\*Byrnes, *op. cit., LRUSA,* p. ▪.
\*Byrnes, *LRUSA,* p. ▪.

---

## A National Magazine Editor: Voluntary vs. Compulsory Integration under the Law*

FAR AND WIDE we hear the cry: "It's the law of the land—it must be obeyed—the Supreme Court has decided—it is final."

But what really has been decided on "desegregation"? What is "the law of the land" that all citizens are supposed to obey?

The quandary arises when we endeavor to determine whether voluntary or enforced integration in the schools is "the law of the land."

Of particular interest in this regard is the transcript of a recorded interview with Dr. Omer Carmichael, Superintendent of Schools in Louisville, Kentucky, which begins on page 46 of this magazine. Dr. Carmichael says that white children are attending certain schools in Louisville which have no Negro children in them, and Negro children are attending certain schools which have no white children in them, but that both whites and Negroes are attending other schools which are mixed. Under this system parents are allowed to exercise "freedom of choice," and requests for "transfer" are granted insofar as is practicable within the available school facilities.

This is "permissive" segregation. It is also being called "voluntary" integration. In any event, authority is being exercised by a subdivision of a

---

* From "What Is the Law of the Land?" by David Lawrence, editor, reprinted from *U.S. News & World Report,* an independent weekly news magazine published at Washington, October 5, 1956, pp. 151-152. Copyright 1956 United States News Publishing Corporation. For model documentation see p. 47.

State government—the school board—to assign pupils on a basis conforming to local conditions and local sentiment on the race question.

It is a noble experiment. But is it really constitutional? If it is, then the Supreme Court of the United States must say so and, if it someday does, it will, in effect, be reversing a vital point in its decision of May 17, 1954.

The Louisville plan happens to be buttressed for the time being by a significant ruling rendered on July 15, 1955, by a federal court in South Carolina composed of two members of the U.S. Circuit Court of Appeals and one U.S. District Court judge. This ruling, which has not been passed upon by the highest court one way or the other, says in part:

"It (the Supreme Court) has not decided that the federal courts are to take over or regulate the public schools of the States.

"It has not decided that the States must mix persons of different races in the schools or must require them to attend schools or must deprive them of the right of choosing the schools they attend.

"What it has decided, and all that it has decided, is that a State may not deny to any person on account of race the right to attend any school that it maintains. This, under the decision of the Supreme Court, the State may not do directly or indirectly; but if the schools which it maintains are open to children of all races, no violation of the Constitution is involved even though the children of different races voluntarily attend different schools, as they attend different churches.

"Nothing in the Constitution or in the decision of the Supreme Court takes away from the people freedom to choose the schools they attend. The Constitution, in other words, does not require integration. It merely forbids discrimination. It does not forbid such segregation as occurs as the result of voluntary action. It merely forbids the use of governmental power to enforce segregation."

But, after we have read the above, we must compare it with what the Supreme Court of the United States said in its famous decision of May 17, 1954. The Court confessed its inability to find anywhere in the Congressional debate on the Fourteenth Amendment anything conclusive to support the theory that desegregation in the schools was the intent of the sponsors of the Amendment.

Then, without any basis in precedent or in constitutional history, the Court arbitrarily decided that the time had come to adopt a psychological rather than a legal yardstick for measuring the effect of segregation on school children. The Court said:

"Does segregation of children in public schools solely on the basis of race, even though the physical facilities and other 'tangible' factors may be equal, deprive the children of the minority group of equal educational opportunities? We believe that it does. . . .

"To separate them from others of similar age and qualifications solely because of their race generates a feeling of inferiority as to their status in the community that may affect their hearts and minds in a way unlikely ever to be undone. . . .

"Whatever may have been the extent of psychological knowledge at the time of *Plessy* v. *Ferguson,* this finding is amply supported by modern authority. Any language in *Plessy* v. *Ferguson* contrary to this finding is rejected."

In the *Plessy* v. *Ferguson* case—decided in 1896 by the Supreme Court —the doctrine of "separate but equal" facilities had been upheld. It remained "the law of the land" for 58 years thereafter.

How has the new "law of the land" been determined? By Congress? By "judge made" rules? In spite of the fact that no testimony whatsoever from experts was taken in the trial court, the Supreme Court set itself up as the final authority on "psychological" matters and handed down a mandate based upon its own examination of these same "psychological" factors.

The opinion of the nine Justices declared frankly that they relied on out-of-court assertions contained in the writings of a few sociologists. These were primarily critics of segregation. It is axiomatic that "expert" opinion cannot be considered in court unless the testimony is subject to refutation in cross-examination.

But what will the Supreme Court say now about the actual experience in the Louisville schools? There, by reason of freedom of choice and parents' preference, certain children are permitted to attend all-white schools, and certain parents have selected all-Negro schools. So far as legal authority is concerned, the parent of a child cannot insist upon his choice, and the school superintendent may put Negro children and white children in any school he pleases. This may, in a broad sense, satisfy the legalities. But on the "psychological" front—does it not disprove the Supreme Court's "finding"?

Thus, for example, if the Court is right, will not the children who are in all-Negro schools have a "feeling of inferiority" to whites because they have been persuaded by one means or another not to go to the same school with whites? How is it proposed to remove such "psychological" barriers? Isn't it "the law of the land" that these barriers must be removed?

Likewise, what will be said as to the effect hereafter on the white children who are compelled to attend school with Negro children, especially when the cultural training of the white children and the whole philosophy of Southern families has been psychologically set against mingling of the races on a social or quasi-social basis?

Can it be persuasively argued that Negro children are adversely affected by enforced segregation but not by voluntary segregation? Can it be logically contended that some white children are not unfavorably affected in their educational opportunities when integration is ordered by the school authorities? The testimony before a House subcommittee last week on the experiences in the integrated schools of the District of Columbia revealed some startling facts on these points.

Surely the Supreme Court cannot now refuse to consider evidence on "achievement" tests and other related factors which it failed to request in the first instance as the Court constituted itself virtually a commission on psychology, without regard to testimony or cross-examination of witnesses on both sides. Was this really "due process"? . . .

To say the least, "the law of the land" on the school question is far from clear today. Proposals to achieve "equality" among unequals amid the vicissitudes of the classroom are not susceptible of enforcement by law. To engage in such empiric adventures is hardly the function of the Supreme Court of the United States as prescribed in the Constitution itself. Plainly this is a departure from our accustomed reliance on constitutional law and historic procedure.

Voluntarism, instead of coercion, is certainly a desirable means whereby the States can handle their school problems. But is voluntarism sanctioned by the Supreme Court of the United States?

We must, therefore, still ask: Just what is "the law of the land" on "desegregation"?

## Eighteen Social Scientists: Race Differences and Intelligence*

IN CONNECTION with the process of school desegregation and the difficulties with which it has been accompanied in certain areas, the question has again arisen as to the existence of innate differences in intelligence be-

---

* The full text of "Does Race Really Make a Difference in Intelligence?" a joint statement by 18 social scientists, most of them members of the American Psychological Association, released October 16, 1956. Reprinted from *U.S. News & World Report*, October 26, 1956, pp. 74-76. For model documentation see p. 47.

tween Negroes and whites. The present statement is directed to that question.

Those who have signed it are not on this occasion taking sides with regard to the problem of desegregation as a whole, nor with the manner or the rapidity with which it should be accomplished. They are for the moment concerned only with the facts and conclusions accepted by scientists with regard to racial comparisons in inborn intellectual capacity.

A number of years ago, at a time when Nazi race theories were receiving much publicity, several scientific organizations placed themselves on record as opposed to the conclusion that race was a determiner of innate psychological characteristics; their position was that no such relationship had ever been scientifically demonstrated.

These organizations included, among others, the American Anthropological Association, in 1939, and the Society for the Psychological Study of Social Issues, a division of the American Psychological Association, in 1938.

More recently, in 1950, a group of distinguished social scientists meeting in UNESCO House in Paris issued a statement on race which reads in part as follows:

> "Whatever classification the anthropologist makes of man, he never includes mental characteristics as part of those classifications. It is now generally recognized that intelligence tests do not in themselves enable us to differentiate safely between what is due to innate capacity and what is the result of environmental influences, training and education.
>
> "Wherever it has been possible to make allowances for differences in environmental opportunities, the tests have shown essential similarity in mental characters among all human groups. In short, given similar degrees of cultural opportunity to realize their potentialities, the average achievement of the members of each ethnic group is about the same."

Two years later an equally distinguished assembly of geneticists and physical anthropologists, also meeting in Paris, pointed out that:

> "The scientific material available to us at present does not justify the conclusion that inherited genetic differences are a major factor in producing the differences between the cultures and cultural achievements of different peoples or groups. It does indicate, on the contrary, that a major factor in explaining such differences is the cultural experience which each group has undergone."

In 1953, a statement submitted to the United States Supreme Court by more than 30 American social scientists included the following:

> "The available scientific evidence indicates that much, perhaps all, of the observable differences among various racial and national groups may be adequately explained in terms of environmental differences. . . . It seems clear, therefore, that fears based on the assumption of innate racial differences in intelligence are not well founded."

These statements still stand, and in our judgment represent the consensus among experts who have studied this question as objectively and as scientifically as is at present possible. We know of no new research which would reverse these conclusions.

Those few specialists who take a different position usually do so on two major grounds. The first is that Negro-white differences in intelligence-test scores persist even when the two groups are "equated" for social and educational opportunities. To this we would point out that such "equation" is exceedingly difficult to achieve, since the opportunities related to test performances are by no means easy to assess in quantitative terms.

We do know that the intelligence quotients of Southern Negro children improve markedly after a period of years in the schools available to them in New York or Philadelphia.

In the second place, it has been argued that the differences in I.Q. persist even when "noncultural questions" are used. We would deny the possibility of devising a "noncultural" test in the light of our present understanding of the problem.

In the early days of testing, many psychologists believed that the elimination of the handicap due to language was equivalent to eliminating the influence of culture in general. One psychologist, for example, Prof. Florence L. Goodenough of the University of Minnesota, devised a performance test consisting in "drawing a man." She regarded this test as "culture-free." Many investigators have made use of this test, and they have been able to demonstrate that, contrary to the earlier view, the results are indeed affected by many aspects of previous experience.

Professor Goodenough herself has now recognized this fact, and very honestly and courageously points out her former error. Writing with Dale B. Harris on "Studies in the Psychology of Children's Drawings" in the *Psychological Bulletin* for September, 1950, she expresses the opinion that "the search for a culture-free test, whether of intelligence, artistic ability, personal-social characteristics, or any other measurable trait, is illusory."

She goes on to state that her own earlier study "is certainly no exception to the rule" and adds: "The writer hereby apologizes for it."

No one can deny that at the present time the intellectual achievement of American Negro children, particularly those who come from segregated schools, is lower *on the average* than that of white children, nor that a reasonable amount of time must elapse before the gap can be closed. We would interpret the difference in terms of the *whole* pattern of educational opportunities associated with the social environment, and which may affect both the physical and mental development of the child.

Even those few scholars, however, who prefer an explanation in terms of race indicate that there is "overlapping" between the two racial groups. Overlapping is usually defined technically as the percentage in one group which is superior in test scores to the median or average score obtained by the other. *In every comparison with which we are familiar in this field there is some degree of overlapping.* This means more than that *some* Negro children are better than *some* white children. It means that some Negro children do better than the *average* white child, in spite of all the handicaps to which the former have in the past been subjected.

The conclusion is inescapable that any decision to use differences in the average achievement of the two racial groups as a basis for classifying in advance *any individual child,* Negro or white, is scientifically unjustified.

PROF. OTTO KLINEBERG, Columbia University
PROF. THEODORE NEWCOMB, University of Michigan
DR. GARDNER MURPHY, Menninger Foundation
PROF. NEVITT SANFORD, Vassar College
PROF. ROBIN WILLIAMS, JR., Cornell University
PROF. DAVID KRECH, University of California
PROF. JEROME BRUNER, Harvard University
PROF. ALLISON DAVIS, University of Chicago
PROF. DANIEL KATZ, University of Michigan
PROF. ANNE ANASTASI, Fordham University
PROF. STUART COOK, New York University
PROF. ISIDOR CHEIN, New York University
PROF. MARIE JAHODA, New York University
PROF. KENNETH CLARK, College of the City of New York
PROF. BINGHAM DAI, Duke University School of Medicine
PROF. IRVING LORGE, Teachers College, Columbia University
PROF. SOLOMON ASCH, Swarthmore College
DR. DAVID RAPAPORT, Austen Riggs Foundation

## A Southern Writer: Desegregation and Miscegenation*

WHAT may well be the most important physical fact in the story of the United States is one which is seldom emphasized in our history books. It is the fact that throughout the three and a half centuries of our existence we have kept our several races biologically distinct and separate. . . .

[Now] there lurks in ambush, as it were, another fact: we have suddenly begun to move toward abandonment of our 350-year-old system of keeping our races pure and are preparing to adopt instead a method of racial amalgamation similar to that which has created the mixed-blood nations of this hemisphere; except that the amalgamation being prepared for this country is not Indian and white but Negro and white. It is the deep conviction of nearly all white Southerners in the states which have large Negro populations that the mingling or integration of white and Negro children in the South's primary schools would open the gates to miscegenation and widespread racial amalgamation.

This belief is at the heart of our race problem, and until it is realized that this is the South's basic and compelling motive, there can be no understanding of the South's attitude.

It must be realized too that the Negroes of the U.S.A. are today by far the most fortunate members of their race to be found anywhere on earth. Instead of being the hapless victim of unprecedented oppression, it is nearer the truth that the Negro in the United States is by and large the product of friendliness and helpfulness unequaled in any comparable instance in all history. Nowhere else in the world, at any time of which there is record, has a helpless, backward people of another color been so swiftly uplifted and so greatly benefited by a dominant race.

What America, including the South, has done for the Negro is the truth which should be trumpeted abroad in rebuttal of the Communist propaganda. In failing to utilize this truth we have deliberately put aside a powerful affirmative weapon of enormous potential value to the free world and have allowed ourselves to be thrown on the defensive and placed in an attitude of apologizing for our conduct in a matter where actually our record is one of which we can be very proud.

We have permitted the subject of race relations in the United States to be used not as it should be used, as a weapon for America, but as a

_____

* From "Mixed Schools and Mixed Blood," by Herbert Ravenel Sass, in *The Atlantic*, November 1956, pp. 45-49. For model documentation see p. 47.

weapon for the narrow designs of the new aggressive Negro leadership in the United States. It cannot be so used without damage to this country, and that damage is beyond computation. Instead of winning for America the plaudits and trust of the colored peoples of Asia and Africa in recognition of what we have done for our colored people, our pro-Negro propagandists have seen to it that the United States appears as an international Simon Legree—or rather a Dr. Jekyll and Mr. Hyde with the South in the villainous role. . . .

Segregation is sometimes carelessly listed as a synonym of separation, but it is not a true synonym and the difference between the two words is important.

Segregation, from the Latin *segregatus* (set apart from the flock), implies isolation; separation carries no such implication. Segregation is what we have done to the American Indian—whose grievous wrongs few reformers and still fewer politicians ever bother their heads about. By use of force and against his will we have segregated him, isolated him, on certain small reservations, which had and still have somewhat the character of concentration camps.

The South has not done that to the Negro. On the contrary, it has shared its countryside and its cities with him in amity and understanding, not perfect by any means, and careful of established folk custom, but far exceeding in human friendliness anything of the kind to be found in the North. Not segregation of the Negro race as the Indian is segregated on his reservations—and as the Negro is segregated in the urban Harlems of the North—but simply *separation* of the white and Negro races in certain phases of activity is what the South has always had and feels that it must somehow preserve even though the time-honored, successful, and completely moral "separate but equal" principle no longer has legal sanction.

Until the Supreme Court decision forbidding compulsory racial separation in the public schools, the South was moving steadily toward abandonment or relaxation of the compulsory separation rule in several important fields. This is no longer true. Progress in racial relations has been stopped short by the ill-advised insistence of the Northern-directed Negro leadership upon the one concession which above all the white South will not and cannot make—public school integration.

Another word which is doing grave damage to the South today is prejudice, meaning race prejudice—a causeless hostility often amounting to hatred which white Southerners are alleged to feel in regard to the Negro. Here again the South, forgetful of the lessons of its past, has failed to challenge effectively an inaccurate and injurious word. Not prejudice but preference is the word that truth requires.

Between prejudice and preference there is a vast difference. Prejudice is a preconceived unfavorable judgment or feeling without sound basis. Preference is a natural reaction to facts and conditions observed or experienced, and through the action of heredity generation after generation it becomes instinctive. Like separateness, it exists throughout the animal kingdom. Though the difference between two races of an animal species may be so slight that only a specialist can differentiate between them, the individuals of one race prefer as a rule to associate with other individuals of that race. . . .

[It] is nonsense to say that racial discrimination, the necessary consequence of race preference, is "un-American." Actually it is perhaps the most distinctively American thing there is, the reason why the American people—meaning the people of the United States—are what they are. . . .

The truth is, of course, that there are many different kinds and degrees of racial discrimination. Some of them are bad—outdated relics of an earlier time when conditions were unlike those of today, and these should be, and were being, abolished until the unprecedented decree of the Supreme Court in the school cases halted all progress. But not all kinds of racial discrimination are evil—unless we are prepared to affirm that our forefathers blundered in "keeping the breed pure." . . .

[We] white Southerners prefer our own race and wish to keep it as it is.

This preference should not and in fact cannot be eliminated. It is much bigger than we are, a far greater thing than our racial dilemma. It is —and here is another basic fact of great significance—an essential element in Nature's huge and complex mechanism. It is one of the reasons why evolution, ever diversifying, ever discriminating, ever separating race from race, species from species, has been able to operate in an ascending course so that what began aeons ago as something resembling an amoeba has now become Man. In preferring its own race and in striving to prevent the destruction of that race by amalgamation with another race, the white South is not flouting Nature but is in harmony with her. . . .

. . . Unfortunately the opinion has prevailed outside the South that only a few Southerners hold this conviction—a handful of demagogic politicians and their most ignorant followers—and that "enlightened" white

Southerners recognize the alleged danger of racial amalgamation as a trumped-up thing having no real substance.

Nothing could be farther from the truth. Because the aggressive Northern-Negro leadership continues to drive onward, the white South (except perhaps that part which is now more Western than Southern and in which Negroes are few) is today as united in its conviction that its racial integrity must be protected as it was when the same conviction drove its people—the slaveholder and the non-slaveholder, the high and the low, the educated and the ignorant—to defend the outworn institution of Negro slavery because there seemed to be no other way to preserve the social and political control needed to prevent the Africanization of the South by a combination of fanatical Northern reformers and millions of enfranchised Negroes. The South escaped that fate because after a decade of disastrous experiment the intelligent people of the victorious North realized that the racial program of their social crusaders was unsound, or at least impracticable, and gave up trying to enforce it.

Now in a surging revival of that "Reconstruction" crusade—a revival which is part dedicated idealism, part understandable racial ambition, part political expediency national and international—the same social program is again to be imposed upon the South. There are new conditions which help powerfully to promote it: the Hitlerite excesses in the name of race which have brought all race distinctions into popular disrepute; the notion that the white man, by divesting himself of race consciousness, may appease the peoples of Asia and Africa and wean them away from Communism.

In addition, a fantastic perversion of scientific authority has been publicized in support of the new crusade. Though everywhere else in Nature (as well as in all our plant breeding and animal breeding) race and heredity are recognized as of primary importance, we are told that in the human species race is of no importance and racial differences are due not to heredity but to environment. Science has proved, so we are told, that all races are equal and, in essentials, identical.

Science has most certainly not proved that all races are equal, much less identical; and, as the courageous geneticist, Dr. W. C. George of the University of North Carolina, has recently pointed out, there is overwhelming likelihood that the biological consequences of white and Negro integration in the South would be harmful. It would not be long before these biological consequences became visible. But there is good hope that we shall never see them, because any attempt to force a program of racial integration upon the South would be met with stubborn, determined, and universal opposition, probably taking the form of passive resistance of a hundred kinds. Though secession is not conceivable, persistence in an attempt to compel the South to mingle its white and Negro children in its public schools would split the United States in two as disastrously as in the sixties and perhaps with an even more lamentable aftermath of bitterness.

For the elementary public school is the most critical of those areas of activity where the South must and will at all costs maintain separateness of the races. The South must do this because, although it is a nearly universal instinct, race preference is not active in the very young. Race preference (which the propagandists miscall race prejudice or hate) is one of those instincts which develop gradually as the mind develops and which, if taken in hand early enough, can be prevented from developing at all.

Hence if the small children of the two races in approximately equal numbers—as would be the case in a great many of the South's schools—were brought together intimately and constantly and grew up in close association in integrated schools under teachers necessarily committed to the gospel of racial integration, there would be many in whom race preference would not develop. This would not be, as superficial thinkers might suppose, a good thing, the happy solution of the race problem in America. It might be a solution of a sort, but not one that the American people would desire. It would inevitably result, beginning with the least desirable elements of both races, in a great increase of racial amalgamation, the very process which throughout our history we have most sternly rejected. . . .

That is the compelling reason, though by no means the only reason, why the South will resist, with all its resources of mind and body, the mixing of the races in its public schools. It is a reason which, when its validity is generally recognized, will quickly enlist millions of non-Southerners in support of the South's position. The people of the North and West do not favor the transformation of the United States into a nation composed in considerable part of mixed bloods any more than the people of the South do. Northern support of school integration in the South is due to the failure to realize its inevitable biological effect in regions of large Negro population. If Northerners did realize this, their enthusiasm for mixed schools in the South would evaporate at once. . . .

[The] underlying and compelling reason for the South's refusal to operate mixed schools—its belief that mixed schools will result in ultimate racial amalgamation—has been held virtually taboo and if mentioned in the North is not examined at all but is summarily dismissed as not worthy of consideration. The amalgamation "bogey," it is said, is not really believed by intelligent Southerners but is a smoke screen used to hide the South's real motives, which are variously described, ranging from plain sadism to a shrewd determination to deprive the Negro of education so that he can never displace the Southern white man. Besides, it is confidently alleged, the Negro does not wish to destroy the identity of his race by merging it with the white race.

Both those statements are incorrect. As already pointed out, the fear that mixed schools in the South would open the way to racial amalgamation is not a bogey or a smoke screen or a pretense of any kind but the basic animating motive of the white South in resisting the drive of the N.A.A.C.P. and its supporters. The second statement is as erroneous as the first. The Negro leaders do want racial amalgamation; they not only want the right to amalagamate through legal intermarriage but they want that right to be exercised widely and frequently.

It is only natural and human that they should feel this way. The truth is that these ambitious, intelligent, often amalgamated, and often genuinely dedicated Negro men and women feel about this matter exactly as white men and women would feel if they were similarly constituted and circumstanced—fusion of the two races would solve the Negro's problem at once. How much of the Negro rank and file consciously seeks amalgamation is a question; to the Southern Negro in particular the thought of intermarriage is still new and strange. As for the Northern leaders of the movement, some of them make no bones about it, and when they do evade the question they do so only for reasons of strategy. . . .

It is because there the adolescent and "unprejudiced" mind can be reached that the integrationists have chosen the Southern schools as their primary target; and it is precisely because the adolescent and therefore defenseless mind would there be exposed to brain-washing which it would not know how to refute that the white South will not operate integrated public schools. . . .

Many well-meaning persons have suddenly discovered that the tenets of the Christian religion and the professions of our democratic faith compel us to accept the risks of this hybridization. No one who will face up to the biological facts and really think the problem through can believe any such thing or see the partial suicide of the white race in America (and of the Negro race also) as anything other than a crime against both religion and civilization. . . .

. . . There is good hope that before too long this will begin to be recognized outside the South. The current pseudoscientific buncombe about racial identity is at last being questioned openly. It will be exploded completely with the ending of the leftist-liberal taboo which has practically sealed the lips of geneticists able and willing to discuss racial realities, and our Lysenko-like excursion in the realm of race will come to an end. Then it will be seen that the South, in maintaining the actuality and the great significance of racial differences, has not been "racist" in any evil sense but has been the defender of something permanently important to the whole American people; and that the Supreme Court, in launching the Negro on an offensive which cannot and should not succeed, has dealt a terrible blow to his advancement and his happiness.

## A Florida Sociologist: Conflict and Change in the "Solid" South*

THE SOUTH has been called many things; it is a region which inspires colorful adjectives. Romantic, feudal, gracious, courtly, chivalrous—some observers persist in seeing the South against a background of magnolia blossoms. Fighting, feuding, backward, disease-ridden, illiterate—others can only see Tobacco Road. Even those who strive for objectivity deal in stereotypes—the "Solid South," the "Democratic South," the "one-party South," the "agricultural South." In recent years the South's participation in the general national prosperity has evoked novel characterizations such as industrial, urban, progressive, awakening. These are hopeful adjectives appropriate to a "land of opportunity."

It is evident that the Region defies such simple, short-hand descriptions, just as it is evident that the old descriptions fit even more poorly now than they did in the past. Perhaps the most inept of all characterizations is that of "the solid South." Whether the term had as its referent political allegiance, voting behavior, or a broader complex of attitudes, the fiction that the South was ever "solid" has been maintained [not] only by ignoring the special interests and attitudes of large segments of the Region's citizens, notably Negroes, but also blocs of silent and disenfranchised whites. The elections of 1952 and 1956 served only to highlight a heterogeneity which has long existed in the South to a much greater extent than the defenders of the status quo have cared to admit.

At the risk of triteness, we may observe that the South properly can be described only as "changing." This, too, may be simply another one of

---

* From "Consensus in the Changing South," by Lewis M. Killian, in *The Phylon Quarterly,* second quarter, 1957, pp. 107-117. Presented in the Atlanta University School of Arts and Sciences Lecture-Forum Series, April 4, 1957. For model documentation see p. 47.

the hopeful adjectives which appeal to Chambers of Commerce and optimistic liberals alike. Accurate though the characterization may be, we need to look critically at the nature of this change. It may be satisfying to observe that the South is escaping from isolation and provincialism and that it is becoming more like the rest of America, but this does not mean that things are becoming better every day in every way, as some people seem to assume. . . .

Now when we consider just the mensurable changes which have taken place since 1940, it is evident that the South has come near to losing many of its distinctive regional characteristics. It is rapidly losing its distinctively rural and agricultural character. The rate of urban increase in the Southeast has been consistently higher than that of the United States since 1940. For an even longer period, the rate of increase of workers in industry has been much higher for the Southeast than for the rest of the nation. Furthermore, students of industry in the South have concluded that this industrial development has been not atypical but similar to that in other regions. Although the Region still lags, the gap between southern incomes and educational levels and those of the Nation has been narrowed. And, while the Region still has the largest non-white population in the Nation, every census shows a decrease in the proportion of Negroes in the population. Heavy out-migration of both whites and non-whites is one of the most significant population trends, one which does not seem to be abating. On the other hand, although we lack precise measurements of it, we may be sure that there has been a considerable exchange of population with other regions, particularly of white population.

These developments have been both result and cause of vast changes in the technology of the Region. Technological advances and rural population decline have been intimately related, as machines have displaced thousands of workers from the farm. Increased availability of hydroelectric power, the development of the pulp paper industry, and other developments have been accompanied by a diversification of industry comparable to the diversification of agriculture. Technological changes have reached into southern homes in a significant way in the form of household appliances and television sets.

The burgeoning of the southern economy has been accompanied by a re-alignment of interests and the adoption of new values. Old values, such as "States' Rights," have been joined with new interests such as Tidelands oil. While the causes of the Republican vote in the South in 1952 and 1956 are yet to be defined, we may suspect that the conservative economic policies identified with the Republican party find an increasingly sympathetic response in this new South. It was said of the Dixiecrat movement of 1948, "The ideology was promoted by a distinct social class, the middle class and/or upper middle class which derives its income from the new industries and branches of established northern industries which have arisen in the South." Although the Dixiecrat movement met the fate of so many Third Party movements, the interest groups which provided its leadership still remain as significant elements in the southern power structure. . . .

Keeping in mind the nature of the mores, to say that the mores of the South support segregation is to pretend that only white people can be southerners and that thousands of young white southerners do not find themselves in violent disagreement with their parents. As a matter of fact, the suspicion that Negroes are human beings and that segregation violates basic American values had considerable currency in the South before May 17, 1954. It did not have sufficient currency, particularly in the seats of power, to make it a subject of public discussion, however. Although it was an issue smoldering just below the surface of mass consciousness, the anonymous, impotent individuals who opposed segregation saw no way of bringing the issue to the surface for discussion and resolution. Attitudes opposing segregation, probably widespread among Negroes and scattered among whites, remained in the area of "private opinion" rather than becoming public opinion, which has been defined aptly as "the opinions you will express to a stranger."

Let it be recognized frankly that Negro leaders, rather than waiting for the further spread of these private opinions, chose the tactics of a social movement to bring about the change which they desired. Their strategy has been to use a traditionally prescribed means of requiring changes in overt behavior regardless of the extent of attitudinal support, namely court action.

This movement combines features of both a value-oriented movement and a control movement. Its leaders have sought to gain acceptance of a new definition of certain basic American values. But pending widespread acceptance of this definition, they have sought to secure for their people, through court action, a greater measure of control in the society in which they have so long been silent partners. In obtaining a favorable decision in the Brown case, the National Association for the Advancement of Colored People made important initial accomplishments. It forced into the mass consciousness the conflict of values which constitutes the American dilemma, and it laid the basis for a program of action in which the scattered individuals in the mass could participate. The tremendous increase in recent years in National Association for the Advancement of Colored People membership among Negro Southerners has changed the integration movement from an elite movement to a truly Southern movement with wide popular support.

This social movement has chosen to represent its goals symbolically, or in the form of a "myth" as conceptualized by Georges Sorel. That is, the objective of "complete desegregation by 1963" may be a star to which the followers are encouraged to hitch their wagon rather than a realistic goal. Such an ambitious goal plays an important part in sustaining a long, arduous campaign in the face of great odds. It constitutes an easy-to-visualize objective; its ambitious character is an antidote against the temptation to give up the struggle upon the attainment of intermediate objectives; and its immediacy imparts a sense of urgency that prohibits even a temporary relaxation of efforts.

Another significant feature of this movement is its relative lack of direct access to the agencies of mass communication in the South. This is a serious handicap and makes the proposal that the National Association for the Advancement of Colored People should satisfy itself with "educating the public" unrealistic. There is some compensation, however, in the fact that the newsworthiness of the activities of the movement results in gratuitous publicity. Thus it is reported that even unsympathetic press coverage of the proposal for a bus boycott in Montgomery contributed greatly to its success.

The most important feature of the integration movement that should be noted is its dependence upon organization. With the waging of costly legal battles as the principal tactic, the movement must funnel its support into a fund-raising, strategy-making nucleus. Without this, many of the followers would lapse back into the state of impotent, voiceless members of the mass.

While it forced the conflict of segregation and other values into the consciousness of the South, the National Association for the Advancement of Colored People did not succeed in making this an issue around which a genuine public formed. Instead, it evoked a counter-movement which seeks to deny the legitimacy of the new definition of values that the integration movement espouses and to prevent the followers of this movement from gaining any greater measure of control. The tactics employed by the defenders of segregation show that they constitute a counter-movement and not simply a segment of a true public. The emergence and the vigor of this counter-movement suggest that its members do not have confidence that the mores of the South do indeed support segregation. We may suspect that the vigor with which this movement is being prosecuted reflects the suspicion that a significant portion of both the white and Negro population of the South are no longer convinced of the absolute rightness of segregation. It is not just a movement to repel an invasion of new, non-traditional ideas; it is also a movement to restore and secure traditional values that are beginning to lose their hold in the society. The Agrarians of the late Twenties were the Casandras who predicted that the sort of changes that were beginning in the South would make such a movement necessary. The Dixiecrats of 1948 were the vanguard who sensed that the threat to traditional values and to long-dominant power groups finally had materialized. Those people who did not recognize until May 17, 1954 that the South was in an era of vast turmoil and social change were rather late in waking up!

The fundamental strategy of this counter-movement is to fight a long series of delaying actions. These delaying actions seem designed to exhaust the resources of the integration movement; to weaken its morale by making success seem increasingly remote; and to sustain morale in the segregationist counter-movement. The last objective is served by diverting attention from the conflict of values which is the central issue; offering a series of minor victories which, however, do not resolve the basic conflict; and proposing a variety of unrealistic goals such as interposition or a private school plan, to keep up the hopes of the following. Such realistic goals as resolving the issue by constitutional amendment rarely are proposed, probably because a favorable resolution by this method seems so unlikely to the leaders of the counter-movement. In fact, the counter-movement seems to have no long-range program but to depend upon one expedient after another.

An important tactic which marks this as a counter-movement is the attempt to restrict discussion of the issues. Here the contrast with the process that goes on in a true public is sharpest. The right to disagree is simply not conceded. Restriction of discussion is achieved in various ways. Crude methods, such as cross-burning and physical violence, are relatively unimportant in the total picture. More refined means, such as threats to job security and economic boycotts, are much more effective in that they do not so obviously violate important societal values. Perhaps the most effective measure is the limitation of frank and free discussion on the grounds that it will "cause trouble." This measure is effective because it is used most often by people occupying positions of power. That it precludes the formation of a public is evident, for we expect controversy in a public. That it is a tactic of the counter-movement is evident in the fact that the proponents of integration are so much more frequently defined as "trouble-makers" than are their opponents.

An aspect of the counter-movement that is worthy of serious study of social scientists is its ideology, that is, the conception of society and of history that is fostered to justify the movement and its program. We have seen, in the past two years, some interesting examples, formal and informal, of historical "revisionism." A "Golden Age" existing before May 17, 1954, has been created, in which most Negroes were happy, most white people were busy trying to make them happier, and in which no such thing as race conflict existed. All but forgotten facts concerning the manner in which the Fourteenth Amendment was passed have become suddenly matters of great interest, as have long-forgotten attempts to invoke the principle of interposition. The ideology also includes a projection of history, a prediction of things to come, with all the details of mediocrity in the classroom, violence on the school grounds, amalgamation, and an integrationist Gestapo graphically portrayed. And these are not just the spontaneous products of the imagination of the man on the street. They have been constructed skillfully and spread artfully by the intellectuals of the counter-movement.

Of equal interest to the student of this fascinating era should be the process of symbolization. To destroy effectively the opponents of a social movement it is desirable to define them as irresponsible, villainous, or both. Thus they are denied the right of appeal to the rules that would govern our conduct towards an "honorable opponent." Careful analysis of the contents of the mass media in the South would reveal a process of stereotyping the National Association for the Advancement of Colored People and other organizations as irresponsible and undeserving of "fair play." The implication that any organization which advocates integration is probably communist-dominated is a particularly important part of this process of symbolization. Developing an unfavorable set of symbols relating to the Supreme Court may have an important function as preparation for defiance of the law.

The tactic of discrediting the organized core of the integrationist movement is of special significance in the light of what has been said about the importance of organizations in a mass society. The intuition that the crippling of this organization would be the severest setback to the integration movement is no doubt a correct one. In a mass society the right to organize to advance one's views must be considered an essential freedom. Without it, traditional freedom of speech means little.

Desegregation is not the only issue that faces a changing South, but it is by far the most important. From the standpoint of American and Judaeo-Christian values, what is going on is not pleasant to behold. The challenge to the objectivity of the social scientist who tries to describe it is tremendous. Yet I believe that on whatever side of the issue Americans may find themselves, their idealism will be served best by a healthy admixture of realism. As a social scientist, I have endeavored to present a realistic analysis of the way in which an urban, changing South is undertaking to achieve consensus on this vital issue. What the content of a collective decision may be is not the only thing that is important to the citizens of a democratic society; how the decision is reached is equally important.

## An Arkansas Judge: Regional Tradition and National Law*

... WE COME now to an hour in our history when we must stop and take an inventory of our beliefs; and in this appraisal of our situation we must decide whether we do, in fact, believe in the principle of majority rule for our nation.

Now—in this hour of defeat and travail—just how much do we believe in government of our nation through democratic processes? How strongly do we honestly believe that under the American Way of Life every man must respect and obey the laws?

Are we—now that one of our regional traditions has been repudiated and set aside by the nation as a whole—going to, in turn, repudiate and disown our nation?

We find ourselves in the very uncomfortable position of being compelled to search our souls for a basic, fundamental principle upon which to chart our future course.

Shall we adopt segregation of the races as the bedrock, immutable ideal and cling to it at all costs? Shall we abandon democratic processes in our national government just so we can retain segregation? Shall we, once again, undertake to withdraw the Southland from the Union and create a new nation where segregation can be the law of the land? What is the deep down, underlying, fundamental all-important principle which you are willing to accept as the guiding light and spirit of all governmental decisions? Is it democracy? Is it segregation? What is it? You've got to answer that question for yourself before you are ready to help solve the problem of racial integration. . . .

---

* From a commencement address at Arkansas State College in August 1957 by Judge Lee Ward of Paragould (eastern Arkansas), former Commander of the Arkansas American Legion, *Arkansas Gazette,* August 25, 1957, p. 4E. For model documentation, see p. 12.

## A Virginia Editor: Some Conflicting Rights*

... [BECAUSE the critics of Governor Orval E. Faubus] are more numerous and more articulate than his supporters, the story has gone forth to the country of a "defiant" state executive acting from anti-Negro bias.

Now, ours is the greatest nation on earth for missing the forest in concentrating on the trees. The nine Negro pupils are not really very important in all this; their names will be as lost, one day, as the name of Gavrillo Prinzip, who fired the shot at Sarajevo. It is not important that the Mayor of Little Rock repudiated the Governor, or that earlier the voters of Little Rock had repudiated the Mayor, or that Mr. Faubus wants a third term, or that the judge came from North Dakota. It is not even vital to an understanding of the crisis at Little Rock that we read the rude remarks addressed to Dr. Benjamin Fine.

There are two great conflicts here. One is a conflict of powers. The other is a conflict of rights.

The first of these, contrary to popular impression, does not involve the Supreme Court's power to prohibit to a state the operation of racially separate schools. Other Southern governors have contested that action by the Court. Mr. Faubus has not. On the day that mobs swirled around Central High School in Little Rock, and Guardsmen barred nine Negro pupils from the school, integration began without interference in Fort Smith and Van Buren.

The conflict stems from a state's use of its police power; and on this point, on the basis of what is now known, let this be said without hesitation: So far, the State of Arkansas and Orval Faubus are wholly in the right; they have acted lawfully; they are entitled to those great presumptions of the law which underlie the whole of our judicial tradition. When Mr. Eisenhower assured Governor Faubus that "the Federal Constitution will be upheld by me by every legal means at my command," the assurance might well have been construed as support for the Governor's dramatic action. Mr. Eisenhower did not mean it that way, of course, but if the federal Constitution truly is to be upheld, then Mr. Faubus, at this writing, will have to be upheld. This is why:

The Police Power is an attribute of Sovereignty and a neces-

---

* From "Right and Power in Arkansas," by James Jackson Kilpatrick, editor of the Richmond *News-Leader,* in the *National Review,* September 28, 1957, pp. 273-275. For model documentation see p. 47.

sary attribute of every civilized government. . . . Consequently, it is inherent in the States of the American Union, possessed by every one of them as sovereign, and is not a grant derived from or under any written Constitution.

That is the way the section on "Police Power" begins in *American Jurisprudence*. More than this:

> The police power under the American constitutional system has been left to the States. It has always belonged to them and was not surrendered by them to the general government or directly restricted by the Constitution of the United States. It has repeatedly been held that no provisions of the Federal Constitution and none of the amendments added to that instrument were intended or designed to interfere with the police power of the several States.

And *Corpus Juris Secundum* says the same thing. . . .

[The] essential fact remains and ought not to be obscured: The preservation of public order is a power reserved to the states. . . .

There are not many Supreme Court precedents involving governors who have called out their militia. Three cases may be mentioned, one because it has been widely, and irrelevantly, recalled in the past two weeks, and the others because they shed some light on the issue.

The oldest precedent dates to 1809, when Governor Snyder of Pennsylvania called out a detachment of Guardsmen, under the command of General Michael Bright, to prevent a federal marshal from serving certain papers. The marshal served his papers anyhow; General Bright and his soldiers were tried and found guilty of obstructing justice. There was a colorful yarn behind all this, but it need not concern us here: The point is that Governor Snyder was not relying upon his state's police power to prevent a breach of the peace. He was, in fact, defying judicial authority in a way that Mr. Faubus, who walked upon his driveway and shook hands with the federal marshal, was not.

Considerably more in point is a case that arose a hundred years later in Colorado, when Governor James H. Peabody called out the Guard to maintain order in a bitter labor dispute. Under the Governor's direction, Guardsmen took into custody a union organizer named Mayer, president of the Western Federation of Miners, and held him for two and a half months. Mayer later sued the Governor for damages. The Supreme Court, in an 8-0 opinion by Holmes, stoutly upheld the Governor's action. The Court said that "great weight" must be given to a governor's determination of public unrest, and the Court added: "When it comes to a decision by the head of the state upon a matter involving its life, the ordinary rights of individuals must yield to what he deems the necessities of the moment. *Public danger warrants the substitution of executive process for judicial process.*" (My emphasis)

The case most often recalled in the past few days, however, is the "Sterling case" in Texas. This arose late in the summer of 1931, when the Texas Railroad Commission laid down some stringent regulations on the production of oil. Producers in East Texas objected strenuously—so strenuously, in fact, that Governor Ross Sterling in August issued a proclamation declaring that certain counties were in a "state of insurrection, tumult, riot, and a breach of the peace." He laid down what he termed "martial law," and sent Brigadier General Jacob F. Wolters to the oil fields to take charge. Governor Sterling himself decreed a production limit of 165 barrels per well per day (later reduced to 100 barrels), and Wolters enforced the order. In October, producers asked a three-judge federal court to enjoin the Governor and the General from enforcing military or executive orders "regulating or restricting the production of oil from complainants' wells." The court heard Governor Sterling's argument that a virtual "state of war" existed in the oil fields, and that his orders were "acts of military necessity to suppress actually threatened war." But the court dismissed these contentions, and granted the injunction. From this order Sterling appealed.

On December 12, 1932, a unanimous Supreme Court affirmed the lower court. One paragraph from Chief Justice Hughes' opinion has been widely quoted. Sterling had said his order was unreviewable by a federal court. Hughes said:

> If this extreme position could be deemed to be well taken, it is manifest that the fiat of a State Governor, and not the Constitution of the United States, would be the supreme law of the land; that the restrictions of the Federal Constitution upon the exercise of State power would be but impotent phrases, the futility of which the State may at any time disclose by the simple process of transferring powers of legislation to the Governor to be exercised by him, beyond control, upon his assertion of necessity. Under our system of government, such a conclusion is obviously untenable. There is no such avenue of escape from the paramount authority of the Federal Constitution.

But the critics of Governor Faubus, taking comfort from that paragraph, would do well to read on in the Sterling opinion. Keep in mind, too, that Governor Faubus at no time has contended his orders to the Guard are not subject to judicial review. Hughes went on to say, in the next paragraph:

> The application of these principles does not fail to take into account the distinctive authority of the State. In the performance of its essential functions, promoting the security and well-being of its people, the State must of necessity enjoy a broad discretion. . . . As the State has no more important interest than the maintenance of law and order, the power it confers upon the Governor as Chief Executive and commander-in-chief of its military forces to suppress insurrection and to preserve the peace is of the highest consequence. The determinations that the Governor makes within the range of that authority have all the weight which can be attributed to State action, and they must be viewed in the light of the object to which they may properly be addressed and with full recognition of its importance.

Hughes went on to say that a state governor is "appropriately vested with the discretion to determine whether an exigency requiring military aid . . . has arisen." And he asserted: "His decision to that effect is conclusive. . . . The nature of the power also necessarily implies . . . a range of honest judgment as to the measures to be taken in meeting force with force, in suppressing violence and restoring order." Having delivered itself of this dictum, as is the Court's frequent custom, the Court then brushed all these considerations to one side. The question before the Court, said Hughes grandly, "is simply with respect to the Governor's attempt to regulate by executive order the lawful use of complainants' properties in the production of oil." On that narrow issue, without passing upon the tumult in East Texas at all, the Court upheld the lower tribunal.

The point of all this is that a state is clearly within its lawful powers in calling out militia to maintain public order; the determination by a governor of conditions of turmoil is like a jury's finding of facts, and in such cases courts must act with the greatest care in substituting their judgment for that of a governor. If Governor Faubus can present substantial evidence of public unrest and threatened violence (he has not, like Governor Sterling, declared "martial law" or made bellicose charges of a "state of war"), he will have a strong case. . . .

The distinction between "rights" and "powers" is drawn carefully in the Constitution. The Ninth Amendment covers one, the Tenth the other; and when the Ninth asserts that the enumeration in the Constitution of certain rights shall not be "construed" to deny or disparage other rights retained by the people, it must be taken to mean that the courts, by the device of construction, shall not construe away those rights which are essential to the freedom and happiness of the people. It can mean nothing else.

It seems reasonable to assume that one of these rights, not enumerated, would be roughly the right that in real property is called the right of quiet possession—in general, the right to peace and tranquillity, the right to freedom from tumult and lawlessness. This is a sort of community right, a societal right, one retained not by the individual alone, but "by the people." And to get at the problem at hand, it may be suggested that the white parents of the South have some rights relating to the quiet education of their children under surroundings which they desire.

At the same time, the Supreme Court has created certain "rights" for Negro students. One of them, the right to attend a non-segregated public school, did not exist before May 17, 1954. The Court, taking a rib from the Fourteenth Amendment, simply created the right; and in doing so, the Court had to do a lawless thing. It seized from the states a power plainly reserved to the states. The Court undertook not to interpret the Constitution but to amend it.

Be that as it may, this supposed "right" came into being. Now the right, so created, of the Negro pupils of Arkansas to attend a desegregated school has come into conflict with the right, long established, of the people of Little Rock to enjoy domestic tranquillity. And the question that must be resolved is, Which is superior?

It is by no means a novel question. The Fifth Amendment guarantees that no man's property shall be taken "for public use" without just compensation. That is his right. But Congress and the courts have decided that a man's property may be taken from him for resale to another, willy-nilly, for construction of apartment houses that are not public but private. The right of the community to be free of slums, in brief, has been held to be superior to the right of an individual not to be deprived of his unoffending property. Or in a more familiar example, the Court has noted that the right of free speech gives no man the right to cry "fire!" in a crowded theater; the community's right, again, is superior. The freedom of religion guaranteed in the Constitution does not embrace the freedom of Faith Healers to handle rattlesnakes in public. And so it goes. The Community, no less than the individual, has rights.

It is true that in the past year or so, the Supreme Court, confronting such conflicts, has tended to put the rights of the individual above the rights of society. Thus, the right of a pro-Communist to practice law is superior to the right of California to deny him a license. The right of a

Negro rapist to a speedy trial is superior to the right of women in the District of Columbia to be protected from him. The right of Mr. Watkins to evade questions is superior to the right of Congress to ask questions. The right of Mr. Yates to advocate abstract overthrow of the government is superior to the people's right to internal security.

The crisis in Little Rock is a part of this pattern of conflicting rights. Conceding, for the sake of discussion, that the Negro pupil has these new rights, what of the white community? *Has it none?* Demonstrably, the enrollment of Negro pupils in hitherto white schools leads to far more than what the Court once termed mere "disagreement" with legal principles. Manifestly, race-mixing of certain schools now leads to knifings, dynamitings, and other forms of violence. And thus far, integration has touched only the outer fringes of the Deep South. By far the worst is yet to come. The question thus raised so formidably in Little Rock is whether the rights of the nine pupils override the rights of the 1,900 pupils, whether admission to a desegregrated school is a right superior to the right of a community to peace and order.

Something, somewhere, has to give. Either the states have broad powers to maintain public order, or they do not; either the people have a right to domestic tranquillity, or they do not. If the federal courts choose summarily to override the police power of the states, there is nothing much the states can do about it; and if the courts insist upon unyielding enforcement of the newly created rights of Negro pupils, the communities of the South may be reduced to chaos and blood may flow ankle-deep in the gutters, but there will be nothing much for the Southerners, white and black, to do but to turn to prayer and private schools.

Mr. Warren sowed the wind; he has not yet reaped the whirlwind. But when Mr. Faubus called out the Guard on September 4, Mr. Warren reaped a cold and ominous breeze carrying a hint of the storm ahead.

## A Little Rock Minister on Responsibility for the Crisis*

... THE Little Rock school board and Superintendent Virgil Blossom must share responsibility for the Little Rock debacle. Their whole approach to the task of making a transition from a dual to an integrated school system unwittingly invited the drastic action which Governor Faubus took on September 2 when he called out the national guard.

---

* From "Lesson from Little Rock," by Colbert S. Cartwright, pastor of Little Rock's Pulaski Heights Christian Church, in *The Christian Century*, October 9, 1957, pp. 1193-1194. Copyright 1957 Christian Century Foundation. Reprinted by permission of *The Christian Century*. For model documentation see p. 47.

It has been Faubus' contention that the Little Rock community "is not in the condition to have integration at the moment." This is a judgment impossible to prove or disprove. Many observers are convinced that the transition would have been made with a minimum of trouble if the governor had not interfered. There are other persons of both races who have watched with growing alarm the school board's development of an approach to the problem which disregarded everything experience has taught about human nature.

The general attitude of Dr. Blossom in explaining the plans for integration to white groups was that the prospect was as distasteful to him and the school board as to anyone else. His argument rested solely on the fact that the school board knew no way to get around the Supreme Court decision. He emphasized the wisdom of the school board's designing its own "deliberate" program to avoid having to take a faster route if a federal district court should delineate a plan. The superintendent explained the plan to anyone who would listen. He asked help from no one.

This approach to preparing the community for the mingling of the races in public schools revealed no awareness of the lessons taught by troublesome Clinton, Tennessee, or peaceful Louisville, Kentucky. Superintendent Omer Carmichael of Louisville has said that one thing was plain to him from the beginning: preparation for so radical a change has little hope of success unless it is a communitywide program. In *The Louisville Story* he explains the manner in which he sought to involve the whole community in a discussion of desegregation. He solicited help from parent-teacher associations, the Kentucky council on human relations, churches and church-related groups, women's clubs, civic groups and other organizations. He secured the cooperation of radio stations and disseminated literature on race relations. As the whole Louisville community became involved in thinking about race relations, the problem was seen not only from the legal but from moral, social and psychological points of view. . . .

In relationship to the community the Little Rock school board has consistently taken an autocratic approach. Carefuly avoiding consultation with either Negro or white patrons, the board on May 24, 1955, announced to the public a plan of gradual integration under which high school level grades would be desegregated probably in September 1957. If all went well integration would follow in the other grades over a period of approximately six years. Since no one had been consulted, many persons questioned the plan. Many Negroes wanted a faster plan; many white persons wanted no plan at all. Interested citizens, both Negro and white, went to Dr. Blossom with questions. When any point of the plan was questioned there was only one reaction—a defensive bristling.

Five months after the plan was announced the Arkansas council on human relations convened a meeting at Little Rock at which Dr. Blossom explained his plan. Irene Osborne, who had been working in Washington, D.C., to marshal community support for the school desegregation program there, spoke on the importance of community relations in making the transition. Dr. Blossom exhibited open hostility toward the approach she suggested.

In December 1955 the interdenominational ministerial alliance of Greater Little Rock, composed of Negro ministers, asked the school board to appoint an advisory committee, which would include Negroes, "to work in the direction of racial integration in the schools." The board not only declined, but refused to suggest any alternate way in which the Little Rock community might help in paving the way to a smoother transition. At about the same time, Dr. Blossom presented the plan of gradual integration to the Greater Little Rock ministerial alliance, composed of white ministers. The plan was received with general enthusiasm. But when the alliance suggested that it endorse the plan officially and publicly, Dr. Blossom urged it not to do so. To the present time he has not sought the help of ministers of either race in preparing the community for the board's plan of integration.

During the 1955-1956 school year professional educators in Little Rock became concerned because no preparation was being given high school teachers for the new problems they would face when integration came. They suggested to Dr. Blossom that informal meetings of teachers be arranged to discuss such problems. He did not think well of the suggestions, and at no time has he sought to help teachers face their own prejudices or to provide them with guidance in dealing with problems of group dynamics.

At a luncheon meeting on October 12, 1956, Robert Snyder, for three years chairman of the St. Louis council on human relations, explained to a number of Little Rock civic leaders the way in which 85 organizations in his city worked to help the schools meet the problem of school desegregation. Dr. Blossom was present, but indicated no interest in gaining such support from Little Rock agencies. On March 11, 1957, he explained the school board's plan to the community council, a group made up of representatives from all metropolitan area organizations and agencies concerned for civic betterment. Although he did not emphasize the need for preparing the community for school integration, he did state for the first time publicly that he would call on the various groups to help prepare the community. He did not say when. To date their help has not been requested.

During the past summer the Negro community grew uneasy as it saw the Little Rock school board doing all within its power to discourage Negro pupils from entering the previously all-white high school. A group of concerned Negroes went to Dr. Blossom with a complaint. He admitted that "screening" had been taking place, but defended it as being in the best interests of all. The Negroes suggested that it might be well if some channel of communication could be established between him and the Negro community. He readily agreed that it would be a good idea to have a committee which could help interpret to the Negro community what the school board was trying to do, and said he would call on the group the next week to work out details. But he never called. Throughout the summer months persons of both races, deeply concerned for the problems of human relations, became increasingly disturbed as they realized that the social forces of Little Rock were not being marshaled to aid in a smooth transition to integration. No one knew what might happen. There might be trouble, for which no one was ready.

Had the school board developed adequate plans with law enforcement officials for every eventuality? Several prominent Little Rock citizens investigated the possibility of bringing to the city a law enforcement official nationally known as an expert in the field of police-community relations to counsel quietly with local officials. When Dr. Blossom was approached on the possibility, he replied that he had adequately studied the problem and needed no outside help.

Governor Faubus' decision on September 2 to call out the troops and to block integration was the natural outcome of every step the Little Rock school board had taken. It had insisted all along that the only reason the schools were being integrated was that the federal government was forcing it to do so. It had consistently refused to seek the help of the community in gaining moral support for its reluctant step. Then the governor in shining armor came to the rescue. He said the school board did not need to integrate, that since the community was not prepared for integration there would be violence. He would call out the militia as the "preservator of the peace."

Dr. Blossom, the school board and Little Rock's leading citizens were stunned by Faubus' unprecedented actions. They did not want the governor to interfere. Knowing that some racial mixing in the public schools is inevitable, they would prefer to have it come about peacefully and on their own terms. What they failed to consider was that their whole approach had played directly into the hands of the members of white citizens councils. Having sought to prepare the community solely upon a legalistic basis, they had no defense when the governor, prompted by rabid segregationists in Little Rock, insisted he had found the needed loophole.

Three days after the governor ordered his troops to prevent integration in the name of states' rights, the school board found itself in the position of being on the governor's side. It went to federal court and petitioned the judge to suspend "temporarily" the plan of integration. This was exactly what the governor and his white citizens council cohorts were pleading for. The school board's house of cards had fully collapsed. Citizens who had agreed to compliance if there was no other way out now took fresh hope in the governor's action and the school board's acquiescence. Little Rock became sharply divided.

Arguments among Little Rock citizens will continue for years as to whether Governor Faubus got a square deal in federal court. Few will question why the problem arose in the first place. Fewer still will be aware of the responsibility the school board must share for the ridiculous situation which arose.

The experiences of Washington, Louisville and Clinton all point to the fact that transition, difficult at best, can come about only if all the resources of the community are marshaled to help. They have taught that the moral and social psychological aspects of the problem must be adequately considered. Little Rock tried a different path. On September 2 it was confronted with a "dead end" sign. It is still a question whether the school board can read the sign.

## A Little Rock Minister: Governor Faubus and the Calling of the Guard*

. . . IT IS UNLIKELY, at least at the beginning, that Faubus's primary motive was to capitalize upon the racial issue in Arkansas for political gain. Throughout his career Faubus has been careful to cultivate the steadily increasing Negro vote. He is the first Arkansas governor to appoint Negroes to the state Democratic Central Committee. In last year's campaign for election to a second term as governor, he successfully courted the large majority of the Negro vote.

Whatever else he may have achieved, he has certainly lost any support from that direction.

Nor could the governor have counted on improving his political posi-

---

* From "The Improbable Demagogue of Little Rock, Ark.," by Colbert S. Cartwright, pastor of Little Rock's Pulaski Heights Christian Church, in *The Reporter*, October 17, 1957, pp. 23-25. For model documentation see p. 47.

tion among segregationists by his actions on September 2—although the way events have turned out, he has now become their hero. At the very time he mobilized the militia, he pointed out that he was not opposed to the integration of other school districts in his state. He referred with pride to the peacful integration of state colleges during his administration. Those who have previously criticized his moderate stand still don't entirely trust the man, however much they may support him publicly.

No substantial evidence has been presented that Governor Faubus operated in concert with other Southern politicians to test the validity of the doctrine of "interposition." In the past Faubus has generally been regarded by governors and senators of the Deep South as a moderate on the question of integration, and his recent actions are not enough to convince them that he has made an about-face. He has tolerated and encouraged some integration, and it is doubtful whether extreme segregationists in the Deep South, or even in his own state, can ever really forgive him for that.

To understand why Governor Faubus took steps to defy Federal authority at Little Rock, it is necessary to know the man himself.

Despite a fairly commendable public record, on more than one occasion the governor has landed himself in untenable positions concerning internal problems. In the recent past he has gone down a series of blind alleys in attacking with little apparent foundation the administration of the girls' training school, the state highway department, and the state mental hospital.

On the day before the governor called out the state militia, a Little Rock reporter, George Douthit, raised the question why the governor so often placed himself in these positions. Douthit reported the explanation he had been given by one of Faubus's closest associates: "Faubus will fall for any story, however fantastic, if it is told with sufficient conviction." . . .

The press got a glimpse of Faubus's weakness for fantastic stories at his press conference a few hours after the armed militia turned nine Negro students away from Central High School.

In defending his order to the commander of the National Guard "to place off limits to colored students the schools heretofore operated or recently set up for white students," Faubus commented: "Now this report came to me this morning that when the Negro students, accompanied by parents, were attempting to enter, white students at the door shouted out to them, 'Let them come on in and we'll take care of them.' " The reporters he was talking to knew perfectly well that nothing of the kind had happened. The Negro children had approached school unattended by their parents, and the Guard stopped them a block away from the door, without commotion. . . .

There is a second personality trait that often gets Faubus into trouble: He is strangely reluctant about asking for competent advice.

I asked one of Faubus's closest associates how the governor usually makes his decisions. He replied: "Faubus just does not seek advice. He is possibly the most accessible governor in the Union to those who wish to catch his ear. He will listen to all who come to him. He will weigh their views to the best of his ability. The trouble with him is that often he does not hear all sides—or even the most important sides—to a problem."

I reminded him that when Faubus called out the militia he told his fellow Arkansans: "This is a decision I have reached prayerfully. It has been made after conferences with dozens of people and after the checking and the verification of as many of the reports as possible."

My informant, who is regarded by many to have the greatest single influence upon Faubus, replied that he had not been consulted by the governor in this matter. "Although I have been influential with the governor at many points, I have always had to go to him. Only twice has he called me for advice."

It would have been reasonable to expect that the governor in his "conferences with dozens of people" would have sought the advice of his five-man committee appointed for the purpose of studying the school problem as it relates to integration. None of these men was consulted by Faubus before he called the militia into action.

Nor did Governor Faubus consult the political leaders in eastern Arkansas, where the Negro population is proportionately largest and where the strongest demands have been made for state action against enforced integration.

It is important to note that eastern Arkansas' political leaders have not been happy about Faubus's handling of the Little Rock problem. They have been firm in approving his earlier and oft-repeated stand against "forcible integration." They have also agreed with the governor that "These matters must be left to the will of the people in the various districts. The people must decide on the basis of what is best as a whole for each particular area."

The foremost legal mind of the eastern Arkansas segregationists, R. B. McCulloch, Sr., of Forrest City, has designed all segregationalist legislation upon this basis. But he has publicly stated more than once that a school-assignment law will be upheld by the courts only if there is some at least minimal racial mixing in the schools.

The Little Rock school board's use of the school-assignment law to whittle down a possible integration of 250 Negro pupils to nine—and with Federal court approval—was exactly what eastern Arkansas political leaders wanted. It proved that generally their strategy of keeping racial mixing to the barest minimum would be successful. But they were not consulted.

The simple fact is that a small group of extreme segregationists at Little Rock sized up the governor and sold him a bill of goods based an fabrications. It never crossed the minds of the moderate segregationists that the governor would alter his past strategy in dealing with the Little Rock situation. Everyone but Citizens' Council members assumed he would keep hands off. . . .

According to responsible sources, it was not until Representative Brooks Hays, a fellow Southern Baptist, went to see Faubus that the governor was made to see the impossible position he was in. Hays, a close friend of Presidential Assistant Sherman Adams, knew at first hand that the Federal government in no way could or would back down. He knew there was a stern commitment to use whatever force necessary to uphold the Federal court's ruling that the process of integration should begin immediately at Little Rock.

Up to the time that Hays got in touch with Faubus, the governor had heard nothing from political advisers except the Citizens' Council line. "Until Hays went to Faubus," a person close to both men told me, "it had not crossed the governor's mind that he might not win his battle against the Federal court."

It now appears that Faubus had gone too far before Hays began his efforts to help the governor find a way to retreat gracefully. It might have been a different story if Hays had gotten there sooner, or if Faubus had less of the curious mixture of timidity and rashness that keeps him from seeking advice.

Orval Faubus, stumbling into one of the greatest constitutional crises the United States has faced since the Civil War, has now come to believe that his only salvation lies in gaining whatever political advantage he can from his predicament. And when the state militia was federalized and the troops of the 101st Airborne Division began patrolling Central High School with bayonets, Faubus found it fairly simple to raise himself to his highest crest of popularity, at least among a certain segment of the population.

Whether he planned it that way or not, the role of a segregationist leader was automatically thrust upon him from the moment Federal troops marched into Little Rock.

## A Magazine Reporter on Congressman Hays*

. . . HIS WEARINESS does not proceed from any great fear about his own political future. At fifty-nine, after having been elected to eight consecutive terms, he feels that the voters have enough confidence in him to tolerate the deviations that enable him "to try to hold a Northern audience to plead the South's valid cause." He was pleased by a newsman's report of what an elderly constituent had said when asked if the voters were changing their minds about their congressman: "Mr. Hays finished? No, sir. I don't always agree with him, but he's an institution around here. We don't hold anything against *him.*"

Although he has made quite clear his conviction that the Supreme Court decision on integration must be upheld in Little Rock, he had previously joined with the rest of the Arkansas delegation in signing a manifesto criticizing the decision.

He considers himself a moderate . . .

"It's an awful feeling for me," he remarked, "being introduced as the congressman from Little Rock and having people look at me so strangely." He is troubled by a report that the name of Little Rock was booed during a performance of *South Pacific.* And yet he has managed to maintain his sense of humor: "I heard a story about a double translation. 'Little Rock' was translated into Russian and from Russian back into English and came out 'Small Stone.' I said, 'Let him who is without sin cast the first small stone.' "

He contends that none of us—North or South, white or Negro, Republican or Democrat—is completely without sin in the midst of "the most complex set of social forces in the world's history." The Little Rock affair, he believes, has shown the South that our Constitutional system of government rests on the acceptance of court orders; it has shown the North that the "casual fitting of a revolutionary idea to well-established customs" is not an easy matter. "Since neither military force nor massive resistance works, we must try friendly persuasion." . . .

---

* From "Mr. Hays of Arkansas Meets His Responsibilities," by Natalie Davis Spingarn, in *The Reporter,* November 14, 1957, pp. 25-26. This article was written on the eve of the election, which Mr. Hays, to the surprise of many, lost to Dale Alford, a write-in candidate. For model documentation see p. 47.

"In Little Rock," Mr. Hays remarked, "the governor is not seeking the favor of the city but of the county-courthouse politicians. In his bid for their support, he is making a coldly calculated response to a political situation." . . .

## A Magazine Writer: Behind the Governor's Decision*

THE DAY Gov. Orval Eugene Faubus called out the Arkansas National Guard, he told William J. Smith, his personal attorney and close friend: "I can't win, Bill." . . .

"If there's trouble or violence out there tomorrow, the integration crowd will say I provoked it by bringing in troops," said Faubus.

"But if I don't call the guard and some children are killed, the other side will say the blood is on my hands. I've got to act on the side of safety. When I testified in Chancery Court last week, I said there might be violence. Now, I'm convinced of it."

Was this a sincere man voicing the dilemma of authority, or was he a man who had yielded to the pressure of racial extremists and who sought to rationalize his surrender? Only Orval Faubus knows the true answer, but his countrymen may judge him by what actually happened.

Events leading to the dreadful showdown that wise men hoped could be avoided had rushed with a kind of Wagnerian fatalism in the last 13 days in the slow, orderly city of Little Rock.

The first incident occurred August 20, when Governor Faubus telephoned Gov. Marvin Griffin of Georgia, No. 1 spokesman of Dixie resistance, at Atlanta. Griffin was due in Little Rock two days later to address the Capital Citizens Council, which was fighting integration in Little Rock.

"Governor," said Faubus, "I've heard that one of your party may make inflammatory statements here. Our town is tense. If that's true, I'd rather you wouldn't come."

"Naw," said Griffin. "I'm gonna give 'em hell on the Constitution and Roy (Roy V. Harris, former Georgia state senator and Citizens Council leader) is gonna give 'em hell on the civil-rights thing. But nobody will advocate violence."

"In that case," said Faubus, "you're welcome. You and your party

---

* From "The Real Little Rock Story," by Fletcher Knebel, in *Look*, November 12, 1957, pp. 31-33. Copyright © 1957 by Cowles Magazines, Inc. For model documentation see p. 47.

come stay at the mansion. I'm speaking out of town that night, but you have breakfast with me."

When the Georgians arrived at Little Rock Municipal Airport, state troopers met them. Governor Griffin took the honors. Harris pulled a Capital Citizens Council delegation aside. He explained why his party had accepted the mansion invitation from Faubus, then considered by segregationists to be a "moderate" in the grip of enemy advocates of integration.

"Why," said the exuberant Harris, "havin' us at the mansion's the worst thing could happen to Faubus. It'll ruin him with the integrationists and the liberals."

That night of August 22, Griffin and Harris spoke at a $10-a-plate Capital Citizens Council dinner to raise funds to fight entry of Negroes in the schools. A crowd of 350 heard Griffin vow that Georgia public schools would never be integrated while he was governor. Harris went further and said the guard, state patrol and posses would be used to keep Negroes out of the schools.

"That's what put Faubus on the spot," Harris recalled later. . . .

At the CCC rally, Governor Griffin had heard complaints that Governor Faubus wouldn't come over to the segregation side. A group decided to call on the governor individually and "put some backbone in him," as one expressed it. Other segregation leaders pounded at Faubus, declaring his political future was nil if he failed to halt Negroes at the doors of Central High. Little Rock heard that political backers in the east Arkansas planters' country, where the word "integration" is poison to the tongue, were hammering at him.

No evidence of such calls has been produced, but words were not needed to tell Faubus that his political future did not lie in Little Rock, which had accepted the coming of integration, however reluctantly, but in the state of Arkansas. The facts seemed apparent. No man who failed to side with the segregationists could hope to carry Arkansas in 1958, when Faubus' present term ends. . . .

Letters, wires and phone calls drummed on the executive mansion after the CCC rally. Most stressed one theme: Keep the Negroes out. Jimmy Karam, who had conferred quietly with segregation leaders around the time of the CCC rally, was in and out of the mansion.

Was Faubus' mind already made up by Thursday, August 29, to call out the guard? There is one solid clue. Some time during that day— the day he testified in Chancery Court—he got in touch with Maj. Gen.

Sherman T. Clinger, state adjutant general and commander of the Arkansas National Guard, and gave him secret orders to "prepare" the guard for possible action.

The exact content of what Faubus said to Clinger remains hidden, but General Clinger says it was of such a nature that the official guard call, shortly after 3 p.m. Monday, came as no surprise. . . .

At no time in this hectic week end did Faubus tell callers that he had informed General Clinger as early as Thursday to be "prepared" to muster the guard. At no time did he consult on the legality of the move with Bruce Bennett, Arkansas attorney general and prospective candidate against Faubus for governor next year.

Labor Day morning, September 2, was a period of growing resolution for Faubus. It was at noon, as he later recalled, that he decided finally to call out the National Guard.

He telephoned his lawyer, Bill Smith, found he was playing golf. Faubus sent an emissary to wait at the 18th green of Riverdale Country Club.

Smith called Faubus from the home of Ted Morley, who had played in the day's foursome. "I've tried to get you since noon, Bill," said Faubus. "I need you at the office in the capitol."

"I'm going to call out the guard," the governor said simply when Smith arrived. The lawyer was surprised. Only 24 hours before, Faubus had indicated, in a lengthy conversation with Smith, that he would make no move until after Central High opened Tuesday—presumably with Negroes sitting beside white children for the first time. . . .

Clinger asked for his orders, was told to use his "discretion." (The governor and the general say there was no order Monday to bar the entry of Negroes. Faubus issued such an order Tuesday.)

Faubus arranged for TV time, began work on a speech. He said not a word to local authorities. First word that the guard had been called came at 9 p.m., when an *Arkansas Gazette* newsman, on his way home, saw troops surrounding Central.

The school board was in emergency session at the Albert Pike Hotel. Harry Ashmore, executive editor of the *Gazette,* called Superintendent of Schools Virgil T. Blossom out of the meeting. "The governor's called the guard," said Ashmore. "My God!" said Blossom. The meeting broke up, to hear Faubus on TV. Board members were stunned. So was the nation. . . .

## A Harvard Historian: Some Causes and Consequences of the Little Rock Episode*

THE PUZZLING course, in recent months, of the struggle for equal rights for the Negro reflects the dominant mood of American politicians today. The conjunction of victory with defeat, of crablike advance and prudent withdrawal, is the consequence of the overwhelming acceptance of the politics of moderation.

It has become a truism that effective political action depends upon compromise. Only by evading issues, and particularly ideological issues, can a statesman retain enough support to permit the placid operation of government. Any showdown is to be avoided as far as possible, for it alienates substantial segments of power and opinion.

Yet a policy that makes moderation the highest virtue runs the grave risk of exposing itself to the pressures of extremists who keep raising the price of their acquiescence. Moderation is often mistaken for weakness, and thus becomes a standing temptation to the blackmailer. This has been the history of Negro rights since 1954. . . .

It is easy today to lose sight of the fact that the Supreme Court decision of 1954 was a moderate one. While the Court struck down the principle of segregation, its ruling permitted such latitude of adjustment as to make almost any outcome possible. On the question of segregation in the public school system it could hardly have ruled otherwise than it did, and its ruling was unanimous. The right of all citizens to equal education, after all, had been established more than eighty years earlier, when the Fourteenth Amendment forbade states to discriminate among citizens on the basis of race; and no one, then or now, has challenged this constitutional provision. In 1954 the Court did no more than review its own opinion, expressed sixty years earlier, that segregated institutions might provide equality of treatment. It found, as a matter of fact, that segregation had actually borne the implication of inequality, and ordered the abolition of the existing system of separate schools. But it did not prescribe the exact manner in which abolition should be effected. It expected that local conditions would dictate the mode of enforcement; and it hoped that, given good will, a gradual process of accommodation would

---

* From "Civil Rights after Little Rock—the Failure of Moderation," by Oscar Handlin, professor and Pulitzer Prize historian, in *Commentary,* November 1957, pp. 392-396. For model documentation see p. 47.

adjust the Southern educational system to the requirements of the law with "all deliberate speed."

In retrospect, it is arguable that this vagueness may have been unfortunate. If the Court had prescribed a firm line of action, as it did in the cases of higher education and transportation, it might have secured quicker compliance. The segregationists would certainly have found it more difficult to mobilize the forces of resistance. No doubt the public elementary and high schools involved more touchy issues and called for a more painful transition than did the universities or interstate trains. But the interval between the decision and the effort at enforcement gave the enemies of the decision an opportunity to explore the means of frustrating it.

In areas where compliance was prompt, the decision evoked least opposition. The pattern of segregation simply fell away. Perhaps the problem was less complicated in the Border states than in the Deep South. Yet Baltimore and the District of Columbia have Negro populations as dense as in most Georgia counties, and the habits of segregation had been almost as fixed in those cities as in the rural South. The certainty of integration, however, was so strong that the opposition never took shape. In Delaware, a protest movement developed too late to be effective, and collapsed. But elsewhere there was delay, and this enabled the segregationists to gather strength and stir up public opposition. In doing so they were encouraged by the period of indecisive political maneuvering that began with President Eisenhower's illness in October 1955. . . .

The whole issue acquired a new cast in the fall of 1955. President Eisenhower's illness in effect advanced the Presidential election by a whole year. In the months that followed, uncertainty as to the President's health dominated the nation's political thinking. In the Democratic party, and particularly in the Stevenson camp, there was considerable confidence —in which the wish was father to the calculation—that Eisenhower would not run. Relieved of the necessity of dealing with the magic of Ike's name, and cheered on by discontent in the farm belt, the Democrats imagined they could readily regain their primacy of the 1930's and 1940's. The Congressional elections of 1954 seemed to confirm that estimate of the situation. It therefore seemed more important to concentrate on the nomination than on the election. Stevenson had few doubts that he could be renominated, but he wished to lead a united party that would be certain to win in November. And to keep the party united meant to appease the Southerners who had bolted openly in 1948 and defected surreptitiously to the GOP in 1952.

Stevenson himself had always been a moderate. But moderation in 1952 had been located somewhere between the strong desegregationist position of Governor Williams of Michigan and the strong pro-segregationist position of Senator Russell of Georgia. By the end of 1955, however, moderation had moved over to some point between the positions of Stevenson and Russell. Stevenson therefore found it necessary to soothe Southern sensibilities; and the convention of 1956 witnessed a further retreat on the civil rights issue. By the time it became clear that Eisenhower would run and that the election would be a serious contest, it was too late to shift the grounds of the campaign. The net result was to encourage the intransigent Southern wing of the Democratic party. The Republicans were under no pressure to take a vigorous stand; and the liberal Northern Democrats were isolated by the resounding defeat of the Truman-Harriman group. Certainly nothing in the vague platitudes uttered in the course of the campaign of 1956 was likely to arouse Southern fears that the government, whether Republican or Democratic, would act positively to enforce the law. . . .

As in the decade before the Civil War, the extremists of the Deep South were above all anxious to avoid isolation from the Border states. Alone, they counted for little in national affairs; that had been demonstrated in 1850 and again in 1948. Only association with the larger Southern grouping enabled the die-hards to make their weight felt. And the Civil Rights Bill was an ominous foreshadowing of what might come, precisely because the Border-state Congressmen had taken an independent line. If this persisted it might lead to a broad realignment in which the Deep Southerners would suffer. Hence the importance of the school issue. Not only was integration in the Border states a threat to segregation everywhere, it was also the decisive test of whether the extremists in the Deep South would be isolated or not. Their strategy was to provoke a conflict over integration that would mobilize the broadest possible range of opinion in their support.

This was the meaning of Little Rock. Few contemporary social crises have been as well reported as that which began with the visit by Governor Griffin of Georgia to Governor Faubus of Arkansas. The facts are clear, and only the deep dismay at the way in which they unfolded has prevented an accurate assessment of their meaning.

Little Rock is not a Deep Southern, but a Border city; the percentage of Negroes in its population is smaller than in Washington or in Baltimore. The problem of adjusting its schools to the Court's decision should have been no more difficult there than in the District of Columbia or in Maryland. The integration plan adopted in Little Rock was moderate, to be slowly worked out over a long period; indeed, it was challenged in the courts by Negroes unhappy at the snail-like pace it anticipated. There is every indication that the public was fully prepared to accept it. Why then the conflict which led ultimately to the use of Federal troops? Not, we may be sure, out of fear of integration as such, which elsewhere in Arkansas proceeded peacefully, but from a desire to make political capital out of the problem. This was the riposte of the extremists.

The fear of the politicians of the Deep South that they might be isolated underlay the situation; the ambitious demagogy of Governor Faubus precipitated the crisis. Every step taken by the Governor has shown not only lack of candor but also a determination not to allow the problem which he created to be resolved peacefully. In the face of such determination the moderates were helpless. Having abjured the use of force to implement the law, the President at first saw no means of acting at all. In the hope that moderation would lead to a compromise, he consented to negotiate with the Governor rather than condemning him out of hand. This temperate attitude encouraged Faubus to violate the agreement that seems to have been reached at his meeting with the President at Newport. Then at last Eisenhower lost patience and ordered the troops to act.

But the course of moderation had even then not run out. The eagerness for compromise asserted itself again at the President's conference with the four Southern governors, until once more Faubus showed he was not to be compromised with. The President had originally announced that the conference would deal with the whole issue of integration. When the governors appeared, however, he acquiesced to having the question narrowed to that of troop withdrawal. But Eisenhower found that the only reward of moderation was to encourage the Governor of Arkansas in his intransigence.

The Little Rock incident has shown clearly—what the long experience with demagogues in a democracy should long since have revealed—that moderation works only with moderates. Extremists are ruthless, and moderation (which they identify with weakness) only stimulates them to increase their demands. At some point the moderate must either take a stand and fight back, or yield entirely. There is a striking parallel in this respect between the administration's handling of the segregationists and its handling of McCarthy. And in the final showdown, the one may prove to be as empty a threat as the other. . . .

## *A Southern Author on a New Kind of Mob**

WITH A FEW shining exceptions, when crisis has come to the Southern community the mob has come also; agitators have moved in; the people have seemed indifferent to law and order; the demagogues have put on their usual subversive act; the unwashed and illiterate and criminal and psychotic elements have taken over our streets. And we who think we are free and strong and intelligent suddenly realize we are dominated—not by a dictator but by a dictating idea.

The realization comes to us slowly but it finally strikes deep: that this dictating idea is embodied in a rabble so powerful that the police force, the churches, the best leadership of the community are helpless to deal with it.

How is this possible? Where does the mob's strength come from? It must have enormous strength to paralyze the people as it seems to do. It, apparently, has an almost magic power over men's minds for again and again we have watched a community grow mute and helpless when the mob gathers on the street.

But, when one looks for its strength one is puzzled. Actually, this mob which I shall call Mob No. 1, is few in number, its members are weak in community influence, many of them have criminal records, their intelligence quotients would certainly run pretty low; they are nothing but the riffraff, the hoodlums with no visible source of strength at all.

Then where on earth does their power come from?

To find its source, we must take two journeys:

The first one will be short. All we need do is walk over to Main Street and enter a few modern air-conditioned offices. There, sitting at their desks, are the men who quietly protect the rabble and give it its hidden strength. Some of these men are bankers, doctors, lawyers, engineers, newspaper editors and publishers; a few are preachers; some are powerful industrial leaders; most are known only in their home towns and state; but others have important connections in New York City and Washington. They hold not only economic power but moral and civic power, for they sit on church and education boards, on health boards, on various local and state planning committees.

This is Mob No. 2. Not all our business and professional men be-

---

* From "No Easy Way, Now," by Lillian Smith, Southern author, in *The New Republic*, December 16, 1957, pp. 12-14. For model documentation see p. 47.

long to it, by any means. But many do. It is a quiet well-bred mob. Its members speak in cultivated voices, have courteous manners, some have university degrees, and a few wear Brooks Brothers suits. But they are a mob, nevertheless. For they not only protect the rabble, and tolerate its violence, they *think in the same primitive mode,* they share the same irrational anxieties, they are *just as lawless in their own quiet way,* and they are dominated by the same "holy idea" of white supremacy.

They don't dynamite houses and churches—they leave that to Mob No. 1. They smother: By their use of boycott, by their quiet threats, and economic pressures, by suppression of news, they strip college professors, school teachers, preachers, writers, reporters, editors, students, their own employees, and many other white Southerners of their Constitutional rights to speak and write—and to be heard. These are precious rights to Americans. A man who takes them away from us is a law-breaker, as much one as is the rough-neck who throws his weight around on the street. And, in my opinion, far more dangerous.

Yet, because most people think only something noisy is violent, they tend to be deaf to this insidious form of spiritual violence, this whispered contempt for law—which is taking over much of our South, and is creeping into the North, also.

The men in Mob No. 2 are, for the most part, responsible, sensible, professional and businessmen who have often shown a generous concern for the welfare of their community. They are usually completely reliable in their business affairs. Then why would they play this shabby role of protector of the street mob? Why would they be willing to strip their fellow-citizens of their freedom of speech and belief? Do we know? I am not sure that they, or we, understand their motivations.

But we need to understand. We need to find out why they are willing to risk so much of our future for so little of our past.

To find the answer, we must search for Mob No. 3.

This will take us on a much longer journey. For it leads us back home into the secret places of our hearts and minds. Mob No. 3 lives in the depths of every man's mind: It is activated by primitive fears, hatreds, guilts, some of which have nothing whatever to do with race. It is nourished on anxiety about the body image, on anxiety about our personal relationships, and on the terrors that rise like a miasma from ancient myths of birth, death, blood, heredity, animals, darkness.

Mob No. 3 makes its home on the prehistoric, mythical level of the human mind. We are born possessing that symbolizing layer of mind

—and everybody in the South seems to have an extra amount of it! It is a pity that reason is not also born in us. But we know . . . that it is not: It is a talent, a skill, a method that has to be developed; . . .

In the South, we long to be good; but we rarely tolerate criticism when we are bad. We want to be Christian; but we rarely permit clergymen to subject our way of life to the spiritual test of Christ's teachings. We long to be learned and we admire the physical sciences and the technologies, but we turn away from knowledge of our own minds and hearts and human relationships. We are not only afraid to talk about race we are afraid of all inquiry that comes close to man, himself. We are afraid of biology, psychology, psychiatry, psychoanalysis, afraid of all the social sciences. We are profoundly embarrassed when someone suggests that we look at the human condition as the existentialists are, today, urging us to do. We shudder and turn away as if we were shown a dirty picture.

Above all else, we are sensitive to criticism from our own fellow-Southerners; so much so, that we try to punish them if they dare warn us that we are close to disaster. We Southerners are endowed with a powerful and potentially creative imagination that could produce a rich culture and a great people. I believe that. But because we refuse to let it mate with critical intelligence and ethics, with poetry and mysticism, and compassion, it tends to produce not strong, vital, free creative individuals but sex-obsessed mobs; it thrusts up out of our soil not great leaders but irrational obscene demagogues; it produces not healthy-minded, morally strong children but children torn and ambivalent—weakened by learning to love ideals which they are commanded, even by state laws, not to live; confused, and made apathetic by their culture's inexorable directive to fit the moral necessities of the atomic age to the narrow framework of their grandfather's code.

It is such a pity. It is more: It is our great tragedy. Like Medea, when she brought her murdered children to their father, we can cry: *I have done it: because I loathed you more than I loved them. Mine is the triumph. . . . I tore my own heart and laughed: I was tearing yours.*

Are all Southerners like these I have described? Are we all bereft of self-criticism? and blind? and complacent? and avenging? Aren't some of us decent, sensitive, reasoning, honest, compassionate human beings who measure up well when compared to the best in our nation and other countries?

Of course. There are hundreds of thousands of Southerners who do. Perhaps millions. But their moral weight in their own region is as light as a handful of feathers. For they are hushed and silent. They do not speak out. They know: but they do not say what they know. They feel: but they do not act out what they feel.

Why don't we Southerners speak, in time?

Because we fear economic reprisals from Mob No. 2? Yes. Because we fear physical violence from Mob No. 1? Yes. But there is another reason:

To speak against segregation is taboo. More of a taboo than to break segregation by our acts. There are reasons why we feel the strength of this taboo: We were taught from early childhood never to speak against segregation and never to question it. Our honest young eyes might see its cruelty and did. But we must not admit it. It was our Lesson No. 1; and most of us learned it well. . . .

## A Washington Journalist: The Pace of Integration*

THE greatest single reward I have had as a result of my long and continuous efforts on behalf of our Negro fellow citizens is that we tell one another the truth—a rare achievement between the two races. Just after World War II, I was dining with seven members of the faculty at one of our Negro universities. In the course of conversation a young instructor said to me: "Mrs. Meyer, after Pearl Harbor I couldn't help feeling a secret exultation that a colored race had clobbered the white man." "My friend" I replied, "never forget that despite failures and injustices, Americans have done more for the Negro than any other nation on the face of the globe. We fought a civil war to establish his freedom. Since then thousands of whites in high and low positions have exhibited an interest in the Negro's welfare and development never before shown by a dominant race. On the whole the treatment of the Negro in America constitutes not an indictment but one of the greatest achievements of a democratic nation." . . .

. . . Instead of lamenting over Little Rock, we should emphasize that in the Border States from Maryland to west Texas more than 350,000 Negro children who formerly went to segregated schools have already entered mixed classes.

This is a good beginning. But I am deeply concerned that so few

* From "Race and the Schools—A Crisis North and South," by Agnes E. Meyer, author and authority on public schools, in *The Atlantic,* January 1958, pp. 29-34. Copyright © 1957 by The Atlantic Monthly Company. For model documentation see p. 47.

people recognize the extent to which the burden of guiding this major revolution is being thrown upon school boards, administrators, and teachers unprepared for so gigantic a task of social engineering. All this at a time when our schools are already bulging with pupils and our overworked and underpaid teachers are struggling to maintain educational standards in badly equipped schools. Ill-considered, hasty attempts at integration, especially when carried out in impoverished and overcrowded schools, instead of furthering the education of the Negro will surely result in the retardation of all students, white and Negro, and increase rather than alleviate racial tensions.

Before our emotions became overwrought, we were committed to the *expansion and improvement* of our public schools as educational institutions where the young can learn to live together not as blacks and whites but as American citizens. This is still our first objective. The education of the white child must not be sacrificed for the Negro, nor that of the Negro for the white, or both races will lose and the future of our nation be imperiled.

I shall not argue the right or wrong of a question to which a democratic people can make but one answer. Instead I shall make a plea both to Northerners and Southerners and especially to Negro leaders for moderation in their attitudes toward this difficult problem and in the interpretation of those words, "deliberate speed." The chief responsibility for leadership is still that of the white population. And the Negro should realize, now that the power of the law supports his demands, that he is no longer in the position of an aggressor but of a partner in its orderly implementation. . . .

The public school has always been the mainstay of our social and industrial fabric. But today it has an increased and vital importance in our complex, interrelated technological society, due to our need for more and more highly trained people. Education is now *the prime function of the modern state*. The serious defeat we suffered when the Russians launched their satellites has belatedly awakened us to this elementary truth.

For the first time in our history we are running short not only of scientists, engineers, and technologists but of the brain power required to maintain and develop our massive and infinitely complex industrial organization. We need this educated man power, and the source of supply begins in the public schools! . . .

Can it be done? Can we absorb millions of Negro children, many of them retarded, into our schools and at the same time improve the educational process for both races? Only if the American conscience is aroused and responds to the enormity of the problem. Large amounts of money will be needed by the states and communities to make a success of integration: We shall need more classrooms, smaller classes wherever possible, better school equipment, health programs, and auxiliary services, more and better-trained teachers, and psychiatric consultants and guidance experts aware of the stresses and strains to which the children, their parents, and the teachers themselves are exposed, especially during the transition period.

Skilled personnel in such numbers obviously cannot be produced overnight. The size of the problem that confronts us is alarming, and its very complexity tells us that progress is bound to be slow, especially in the plantation states of the South and in our big Northern cities where the Negro population is heaviest.

In the underprivileged communities, the school program will have to be supplemented by recreational facilities, especially for teen-agers, where Negroes and whites can learn to play together and by closer coöperation between the schools and the homes through a staff of visiting teachers. For the child's environment is far more educational than the school, as our rates of crime and delinquency have long demonstrated. Actually one of the most valuable by-products of desegregation will be the revelation of our unrealized, unmet educational needs. . . .

The calm deliberation of Negro leadership is urgently needed at this critical juncture when the emotional situation could improve or degenerate so rapidly. In several conversations with Negro intellectuals and officials of the National Association for the Advancement of Colored People and the Urban League, I had the impression that the Negro leaders themselves cannot agree on what they wish to achieve. In one Southern city which had done an admirable job of desegregation, even to the point of granting all students complete freedom of choice as to which school they preferred to attend, none of the local Negro leaders was satisfied with the "permissiveness," as it is called, although the Negro parents were contented. All the leaders were critical of the Negro teachers who urged their pupils, especially the bright ones and the good athletes, to remain in the Negro schools. Another disappointment to these Negro leaders was the fact that numerous Negro children after attending the white schools for a year chose to return to their segregated schools. In other words the permissiveness for which the Negroes are fighting in New York City is anathema to the Negro leaders in cities that have adopted it. After one such lengthy discussion, in which I was the only white person, I said:

"If God Almighty came down from heaven to do this desegregation job none of you would be satisfied with it." My friends laughed heartily and agreed.

I believe that the Negro leaders who are pressing for immediate and radical desegregation are too unaware of its effects upon the schools and of the tensions to which it exposes the Negro child. They are too indifferent to the human problem involved. If retarded Negro children are demoted when they are transferred to a white school, this has a discouraging effect. If they are not demoted, many Negro children leave the white schools when they find they cannot keep up with their age group. Even under the most favorable conditions, such as those I have described in Louisville and Washington, the pressure on the Negro child confronted for the first time with a strange environment, higher achievement standards, and new social or cultural values is hard to bear for all but the most courageous and talented.

The teachers and the Negro parents are keenly aware of these psychological problems, but the leaders of the NAACP ignore them in deciding their policies. If the interests of the Negro child were more of an influence on these leaders, they would not persist in aggressive tactics in Southern counties where the predominance of Negro population makes the task of desegregation an extremely difficult social, psychological, and educational problem.

The words "deliberate speed" clearly indicate that the Supreme Court Justices did not insist upon immediate, drastic enforcement of their decision. These words are the equivalent of the Roman adage *festina lente,* make haste slowly. In a democracy, sound progress has never come about in any other way.

## A Psychologist on the Temper of the Little Rock Negroes*

. . . [THE] MORALE of Negroes in Little Rock appeared to be quite high. The present high morale seems to be supported by a sense of pride in the dignity and courage of the Negro students, admiration for the leadership and skill of Mrs. L. C. Bates, Arkansas N.A.A.C.P. leader who aided the Negro students, and a firm determination on the part of all segments of the Negro community that there shall be no retreat in the process of school integration.

---

* From "Observations on Little Rock," by Kenneth B. Clark, psychologist, in *New South,* official magazine of the Southern Regional Council, June 1958, pp. 3-7. For model documentation see p. 47.

In general, it appears that the Negro community in Little Rock has become more unified as a consequence of these recent tensions. There seems to be no significant differences of opinion between the upper middle-class, professional group of Negroes, and the working-class Negroes. What differences there are seem superficial. Working-class Negroes are more likely to express their feelings about the presence of Negroes in Central High School in a little more flamboyant terms. For example, a Negro bootblack stated: "I know one thing. Those white people better not be foolish enough to hurt one of those colored children. They're not bothering anybody. They better leave them alone. It'll be hell in Little Rock if they lay a hand on one of those kids." A Negro waitress in one of the night clubs in Little Rock stated in fluent language her admiration of the nine Negro students who were then attending Central High School. After expressing her admiration, she said: "When you gonna get some more of our children in that school? They can always pick on a few. They wouldn't be smart if we had a couple of hundred kids there. I sure wish that my child was old enough to go to that school."

Upper middle-class, professional Negroes are more restrained in their expression of admiration and respect for the children and Mr. and Mrs. L. C. Bates. They generally indicate their support by calling the Bates' and inquiring whether there is anything that they can do to help. They also have increased their general interest in the affairs of the NAACP and their financial support of the organization's effort. . . .

From one perspective, it may be stated that the Negro community has become more isolated from the white community. There is evidence that some types of peripheral contacts with whites have become strained or have been terminated by the tensions surrounding the integration of Central High School. On the other hand, many of the upper middle-class Negroes contend that this is more apparent than real. They argue that there were really no genuine and meaningful contacts between the white and the Negro community prior to the recent tensions; that what appeared to be a fairly smooth and adequate relationship was merely the Negroes' accommodation to an inferior status and the whites' willingness to accept this accommodation as evidence of good relations between the two groups. The changes which have developed since the difficulties at Central High School are seen by these individuals as the understandable reaction of many whites when Negroes seek to improve their status in the community. Rather than seeing these changes as negative, Negroes tend to see them as inevitable manifestations of the true nature of the relationship between the groups. . . .

. . . These Negroes seem quite clear in their evaluation of the moderate, less extreme whites. They do not have very much compassion or respect for them. They tend to believe that their lack of courage and the ease with which the extreme pro-segregationist whites were able to immobilize them reflected a basic lack of conviction on the part of the moderate whites and a tendency not to jeopardize their own status by taking a position for justice and law and order when it involved problems of race relations.

There are some exceptions which Negroes in general tend to recognize. There are some whites who maintain positive and close relations with the leaders of the Negro community. Their aid has been invaluable although, for obvious reasons, most cannot be publicly identified.

While there appeared to be no direct, overt, and systematic collaboration between Negroes and white groups in Little Rock at the time of my observations, some of the Negro leaders believed that the majority of the white people are determined that there shall be no further incidents which will add to the difficulties and stigma that the city has already received in the national and international press. The following incidents illustrate the basis for their opinion:

A Negro girl boarded one of the desegregated buses in Little Rock and took a seat beside a white woman. The woman, who was obviously an extreme pro-segregationist, began to berate the Negro girl and insisted that she should move to the back of the bus. When the Negro girl refused to move, the white woman became more extreme in her denunciation and name-calling. A majority of the people who were on the bus were white. As the woman threatened and raved, they became more and more tense and seemingly embarrassed. The white woman got up and made a threatening gesture toward the Negro girl as if she were going to strike her. As she did this, a number of white people jumped up and restrained the white woman. Another white woman led the Negro girl to a seat beside her. As this was done, the whole bus relaxed and the incident was closed, except that the pro-segregationist woman kept muttering something about the large number of "nigger-lovers" who now infested Little Rock. It may be of further interest to note that this incident was reported to Negro leaders by one of the white people on the bus and later confirmed by the Negro girl who was involved.

There is little or no indication that the Negroes of Little Rock have been intimidated by the intense and at times violent behavior of the pro-segregationist whites. They look upon the activities of these pro-segregationists as pathetic and ridiculous attempts to save a lost cause. They even have a tendency to look upon the violence as essentially ridiculous even though cruel.

The Negro community may be characterized as fearless, determined, and stolid. There is a relentless refusal to move backwards. . . .

[The nine] students have reacted extraordinarily well to the tensions, threats and anxiety surrounding their attendance at Central High School. . . .

. . . being different personalities they differ in the weight that they give to this harassment. Some tend to minimize the significance of this ordeal and dismiss all but the most severe incidents as being petty. . . .

Others are quite disturbed by the cumulative cruelties which they had had to bear. They seem too proud to whine about it, but they reveal their anxiety by indirect indications of dread. . . .

They accept with a quiet grace and dignity the many indications of respect and admiration which come from the Negro community. It is my belief that they have been helped to maintain an even balance in this regard by the keen insights and guidance of Mrs. Bates and their seemingly excellent relationships with their parents and brothers and sisters.

Their relations with their former classmates and the community in general also seem to be quite good. . . .

. . . some of the Negro children—presumably a small minority—who are still attending Horace Mann School have expressed rivalry or jealousy by indicating that they would not want to go to Central High School. All of the students are aware that this sentiment exists, but none of them seems unduly disturbed by it. They tend to dismiss it as a sign of acceptance of segregation on the part of the individuals who hold this opinion. They are supported by the fact that the majority opinion in the Negro community rejects this negativistic point of view. . . .

There seems to be little or no evidence that they have suffered significantly so far. They have received a great deal of public attention, support, and acclaim. They have managed to maintain their personal balance and stability. If there is a significant danger inherent in this situation and their relationship to it, it is the danger that they do not seem sufficiently aware of the very real possibility of physical harm which might be inflicted upon them. . . .

## A Little Rock Editor on the Reporting of the School Story*

FOR SOME months now I have served, in addition to my other duties, as something of a public monument, a sight to be seen by distinguished visi-

* From "The Untold Story Behind Little Rock," by Harry S. Ashmore. in *Harper's*, June 1958, distributed by the Southern Regional Council in a reprint from which this selection is taken. For model documentation see p. 47.

tors on safari to Darkest Arkansas. They still come in a seemingly endless stream to view the scene of the Battle of Little Rock—small, brown men from the Orient, lady parliament members from Norway, earnest students from Eastern universities, pipe-smoking professors of sociology, ecclesiastics of every rank and denomination, and journalists without number. They go, usually to look upon the site of Faubus' charge and Eisenhower's envelopment, visit the governor in his marble sanctuary, and come finally to what a friend of mine has termed, inaccurately I hope, Ashmore's Tomb. . . .

. . . With only rare exceptions the visitors—domestic no less than foreign—come with an image of Little Rock firmly fixed in their minds, an image fashioned by the millions of words sprayed through the communications media since the balloon went up last September. And I doubt that the image is perceptibly altered even when they gaze upon a quiet, attractive city built upon tree-clad hills where civilized people still go about their ordinary business without visible trepidation. . . .

. . . "Remember Little Rock" proclaims the great seal that adorns propaganda-bearing envelopes going out from the headquarters of the Southern Citizens Councils. The same words have been sounded by Negro hoodlums moving with drawn knives against whites in the slum streets of Northern cities. . . .

. . . Little Rock was about as handy a package as the Russians have had handed them since they set out to woo the colored peoples of the earth. In the South (and among some of the copperhead columnists who espouse states' rights above Mason and Dixon's line) a whole new mythology has evolved to fit extant prejudices against the central government. Westbrook Pegler, for example, has solemnly contended that Old Applehead sent his stormtroopers into Little Rock to assault innocent citizens not only without legal sanction but without cause, . . . The effort is far advanced to expunge from pliant Southern memories the salient fact that Orval Faubus moved first with force of arms when he sent his state militia to seize Central High School in naked defiance of a federal court. . . .

The Little Rock story . . . was, by universal judgment, the second biggest news story of the year—topped only by Sputnik. It attracted a concentration of correspondents, photographers, and radio and television technicians comparable to that which assembles for a national political convention. The newspapers, wire services, and networks sent their best men, too—seasoned hands to handle the fast-breaking spot news and think-piece experts to back them up. For many days the story had top priority on every news desk in this country and abroad—which meant the men on the ground could count on whatever space or time it took to report their findings in full. It is fair to say that contemporary journalism's best effort went into the Little Rock story.

Yet Harold C. Fleming, the perceptive executive director of the Southern Regional Council, whose business it is to chart the shifting pattern of race relations in the South, has written of the result:

. . . what do the millions of words and television images add up to? Have they given Americans—to say nothing of foreigners —a clearer understanding of the South's malaise? As a result of them, will the national shock be less or the insight greater if a similar eruption accompanies desegregation in Dallas or Charlottesville or Knoxville? We can hope so, but not with much optimism. Only a few major newspapers, like the *New York Times,* a few thoughtful television and radio commentators, and a few good magazines sought to give a meaningful perspective to their reports from Little Rock.

Conspicuously lacking in most interpretations is any sense of continuity. The upheavals in Tuscaloosa, Clinton, and Little Rock were not isolated events, but episodes in an unfolding drama of social change. . . .

I can file no dissent from Fleming's verdict. I was there when the cowboy reporters rode in to the scent of blood. They did not have to seek for drama; it was thrust upon them, with a complete set of heroes and villains—and these readily interchangeable, depending upon your point of view. I do not charge that the press sensationalized the Little Rock story; the facts themselves were sensational enough to answer any circulation manager's dream. Moreover, I believe that—with rare exceptions—the men and women who reported the Little Rock story were competent and conscientious. Similarly, I have no reason to believe that any but a tiny handful were bound by home-office policy or blinded by their personal prejudices.

They performed their traditional function, within the traditional limits. They braved the mob that formed for some days around the high school, they interviewed the principals on both sides and many of the minor characters, they sketched in personalities and filled in color, and some at least tried hard to define the feeling of the community. Over a period of weeks they did a reasonably accurate job of reporting what happened at Little Rock—but as Fleming has said, they have failed to tell why it happened.

And the reason, I think, is that to American journalism the Little Rock story had an arbitrary beginning and end. It began the day Governor

Faubus surrounded Central High School with his state guard. It continued so long as there was a naked edge of violence. It ended when federal troops restored a surface order to the troubled city. It has had subsequent footnotes only when the edge of violence re-emerged in clashes between white and Negro children inside the school. It survives in the press today largely in the sort of occasional oblique reference that passes for background of more immediate news.

Yet it is quite obvious that the Little Rock story did not begin in September. It is equally obvious that it has not ended yet. For Little Rock was simply the temporary focus of a great, continuing, and unresolved American dilemma which touches upon fundamental concepts of morality, of social change, and of law. Journalism has concentrated on only the exposed portion of the iceberg; the great, submerged mass remains uncharted. . . .

. . . this was a controversy that had three sides. Caught between the committed and dedicated partisans was a substantial and silent mass of plain citizens—confused and deeply disturbed. They were people who deplored desegregation and also deplored violence. They felt, many of them, a deep compassion for the nine Negro children exposed to the anger and contempt of a white mob. But they also felt that the Negro children should not be attending the white school in the first place. They had been, most of them, willing to undertake what they considered the unpleasant duty that had been required by the courts.

But then, at the last moment, their governor had stepped forward and proclaimed that what they had accepted as the law was without substance— and that their failure to resist desegregation amounted to treason to their own traditions and to their own people.

It is true that most of those who accepted this thesis (and the majority have, to some degree) did so with conscious rationalization. But it is also true that when emotion triumphed over reason they did not actively join the crusade of the governor and the Citizens' Councils; rather they simply subsided into troubled silence and by so doing withdrew their support from those few who attempted to stand against the tide. And because they were silent, their attitude went largely unreported. The press took due note of the fact that in fairly short order Governor Faubus was in command of the field; but here again it did not explain why—which is the heart of the story. . . .

. . . there were other aspects of the Little Rock story that were equally vital and by no means so elusive. There was, conspicuously, the failure of leadership in Washington which matched the default of Southern leadership, and made the ultimate showdown between state and federal force inevitable. . . .

. . . making all due allowance for my [Democratic] prejudice, I submit that the record shows that from May 1954, when the United States Supreme Court reversed the old Plessy doctrine, until September 1957, when the chickens finally fluttered in to roost in Little Rock, the Eisenhower Administration took no affirmative action to pave the way for the sweeping legal change the Court required or to temper the inevitable dislocations it would occasion. Indeed, the incredible fact is that the Administration, without preliminary, moved directly to the ultimate resort of armed force, and then was confounded by its own belated audacity.

It required no delicate fingering of the public pulse to chart the course of growing defiance in the South. It was evident in violent utterances by some of the South's public men and in the silence of others. It was made a matter of record in the passage of a variety of restrictive laws in the Southern legislatures. A conspicuous public monument was erected in Washington when one hundred Southern members of the Senate and House signed their breast-beating Manifesto in the spring of 1956.

Yet Mr. Eisenhower's only reaction to all this was an occasional bemused press conference statement about the difficulties of changing the minds and hearts of men. His Administration, it is true, made token efforts to pass stringent civil-rights legislation—which only served to lacerate the Southerners in Congress and certainly had an adverse effect upon their minds, hearts, and spleens. And of course, Vice President Nixon, in the days before he sheathed his hatchet, joined other Administration spokesmen in making proper obeisance to their party's Abolitionist tradition when campaigning in those areas where the Negro vote is heavy.

But at no time did Mr. Eisenhower attempt to use the moral force of his office to persuade Southerners of the justice of the course the Supreme Court required of them, or his great personal prestige in the region to allay their fears that they were being forced into a revolutionary rather than an evolutionary course. Nor did he employ the vast political powers of his office to negotiate with the recalcitrant Southern political leaders from a position of strength. . . .

If the reporting of the prelude to Little Rock was conspicuously inadequate, it seems to me that the postlude provides an even more distressing example. The stirring martial events of September were, it is true, somewhat confusing—particularly when President Eisenhower and Governor Faubus held their historic peace conference at Newport and there remained some doubt as to who emerged with whose sword. Out of the communiques issued by the White House on this occasion, however, and the later meeting with envoys from the Southern Governors' Conference, there emerged an assumption that the executive department of the federal government was prepared to back to the utmost the orders of the federal judiciary.

This notion was reinforced by the arrival of the 101st Airborne Infantry, and by the presence in Little Rock of so many FBI agents they created a problem of hotel accommodations. Indeed, there was public and official talk of a vast document compiled by the FBI, at the direction of the United States Attorney General, presumably in preparation for court action against those who were clearly defying the injunctions of a federal judge. During those fall days the embattled Little Rock School Board—under fire from the state government for carrying out the judge's order and deserted by a city administration intimidated by a show of political strength by the Citizens' Council—waited for the federals to ride to their aid. All they got, as it turned out, was withdrawal of the regulars of the 101st and a perfunctory detail of federalized national guardsmen, under orders to observe but not to arrest any malefactors within the school.

It soon became apparent that this was far from enough to preserve any semblance of order. The mob which once came close to forcing entry into the school did not re-form, it is true, but it didn't need to. A far safer course was to inspire a small group of white students to undertake a campaign of harassment against the isolated Negroes. And as it became apparent that Washington had done all it was going to do, the Citizens' Councils became bolder and bolder in their campaign of intimidation, coercion, and boycott directed against any who dared dissent from the defiant course they had charted. The campaign bore tangible fruit in the expulsion of one of the nine Negro children who had responded in kind to calculated mistreatment. . . .

. . . In Washington, the decision to leave to the Little Rock School Board the entire burden of carrying out the court order against impossible odds has never been officially announced, but has been clearly acknowledged by the Department of Justice. The new Attorney General, William P. Rogers, said that there were no present plans for further legal action in Little Rock. He further noted that the Administration would not press for additional civil-rights legislation at this session of Congress—a matter of some moment since the Justice Department had previously used as an excuse for inaction at Little Rock the failure of the enforcement provisions in the last civil-rights bill.

These pronouncements were followed by one of the most remarkable scenes enacted on Capitol Hill since the passage of the Missouri Compromise. Mr. Rogers appeared before the Senate Judiciary Committee to be interrogated as to his fitness as Attorney General, received cordial greetings, and was recommended for confirmation without a single question being addressed to him regarding his past or future course in the Little Rock case—and this before a committee that counts among its members Senators James Eastland of Mississippi and Olin Johnston of South Carolina. This singular occurrence was accorded no more than passing mention in the press and no one of consequence speculated in print or on a television tube as to the dimensions of what must have been one of the most singular political deals in recent years.

Just as the Little Rock story did not begin in Little Rock, it will not end there—whatever the ultimate fate of the eight children still remaining in the beleaguered high school at this writing. These events have already had tragic consequences in Arkansas and the South; those who were disposed to support an orderly adjustment to the new public policy have been discredited and disarmed—not alone by the extremists who are now in control, but by a national Administration which deserted them in the first collision between federal and state force and declared in effect that the rule of law propounded by its own courts is not enforceable. And so, by default, what began as a local issue has been built into a national constitutional crisis. . . .

I am the first to argue that time is of the essence in any resolution of the problem. In so delicate an area of human relations change must be evolutionary. Yet time is of value only if it is put to some practical use; perhaps the most cogent single question yet raised was that put by Francis Pickens Miller of Virginia to a group of Southerners who at a national conference were pleading for a breathing spell.

What, he asked, did they propose to do with it?

It is clear that the Southern leadership has no program and no policy except the negative one of delay at any price—and part of that price will be a steady deterioration of race relations across the whole of the nation, with a corollary impact of great significance on our sagging foreign policy. In the face of this, the Administration has offered nothing except the politician's usual device for postponing unpleasant decisions—the creation of a study commission. . . .

## A Letter Writer's Disagreement*

THE almost pathological espousal of the Democratic party by Southerners
. . . was nowhere better illustrated than in the June Easy Chair. When the
brilliant and courageous editor of the Arkansas *Gazette* can convince himself that the mess at Little Rock was largely a Republican responsibility,
one can appreciate the pervasiveness of Yankee-hating in the post-Recon-
struction South. . . .

Mr. Ashmore blames President Eisenhower for not changing in the
four years since the crucial Supreme Court decision what hundreds of
Southern intellectuals like the good editor himself have failed to do in a
century.

WARREN S. WALKER
*Carlinville, Illinois*

## A Law Professor: The Problem of Enforcement†

IF THE South will not end segregation because it is contrary to law, if the
South will not end segregation because it is immoral, there remains the
possibility that segregation will be ended by orders of the federal courts.
Such orders there surely will be. That they will end segregation is far less
clear. Mansfield, Texas, was ordered to end segregation in its schools by the
federal court in August, 1956. No Negro child has yet attended those
schools. A threatening mob, unrestrained by local and state authorities, was
enough to intimidate would-be Negro applicants, and to keep the school
for white students only. The University of Alabama was ordered to admit
Negroes in 1955. No Negro has yet attended that university, except for the
day or two that Autherine Lucy risked her life to get to the classroom. . . .

Violence may be the principal weapon for keeping schools segregated,
despite orders of the federal courts, but it has a powerful ally in the delaying legalism. It has been two and a half years since the U.S. Supreme
Court ruled, after years of litigation, that Virgil D. Hawkins cannot be
denied admission to the University of Florida Law School because of his
race. Since the Court spoke, Hawkins' case has been back and forth through

---

* A letter to the editor of *Harper's*, published in the issue of August 1958. For
model documentation see p. 172.

† From "School Integration: An Almost Lost Cause," by Charles Alan Wright,
University of Texas professor of constitutional law, in *The Progressive*, August
1958, pp. 7-10. For model documentation see p. 47.

the Florida courts again, has gone once more to the Supreme Court, and now is in a lower federal court. Hawkins has helped make a good deal of law, but he has not yet been admitted to law school. Last winter a federal court in Dallas finally issued a decree, after the case had been appealed three separate times, calling for an end of segregation in that city. But the Dallas school board has announced that there will be no integration there next year because, so it says with breathtaking hypocrisy, it does not know which is controlling, the federal court order or a Texas law, enacted since the litigation began, requiring continued segregation!

The problem of integration is, in ultimate analysis, a simple question of law enforcement. A state which discriminates according to race in admissions to its schools is breaking the law. Usually when a government has a law forbidding certain conduct, the full resources of that government, including its police and its prosecutors, are devoted to preventing and punishing such conduct. Quite frequently private persons who have a special concern with the unlawful conduct may also bring their own lawsuit, but this is a supplement to the efforts of the government to enforce the law, rather than a substitute for such effort. It is virtually unprecedented to leave enforcement of the law of the land exclusively to private lawsuits, brought and financed by private persons, as we now are doing with that provision of the Fourteenth Amendment prohibiting school segregation.

There are special reasons why private law enforcement will not suffice to end segregation. Individual Negroes, denied their constitutional right to attend an integrated school, cannot possibly be expected to carry the brunt of litigation. The cost of these lawsuits is prohibitive. Necessarily they must combine their efforts, as they have done in the National Association for the Advancement of Colored People, but such an organization immediately becomes an obvious target for harassing investigations and legislation, and is forced to divert much of its energy and its resources into battling for its right to exist.

Even were the NAACP free to pursue its course unmolested, it is a rather puny David forced to do battle simultaneously with a number of alert Goliaths. In this battle the Southern states have every advantage. These lawsuits are extremely expensive, and the funds which the NAACP is able to raise by private contribution are a pittance compared to what Southern legislatures are willing to appropriate from otherwise-impoverished state treasuries for the cause of preserving segregation. The states resisting integration have the edge with regard to legal talent. It is no disparagement of the dedicated lawyers who have worked tirelessly for the

NAACP to say that, good as they are, they are not the outstanding lawyers of the South.

The South has the tremendous advantage of being able to revise at will the rules of the game. Let one segregation statute be held unconstitutional by a federal court and the legislature in that state will hasten to enact a new package of laws which must be attacked and invalidated one by one before an end to segregation can be ordered. Finally, the South has the advantage of the seeming neutrality of the federal government. It is the Constitution of the United States which the NAACP is seeking to enforce, but the government of the United States acts as if it is a matter of complete indifference to it whether segregation continues, in defiance of the Constitution, or whether it is ended. It is true that the federal government did intervene, effectively and powerfully, at Little Rock, but its intervention came at the wrong time and for the wrong reason. Segregation in the public schools is fully as unlawful in Biloxi, Mississippi, where no court action has even been begun, as it is in Little Rock, Arkansas, where a court has decreed its end.

Court orders must be obeyed, in a law-abiding country, and it is right that the government should see to it that they are, but a court order has no stronger claims to obedience than does the Constitution itself, from which the courts derive their authority. For the federal government to remain idle in the face of open violation of its supreme law, except in the rare case where private persons have secured a court order calling for compliance with the law, is, in effect, to concede the ultimate victory to those states which are determined not to obey the law.

The South will not end segregation because the Supreme Court says it must, nor because the churches denounce segregation as immoral, nor because the NAACP, laboring manfully with inadequate resources, brings a pitifully few lawsuits looking toward this end. Segregation will be ended in the South only if the government of the United States recognizes that it is its function and its responsibility to require compliance with the Constitution. The federal government alone has the money and the legal manpower and the patience and the power to force recalcitrant states to obey the law. Decisive federal action in support of integration is the only thing which will persuade the South that the end of segregation is inevitable, and that nothing is to be gained by throwing stones outside a Central High School or spitballs within. And, not irrelevantly, the federal government has express constitutional authority, conferred by section five of the Fourteenth Amendment, to see to it that every person in the land enjoys the rights that Amendment guarantees. . . .

## *A News Story: Administration Attitudes on School Integration**

WHILE President Eisenhower steadfastly has declined to give his opinion on the Supreme Court decision outlawing racial segregation in public schools, his legal speakesmen have been ouspoken advocates of desegregation.

Herbert Brownell Jr., the Eisenhower administration's first attorney general, contended that the high Court had the authority and the duty to strike down the color line in public schools. . . .

J. Lee Rankin, now solicitor general but at one time head of the Justice Department's Office of Legal Counsel, told the Supreme Court orally in December 1953 that the Justice Department adopted the views of segregation expressed in a legal brief filed by the Truman administration in 1952. The brief said the historic "separate but equal doctrine" of 1896 was wrong and asked the Court to overturn it. The Justice Department said at the time that Rankin was speaking for the Eisenhower administration.

The separate but equal doctrine, handed down in a transportation case, allowed states to enforce segregation in schools provided that separate facilities for Negroes were equal to those provided whites.

The Supreme Court's decision of May 17, 1954, struck down the separate but equal docrine, holding racial segregation in public schools to be unconstitutional.

During arguments in April 1955 on implementation of this decision, Solicitor General Simon E. Sobeloff, now chief judge of the United States Fourth Circuit Court of Appeals, took what he called a middle course.

Thurgood Marshall, counsel for the National Association for the Advancement of Colored People, argued for a decree fixing a firm deadline for ending segregation. . . .

## *A Catholic Editorial†*

THE SUBJECT of interracial justice has been discussed in countless Catholic gatherings over the years, but for some reason or other there had never been a national Catholic convention devoted exclusively to this sub-

---

* *Arkansas Gazette,* from "Eisenhower Mum on Integration but His Legal Spokesmen Favor It," Associated Press news item from Washington dated August 25, published August 26, 1958, p. 1B. For model documentation see p. 51.

† From an editorial report, "Catholics on Interracial Justice," in *The Commonweal,* September 28, 1958, pp. 630-631. For model documentation see p. 47.

ject. This year the two oldest Catholic Interracial Councils in the country, New York and Chicago, decided to remedy this omission. The result was the first National Catholic Conference for Interracial Justice, which took place in Chicago on the last three days of August. . . .

While the Conference was in session, the Chicago papers were carrying front-page stories on the newest developments in the Little Rock crisis. Almost as if in reply, Father William J. Kenealy, S.J., of the Law School at Loyola University in New Orleans, early in the meeting restated the teaching of the Church on this basic question of race.

"The fundamental principal of the essential equality and dignity of every human being, and the essential unity of the entire human race, has been sanctified by the sacrifice of Calvary, illumined by the dawn of Easter, emblazoned by the fires of Pentecost, and heralded to the corners of the earth by the voice of Catholicism—proclaiming our common origin in the First Adam, our common redemption by the Second Adam, and our common sanctification in the Mystical Body of Christ," Father Kenealy said. "Popes, archbishops, bishops, dogmatic and moral theologians, the unanimous judgment of the teaching Church is that compulsory segregation is objectively and morally wrong. It is a cancer in the body politic. It is a desecration of Christian civilization. . . . In the eyes of God there is neither white nor black nor red nor yellow nor brown; neither Jew nor Gentile nor Barbarian nor Scythian, but all are brothers in Christ Jesus. 'By this will all men know that you are my disciples, if you have love one for another.' " . . .

What was the temper of the Conference? If I read the sentiments of the participants correctly, most of them are tired of being told that they must not expect "too much, too soon," that they must be "patient." Father LaFarge reflected this point of view, I think, when he expressed his sorrow over the passing of the Catholic Committee of the South and when he said, in another connection: "Caution and patience are basic virtues, but exhortations to prolonged inaction are meaningless if they are used, as is not infrequently the case, as a mere excuse for doing nothing. . . . Many of the worst interracial situations that exist today would not have come to pass if such reasonably prompt action had been exerted a couple of decades ago." . . .

## A Civil-Rights Authority: The Supreme Court Decision and the White House*

. . . UNFORTUNATELY, THE Court decision made no mention of the Executive's role or of the range of the Federal Government's duties in

---

* From "The Integration Crisis," by Charles Abrams, Chairman, New York

"enforcing the Constitution." For a critically long period, enforcement was considered exclusively a judicial affair. While this might work in times and places where law is obeyed automatically, the problem became vastly different when it was flaunted.

A court is neither an administrative nor an executive agency. It has no public-relations staff to defend its actions, no budget to maintain its prestige in crisis. It functions in an aura of judicial sublimity in which administration of justice conforms to an impressive and a solemn ritual. It operates with a court attendant and a few clerks and stenographers. Its orders are automatically complied with on the great majority of cases and are executed in a few by a U. S. Marshal, who is generally an affable, elderly gentleman in the nature of a process-server. If he encounters resistance in carrying out the court's mandate, he may call on Federal troops to help.

The court's power to enforce compliance with its orders stems from its contempt power, a power rarely used and historically limited in its scope to punishing those who insult the court *in facie curiae* or to compelling an individual to conform to its decrees. While the contempt power could conceivably function against a single offender or a score of them, it is hard to see how the power could be used to compel parents to send their children to school, prevent a closing of schools, cope realistically with the tirades of irresponsible but widely-read journals, curb mass violence, or contend with the day-to-day stratagems of Southern opportunists operating in one of the most sensitive, complex and eccentric areas of American social life.

In assuming enforcement, the Supreme Court made no reference to the Executive assistance promised by Attorney General Brownell. Soon, the general feeling came to be that the Executive as well as Congress could now forget the whole business and let the Court do the job unaided. If new circumstances had not supervened, it might have done it. But there were three developments which neither the Court nor anyone else could foresee:

1. The power of Southern dissidence and the subsequent wavering on the part of both parties during the 1956 political conventions. Unlike the Truman campaign of 1948, when the Southern diehards walked out in protest, the Democratic party, despite some bitter opposition from the North, succumbed to the pressures of the South and in the 1956 platform rejected "all proposals for the use of force to interfere with the orderly

State Commission Against Discrimination, in *The New Leader,* October 27, 1958, pp. 3-5. Mr. Abrams is best known in the fields of race relations and housing. For model documentation see p. 47.

determination of these matters by the courts." The Republicans were even more solicitous of Southern feelings and coupled force by any official agency with mob violence, declaring that "use of force or violence by any group or *agency* will tend only to worsen the many problems inherent in the situation." While the Democrats left enforcement to the courts alone, the Republicans advocated nothing more than "intelligent study, understanding, education and good will." Thus neither party acknowledged any responsibility to help enforce the decree, and both in fact repudiated any such idea.

2. Wavering on the part of President Eisenhower. His frequent references to the fact that he wished the Court had gone slower, to the need for changing the "hearts of men" first, his notorious refusal to support the morality of the decision and his lack of a program to implement it in accordance with his Attorney General's promise helped build up the opportunistic and irrational segregationists to a position of prominence. It simultaneously submerged the more responsible elements who were seeking a practical means of complying with the Court's orders.

3. The rise of Orval Faubus. The Governor of Arkansas is the official embodiment of the opportunism, lawlessness and subversion which will not be snuffed out by all the forces of Northern oratory or scholastic logic. The premonitory bubble that signalled official resistance to the Court's decree had already appeared with the resolutions of six states "annulling" it. But the spectacle of a Governor calling out the militia to shut the schools, and virtually inviting mob violence to justify his illegal action, was unexpected. It poses the question as to whether the courts will enforce contempt proceedings against a state executive, whether his acts in fact warrant such proceedings and above all, whether this is advisable and whether it will set at rest the issue of defiance in Virginia, Mississippi and elsewhere. . . .

. . . "There can be no successful government," Woodrow Wilson said, "without the intimate, almost instructive [instinctive?] coordination of the organs of life and action." The Executive's duty is to execute the laws and keep the organism whole and alive. Once the law has been laid down, whether by Congress or by the Judiciary, it is primarily the Executive upon whom the obligation rests to help implement the law within reasonable and practical bounds.

I think President Eisenhower, however, has only vaguely sensed the general principle and has been extremely uncertain about the manner of its application. For one thing, any implied disagreement with a court's decision by the Executive can never help win popular support. If Mr.

Eisenhower had any qualms, he should have conveyed them to his Attorney General before argument of the case. Presumably, the Attorney General carried his superior's position to the Supreme Court when asking it to outlaw segregation; it is now neither appropriate nor dignified to punctuate the national atmosphere with unsolicited doubts or to re-argue the morals of a case which the Government established and won in 1954 and 1955.

The calling out of troops in Little Rock would probably have been unnecessary had the President stated unequivocally at the start that he intended to enforce the law. Wavering both by him and by the two political parties at the use of force emboldened the violation of law, gave a moral base to immoral disobedience and ultimately invoked the very use of armed force which would have been unnecessary had it been made clear in the first place that force would be used to support the Court's orders. His calling out of the troops in Little Rock, while it belatedly recognized Executive responsibility, was a serious mistake, and indicated a lack of familiarity with both the nature of the problem and the devices best suited to tackle it.

The Federal Government is the greatest single source for spending and lending for new ventures; it finances housing and city development, controls credit, insures investments, grants huge subsidies to private and public agencies; it builds dams, atom plants, roads and public works. Its influence permeates almost every phase of enterprise and touches every local official and citizen.

Accordingly, a whole arsenal of devices exists upon which the President may draw to assert his vast prestige, influence and power. Military force is the first resort of generals and the last of statesmen. . . .

## A Magazine Staff Writer: Consequences of Resistance*

. . . CAN AN orderly line of progress for the South be discovered? A start at least would be for each of those engaged in the present struggle to realize the uses and limitations of the weapons with which he fights.

The Southern white man has massive weapons for stalling and delay. But he knows he lacks an ultimate weapon. Harry Ashmore has ridiculed the notion of his "fellow townsmen lining up in double rank while the chairman of the local White Citizens' Council checks their bandoliers in preparation for a second march to turn back the Federals at Pea Ridge."

---

* From "The Bitter Fruits of Southern Bitter-Endism," by Douglass Cater, in *The Reporter,* January 22, 1959, p. 31. For model documentation see p. 47.

It is equally farfetched to imagine the white citizens of the South taking to the hills for extended guerrilla warfare. The South is still overwhelmingly their land—their homes, their businesses, their institutions. By bitter-endism, as the experience of Little Rock and Tuskegee has shown, they can only hurt themselves.

The Southern Negro, despite his impressive victories in court, should also give thought to the limitations of a legal victory that may turn out to be more symbolic than real. Thurgood Marshall, the most brilliant of the Negro courtroom pioneers, once stated his aim to a reporter for the *New Yorker:* "If ninety-nine Negro children out of a hundred should be found to be stupid, that hundredth one still has a right to equal educational opportunities. All I'm saying is this, and it really says just about everything I have to say on civil rights. Any tests the school wishes to give the children to separate them for one reason or another are O.K. with me except for one test—the racial test. That's all it comes down to. Not the racial test. It is possible to sympathize with Marshall's concern for that hundredth child and still to realize that in the South it must be accompanied by an acceptance of the heavy burden of bringing along the ninety-nine.

The recent Supreme Court decision upholding the Alabama Pupil Placement Law, at least for the present, raises the prospect that token integration may meet the Court's requirements. But, even if the Deep South yielded this much, there could be danger for both races in this development. Cynically applied, pupil placement could be used to cultivate an educational aristocracy which, mainly prejudicial to the Negro, might also work a hardship on great numbers of underprivileged white children. A handful of Negro children in white schools may satisfy the Supreme Court and Thurgood Marshall, but no one should forget—as the concentration on legalistic battles and legalistic triumphs tempts us to forget—that the South's continuing problem remains the improvement of its whole public-school system. . . .

## A Tennessee Author: Conformity and Resistance*

IN THE MANY millions of words that have poured from the presses since the Supreme Court's school desegregation decision in 1954—reporting, analyzing, describing, predicting, deploring, applauding, and questioning —one man more than any other has been the center of discussion and

---

* From "The Man in the Gray Flannel Sheet," by Wilma Dykeman, a Tennessee author, in *The Progressive,* February 1959, pp. 8-9. For model documentation see p. 47.

speculation. He is the man-in-the-middle. He is the man who has neither affirmed the necessity to uphold the black-robed justice of the highest court in the land, nor yet totally neglected that justice by resorting to the white robes of the lowest lawlessness in the region.

The antics of that lunatic fringe, who drape themselves in white sheets and seek to intimidate individuals and communities, make lively news, but it seems likely that the final resolution to conflict in the South—and the cost or ease with which that outcome is effected—will be determined largely by the middle-of-the-road man, who so far has drawn what might whimsically be called his gray flannel sheet around himself and by his own timidity invited further intimidation.

The term gray flannel is appropriate here. It is a national symbol, suggesting a certain status, a set of habits and attitudes, indeed, a way of life. And it is the arrival of this way, influencing and altering the "Southern way of life," which has numerous implications for the present and future.

It may be that in the effort to identify and understand the South, outsiders have sometimes tended to make its problems appear more isolated than they are, and its people more unique than they are. . . . In fact, it is the familiarity of their responses that is often most striking: their care to shun controversy, their desire to avoid "trouble," their need to win friends and peace of mind. These are not purely, or even chiefly, Southern characteristics, but they are influencing the silent middle people in the South today. No one seems to have noticed that these are the same people who are silent everywhere on the major issues of our time. . . .

"I'm sick to death of cocktail party liberals," a young Southern matron said recently, a woman whose husband has business alliances which require frequent trips to New York. "People who wouldn't dream of being different in their own little circle, of ordering bourbon and water if the boss had set the pace at dry martinis, these organization men ask you with real amazement why more Southerners don't 'speak out' on racial matters. Well, some day I'm going to tell them. It's simple. We like to be executive vice presidents, too!" . . .

The man in gray flannel is a product of the New South. Jeter Lester's Tobacco Road and Scarlett O'Hara's Tara may still dominate the public imagination, but split-levels and ranch styles dominate the local landscapes. The magnolias on Main Street have more often than not been replaced by concrete block cubicles dispensing Dairi-Creme or Tastee-Freez or their kissin' kin. Whether or not this is desirable is a matter of debate; that it is so is a matter of fact. . . .

Yet, as the face of a region is changed, is the mind changed too, simultaneously and in equal degrees? Are the current symbols of success—

the key to the executive wash room, the wall-to-wall carpeting, the locker at the country club—merely new chains forged from the old needs to maintain community (in this case racial) solidarity and individual status at all costs? The man in the South today who is pulling the gray flannel sheet over his head may be vaguely concerned about a hypothetical daughter some day marrying an imaginary Negro; he may be occasionally worried about a concept of states' rights he doesn't very clearly understand—but like his Northern counterpart he is sharply concerned about his job and a promotion, or his business and its increase. And in segregation-integration he recognizes an issue of such emotional proportions that deep involvement on either side can mean only trouble for his own ambitions.

A shrewd and successful lawyer from a small town in the Deep South said in conversation not long ago, "A few of the really first-class people in my county belong to the White Citizens' Councils because of business. They tell me they don't have anything to do with the organization, only keep their names on the rolls because it means financial life or death to them. I disagree and tell them, 'If you're going to belong, you'd better have something to do with it. Some of these days those boys will break loose and do something you don't like, and then you'll be implicated, too. You'd better get in, or get out.'"

When turmoil developed a couple of years ago in the small town of Mansfield, Texas, a man who followed closely the pattern of developments recalls, "Most of the leading business people of Mansfield managed to be absent during the conflict. Suddenly they had business out of town, a relative to visit, a trip to make. In years to come they can tell their children they were away during the trouble. They took no side in it." . . .

. . . it is in large part the so-called "comfortably fixed" people who are huddling so close on no-man's-land today that it has suddenly become "every-man's-land." And some of the basic forces holding them in thrall are the same forces enervating their counterparts everywhere. These are (1) the dedication to security and its Siamese twin, conformity; (2) the vogue of anti-intellectualism; and (3) the relinquishment of deep human issues to purely political leadership. . . .

## Little Rock's Congressman: More Communist Influence?*

I AM SURE that many Members of this House will recall, when Federal troops occupied Little Rock in the fall of 1957, that the television news-

---

* From an address to the United States House of Representatives by Congressman Dale Alford of Little Rock, as reported in *The Solid South*, a paper which de-

reels and press of the Nation carried a scene that purported to show a white woman "befriending and comforting" a young Negro girl who had left her new modern Horace Mann High School to enter the 33-year-old Central High School. Of course, the reporters and photographers had no way of knowing that the scene was a staged affair. However, an inquiry would have revealed that the white woman was Grace Lorch—the well-known former Grace Lonergan, a Communist functionary, whose record is in the files of the FBI, the Senate Internal Security Committee and the House Committee on Un-American Activities. Files of both the House and Senate committees mentioned contain evidence that Mrs. Lorch was identified in Boston, 9 years ago, as a Communist organizer, that she attended the Massachusetts Communist Convention in 1943, and that she was a member of the New England District of the Communist Party in 1945. Her yeoman service to the Communist apparatus was so great that she was sent to Arkansas, via Nashville, Tenn., and other points, to help create racial incidents in my state.

. . . Grace Lorch proved she is an expert at racial agitation when she staged the exhibition of alleged friendship by putting her arms around the Negro girl, being very careful to receive the full attention of unsuspecting newsreel cameramen. Grace Lorch performed her assignment well, for she was rewarded for this stunt when the Emergency Civil Liberties Committee transported her to New York and there sponsored a $10 per plate dinner in her honor. The Emergency Civil Liberties Committee is a shock-troop or commando-type group allied with Communist-dominated civil liberties agitation. The Communists have developed a great money-raising vehicle in their program of race agitation in the South. They encourage and promote racial incidents, create and ballyhoo a hero or heroine, then bring them to the East for a series of rabble-rousing dinners and rallies.

## A Segregationist View on Race Relations, Equality, and Integration*

. . . IT IS MY personal conviction that the local customs in this case were "hardened by time" for a very good reason, and that while they may not,

---

scribes itself as "Defending the U.S. Constitution" and "Advocating Conservative Principles of Government," March-April 1959, p. 3. For suitable documentation see p. 67.

* From a letter to President Eisenhower by Carleton Putnam, author and airlines executive, as reprinted without date in *The Solid South*, April-May 1959, p. 3, where Mr. Putnam is described as "a member of the famous New England Putnam family, a native of New York City, a graduate of Princeton and Columbia, . . ." For suitable documentation see p. 172.

as Frankfurter says, have been decreed in heaven, they come closer to it than the current view of the supreme court. I was particularly puzzled by Frankfurter's remark that "the Constitution is not the formulation of the merely personal views of the members of this court." Five minutes before the court's desegregation decision, the Constitution meant one thing; five minutes later, it meant something else. Only one thing intervened, namely, an expression of the personal views of the members of the court.

It is not my purpose to dispute the point with which the greater part of Frankfurter's opinion is concerned. The law must be obeyed. But I think the original desegregation decision was wrong, that it ought to be reversed, and that meanwhile every legal means should be found, not to disobey it but to avoid it. Failing this, the situation should be corrected by constitutional amendment. . . .

To me there is a frightening arrogance in this performance. Neither the North, nor the court, has any holy mandate inherent in the trend of the times or the progress of liberalism to reform society in the South. In the matter of schools, rights to equal education are inseparably bound up with rights to freedom of association and, in the South at least, may require that both be considered simultaneously. (In using the word "association" here, I mean the right to associate with whom you please, and the right not to associate with whom you please.) Moreover, am I not correct in my recollection that it was the social stigma of segregation and its effect upon the Negro's "mind and heart" to which the court objected as much as to any other, and thus that the court, in forcing the black man's right to equal education, was actually determined to violate the white man's right to freedom of association?

In any case the crux of this issue would seem obvious: social status has to be earned. Or, to put [it] in another way, equality of association has to be mutually agreed to and mutually desired. It cannot be achieved by legal fiat. Personally, I feel only affection for the Negro. But there are facts that have to be faced. Any man with two eyes in his head can observe a Negro settlement in the Congo, can study the pure-blooded African in his native habitat as he exists when left on his own resources, can compare this settlement with London or Paris, and can draw his own conclusions regarding relative levels of character and intelligence—or that combination of character and intelligence which is civilization. Finally, he can inquire as to the number of pure-blooded blacks who have made contributions to great literature or engineering or medicine or philosophy or abstract science. (I do not include singing or athletics as these are not primarily matters of character and intelligence.) Nor is there any validity to the argument that the Negro "hasn't been given a chance." We were all in caves or trees originally. The progress which the pure-blooded black has made when left to himself, with a minimum of white help or hindrance, genetically or otherwise, can be measured today in the Congo. . . .

I would emphatically support improvement of education in Negro schools, if and where it is inferior. Equality of opportunity and equality before the law, when not strained to cover other situations, are acceptable ideals because they provide the chance to earn and to progress—and consequently should be enforced by legal fiat as far as is humanly possible. . . .

Throughout this controversy there has been frequent mention of the equality of man as a broad social objective. No proposition in recent years has been clouded by more loose thinking. Not many of us would care to enter a poetry contest with Keats, nor play chess with the national champion, nor set our character beside Albert Schweitzer's. When we see the doctrine of equality contradicted everywhere around us in fact, it remains a mystery why so many of us continue to give it lip service in theory, and why we tolerate the vicious notion that status in any field need not be earned.

Pin down the man who uses the word "equality," and at once the evasions and qualifications begin. As I recall, you, yourself, in a recent statement used some phrase to the effect that men were "equal in the sight of God." I would be interested to know where in the Bible you get your authority for this conception. There is doubtless authority in Scripture for the concept of potential equality in the sight of God—after earning that status, and with various further qualifications—but where is the authority for the sort of ipso facto equality suggested by your context? The whole idea contradicts the basic tenet of the Christian and Jewish religions that status is earned through righteousness and is not an automatic matter. What is true of religion and righteousness is just as true of achievement in other fields. And what is true among individuals is just as true of averages among races.

The confusion here is not unlike the confusion created by some left-wing writers between the doctrine of equality and the doctrine of Christian love. The command to love your neighbor is not a command either to consider your neighbor your equal, or yourself his equal: Perhaps the purest example of great love without equality is the love between parent and child. In fact the equality doctrine as a whole, except when surrounded by a plethora of qualifications, is so untenable that it falls to pieces at the slightest thoughtful examination.

Frankfurter closes his opinion with a quotation from Abraham Lincoln, to whom the Negro owes more than to any other man. I, too, would like to quote from Lincoln. At Charleston, Ill., in September 1858 in a debate with Douglas, Lincoln said:

"I am not, nor ever have been, in favor of bringing about in any way the social and political equality of the white and black races; I am not nor ever have been in favor of making voters or jurors of Negroes, nor qualifying them to hold office. . . . I will say in addition to this that there is a physical difference between the white and black races which I believe will ever forbid the two races living together on terms of social and political equality. And in as much as they cannot so live, while they do remain together, there must be the position of superior and inferior, and I as much as any other man am in favor of having the superior position assigned to the white race." . . .

Perhaps the most discouraging spectacle is the spectacle of Northern newspapers dwelling with pleasure upon the predicament of the Southern parent who is forced to choose between desegregation and no school at all for his children. It does not seem to occur to these papers that this is the cruelest sort of blackmail; that the North is virtually putting a pistol at the head of the Southern parent in a gesture which every Northerner must contemplate with shame.

Indeed there now seems little doubt that the court's recent decision has set back the cause of the Negro in the South by a generation. He may force his way into white schools, but he will not force his way into white hearts nor earn the respect he seeks. What evolution was slowly and wisely achieving, revolution has now arrested, and the trail of bitterness will lead far.

## A Tennessee Newsman: Economic Aftermath*

FIVE NEW industrial plants, worth a million dollars and employing a total of 300 persons—that's what Little Rock has probably lost because of its school crisis.

Businessmen lined up solidly behind the recent campaign to oust three extreme segregationists from the Little Rock school board. They did it because they were outraged as citizens by the "purge" of 44 of the city's best teachers. But another reason for their actions lay in this one ugly fact:

---

* From "New Factories Thing of Past in Little Rock," a story by Garry Fullerton in the *Nashville Tennesseean,* May 31, 1959, pp. 1, 6; this selection is taken from a reprint. For suitable documentation see p. 35.

Since September, 1957, when desegregation violence at Central high school made Little Rock the center of world attention, not a single new factory has located in that city.

Based on recent experience, if 1958 had been a typical year, Little Rock might have welcomed five new plants, with a total value of $1 million and employing 300 persons. Actually, it could well have been

## LITTLE ROCK INDUSTRY

| Year | No. of New Plants | Value | No. of New Jobs | No. of Expansions | Value | No. of Jobs |
|------|-------------------|-------|-----------------|-------------------|-------|-------------|
| 1950 | 7 | $ 835,000 | 143 | 6 | $2,110,000 | .. |
| 1951 | 7 | 945,000 | 255 | 3 | 475,000 | .. |
| 1952 | 6 | 295,000 | 163 | 9 | 2,150,000 | .. |
| 1953 | 2 | 100,000 | 30 | 7 | 820,000 | .. |
| 1954 | 3 | 1,350,000 | 150 | 1 | 500,000 | .. |
| 1955 | 5 | 1,393,000 | 565 | 8 | 1,250,000 | 192 |
| 1956 | 2 | 325,000 | 70 | 8 | 1,350,000 | 213 |
| 1957 | 8 | 3,092,000 | 1002 | 3 | 913,985 | 70 |

September, 1957—Trouble at Central high school

| Year | No. of New Plants | Value | No. of New Jobs | No. of Expansions | Value | No. of Jobs |
|------|-------------------|-------|-----------------|-------------------|-------|-------------|
| 1958 | | NONE | | 1 | 325,000 | 50 |
| 1959 | | NONE | | 1 | 268,000 | .. |

These figures were furnished by the Little Rock Industrial Development company. The plant values and the numbers of employees are mainly estimates, particularly in more recent years.

more than this, since the city was developing an industrial boom before the school crisis struck.

"We don't say it's all because of the school business," said Everett Tucker Jr., secretary and executive director of the Little Rock Industrial Development company [and also an anti-Faubus school board member]. "There may be other factors, too. But you don't just all of a sudden run up against a blank wall like that." . . .

## An Arkansas Professor: The NAACP and the Grass Roots*

ALTHOUGH newspapers, periodicals, and, more recently, several books have given a fairly adequate background of the Little Rock school-integration crisis, they have thrown only limited light on the part played by the local branch of the National Association for the Advancement of Colored Peo-

* A statement prepared in 1959 for this collection of materials by Professor George C. Iggers, a white historian who was a leader in the Little Rock NAACP from 1952 to 1956 and in 1960 is teaching at Dillard University, New Orleans.

ple (NAACP). Such neglect has given rise to a number of popular mis-conceptions, the most serious and widespread being that the national office of the Association pressed litigation upon the Little Rock branch as part of a Southwide strategy to secure compliance with the Supreme Court's decisions of 1954 and 1955.

Actually, the pressure for the suit came from the Little Rock branch itself, which, like other local units, possessed a large degree of autonomy and freedom of action. Moreover, the Little Rock branch had been working for a number of years previously to bring about racial integration in the local public-school system. In February, 1956 the branch filed a suit against the Little Rock School Board, not because it rejected a moderate program of integration but because slowly but surely it had lost confidence in the good faith of the Board to implement voluntarily any program that would bring an end to the so-called "separate but equal" system.

The first active demand for gradual integration of the Little Rock public schools came in early 1952, more than two years before the Supreme Court decision of May, 1954. During the early years after World War II developments in local race relations provided considerable grounds for optimism. Peaceful and voluntary admission of Negro students to the University of Arkansas Law School in Fayetteville was accomplished; Negroes were accepted as students at the University's Medical School in Little Rock; Negroes had experienced no difficulty in enrolling in the University of Arkansas Graduate Center in Little Rock, where they constituted approximately one-half the total students. Further, the main branch of the Little Rock Library opened its doors and shelves to Negroes; and the Rock Island Railroad abolished its separate waiting rooms. In the downtown area, department stores, following a request by a local, informal interracial group, removed "white" and "colored" signs from drinking fountains. New and more systematic channels of interracial communication developed, carrying the prospect for common cooperation on a variety of human problems and issues in the future. In 1954 the Arkansas Chapter of the Southern Regional Council was reorganized as the Arkansas Council on Human Relations. Its luncheon and dinner meetings, some of which were held in downtown hotels on an unsegregated basis, brought together both White and Negro local leaders to discuss and act on problems of mutual concern. Informal contacts between white and Negro ministers increased, leading to plans for a merger of the respective ministerial alliances, a goal that was realized—and held—inspite of subsequent strains and tensions.

In early 1952 the Education Committee of the Little Rock NAACP, of which I had just been named chairman, did a study of local schools and found that those serving Negro children were generally inferior with respect to classroom space, library facilities, teacher salaries, per capita appropriations, curriculum, quality of instruction, and other indices. We found that the gap between median Negro and white achievement on standardized national tests administered in Little Rock grew continuously larger from year to year and from grade to grade.

With the approval of the Education Committee of the local NAACP I recommended as a starter that instead of attempting to duplicate courses and facilities, the Little Rock School Board experiment with admission of selected Negro students from Dunbar High to specific courses at the nearby Little Rock Senior High. Interestingly enough, the report was given serious attention in both Negro and white communities. It was published, not by the NAACP but by a local interracial organization called the Little Rock Committee on Schools, which was supported by individuals and organizations in addition to the NAACP. The Reverend Harry Bass, Executive Secretary of the Little Rock Urban League, and the Reverend Lewis Deer, pastor of the white Pulaski Heights Christian Church and president of the Arkansas chapter of the Southern Regional Council, served with me on the steering committee, which quickly established contact with one member of the Little Rock School Board who appeared quite sympathetic to the approach suggested in the report. Through him arrangements were made for the Committee to meet informally and quietly with the Little Rock School Board on February 20, 1952. Much to our dismay plans for the meeting were discussed with representatives of the local press by Thaddeus Williams, an attorney and president of the local NAACP, and subsequent fear of public reaction led the Board to cancel the scheduled meeting. This produced a certain amount of consternation within the local NAACP branch.

However, it was possible to resume highly informal negotiations. Mr. A. B. Bonds, Jr., the Arkansas State Commissioner of Education, indicated to members of the committee his sympathy with the study and with the concluding recommendations. After a lapse of more than two months another meeting was scheduled with the Little Rock School Board. This was a formal gathering at which the Reverend Lewis Deer was spokesman for a committee which included several prominent white leaders. After listening to our presentation the Board went into closed session, turning down our request. While I do not know details of the Board's discussion in this restricted meeting, I did learn through our original contact on the Board that three members of the six-man Board, including himself, were sympathetic with the plan; the other three opposed it, and Mr. Harry A. Little, then Superintendent of Little Rock Schools, was very outspoken against any integration whatsoever. Only after this meeting and a consequent conviction that further negotiations for even a limited, experimental school desegregation program would be fruitless did the Little Rock branch of the NAACP vote to support a suit against the Board for the objectives implicit in the report.

This was in 1952. The national office counseled against such a move, urging that we wait until the Supreme Court ruled on the five cases which were to become the basis for the May, 1954 decision. This advice was followed, and the local branch of the NAACP took no further action through the courts until much later.

Soon after the high court's 1954 decision the Little Rock School Board announced it would comply just as soon as the Court gave instructions on implementation. In September of 1954 the Executive Board of the Little Rock NAACP, of which I was then chairman, met with the School Board and the new Superintendent of Schools, Mr. Virgil Blossom. At this meeting the Superintendent outlined the original "Blossom Plan" for public school integration in the city. In the East End was being constructed a new school building which had been planned as a junior high school for Negroes. Now Mr. Blossom proposed that it serve as a general high school to which Negroes and whites would be admitted. Dunbar High would be converted into a junior high school, presumably for Negroes only. At the high-school level integration would begin with completion—probably in September, 1956—of the East End high-school building, subsequently named Horace Mann High, and of a West End high school subsequently named Hall High. The following year integration would be undertaken in the junior high schools, and still later, and more slowly, in the elementary schools. Meanwhile the Board would draw up one set of city school zones which would serve as a basis for assignment of pupils regardless of race.

This original "Blossom Plan" was well publicized, primarily by the Superintendent himself in talks before many Negro, white, and mixed groups throughout the city. Significantly, there was little public criticism of his proposals. The Capital White Citizens Council, which was organized in early 1955, strongly objected, but it showed little strength until the gubernatorial campaign of 1956.

Within the Little Rock Branch of the NAACP sentiment on the Blossom proposal was sharply divided. The more militant members opposed it on the grounds that it was vague, indefinite, slow-moving, and indicative of an intent to stall further on public-school integration. However, these contentions were rejected by a very clear majority who cautioned against moving too fast and held that the Superintendent and the Board should be given adequate time to demonstrate their good faith in effectuating the plans drawn up by Mr. Blossom. The militants wanted to file a suit against the Board immediately. The moderates thought a suit ought to be avoided, if possible, so that Little Rock might show the rest of the South that peaceful and voluntary compliance with the Supreme Court decision could be realized. Officers of the local NAACP branch continued to keep in touch with the Board and with the Superintendent, indicating their support for the program and urging that the necessary steps for its realization be taken as quickly as possible.

However, during the summer of 1955 the school board publicly announced some modification in the original Blossom program, evoking serious doubt among NAACP members who had assumed the good faith of the school officials. Under a new voluntary transfer plan children would not have to go to the school in their zone, but could apply, and get approval for, attendance elsewhere. Moreover, only Negro teachers were to be assigned to the Horace Mann High School, a move which would presumably lead most, if not all, whites considering attendance at Mann to change their minds. Only white teachers were to be assigned to Central High, Technical High, and a fourth school, Hall High, being built on the West Side. Further, although the publicly supported Dunbar Junior College for Negroes was abolished, colored students were denied admission by the Little Rock School Board to the Little Rock Junior College (white). Finally, the starting date of high-school integration was set back until 1957 or 1958. Perhaps the most disturbing of these developments from the NAACP's point of view was the Board's decision to open the new Horace Mann High School in February 1956 as a segregated Negro institution.

Had the original Blossom plan been placed in effect, even with the somewhat gerrymandered school zones which put from 500 to 800 Negroes in the Horace Mann district notwithstanding the fact that a majority of them lived closer to Central High, both Central and Horace Mann would have been substantially integrated. These drastic modifications of the original plan, undertaken without the advice or consent of the many Negroes who had been inclined to go along with the first proposal even though it left much to be desired, forced upon them the conclusion that the Board and the Superintendent now intended to integrate the public schools only on a token basis, if at all.

By this time a majority of the NAACP members felt that their only alternative was legal action seeking to enjoin the Board from opening Horace Mann on a segregated basis. Too, the conviction was growing among those of us who had previously opposed a suit from the standpoint of community relations that without a court order the Board would never integrate a single school. Adding to our consternation was the fact that many Negro students who previously had attended Dunbar High School, which was only a few blocks from Central High, would now pass by the latter (built for 3,000 students but with an enrollment of less than 2,000) in walking at least two miles east to Horace Mann. In considering the suit we were advised by Mr. U. S. Tate, the Regional Counsel for the NAACP from Dallas. He held that the attempt to prevent the opening of Horace Mann by injunction would be psychologically unfortunate and bad in terms of public relations both within and outside the Negro community. Instead, he suggested that students not wishing to attend Horace Mann attempt to register at Central High.

At a pre-trial hearing the attorneys for the Little Rock School Board pursued a line of questioning that indicated clearly that they and the Board believed that the national office of the NAACP had picked Little Rock as a strategic spot for an integration suit. Such was not the case, for neither the NAACP attorneys nor the national office was entirely enthusiastic about the type of suit the local branch had in mind.

Members of the Little Rock branch of the NAACP had lived in the community most of their lives; they had been active in Negro civic affairs, expressing their concerns through various movements and organizations of which the NAACP was one. Verbally and publicly they tended to be considerably more moderate than the spokesmen for the national office, judging from the official pronouncements of the latter. At the same time, however, they were, in fact, much more impatient and much more determined to attain their limited objectives than were the national officials and some of the local lawyers. It was my impression that while they would only reluctantly undertake the suit, they felt it was the sole course in the circumstances, unless they were willing to abandon for an indefinite time all attempts to secure public-school integration.

Nevertheless, they clung to the hope that there would be some good-faith demonstration by the Board, and through a white lawyer attempts were made up until the last minute to arrange another meeting with the Board, at which time, it was hoped, serious differences might be resolved. For the NAACP members the suit was viewed as a last resort to salvage the original Blossom Plan. The School Board was unresponsive to the overtures of the NAACP, and plans for filing suit against it were developed in December 1955 and January 1956. Urgency was dictated by the fact that the Horace Mann High School was scheduled to open on a segregated basis on January 23, 1956.

The NAACP Field Secretary, whose duties were servicing and advising local branches in the area, and who was responsible to the national office, offered no assistance whatever. Consequently, all the detailed organizational work to register Negro students at Central High and to file the suit had to be done by local NAACP members, primarily a core group of hard workers who already had full-time jobs. The national office did agree to furnish the services of its legal staff if we would hire a local lawyer, pay his fee, and cover court costs.

In December, 1955 the local branch voted to file the suit, provided certain conditions were met. First, a sufficient number of parents would have to attempt to register their children at the Central High School, and upon being refused, apply to the local branch for legal aid. Second, the Executive Board of the local NAACP would have to raise at least $300 by January 23, the day of registration for the second semester and the opening date for Horace Mann High School. Third, a lawyer who would take the case for the fee the local branch could afford would have to be found. To our suprise these conditions were readily met.

The response to our search for registrants was overwhelming, reflecting the changed attitudes of the moderate elements in the Negro community and their determination to assume what for them were serious risks in an effort to secure minimal public-school integration. Members of the Executive Committee visited only a limited number of parents of Negro children, selecting those who lived near white schools, emphasizing the principle of registration at the closest school, regardless of race. On the morning of January 23, 1956, practically all the Negro parents we had contacted and their children appeared at the respective schools for registration. Apparently the word had spread in the Negro community and a number of parents whom we had not talked with also appeared with their children and attempted to register. Upon being refused admission for their children, most of the parents applied to the local NAACP branch for legal aid.

The financial problem was more readily solved than we expected. Very quickly the $300 was raised, some of it coming from white sympathizers in the local community. Within four weeks after the filing of the suit we were able to raise an additional $1,000 from local Negroes, who in the past had shown no great disposition to underwrite Negro protest and betterment causes.

Securing an attorney proved less difficult than we had anticipated. Shortly after the decision of the local branch to file the suit, and before more than a few dollars had been raised with which to finance the case, Attorney Wiley Branton of Pine Bluff agreed to serve as our lawyer for a quite modest fee.

In the registration move the Executive Board of the local NAACP was careful not to challenge the Blossom Plan, which we suspected was constitutional. Rather, we pursued the limited objective of obtaining immediate relief in obvious hardship cases. Those Negroes who attempted to register fell into four distinct categories: (1) high-school students who would have to pass Central High on their way to Horace Mann or who lived very close to Central High, (2) students who wished to take courses offered at Central High but not available at Horace Mann, (3) students who wanted to enroll in courses available only at Technical High, and (4) junior-high and elementary students living in a small Negro enclave, West Rock, in the suburban Pulaski Heights district, who each day were transported by bus to a segregated school five miles away, although they lived within easy walking distance of white schools.

The handling of the Little Rock case and the developments in several other projected cases in the state were indicative of the serious lack of communications existing between the Little Rock branch of the NAACP and the attorney of the national staff.

Efforts of the Little Rock branch, for example, to arrange a conference with Attorney Tate regarding strategy in the Little Rock case were unsuccessful. The regional counsel did not arrive in Little Rock until the evening before the court hearing scheduled for the following morning. Upon his arrival he went immediately to bed. Then to the dismay of local NAACP members, he appeared in court the next morning and argued that any gradual plan was unconstitutional, rather than supporting the argument for relief in specific instances around which Little Rock Negroes had built their case. The suit was lost, and the Blossom Plan, now considerably modified from the original, upheld; however, the Court ordered that high-school integration begin in September, 1957.

In the late summer the School Board again fundamentally revised the court-approved Blossom Plan, which had provided for voluntary transfer of students who did not wish to attend the school in their zone. Now the Board assigned all but nine Negro children—including children living in the Central High and Hall zones—to Horace Mann, and all white children in the Horace Mann zone to Central High. More than fifty Negro children had expressed a desire to go to Central.

In retrospect I find it difficult to escape the conclusion that the crisis in September was not the result of premature integration but of the breakdown of authority and the weakness of a false sort of gradualism. The Little Rock School Board in following the erroneous belief that by progressively weakening its own plan and by emphasizing its own reluctance to follow the Supreme Court decision it would make the bitter pill more palatable, actually helped to consolidate extremist opposition.

## DOCUMENTATION SUITABLE FOR RESEARCH PAPERS

BIBLIOGRAPHY ENTRY

Iggers, George C. "The Race Question in Little Rock's Schools before 1956." *LRUSA.*

FIRST FOOTNOTE

*George C. Iggers, "The Race Question in Little Rock's Schools before 1956," *LRUSA,* pp. 283-291.

SUBSEQUENT FOOTNOTES

*Iggers, *op. cit.,* p. ■.
*Iggers, "The Race Question," p. ■.
*Iggers, p. ■.

These examples are models for materials first published in this collection.

## Little Rock's School Superintendent: An Inside View*

. . . ORVAL E. FAUBUS, regarded then as a liberal Democrat, was elected governor in 1954. Faubus made it unmistakably clear that, while he felt Arkansas was not yet ready for sudden integration, the issue was a local one to be decided locally. He pledged "the facilities of the governor's office to implement and assist in any way possible" the decisions of each local school district in regard to integration. That suited the Little Rock School Board exactly.

I might also mention that after our phase plan of integration had been thoroughly discussed by the public and officially adopted by the board, I was chosen as Man of the Year in Little Rock for 1955 in the

* From "The Untold Story of Little Rock," by Virgil T. Blossom, in *The Saturday Evening Post,* May 30-June 27, 1959. For model documentation see p. 47.

annual popularity election staged by the Arkansas Democrat. In the same election, Winthrop Rockefeller, who had become a cattle breeder in Arkansas and was chairman of the Arkansas Industrial Development Commission, was named Man of the Year for the state. His support of greater opportunity for all was well known. . . .

. . . on Feb. 8 [1956] officers of the NAACP filed suit against the school board in an effort to upset our phase program and force immediate integration. The net results of this suit, which was dismissed in Federal District Court and also by the United States Eighth Circuit Court of Appeals in St. Louis, were in our favor. For example, the NAACP did not carry the case to the United States Supreme Court, presumably because they feared our program would be upheld and would set a pattern of gradual integration everywhere. At the same time, the legal action by the NAACP strengthened support of our plan in Little Rock, where the public generally concluded that we had devised the best possible program for giving them the least possible integration in the longest possible period of time.

Governor Faubus was re-elected in 1956, and it was significant that he defeated in the Democratic primaries a rabid segregationist, Jim Johnson. But these triumphs for moderation did not mean that the segregation extremists—mainly in eastern Arkansas—were yielding. On the contrary, they were busy behind the scenes and, still more important, leaders of the bitterly segregationist White Citizens' Council throughout the South were closely studying developments and trying to decide whether they could keep the integration problem off their own doorsteps by joining in a fight to the finish at Little Rock. . . .

Faubus did not want these bills [introduced in the Arkansas Legislature in 1957 by Attorney-General Bennett] and in several casual conversations with him I got the strong impression that he regarded Bennett as an extreme segregationist and did not want to see him come into power. The governor, however, was subject to some complex political pressures. There were, for example, certain powerful business interests which had opposed him in 1954 but later joined him, and in doing so acquired considerable backstage power. These few men were not concerned with the integration issue so much as they were with extending their own political influence.

In addition, Governor Faubus had a comprehensive tax program that he was determined to get through the 1957 legislature. Representatives from Eastern Arkansas usually were able to dominate the legislature and they could block his tax program unless he accepted the segregation bills. . . .

[May 30, 1959 issue]

. . . THAT EVENING [four days before school opened in 1957] the school board once more tried to enlist the aid of the governor, who met with us at a hotel. Gov. Luther Hodges of North Carolina had just issued a warning that he would not tolerate violence in connection with school integration in that state, and we hoped Faubus would follow his example.

"We are concerned only about possible violence from the outside," R. A. Lile, a member of the board, told the governor. "We don't know whether we could get the help of the National Guard if it is needed. But if you would issue a statement like the Hodges' statement, we won't need the National Guard."

"If I make such a statement," Faubus replied, "it would make me look like an integrationist."

"Well, issue the statement," Upton suggested, "but add that you will use any legal means under the state segregation laws to oppose integration. That will make your position clear."

Faubus was angry, almost belligerent, as he arose to leave. "I don't know what I'll do," he exclaimed, looking at me, "but when I decide I'll tell Virgil." . . .

[June 6, 1959 issue]

. . . ON THE evening of Oct. 2 [1957] I was informed that the Mothers League was conducting a telephone campaign for a mass walkout of students the next day. School attendance had been improving steadily, and about 1700 children were attending regularly, despite segregationist efforts to keep them away. A rumor had been circulated, however, quoting Faubus as saying that if half of the enrolled pupils stayed away, the school would be forced to close. The Mothers League apparently hoped to achieve that goal, but the scheduled "walkout" was not successful. A total of 1651 students reported for classes the next day. When the Negroes appeared, about eighty-five boys and girls walked out, some of them wearing Confederate caps or wearing Confederate flags on their jackets. . . .

Outside about twenty-five adults were waiting. Somebody produced a straw-stuffed effigy of a Negro, which was hung from a tree and set afire.

Guardsmen cut it down. A boy and girl who had taunted the soldiers were arrested. All who walked out were suspended for three days, and some of the leaders for a week or for the rest of the term.

Neither suspensions nor expulsions stopped the disturbances inside the school during the late fall and early winter months. I do not want to single out any youngsters who were involved because some of them later changed their attitude and became very well behaved. But I cannot avoid saying that all of the Negro students conducted themselves well, with the exception of one girl who was the main target of harassment by segregation-minded youngsters—probably just because she was bright and high-strung and most likely to show her resentment when abused.

Early in October she and another Negro girl were pushed around in a corridor and blocked by several white boys as they tried to enter a classroom. After that there were more frequent incidents, and soldiers usually accompanied the Negro students from one class to another as a protective measure. One girl angered some white students by treating her guard rather imperiously and often saying, "Come on, guard! I'm going to another class now." As a result she was painfully kicked as she went to her seat in assembly, and sometimes boys called her names to which she replied once in similar language.

Once when everybody's nerves were on edge, a chair was shoved in front of a Negro girl—by accident, it turned out—in the cafeteria, and she retaliated by throwing her tray on the head of a white boy and spilling food on several students. . . .

[June 20, 1959 issue]

. . . WHY, THEN, did our plan fail? Looking back, I suppose an objective observer would see where we had to improvise to meet unexpected developments and we made mistakes. But I believe the basic reasons for failure must be found in the vacillation of political leaders at state and Federal levels and in a deliberate plot by extreme segregationists all over the South to force a finish fight in Little Rock to delay or prevent a showdown on their own home grounds.

The Supreme Court's order for integration with "all deliberate speed" seemed to recognize that compliance would take longer in some areas than in others. This gave the extremists a legal opportunity to delay and to make a test fight in our schools, using the persuasive argument to local people that they did not have to accept integration because other areas in the South had no integration plan. The argument fell on fertile ground.

"We won't comply with the Supreme Court decisions," a Mississippi orator summed up for a cheering Little Rock audience. "We will resist as long as we can. Then we will defy the court and secede from the Union. And then we will apply to Washington for foreign aid!"

Even so, politics was the most important single factor in our defeat. The Supreme Court decisions put politicians at all levels on "the hot seat," and most of them were busier trying to get off the seat than trying to inspire respect for law obedience. The fate of a few officials who sought to observe the law or find a compromise solution was enough to convince many others that moderation was political suicide. Gov. Frank Clement of Tennessee, who stood firm against segregationist threats, did not even run for re-election. Congressman Brooks Hays of Little Rock, who sought a sensible solution, was defeated in 1958 by Dale Alford, the school board's outspoken segregationist.

By 1958 moderation had become a liability, and cleverness at evading the law a key to political survival. "You have to be an extremist to survive in Arkansas," a veteran politician remarked to me. "You have to out-Faubus Faubus to get the votes."

On the Federal level, the Department of Justice presented no plan for supporting local attempts to carry out integration, and a Federal judge refused to supply United States marshals to protect Central High School at a time when, I am confident, any show of action by the Federal Government would have been more than welcome to Faubus. "What are the Federals going to do?" he asked me repeatedly before throwing himself into the arms of the segregationists. I could only assume he hoped the "Federals" would take vigorous enforcement action, thus rescuing him from the hot seat and enabling him to evade responsibility for enforcement or nonenforcement.

After disorders occurred the Justice Department did not release the FBI report on responsibility for the demonstrations, nor did it take action against a single known participant, although even in Little Rock Municipal Court six of them were fined.

Attorney General Brownell resigned in October, 1957, and dispatches from Washington said that "settling" of Federal policy in the Little Rock crisis—whatever that meant—had freed him to return to private law practice. In December, when extremists were trying vigorously to close Central High School, dispatches quoted William P. Rogers, who succeeded Brownell, as saying that "we ought to give the Little Rock matter a chance to rest a while."

Finally, the Little Rock integration program suffered severely from lack of positive leadership in the city government. Mayor Mann spoke out for law and order, but we were in the middle of a change to a city-manager form of government, and Mann was a lame-duck mayor without real political power or prestige. He feuded with the city council and with the governor, and political bickering further weakened local leadership in a crisis.

All of these things combined to contribute to the success—however temporary—of the extremists. Even the fact that the majority of the people of Little Rock originally were ready to accept our integration plan worked against us in the end because we did not expect real trouble and were surprised and unprepared when, as I have related, trouble was thrust upon us by extremists in the community and from the outside.

Where do we go from here?

I can speak only as a school administrator who believes in the dignity of the individual as a fundamental part of our American heritage. I believe that, first, we must face the existing facts. The Supreme Court's school-integration decisions are here to stay, as demonstrated by its findings in the Little Rock appeal. At the same time, the court's approval of the Alabama pupil-placement law, permitting school boards to transfer students for reasons other than race, means that a high degree of segregation can sometimes be maintained to preserve educational standards. Thus, the way is open to accept the inevitable in a lawful manner with intelligence instead of emotion. And one thing is obvious—if the South does not plan the future of its system of public education in line with the main stream of progress, then the Federal Government will step in to do it for us. . . .

[June 27, 1959 issue]

## *Two Tennessee Authors: A McCarthy Revival?**

"AT A TIME when the South might well use a renewed vision of Robert E. Lee's virtue or Andy Jackson's vigor," a young Southern liberal said recently, "it seems a shame that we should choose to start reviving the spirit of Joe McCarthy."

An embattled social scientist in Atlanta summed up the situation during a conversation: "One trouble outsiders have in understanding our present difficulties is the culture-lag in the South. McCarthy never caught

---

* From "McCarthyism under the Magnolias," by Wilma Dykeman and James Stokely, Tennessee authors, in *The Progressive,* July 1959, p. 6. For model documentation see p. 47.

on down here back in his heyday, but as the last-ditch fight for segregation grows more desperate, all his ugly techniques are revived. At the end of the decade we're in the throes of an experience the rest of the country put behind it in the early Fifties." . . .

As McCarthyism moves South under the magnolias, most of those against whom the search for subversives appears to be directed are not political Communists as much as racial non-conformists, people who seek a reasonable way of abiding by the Supreme Court ruling on desegregation of the public schools, while those who would subvert the law by defiance and maneuver designate themselves the super-patriots and inquisitors. By their words the investigators are seeking out Southerners 'soft on Communism"; by their acts they are singling out Southerners "soft on segregation."

Of course, the very fact that they feel this necessary indicates the absence of a monolithic South, and reveals that there are many Southerners who abhor the present dilemma and are willing to work for a solution. But the nature of this crisis, with its pull from the past and its emotional undertow, makes it especially susceptible to McCarthyism. In a time of tremendous change at the regional level (involving integration), and deep apprehension at the national level (involving Communism), where these regional racial tensions coincide with our national survival fears, there is created a no-man's land of uncertainty and suspicion. In such an atmosphere, threats and innuendo serve well to intimidate and immobilize creative thought and action on controversial problems. . . .

## An Atlanta Professor: Too High a Price for Segregation?*

EVEN before this year's court decision compelling Virginia's schools to open on an integrated basis, parents in Norfolk County were carrying placards which read:

"We are not for integration or segregation but we want our schools open."

They may also have been carrying with them the hint of a solution to the largely unvoiced but fundamental dilemma over integration which has been worrying both the Negroes seeking entry into the schools and white liberals in both the North and the South.

I say "unvoiced" dilemma because there is no issue on which liberals

---

* From "A Fate Worse than Integration," by Howard Zinn, Atlanta University faculty member, in *Harper's*, August 1959, pp. 53-56. For model documentation see p. 47.

are more certain than that of racial equality. They may disagree about
Formosa or Suez or regulating the unions, but concerning racial discrimination they are unified and altogether free of doubt. At least outwardly.
Underneath, however, liberals have often been more uneasy than they
will admit. They know that the vast majority of Southern whites favor
segregation, that the enforcement of integration below the border states
may well cause mob protests, beatings, dynamiting, and other forms of
violence. And even those who are able to suppress their qualms about
bloodshed cannot escape practical doubts about success: "How in the
world are we going to have integration in South Carolina, Georgia, Alabama, Mississippi—Supreme Court or no Supreme Court—if local leaders
and the population are fiercely opposed?"

The placard displayed in Virginia suggests, I believe, the solution to
this dilemma: *that white Southerners are not in effect for segregation
when it means losing something they value even more than the separation
of the races.* In their unconscious hierarchy of values, segregation does not
hold the highest rank. This is the crucial fact which has permitted integration to take place in many areas of Southern life and which promises
to soften the determination to put up "massive resistance" even in the
Deep South.

Any pollster, any white Southerner, or any Negro will tell you that
white Southerners are overwhelmingly for segregation if the question is
put to them in isolation. What is often overlooked, however, is that, like
everyone else, the white Southerners cherish a large number of values;
that these values are arranged roughly and unconsciously on a kind of
ladder of importance; and that although the Southerner may not consciously acknowledge it, segregation is scarcely ever at the top. . . .

Public-opinion polls are very poor guides to questions like integration because they present so narrow a choice of alternatives. . . .

. . . If we explore the full range of Southern preferences and values
realistically, the strategy necessary for successful integration becomes
clear and the weirdly illogical and uneven pattern of segregation in the
Deep South becomes more comprehensible. Here are some examples of
the values which white Southerners may consider more precious than
continued segregation:

*The most obvious is money—the simple drive to make a profit.* The
power of the boycott, directed against the bus companies in Montgomery,
and the white tradesmen of Tuskegee, needs no elaboration. . . .

. . . A white plumbing contractor will hire a Negro helper and sit beside him on the front seat of his half-ton truck rather than hire a white helper and pay ten dollars more per week. . . .

Negroes, it should be noted, are often respected customers in the stores of the Deep South. . . . At Rich's in Atlanta—the South's largest department store—Negroes and whites rub shoulders at the crowded counters. Women of all shades try on the same hats, the same dresses, and even the same foundation garments. . . .

Another proof of the power of economic pressures to break down racial barriers is the increasing amount of service being given to middle-class Negroes by white menial laborers. . . . There are countless examples: the white telephone repairman wiping his feet as he enters the home of a Negro businessman; the white employees of a contractor digging ditches on the campus of a Negro university; the white deliveryman unloading his wares at the back entrance of a Negro lawyer's home. . . .

[There is a second] key value—*the importance Americans attach to their sports.* Many Southerners will not cling to segregation if it means giving up popular sports. Georgia Tech students showed this three years ago by their near-violent reaction when it appeared that segregation would cause cancellation of an important game. And the successful integration of golf courses in Atlanta was possible because whites refused to give up golf to keep Negroes away. . . .

There are still other values more treasured in the South than segregation. *One of these is social peace, or "law and order."* Even in the most flagrant cases of violent opposition to integration—Little Rock, Clinton, the Nashville school dynamiting, the Autherine Lucy affair— only a small minority of Southerners has preferred violence to quiet if unhappy acceptance. More and more Southerners who strongly defend the idea of segregation are resigning themselves to compliance as the legal structure erected by the courts becomes increasingly formidable. . . .

*The traditional Southern qualities of hospitality, courtliness, and good manners* come into conflict with segregation at many points, and increasingly they triumph. Many Northerners have noted with surprise a phenomenon which the south takes for granted: a vociferous segregationist, in personal contact with a Negro, can often be gentle and courteous. Such displays of courtesy had no real effect on living conditions in the South so long as the Negro remained "in his place." But as the Negro dares to appear in places and situations where he has never been, the courtesy will face a genuine test for the first time. And in many cases the individual white, facing a situation where he must violate ordinary rules of courtesy in order to defend racial separation, will maintain his conduct at the cost of permitting a breach in racial tradition. . . .

*Political power is another value that may prove more important than segregation*—at least so far as Southern leaders are concerned. So long as few Negroes voted, Southern politicians could successfully exploit the race issue. But with the increase in Negro voting, the South is beginning to approach the point where political power may depend more on concessions to the Negro than on the kind of demagoguery that John Rankin and Eugene Talmadge made their specialty. The friendly new attitude of city officials in Atlanta is attributable in large part to their dependence on the Negro electorate. . . .

*Now, to many Southern parents, the education of their children is beginning to seem more important than the maintenance of segregation.* . . .

The South undoubtedly has a long way to go before it solves its race problems and it would be false to pretend that the way will be easy. But, as I have tried to show, many of the values to which Southerners are deeply attached are operating to remove the barriers between races in the South and not violently to reinforce them—even while the cries for continued segregation remain loud and bitter. This principle is a powerful one: whether or not it is used deliberately to deal with crises over Negro rights as they arise, I believe it must ultimately assert itself throughout the South. For the white Southerner it is becoming increasingly clear that there are many fates worse than integration.

## *A Charleston Attorney: A Nation within a Nation?**

IN THE current turmoil which is agitating the South, the bare question of whether Negro children shall attend school with whites is far from being the only, or even the main, issue at stake. There is more to it, too, than the constitutional issue so generally cited by Southern Congressmen, the question of States' Rights versus encroaching Federal power. There is a third factor involved. . . .

Briefly stated, the issue is this:

Shall there continue to exist in America a land, a society, a distinct cultural entity, known as The South?—or shall there be instead only a geographical region, a "southern portion of the USA"? In short—shall the South, as such, survive?

---

* By M. H. Sass, Charleston, S.C. Written in 1959; here first published, in shortened form. For model documentation see p. 291.

Southerners are grimly aware of the fact that their "national" survival is at stake. This awareness is seldom openly or directly expressed, especially to outsiders. It is something which, so far as the average Southerner is concerned, is felt rather than reasoned—but it is widely, deeply, passionately felt. It is this awareness of the mortal peril confronting the South, as a distinct civilization, that accounts for the peculiar sense of urgency which has pervaded the whole Southern resistance movement. And, far more than any strong devotion to this or that constitutional theory, more even than the powerful dislike of the prospect of Negroes being in the schools with whites, it is the Southerner's speechless rage against the outside forces seeking, as he sees it, to destroy the South's very identity, which accounts for the high degree of emotional intensity, the sense of outrage and resentment, the fury and passion and crusade-like fervor that characterize the resisting South today.

These are the emotional qualities which one finds in a man engaged in a grim struggle to defend his home and country against a destroying enemy. And so the beleaguered Southerner of today sees himself: defender of the homeland. . . .

The closest parallel . . . to Southern nationalism can be found right here on our own North American continent, in French Canada.

No parallels are exact, of course, and this one is no exception. In the matter of language, for example, the French Canadian has the advantage (from the standpoint of nationalism) of having a completely distinct tongue from that spoken by other Canadians; while the Southerner has only a different, albeit markedly different, accent and manner of speech.

And, while race is by no means the decisive factor in French Canadian nationalism—there are plenty of French Canadians named Robinson and Gillespie—(nor, for that matter, is religion; a good many British Canadians are Catholics, and there are some French Canadian Huguenots), nevertheless it is generally easier to tell a French Canadian from an English Canadian at first sight than it is to tell a Southerner from a Yankee.

But if the basic difference between South and North is largely cultural and psychological, rather than racial or linguistic—if the distinctions between Southerner and Yankee are somewhat more subtle than those that set off the English-descended Ontarian from the *habitant,* they are nonetheless meaningful, nonetheless real. It can truly be said that, to all intents and purposes, the South is to the North as French Canada is to British Canada.

In Southern life, as in French Canadian, religion plays a dominant role. And while no single church in the South can match the power and position of the Roman Catholic Church in Quebec, orthodox Protestantism in general, and the uncompromisingly orthodox Southern Baptist Church in particular, fulfills much the same function as guardian and propagator of Southern culture and Southern folkways that the Roman church does in Canada.

Both the South and French Canada are rooted in a conservative, rural, agrarian tradition; both societies are considered "backward," by New York and by Toronto; both are societies to which industrialization came late and, when it did come, largely from without and under outside control. As French Canada was conquered by the English, so, later, the South knew conquest at the hands of the North; and the same sort of "conqueror's guilt-fear complex," as it has been spoken of in Canada, "that so bedevils English-French-Canadian relations" certainly is discernible in North-South relations also—business and social, as well as political.

In each case, there is a "homeland"—Quebec to the French Canadian, the area south of the Mason-Dixon line and the Ohio to the Southerner; but both the *habitants'* and the Southerners' birth rates have been much higher than those of their respective neighbors, the result being that the French Canadians have spilled across the prairies of the western provinces, while Southerners in large numbers have overflowed into the western and midwestern United States.

The Southerner, again like his *Canadien* counterpart, is very tenacious of his folkways (and of his religion as well—witness the phenomenal growth, during the past two decades, of the Southern Baptist Church in the Middle West and Far West). The French Canadian, who has spilled into the northeastern United States in even greater numbers than he has into western Canada, has been termed "the least assimilable of immigrants." The Southerner probably runs him a close second. Describing conditions in an Ohio city which over the past few decades has had a considerable influx of white upland Southerners, a Northern newspaper in 1958 commented: "It has been argued, persuasively, that the mountain white family from eastern Kentucky is less assimilable today than was the German family from Württemberg two generations ago."

There is yet another respect in which a parallel can be drawn between French Canada and the South: the probable direction in which their respective nationalisms are headed. Generally speaking, both are mature, level-headed nationalisms. Both seek the protection and perpetuation of their respective cultural identities—and, concurrently, the attainment of economic and political equality with the dominant group—rather than outright separation.

. . . The South fundamentally desires two things: First, it wants *recognition* of its differentness—recognition of the fact that the South *is* different, different from the rest of the USA. Second, the South wants *security* in its differentness; or, to put it another way, it wants recognition of its *right* to be different and to remain different. . . .

And it is on this demand, of *security* for the South's identity, that the Southerner meets opposition, apparently implacable opposition, from the North. This opposition is nothing new. Writing of *The War and Reconstruction,* Cash singled out, as being "the most fundamental drive behind the Yankee's behavior," "that will to wean the South from its divergences and bring it into the flow of the nation."

. . . It is this spirit in the North that both angers and alarms the Southerner. He cannot understand, much less share in, this spirit of American cultural monolithism, this idea—apparently held by most Northern Americans—that the United States must comprise a single monolithic culture, with no room nor toleration for any major divergence. Why, the Southerner complains, does the Northerner insist on a unity built on suppression and monolithism, when we could instead have unity built on diversity, as is the case in the United Kingdom?

In Britain, even though virtually all governmental power is centralized in London, it is recognized that England and Scotland are different *countries*—that Scotland, by virtue of its historical and cultural differences, is a *country* in its own right, as indeed also are Northern Ireland and even long-conquered Wales. And even with the lawmaking power completely centralized in one Parliament, the differences between the four countries which comprise the United Kingdom are recognized in law. What is law for England need not necessarily be law for Scotland. For example, the Church of England enjoys the right of Establishment, in England; but north of the Tweed the Established Church is the Church of Scotland (Presbyterian).

This unity-in-diversity has worked well for Britain—certainly no one can say that the Scots or the Ulstermen were any less conspicuous than the English in the defense of the United Kingdom during the Second World War; it has worked far better, it is safe to say, than any policy of suppression or cultural monolithism could possibly work. Yet any suggestion that here in the USA it might be more fair and just, as well as wise and expedient, for us to devise a system whereby certain general laws would apply to the rest of the country but not to the region south of the Ohio and the Potomac—any such suggestion, it can safely be said, would be damned and denounced in the North as an outrageous blasphemy; for even the idea that the South should be permitted to have a different social and cultural pattern seems to be blasphemy.

Blasphemy to the Northern mind or not, that is what the South wants and that is what it is going to have, if Southern nationalism has its way. With practically every country in the world, every former colonial possession in sight, from Ghana and Morocco to Burma and Indonesia, demanding and getting full independence (almost always with United States support, it might be added), it is rather handsome of the South, Southerners feel, not be raising the question of outright total independence. Certainly, they say, to demand for their homeland simply a recognized status comparable to that of Scotland is not asking too much. In any event, that is the least that the new Southern nationalism is of a mind to accept.

## A Little Rock Minister: A Change of Climate*

LITTLE ROCK'S business, professional, and civic leaders are working hard this summer in a concerted effort to open the city's four senior high schools in September—even if it means accepting desegregation. This is in sharp contrast to the sea of fear and silence which engulfed the community a year ago and inundated the hopes of some 3,400 pupils for public education within their community. Little Rock's leading citizens have awakened to the need to take a public and positive stand for the preservation of their school system.

The shift in attitude may be seen most clearly by comparing the reaction of community leaders to events of last November and their response to those taking place just seven months later in June.

In November the Little Rock school board surrendered to Governor Faubus by buying up Superintendent Virgil Blossom's contract and then resigning en masse. The Arkansas *Gazette* commented, "Their mass resignation stands as a monument to the five members' recognition that they have not had, at any critical point in their tenure, any effective support from the leaders of the community, who have largely remained silent through their ordeal."

A few weeks later the *Gazette's* Pulitzer Prize-winning editor, Harry Ashmore, concluded publicly that Governor Faubus had the support of the people of Little Rock and that the position of moderates such as himself was untenable. "We have lost at every turn," he declared, adding: "Gov-

---

* From "Hope Comes to Little Rock," by Colbert S. Cartwright, pastor of Little Rock's Pulaski Heights Christian Church, in *The Progressive*, August 1959, pp. 7-9. For model documentation see p. 47.

ernor Faubus is in the saddle and is telling the people what they want to hear in a deep emotional situation. They are having temper tantrums and are shouting and hollering. But their position also is untenable. It can't go on forever. Some day the schools will be reopened and they will be integrated."

The battle-worn editor who in those days spoke of his editorial desk as his "foxhole" could not have predicted that in only a few months the city's leading citizens would be clamoring for the opening of the schools on a desegregated basis. Yet this is what happened.

On June 18 [1959] a three-judge federal court voided the governor's proclamation which had closed the high schools, and permanently enjoined him and others from interfering with the "approved plan for the gradual integration of the city's public schools." Community leaders openly welcomed the decision. When the federal court's ruling was announced to a Rotary Club meeting the members greeted the hoped for decision with unprecedented applause.

The catalytic agent which moved Little Rock's leadership to action was the May 5 attempt of the three-man Faubus bloc of the six-man school board to fire summarily 44 of Little Rock's 800 administrators and teachers and to demote the school superintendent to the position of principal. . . .

For the first time during the Little Rock school crisis the city's best known and most influential men united publicly to take a hand in the school problem. Two days after the purge attempt 179 business and professional men met to form the "Committee to Stop This Outrageous Purge" (STOP). Before the meeting ended they had contributed $6,000 in cash and pledges, and gladly gave their names to the press as those responsible for and dedicated to the circulation of petitions to oust the three pro-Faubus board members.

The attempted purge projected the politically influential Arkansas Education Association into the Little Rock crisis as it rose to the defense of the purged teachers. Its executive secretary, Forrest Rozzell, who had been hesitant to make a public break with Governor Faubus, now turned his political deftness toward winning the recall election, regardless of political consequences. . . .

The key to understanding the magnitude of the public response lies in realizing that the anti-purge forces generally did not at first regard the protest as having anything to do with the racial issue facing the schools. They saw themselves as fighting a battle solely on the grounds of justice and fair play for the teachers.

In reality the teacher purge was directly related to Little Rock's ultimate answer to the consistently reiterated demand of the federal courts to desegregate its public schools. The teacher purge had come as a direct result of the extreme segregationists' answer to the question. When Little Rock's prominent leadership chose to fight for the recall of the pro-Faubus bloc in defense of their teachers, they were repudiating the whole tumultuous approach that these extremist forces had taken in the past two years. By defeating the rabid segregationists the STOP leadership not only had saved their teachers from an outrageous purge but were responsible for creating a united school board composed of moderates wanting to open all of Little Rock's public schools as soon as possible.

As a result of their efforts in the STOP movement, the very civic leaders who had refused during the past two years publicly to support Superintendent Blossom's plan of minimum desegregation are now promoting that plan with a crusade-like spirit. Their experiences in the STOP campaign had a significantly transforming effect upon them:

*One*—The civic leadership came to appreciate the indispensability of public schools in modern life. . . .

*Two*—In the STOP campaign the civic leadership rediscovered its moral courage. At the organizational meeting of the STOP organization its chairman, Dr. Drew F. Agar, observed that many persons had kept quiet about the school crisis for nearly two years because they feared it would hurt their business if they spoke up. He said he was sorry to say that he had been in that category. "But I am not any longer," he declared. "Something very malevolent and dangerous has occurred and it is our duty to stop it."

It was obvious from the beginning that the teacher purge had triggered public righteous indignation over the countless other outrageous indignities perpetrated upon the community by the extreme segregationists. As incidents of deceit were visited upon STOP's leadership in the campaign, a growing desire developed to rid the community of this element. Recalling these indignities as he spoke to a rally of 2,000 persons gathered to honor Little Rock's public school teachers, W. S. (Will) Mitchell, campaign chairman for STOP, brought shouts of audience approval when he said: "I think we are ready to take positive action. Too long irresponsible statements have gone unchallenged. What this community needs is the restoration of its self-respect." . . .

. . . One civic leader who found his voice during the STOP campaign said privately to his pastor, "I feel like I have just gotten out from a long jail sentence." . . .

*Three*—In the STOP campaign business and professional men found that their nightmarish fears of economic ruin if they publicly stood against the extreme segregationists did not materialize. Neither did they find that being labeled "left-wingers," "Communist-dupes," and "integrationists" by their opponents was particularly harmful to their prestige.

Instead, the Little Rock business and professional community discovered that when it stood united, as it did in the STOP campaign, attempts at smearing and economic reprisal were ineffective. . . .

*Four*—Little Rock's leadership in the STOP campaign discovered that Governor Faubus is not invincible. . . .

*Five*—The STOP campaign brought about a renewal of open discussion among Little Rock's leadership concerning the plight of the public schools. Little Rock had long been enveloped in a silence begotten by fear. Now men at coffee breaks and at the clubs spontaneously began discussing the previously tacitly forbidden school question. At first discussion centered on the teacher purge, but once that issue was resolved men found they still wanted to talk about the problem of the schools. They had become personally involved in finding an orderly resolution of the entire ugly crisis. . . .

In announcing the school board's reaction the board president, Everett Tucker, Jr., reasoned: "In the judgment of those of us on the board, we now—for the first time in nearly two years—have the opportunity to take over the operation of the public schools and to run them in the best manner possible. Ever since early September 1957 the school board has been hampered and handicapped in everything it has tried to do. Its every action has been attacked or impeded by court actions, and by interference from various sources including the federal government, the state government, the NAACP, and others." . . .

Many imponderables remain on the Little Rock scene, but one thing appears certain: Little Rock's civic leadership will not again abdicate its responsibility for the preservation of the public school system.

# Suggested Additional Readings

PERIODICALS

*Phylon: Review of Race and Culture.* Atlanta University, Atlanta 3, Georgia. A quarterly devoted to literary as well as historical and sociological examination of race relations in the United States. Particularly concerned with Negro-white relations in the South and the role of the Negro in American life.

*New South.* A monthly, the official publication of the Southern Regional Council with central offices in Atlanta, Georgia. Carries brief articles, reports, and public documents concerning various aspects of race relations in the Southern states. It has published many items relating to school segregation and desegregation, including pieces on Little Rock.

*Journal of Negro Education.* School of Education, Howard University, Washington, D.C. A quarterly carrying authoritative articles on various aspects of Negro education in the United States. One of the best sources for intensive studies of the school desegregation process in various Southern states and in specific communities. Each issue in addition carries a comprehensive bibliography of recent literature on race and education. Highly recommended.

*The Crisis.* National Association for the Advancement of Colored People, 20 West 40th Street, New York 18, N.Y. A monthly publication, official organ of the NAACP. *Crisis* has been published for some fifty years. It has varied its orientation and content, and in recent years it has been primarily a medium for reporting the activities of the national organization and of various local branches. However, it does carry articles of substantive and theoretical interest and editorials reflecting the opinions of the NAACP officials. Essential to any comprehensive examination of the NAACP in the school-integration process.

*Southern School News.* Southern Education Reporting Service, Box 6156,

Acklen Station, Nashville, Tennessee. A monthly publication providing a comprehensive coverage of developments in the school integration picture in all the Southern and border states. Its reporting is objective and factual and skillfully done by experienced newspapermen. In addition to its regular reports it reproduces some of the more important documents, speeches, and proposals relevant to public-school segregation and desegregation. Extremely useful in following current developments. Summaries of major trends are also included.

*Race Relations Law Reporter.* Vanderbilt University Law School, Nashville, Tennessee. A quarterly publication that provides a comprehensive summary of legal developments in all aspects of race relations. Deals not only with court cases but with legislative, administrative, and related official actions of local, state and national governments with reference to race relations in the United States. Required for those who have an interest in the legal aspects of race relations.

Other periodicals that may be consulted, depending on the student's particular interest in school segregation and desegregation are:

*American Journal of Sociology*
*American Sociological Review*
*Annals of the American Academy of Political and Social Science*
*Journal of Educational Sociology*
*Journal of Human Relations*
*Journal of Negro History*
*Journal of Social Issues*
*Social Forces*
*Social Problems*

## BOOKS

Blossom, Virgil T. *It Has Happened Here* (New York: Harper and Bros., 1959). The superintendent of public schools in Little Rock during the period when the integration program was developed and carried into practice provides a detailed account of efforts to desegregate schools and of the role he played in it.

Brown, Robert R. *Bigger than Little Rock* (Greenwich: Seabury Books, 1958). The Episcopal bishop of Arkansas gives a first-hand account of events leading to the crisis in Little Rock, weighs the involvement of various local groups, including the "extremists" on both sides, and explains the general ineffectiveness of Little Rock ministers and churchmen in influencing developments.

Burges, Austin Earle. *What Price Integration?* (Dallas: American Guild Press, 1956). A confirmed segregationist views with alarm the trends toward integration of public institutions, fearing that it will lead to Negro-white intermarriage and the "mongrelization" of the population. The work is useful because it gives public expression to beliefs shared, but rarely articulated so directly, by many Southern whites.

Carmichael, Omer, and Weldon James. *The Louisville Story* (New York: Simon and Schuster, 1957). The superintendent of schools in Louisville, Kentucky, and the associate editor of the *Louisville Courier-Journal* provide a brief but complete first-hand account of the desegregation of that city's schools during the years 1954-1956, emphasizing the involvement of white and Negro groups in developing and implementing the successful plan.

Green, Donald Ross, and Warren E. Gauerke. *If the Schools Are Closed* (Atlanta: Southern Regional Council, 1959). The authors of this study, professors at Emory University, Atlanta, point out many implications of closing of public schools as a means of avoiding integration, concluding that mass education on a private basis is not a feasible alternative.

Hays, Brooks. *A Southern Moderate Speaks* (Chapel Hill: University of North Carolina Press, 1959). The former congressman from Little Rock, who sought to bring the governor of Arkansas and the president of the United States to an understanding that would prevent the use of federal troops in the Little Rock crisis, reports on his efforts—and their failure. Additionally, he voices the position of "moderates" on other issues affecting race relations in his native region.

Holley, Joseph Winthrop. *Education and the Segregation Issue* (New York: William Frederick Press, 1955). The president emeritus of Albany (Georgia) State College, a Negro, defends the segregated school system, criticizes the proponents of integration, and sees the best future for southern Negroes in a continuation of the bi-racial system.

Martin, John Bartlow. *The Deep South Says 'Never'* (New York: Ballentine Books, 1957). One of America's outstanding journalists examines the development of white Southern resistance to the Supreme Court decisions outlawing racial segregation in the public schools. Appearing originaly as series of articles in the *Saturday Evening Post*, the material presented here underscores the depth of feeling against integration on the part of various segments of the white population.

Shoemaker, Don, ed. *With All Deliberate Speed* (New York: Harper and Brothers, 1957). Eleven members of the staff of the Southern Education Reporting Service, publisher of the *Southern School News*, analyze various aspects of the school-desegregation process. Particularly useful will be the chapter by Wallace Westfeldt dealing with communities where there was violent resistance to integration.

Shannon, Karr. *Integration Decision Is Unconstitutional* (Little Rock: *Arkansas Democrat*). A widely read columnist for the *Arkansas Democrat*, one of the Little Rock daily papers, brings together a series of articles written for that publication and argues, as the title indicates, that public-school integration is not consistent with an appropriate interpretation of the Constitution.

Woodward, C. Vann. *The Strange Career of Jim Crow* (New York: Oxford University Press, 1957). An outstanding American historian shows that racial segregation in the South is of relatively recent origin and describes the social and political mechanism of its establishment.

## ARTICLES AND PAMPHLETS

*America: National Catholic Weekly.* "Mob Law in Arkansas," September 21, 1957. The editors review the relationships between President Eisenhower and Governor Faubus during the Little Rock crisis and support the actions of the president, noting that "the day that the writ of Federal Courts can be successfully defied in this country, that day organized irresponsibility and mob rule begin."

*America: National Catholic Weekly.* "Faubian Tactics," September 28, 1957. The editors hold that "Governor Faubus let himself be blackmailed by the troublemakers into doing their will. . . . But the price he paid was ruinous; and what he got was not peace."

Bickel, Alexander M., "An Inexplicable Document," *The New Republic,* September 29, 1959. Analyzes the legal content of a speech by Governor Orval Faubus of Arkansas in which the chief executive charged that the Supreme Court had usurped authority, specifically the prerogatives of the states in the public-school area.

Black, Charles L., Jr., "Paths to Desegregation," *The New Republic,* October 21, 1957. A native Texan and Harvard Law School professor analyses the Supreme Court decisions, their interpretation by district courts, and efforts of segregationists to prevent their application, concluding that neither the NAACP, nor the courts, nor the executive branch has moved too far too fast in the desegregation of public schools.

*Business Week.* "Cost of High Tension," September 21, 1957. Reports a

Survey conducted in Little Rock and Arkansas on the effects of the school crisis on business and industrial development and concludes that both retail and wholesale enterprises have been adversely affected; moreover, future industrial development of the area is now in doubt.

Carter, Robert L., and Thurgood Marshall, "The Meaning and Significance of the Supreme Court Decree," *Journal of Negro Education*, Summer 1955. Two NAACP attorneys who were directly involved in the segregation cases ruled on by the Supreme Court examine the implications of the second decision (May, 1955) and indicate steps which members of the NAACP should take in securing compliance with the Court's implementation decree.

Carter, Roy E., Jr. "Segregation and the News," *Journalism Quarterly*, Winter 1957. A lengthy and careful analysis of the way newspapers, magazines and other media have treated public-school segregation and desegregation, particularly since the Supreme Court decisions of 1954 and 1955.

*Congressional Quarterly Weekly Report.* "NAACP Reaction to Faubus Vcitory," August 8, 1958. An interview with Clarence Mitchell, director of the Washington bureau of the NAACP, on the re-election of Governor Orval Faubus to an unprecedented third term. Mitchell expresses determination of the NAACP to continue to seek public-school integration in Arkansas and elsewhere in accordance with court rulings and orders.

Cunningham, Merriman. "The Southern Temper," *New South*, July-August 1958. The dean of Perkins School of Theology at Southern Methodist University reviews the dilemma of the Southern churches in the segregation-desegregation controversy and concludes that the "conscience of churchmen is stirring and beginning to move" in the direction of forthright affirmation of Christian principles.

Current, Gloster. "Crisis in Little Rock," *The Crisis*, October 1957. The NAACP's director of branches provides a first-hand and well-documented account of events in the Little Rock school crisis during the previous month, emphasizing the roles played by local leaders of the organization and the failure of officials to take more affirmative action in carrying out the integration plan.

Dugger, Ronnie. "They Like Faubus," *The New Republic*, October 14, 1957. The author, who accompanied Governor Faubus and members of his staff on a trip to smaller cities and communities in Arkansas, shows that among rural and small-town whites in the state the governor has much popularity.

Fichter, Joseph H., S.J. "The Reluctant South," *The Commonweal*, May

15, 1959. An outstanding Catholic sociologist in the South emphasizes that people who ordinarily are leaders of political, social, educational, and economic forces in the South have been silenced by the bigots and by their own fears.

Fleming, A. S. "The Effects of School Closing," *School Life,* December 1958. An outstanding federal administrator points out some of the probable major consequences of the closing of public schools in an effort to prevent desegregation, emphasizing that mass education of a high quality is impossible in the absence of public financing; reviews also consequences for students whose education is terminated, postponed, or diluted.

Hays, Brooks. "Little Rock from the Inside," *Look,* March 17, 1959. The Arkansas congressman who was defeated by a segregationist favorite of Governor Faubus, and who sought to mediate between the federal and state authorities in the 1957 crisis, describes his role in the Little Rock school situation. He writes as a southern churchman as well, being prominent in the Southern Baptist organization.

Isaacs, Harold R. "World Affairs and U. S. Race Relations: A Note on Little Rock," *Public Opinion Quarterly,* Fall 1958. An exploratory study of the significance of the school crisis in Little Rock on world opinion concerning American society and its government; also, suggests the necessity of trying to understand the impact of that opinion on national, state, and local leaders involved in the Little Rock affair.

Johnson, Guy B. "Segregation versus Integration," *The Crisis,* December 1953. Perhaps the outstanding sociologists in the South, Dr. Johnson reviews the issues at stake in the school cases pending before the Supreme Court, indicating the likely rulings and suggestings some of their implications for race relations generally and for public schools in those states maintaining a biracial system.

Johnson, Manning. "Wanted, Another Booker T. Washington," *American Mercury,* September 1958. A Negro former Communist and frequent witness before federal and state investigating committees attacks the NAACP as being Communist-influenced and argues that "reds" in the organization were largely responsible for the tensions and violence that occurred in Little Rock in September 1957.

Kennedy, William V. "Governor Faubus and the Guard," *America: National Catholic Weekly,* October 12, 1957. A brief account and analysis of the governor's calling out the national guard in the Little Rock school-integration crisis in September 1957.

Laws, Clarence. "Nine Courageous Students," *The Crisis,* May 1958. A field representative of the NAACP who advised the Little Rock branch concerning integration moves at Central High reviews the experience of the nine Negro students who were eventually admitted and emphasizes the hostility of administrators and teachers as well as of troublemaking white students.

Lee, Frank. "The Changing Character of Negro Leadership," *The Crisis*, April 1958. A sociologist and student of racial movements criticizes the leaders of the NAACP for their failure to initiate protest action at the grass-roots level in the South and explains this shortcoming in terms of the smugness and middle-class character of the top officials. (For a reply to Lee see the article, "Comment on Frank Lee's Article," *Crisis*, May, 1958.)

*Look*. "Inside the NAACP: Ruby Hurley's South," August 6, 1957. An illustrated account of the activities of Miss Ruby Hurley, Regional Secretary of the National Association for the Advancement of Colored People, whose headquarters are in Atlanta and who since 1951 has traveled over the entire southeastern states continuously, assisting local branches and leaders of the NAACP with their activities. Excellent photographs.

McKay, Robert. "Little Rock: Power Showdown," *The Nation*, September 28, 1957. Analyzes legal aspects of Faubus's orders calling out the troops in Little Rock and suggests that, once the move was taken, anarchy was the only alternative to the assertion of federal power by the president.

McNeil, Robert B. "A Georgia Minister Offers a Solution for the South," *Look*, May 28, 1957. The white pastor of the First Presbyterian Church in Columbus, Georgia (who was later dismissed from his pulpit) argues that closer contact between Negroes and whites in work on common problems, including school integration, offers the only durable solution to race relations in the region.

Neil, James. "The Education of Governor Faubus," *The Nation*, June 6, 1959. A brief review of Governor Faubus's continuing resistance to public-school integration in Arkansas and an attempt to suggest changes that have taken place in his outlook.

Perlmutter, Nathan. "Florida's 'Moderate' Segregation Formula," *The New Leader*, July 20-27, 1959. The Florida Director of the Anti-Defamation League analyzes critically the state's recently-enacted pupil-assignment law which was designed primarily to maintain segregation legally; a similar measure was adopted in Arkansas and applied by the Little Rock School Board in 1959.

Rowland, Stanley. "Legal War on the NAACP," *The Nation*, February 9, 1957. Reviews moves made in various states to "outlaw" the NAACP and destroy its effectiveness as a Negro organization attempting to secure compliance with the Supreme Court decisions. Notes especially the efforts of state attorneys general and legislatures to force the NAACP out of business either by invoking old laws or enacting new ones such as were passed in Arkansas at Governor Faubus's insistence.

Southern Regional Council and Department of Racial and Cultural Relations, National Council of the Churches of Christ, U.S.A., "Intimidation, Reprisal, and Violence in the South's Racial Crisis." (Pamphlet.) A state-by-state analysis of the use of intimidation, reprisals, and violence by Southerners, primarily white extremists, to oppose individuals and groups seeking to bring about changes in existing racial patterns, particularly in the school institutions.

Stephan, A. Stephen. "Desegregration of Higher Education in Arkansas," *Journal of Negro Education,* Summer 1958. A professor of sociology at the University of Arkansas provides a brief account of desegregation of colleges and universities in the state on a limited basis and gives useful background information on the increase in Negro participation in public education at various grade levels.

Stephan, A. Stephen, and Charles A. Hinks, "Integration and Segregation in Arkansas—One Year Afterward," *Journal of Negro Education,* Summer 1955. Two Arkansas sociologists examine Negro and white reactions to the Supreme Court decision of May, 1954, pointing out that white resistance is developing and that local officials are taking a "wait and see" attitude, doing little or nothing until required to act by court order, though some integration had already occurred at institutions of higher learning.

Vorspan, Albert. "The Plus Side of Little Rock," *Jewish Frontier,* November 1957. Discussess the impact of the Little Rock episode on the American political scene. Is concerned primarily, however, with the significance of Little Rock for religious groups in American life, holding that racial segregation in America is essentially a moral issue with which religion must deal in specific ways.

Wesley, Charles H. "Do Negroes Believe in Themselves?" *Negro History Bulletin,* October, 1957. A prominent Negro historian and educator raises basic questions about the failure of many Negroes to act decisively in realizing new opportunities in view of legal and institutional changes in American life.

Weaver, G. B. "Liberation: Red Paint for Negroes," *American Mercury,* November, 1958. Attacks the NAACP and other integrationist groups in the South on the grounds that they are strongly influenced by hidden communists in their midst and warns Negroes against involvement with such organizations.

Wilkins, Roy. "Deep South Crisis." (National Association for the Advancement of Colored People, 1957). (Pamphlet.) The NAACP's executive secretary in a speech before the Commonwealth Club of San Francisco replies to Judge Tom Brady of Mississippi, who during the previous month had defended massive resistance to the Supreme Court decisions before the same organization.

Williams, David C. "Miracle in Washington," *The Progressive,* December, 1956. A description of public-school integration in the national capital, which was accomplished with a minimum of friction and with good results, contrary to the claims of a congressional investigating committee.

# Suggestions for Research

The issues growing out of the Little Rock experience are not simple ones. The questions raised are complex and difficult. Many of them would make good essay or term-paper topics. For example:

1. Who were the heroes and who the villains in the Little Rock story? To what extent can the story be adequately told in terms of heroism and villainy?

2. What did the Negro and white communities really want in 1957? Did these wants change over time? If so, in what way and why?

3. If you were asked by an intelligent Yugoslavian or Malayan to explain the events of September 23, 1957, how would you do so?

4. To what extent did class differences and class conflict play a role in the Little Rock story?

5. To what degrees did internal conflict in the Negro and white communities, and in various subgroups, help shape the events at Little Rock?

6. Who were the extremists, who the moderates in the Little Rock situation? How realistic is it to describe the course of events as a victory of extremism over moderation—or vice-versa? As a victory of integration over segregation—or vice versa?

7. The president, the governor, the mayor, the school board, the school superintendent, the NAACP, and the White Citizens Council have been singled out by one or more critics as being at least partly responsible for the action of the mob in September, 1957. How would you assess these charges? What conflicting motivations characterized the principals?

8. How would you define the main issue at stake in the Little Rock situation at the beginning of the 1957 school year? Did the issue shift over time? Had it become sharper or dimmer by the fall of 1959?

9. How many theories can you construct to explain Governor Faubus'

decision to call out the National Guard? Which seems most plausible to you? Why?

10. To what extent can the Little Rock story be adequately told in terms of state rights vs. federal rights, or states rights vs. "city rights"?

11. Should a man obey a law even when he believes it to be immoral, as many southerners believe the integration ruling to be? Is obedience to the law the highest appeal that can be made to citizens of a democracy? Was President Eisenhower right in maintaining a neutral position on the merits of the Supreme Court decisions, grounding his appeal for compliance solely on the obligation of citizens to accept "the law of the land"? Should Southern liberals who believe in integration as a matter of ethical principle have said so publicly instead of using the "law of the land" argument?

12. The Reverend Mr. Pruden, president of the Little Rock White Citzens Council; Congressman Hays, a leading moderate; the Reverend Mr. Cartwright, who apparently accepts school integration as a matter of principle; and Mr. Eldon Dennis (letter on pp. 182-183), who apparently believes in full social equality between the races—all are Christian leaders, who invoke Biblical sanction for their views. How can such a wide disparity of opinion flow from the same basic religious teachings?

13. How would you draw the line between the responsibility of the executive branch of the Federal government and the responsibility of the judicial branch for future enforcement of the integration decisions?

14. Suppose you had been president of the Little Rock Chamber of Commerce during 1957-1959. What would you have done about the school situation? What impact, if any, might your activities have had?

15. Picture yourself as a federal district judge confronted with a desegregation suit in Jackson, Mississippi. On the basis of the Little Rock experience, what kind of facts would you want to have before making your decision? What principles would guide in deciding how far and how fast you would try to push integration in that Deep South city?

You will not find the answers to these questions neatly laid out on one or another page of this book. Queries which could be so simply answered would scarcely deserve treatment in an essay or a term paper. To deal effectively with any one of the fifteen questions listed above, you will need, to begin with, (1) a sound factual background and (2) a conversancy with the main issues. Both can be gotten from the selected readings. Beyond these, you must be able to put complicated factual material, along with your own thinking, into some logical, disciplined, literate form. You must be explicitly conscious of personal value judgements and be able to distinguish them from empirical evidence and logical deductions.

In short, the questions we have set forth lend themselves to speculative papers in which the student uses his imagination, his insight, and his inquisitiveness to range afield, held in check only by a respect for the facts and a dedication to logical consistency.

# DOCUMENTING YOUR RESEARCH PAPER

## Footnotes and Bibliography*

THE READER of your research paper expects to find in it both your work and an accounting of the sources from which you have drawn your information. This accounting is your documentation. It is also your thanks, or at least your acknowledgment, to any people whose writings or other works have furnished you the information that you have organized into your paper.

Whether as thanks or as report of sources, your documentation must be explicit and specific. It must tell your reader where you found your information so that he can, if he wishes, appraise your sources, perhaps go to them himself and see whether you have conveyed their facts faithfully or reasoned soundly from them.

All of your sources are listed together in a bibliography (general documentation) at the end of your paper. Any source you cite is named at the point where you cite it, usually in a footnote (specific documentation).

Most of your sources will be books or magazine articles, aside from the selections in this book.

### DOCUMENTATION REFERRING TO A BOOK

A bibliography entry for a book will be organized thus:

May, Rollo, *Man's Search for Himself*. New York, 1953.

| Period | Period | Comma Period |
|---|---|---|
| Name of the author, surname first for alphabetizing. | Title of book, in italic type or underscored to indicate that it is a publication. | City and year of publication. The name of the publisher may appear between the city and the date. |

First line begins at margin; if there is a second line, indent it 5 spaces.

---

* Prepared for the series by the general editor of Chandler Publishing Corporation.

The footnote for a citation from this book would be organized thus:

¹ Rollo May, *Man's Search for Himself* (New York, 1953), pp. 223-224.

| Comma | | Paren-<br>thesis | | Paren-<br>thesis<br>Comma |
|---|---|---|---|---|
| | | | Comma | Comma |
| Index (num-<br>ber or aster-<br>isk). | Name of author,<br>in normal order,<br>as footnotes are<br>not alphabetized. | Title of book,<br>italic type or under-<br>scored to indicate that<br>it is a publication. | in City and year<br>of publication. | |

Period

Numbers of pages that contain the
information documented. Some people prefer to omit the abbreviation "pp."
First line of footnote indented as paragraph; second line at margin.

The order of the items in this information, the use of the index mark (raised number of asterisk), the punctuation, the parentheses, and the use of italic or underscores are customs that spare a writer the labor of writing many words and his reader some quantity of reading. The footnote would otherwise have to be something like:

This information comes from pages 223-224 of a book by Rollo May, entitled *Man's Search for Himself,* published in New York in 1953.

If you name the publisher of a book, the forms for bibliography and footnote are:

May, Rollo. *Man's Search for Himself.* New York, W. W. Norton & Company, 1953.

¹ Rollo May, *Man's Search for Himself* (New York: W. W. Norton & Company, 1953), pp. 223-224.

## DOCUMENTATION REFERRING TO A PLAY

Any citation of a play almost necessarily refers to it as published in a book. Accordingly you cite a play as you would a book. To specify the location of a passage, the page number may be sufficient. But it may be more useful to give act, scene, and if possible line numbers. Hence:

Shakespeare, William. *The Tragedy of Coriolanus,* ed. William Allan Neilson. New York, 1906.

¹ William Shakespeare, *The Tragedy of Coriolanus,* ed. William Allan Neilson (New York, 1906), Act IV, Sc. vii, lines 2-3.

## DOCUMENTATION REFERRING TO A
## MAGAZINE ARTICLE

If your source is a magazine article, your bibliography entry might read:

Kirstein, Lincoln. "The Future of American Opera," *Atlantic* 199:3 (March, 1957), pp. 50-55.

| Comma | Period | | Comma | |
|---|---|---|---|---|
| Name of author, surname first. | Title of article, in quotation marks to indicate that it is not a separate publication. | | Name of magazine, in italic type or underscored to indicate that it is a publication. | Volume and number. |

| | Comma | Period |
|---|---|---|
| Issue, in parentheses. | Page numbers of the entire article. | |

First line begins at margin; second and subsequent lines indented 5 spaces.

Your footnote to this magazine article as your source might read:

[1] Lincoln Kirstein, "The Future of American Opera," *Atlantic* 199:3 (March, 1957), p. 54.

| Comma | | | Comma | |
|---|---|---|---|---|
| Index (number or asterisk). | Name of author, in normal order. | Title of article in quotation marks. | Name of magazine, italic or underscored. | Volume and number. |

| | Comma | Period |
|---|---|---|
| Issue, in parentheses. | Page number to which the footnote refers. | |

First line of footnote indented as paragraph; second line at margin.

As is documentation from books, documentation from magazines is made briefer and less laborious by the customs of word order and punctuation.


## DOCUMENTATION REFERRING TO A
## NEWSPAPER ARTICLE

Citations from newspapers cannot be so precise as citations from books or magazines, since many newspapers have several editions in a day and the same article may appear on different pages in different editions; even more troublesome, it may be rewritten, reheaded, or dropped in later editions, and it may not appear in the early editions of a given date.

A bibliography entry concerning a newspaper might therefore appear thus:

"State to Up Vet Home Loan Rate," *San Francisco Chronicle,* Sept. 17, 1959. Dated Sacramento, Sept. 16.

The corresponding footnote might be:

[1] "State to Up Vet Home Loan Rate," *San Francisco Chronicle,* Sept. 17, 1959; dated Sacramento, Sept. 16.

If the writer of this newspaper article were named, his name would precede the title of the article in both the bibliography entry and the footnote. If the story were sent to the *Chronicle* by a news service, such as United Press International or Associated Press, this fact should appear in parentheses at the end of both bibliography and footnote, in full or abbreviated:

. . . Sept. 16 (United Press International).
. . . Sept. 16 (UPI).

## THE ESSENTIAL IN DOCUMENTATION

Information comes to the writer from so many sources that specimen bibliography entries and footnotes for all possible needs would overflow any book. So it is necessary to keep in mind the basic reason for documenting: namely, to give the source of a statement so it can be appraised, and located, by the reader. These are basic, though some other details may be put into the documentation.

If your bibliography entries and footnotes answer the following questions, they will be satisfactory:

1. *Who?* Who is the author who made the statement? What individual, collaborating group, or institution is the author? Or is the statement published in a work that does not identify the author?
2. *In what publication?* What book, magazine article, newspaper story, speech, broadcast program, or other? At exactly what point in this work? (Can a reader find your citation, from what the documentation tells him?)
3. *When and whence?* In what city and in what year was the book published? On what date was the periodical published?

The next sections contain numerous models for footnotes and bibliography entries, but all are guided by these three principles. Since almost every research project will require documentation referring to some source not covered by a model, you need to perceive the principles as they are demonstrated in the models.

## EXAMPLES OF BIBLIOGRAPHY ENTRIES

The entries in a bibliography are ordinarily arranged in alphabetical order, as these examples are. To help in comparing them with corresponding footnotes, the footnote examples (pages 326-329) are numbered in series and the explanatory remark that follows each bibliography entry gives the number of the footnote.

Baker, Charles T. "Patients' Perceptions of Psychologists." Unpublished master's thesis, Ohio State University, 1953. [An unpublished doctor's dissertation or other research paper would be treated in this same way. See footnote 18.]

Boddy, Francis M., *et al. Applied Economic Analysis.* New York, 1948. [This book has six authors. If only one author card is carried in a library catalogue for it, the card will be in the name of the senior author, here given. See footnote 3 and pages 334-335. of this book.]

Bowman, Isaiah. *The New World,* 4th ed., Yonkers and Chicago, 1928. [An often revised book in political geography; marked differences between editions make it important to specify the edition used, as here. See footnote 6.]

Brahms, Johannes. *Concerto No. 2 in B Flat Major for Piano.* Alexander Uninsky, piano; Willem van Oterloo conducting The Hague Philharmonic Orchestra. Epic LC-3303, 1958. [For some purposes it might be unnecessary to identify the musicians presented on a phonograph record, but the information usually is significant. The record number and the "publisher" appear on the record label. See footnote 23.]

Doe, John. "Indexing of Dissertations." Paper read at methodology seminar, —— University, October 19, 1962. In —— University Library. [If this paper were not in a library and you were citing from your notes, you would write instead, "Notes of reading," or something of the sort. See footnote 19.]

Dumas, Alexandre, fils. Letter to Joseph Méry, Oct. 18, 1844. Unpublished. Collection of Simone André-Maurois. [Letters of famous men often are microfilmed for study, even if not published. If you use a microfilm letter, mention it; as, "Microfilm in —— Library." See footnote 20.]

"The Good ex-President." *Time,* 74:14 (Oct. 5, 1959), p. 34. [A magazine article published without the author's name. It is therefore alphabetized according to its title, ignoring "The." See footnote 14.]

Gunther, John. "Inside Space." *John Gunther's High Road,* American Broadcasting Company (WABC-TV), Oct. 17, 1959. [A broadcast program in a series. The same form could be used for either radio or television. The station call letters and date might be enough in addition to the program name and the name of its "author." If no author, alphabetize on the program name. See footnote 26.]

Joyce, James. *Finnegan's Wake.* Folkways Records. FDF 934, 1956. Tape. [It might be unnecessary to write "Tape," but may be useful. See footnote 25.]

Keats, John. *The Complete Poetical Works and Letters of John Keats,* [ed. Horace E. Scudder]. Cambridge, Mass., 1899. [Scudder's name does not appear in this book, but he is known to be the editor, hence the information is supplied but enclosed in brackets; if the fact appeared on the title page no brackets would be needed. Note that "Mass." is specified to avoid giving the impression that the book was published in Cambridge, England. See footnote 5.]

Kelly, Alfred H., and Winfred A. Harbison. *The American Constitution.* New York, 1948. [A book by two authors; observe that the second author's name is in normal order. Incidentally, this is the first edition of a book that was later published in a second edition; unless another edition is specified, the edition of a book is assumed to be the first. See footnote 2. See also the entry for Isaiah Bowman's book above.]

Kelly, George A. *The Psychology of Personal Constructs.* 2 vols. New York, 1955. [If your references were to only one of these volumes, you would write "2 vols., vol. 1. New York, 1955." See footnote 7.]

Kirstein, Lincoln. "The Future of American Opera." *Atlantic* 199:3 (March, 1957), pp. 50-55. [Discussed earlier in detail. See footnote 13 and page 322 in this book.]

"Kite." *Encyclopedia Americana,* 1955 ed. [Encyclopedia article by an unnamed author. The names of editors and the like for a well-known reference book are not ordinarily needed. Neither is the page number in a book whose contents are alphabetically arranged. See footnote 12.]

Learned, Philip. Lecture given in English 346, Edwardian Criticism, —— University, May 17, 1962. Tape recording. [If there were no tape recording an equivalent statement should appear: "Notes taken by John Doe, student," or the like. Observe that the course title is not italicized or enclosed in quotation marks. See footnote 21.]

Macaulay, Thomas Babington. "Bunyan, John." *Encyclopædia Britannica,* 11th ed. [Macaulay signed this article simply "M"; the full name was gotten from the list at the end of the last volume. Observe the order of Bunyan's names; he is listed under Bunyan, not John. Observe that there are no page numbers or volume number since neither is needed for locating an article in an alphabetically organized reference book. See also "Kite," above in this list. See footnote 11.]

May, Rollo. *Man's Search for Himself.* New York, 1953. [Discussed earlier in detail. See footnote 1 and page 320 of this book.]

Ohneschatten, Dermann, Director, —— State Hospital. Interview, May 27, 1964. Tape recorded. [The subject of the interview could be mentioned, if important. See footnote 22.]

Poore, Charles. Review of Henry B. Kranz, ed., *Abraham Lincoln: A New Portrait*. *New York Times,* Oct. 17, 1959. [See footnote 16, footnote 17, and "Review . . ." below.]

Quintanilla, Luis. "Basic Tenets of Latin American International Policy." In Philip W. Buck and Martin B. Travis, Jr., eds., *Control of Foreign Relations in Modern Nations.* New York, 1957. [See footnote 8.]

Review, unsigned, of Henry B. Kranz, ed., *Abraham Lincoln: A New Portrait*. *Reviews of the Quarter,* vol. 21, no. 4 (Nov., 1959), p. 37. [To alphabetize the entry for this review at K for Kranz would suggest that Kranz wrote the review or that the entry was for the book rather than for the review. There is much variety of opinion about how to handle this kind of entry. If your reader-instructor has a strong opinion, follow his preference. See footnote 17.]

Shakespeare, William. *The Tragedy of Coriolanus,* ed. William Allan Neilson. New York, 1906. [See page 321 of this book, and see footnote 9.]

"State to Up Vet Home Loan Rate." *San Francisco Chronicle,* Sept. 17, 1959. Dated Sacramento, Sept. 18. [Discussed on page 323 of this book. See footnote 15.]

*Swedish Modern Jazz.* Arne Domnerus and his group. RCA Camden, CAL-417, 1958. Record. ["Record" is unnecessary unless needed to distinguish the described item from a tape recording or other work of similar name. The record is a collection of works performed by one orchestra. If the name of one work or its composer were the important item, this information would be given first, followed by "In *Swedish Modern Jazz.* . . ." See footnote 24.]

Sypher, Wiley, ed. *Enlightened England.* New York, 1947. [An anthology. Any book identified by the name of its editor rather than an author would be presented similarly. See footnote 4.]

*Two Thousand Years of Season's Greetings.* New York: Photogravure and Color Company, 1951. [This is the kind of irregular publication sometimes called a "bulletin." Since it may be hard to locate, you help the reader by giving the name of the publisher. Since no author name is given, alphabetize it by title. See footnote 10.]

*We Discover the Dictionary.* Coronet Films, 16V4906, 1949. Film. [The author's name, if one were given, would precede the title in this entry, and would govern the alphabetical position of the entry. "Film" may be unnecessary. See footnote 27.]

### EXAMPLES OF FOOTNOTES

These specimen footnotes are numbered to help in referring to them for comparison with the corresponding specimen bibliography entries in the section preceding this.

[1] Rollo May, *Man's Search for Himself* (New York, 1953), pp. 223-224. [Book, single author. Discussed on page 320 of this book.]

[2] Alfred H. Kelly and Winfred A. Harbison, *The American Constitution* (New York, 1948), p. 64. [Book, two authors.]

[3] Francis H. Boddy *et al., Applied Economic Analysis* (New York, 1948), p. 346. [Book with many authors, in this instance six. Unless courtesy or other special reason calls for them, the names of the junior authors are replaced by *et al.* See pages 334-335 of this book.]

[4] Wiley Sypher, ed., *Enlightened England* (New York, 1947), p. 451. [Book, single editor. This is an anthology, containing works of numerous writers, who need not be named in this kind of entry. To cite the work of one author included in such a collection, follow the model of footnote 8 below.]

[5] John Keats, *The Complete Poetical Works and Letters of John Keats,* [ed. Horace E. Scudder] (Cambridge, Mass., 1899), p. 232. [Book by a single author in a version edited by another person. Observe the brackets enclosing the editor's name; these are present because Scudder is not named on the title page of the book but is known to be the editor; if the title page bore his name there would be no brackets; compare footnote 9, below. Note the "Mass." to prevent confusion with Cambridge, England, another publishing center.]

[6] Isaiah Bowman, *The New World,* 4th ed. (Yonkers and Chicago, 1928), p. 704. [Book, edition specified. Unless an edition is specified, it is assumed that the first edition is being cited.]

[7] George A. Kelly, *The Psychology of Personal Constructs* (New York, 1955), vol. 1, p. 133. [Book, more than one volume. The citation here is to a page in one volume, and the number of volumes need not be stated; that information is in the bibliography entry. If your paper were to have no bibliography, this kind of footnote should read: ". . . 1955), 2 vols., vol. 1, p. 133."]

[8] Luis Quintanilla, "Basic Tenets of Latin American International Policy," in Philip W. Buck and Martin B. Travis, Jr., eds., *Control of Foreign Relations in Modern Nations* (New York, 1957), p. 188. [Work of one author in an edited collection of works by several authors.]

[9] William Shakespeare, *The Tragedy of Coriolanus,* ed. William Allan Neilson (New York, 1906), Act IV, Sc. vii, lines 2-3. [Play, in book form. Unless the printed version has line numbers, a page number would be given rather than the line numbers. Discussed in the text of this book, page 321.]

[10] *Two Thousand Years of Season's Greetings* (New York: Photogravure and Color Company, 1951), p. 5. [Irregular publication, that is, one not published in the usual course of any publishing enterprise—the named publisher is an engraver-printer and this cited work is an advertising piece. The name of the publisher is therefore given even in a footnote plan which does not include names of publishers of standard books. If it had a named author, his name would be at the beginning, as usual.]

[11] Thomas Babington Macaulay in *Encyclopaedia Britannica,* 11th ed., *s.v.* "Bunyan, John." [Signed article in a reference book alphabetically organized. The abbreviation *"s.v."* means *"sub verbo"* or *"sub voce,"* English "under the word" or "under the heading." The word "Bunyan"

is as accurate a guide as a page number could be, and may be better since encyclopedias are sometimes repaged to make room for new entries inserted late in the life of a numbered edition. Macaulay's article on Bunyan fills two pages; if it were a very long article, and the citation to a single sentence or other brief passage, the reader might be helped by being given a volume and page number: ". . . 'Bunyan, John,' vol. 4, p. 805." Observe the spelling *Encyclopaedia.*]

[12] "Kite," *Encyclopedia Americana,* 1955 ed. [Unsigned article in a reference book alphabetically organized. See footnote 11 concerning the omission of page number. Observe the spelling *Encyclopedia* in the title of the work.]

[13] Lincoln Kirstein, "The Future of American Opera," *Atlantic* 199:3 (March 1957), p. 54. [Magazine article. Discussed at length in this book, page 322.]

[14] "The Good ex-President," *Time* 74:14 (Oct. 5, 1959), p. 34. [Magazine article, unsigned.]

[15] "State to Up Vet Home Loan Rate," *San Francisco Chronicle,* Sept. 17, 1959; dated Sacramento, Sept. 16. [News article in a newspaper. Discussed in this book, page 323.]

[16] Charles Poore, review of Henry B. Kranz, ed., *Abraham Lincoln: A New Portrait, New York Times,* Oct. 17, 1959. [Signed book review. Such reviews often have titles, either individual or departmental; it is usually unnecessary and confusing to give such titles.]

[17] Unsigned review of Henry B. Kranz, ed., *Abraham Lincoln: A New Portrait, Reviews of the Quarter* 21:4 (Nov. 1959), p. 37. [Unsigned review of a book, in a periodical—here an imaginary periodical. The bibliography entry corresponding to this footnote is alphabetized at Review.]

[18] Charles T. Baker, "Patients' Perceptions of Psychologists" (unpublished master's thesis, Ohio State University, 1953), p. 31. [Unpublished work, such as thesis or dissertation.]

[19] John Doe, "Indexing of Dissertations" (paper read at methodology seminar, —— University, October 16, 1962; in —— University Library). [Paper read but not published. See the specimen bibliography entry at Doe.]

[20] Alexandre Dumas fils, letter to Joseph Méry, Oct. 18, 1844, unpublished, in the collection of Simone André-Maurois. [Unpublished letter.]

[21] Philip Learned, lecture given in English 346, Edwardian Criticism, —— University, May 17, 1962, from a tape recording. [Unpublished lecture. If the lecture were cited from memory, or from the writer's notes, or from notes of another listener, that fact should be given instead of the reference to a tape recording.]

[22] Dermann Ohneschatten, Director, —— State Hospital, interview, May 27, 1964, from a tape recording. [Unpublished interview. No interviewer being named, the assumption is that the interview was with the writer. If the citation were not from a recording, that fact should be given instead.]

[23] Johannes Brahms, *Concerto No. 2 in B Flat Major for Piano,*

Alexander Uninsky, piano; Willem van Oterloo conducting The Hague Philharmonic Orchestra (Epic LC-3303, 1958), record. [Phonograph record. The word "record" may be unnecessary, or many distinguish between a disk and a tape recording of the same work and performance.]

²⁴ *Swedish Modern Jazz,* Arne Domnerus and his group, RCA Camden CAL-417, 1958), record. [Phonograph record, title without composer's name. This record has several works by various composers and is thus comparable to a book of the type cited in footnote 8 above.]

²⁵ James Joyce, *Finnegan's Wake* (Folkways Records, FDF 934, 1956), tape recording. [Recorded book. To locate a cited passage more exactly, one might add "at 22 min." or the like. The tape does not contain the entire book. When a recorded work has several tapes, the one concerned may be specified, as "tape 3 at 17 min."]

²⁶ John Gunther, "Inside Space," *John Gunther's High Road,* American Broadcasting Company (WABC-TV, New York), October 17, 1959. [Television or radio broadcast; this footnote is for a television program. The network being named, the station call letters and city are extra information; but the latter would suffice if there were no network or the network were not known.]

²⁷ *We Discover the Dictionary* (Coronet Films, 16V4906, 1949), film. [Film. If the text at the citation does not make it clear that a film is meant, the word "film" is needed in the footnote, since many companies that distribute films also distribute sound tapes, disk records, and books having the same titles. Films usually are the work of writing-producing teams and are published without any "author" name; if an author is named, his name belongs first in the footnote.]

## HOW TO FIND DOCUMENTATION DATA

Where do you get information for documentation?

Most books published in the United States and many published in other countries carry this information in the preliminary pages of the book itself. The title page normally has the name of the author (or authors), the title of the book, the name of the editor instead of or in addition to the name of the author, the name of the publisher, the volume number and number of volumes if the book has more than one, the edition number if later than the first, the city of publication, and sometimes the date. But the date may appear only in the copyright notice on the back of the title page, and there may be several copyright dates owing to renewals and revisions (if there are, use the latest). If the title-page date is other than the copyright date, give both dates (as "New York, 1938; title page dated 1949"). You and your reader, seeing this discrepancy, may reasonably wonder whether the title-page date is an effort to suggest that the book is more recent than it really is.

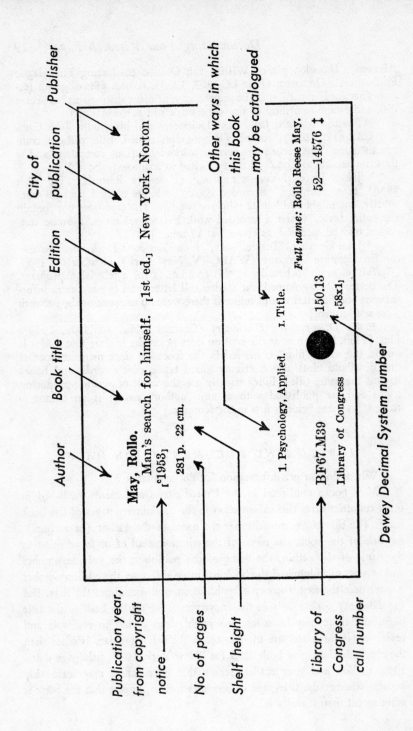

Author

Publication year,
from copyright
notice

No. of pages

Shelf height

Library of
Congress
call number

Book title

City of
publication

Edition

Publisher

Other ways in which
this book
may be catalogued

Dewey Decimal System number

May, Rollo.
   Man's search for himself. [1st ed.] New York, Norton
[c1953]
   281 p. 22 cm.

      1. Psychology, Applied.      1. Title.

Full name: Rollo Reese May.

BF67.M39          150.13
Library of Congress          [58x1]

52—14576 ‡

Often you have documentation information on a book even before you see the book itself, for library cards usually contain all of it, and more, especially those cards prepared by the Library of Congress and distributed to libraries throughout the country. (See page 330.)

Magazines usually provide the bibliographical information in a note somewhere in the early pages, less often on the cover or on a page near the end of the issue. Finding it may take some hunting, since practice is not uniform. In most magazines it will be on the page with the table of contents. Also, as with books, a researcher often gets the information from a library card for the article before he has to search it out from the publication itself. He may also get it from the entry for the article in *The Readers' Guide to Periodical Literature*.

The title page of an unpublished dissertation or thesis will give you all the information you need for documentation, as will the file copy of a paper read at a scholarly meeting but not published. For letters, personal communications, lectures, interviews, and the like, you must formulate the documenting statement from information you get at first hand.

The label of a phonograph record gives you the name of the song, speech, collection, or other work recorded, the names of the composer and of the performing musician or his analogue, the name of the maker, distributor, or publisher of the record, his identifying number or code letters, the date of issue, and sometimes other information. You may have to get some facts from the album cover or record envelope, or from the distributor's list.

Documentation data for tape recordings and films will almost necessarily come from the label. Films usually carry it on the title frames at the beginning.

Radio and television programs contain almost too frequent mention of the program name, its principal personality, the call letters of the broadcasting station, and the name of the broadcasting system. You may thus get this information from the program itself. You may also be able to get it from the program listing in a newspaper or periodical. Sometimes you may get the script of a program from the sponsor or the broadcasting company; if so, the first page or two of the script will contain many of the documentation data.

## RECORDING DOCUMENTATION DATA

You begin documenting your research paper before you begin writing it, even before you begin taking your research notes. If you were to collect material, write your paper, then try to work back to find where you got your material in order to document it, you would find the effort hopeless. When you decide to investigate a book or magazine article or other source, therefore, you should prepare immediately a bibliography card recording all the documenting information you will need if you refer to the source—this before you take your first note! Then, when you write a note card, it should have a record of its source. The record need not be complete to identify it with your bibliography card—a short "slug" something like "May *Man's Search*" is enough. Thus your bibliography card would read:

> May *Man's Search*   M 150.13
>
> May, Rollo. *Man's Search*
> *for Himself*. New York,
> 1953.

Then a note card might look like this:

> May *Man's Search*   224
> "... *Courage is the capacity*
> *to meet the anxiety which arises*
> *as one achieves freedom.* ..."

With the note card and the bibliography card, you are prepared to put accurate documentation into your finished research paper.

## CITATIONS AFTER THE FIRST—BOOKS

When a writer must cite numerous statements from the same source at intervals throughout his paper, repeating long footnotes would become tedious for him and for his reader. When the first footnote has given full information, later footnotes may be shortened in many ways, providing the shortening does not make them confusing.

A second citation from the May book might come immediately after the first one, with no other footnote intervening. For such immediately succeeding footnotes, scholars have long used this style of shortening:

²*Ibid.,* p. 231.

This means "From page 231 of the same source given in the immediately preceding footnote." The abbreviation *Ibid.* for *ibidem* (literally, "in the same") is typical of the many abbreviations and Latin expressions that we have inherited and continued to use since early scholars established them. Because they are in some sense part of an omnilingual scholarly vocabulary, many instructors require their students to learn them and use them. But some people think of them as Latin and, if they or their readers do not know Latin, feel that the use of Latin expressions is pretentious or even dishonest. Such people would prefer to use some equivalent English-language form like

²**May, p. 231.**

—or even, if May's name is mentioned in the text, nothing more than

²P. 231.

The writer of a research paper does well to learn what preference his instructor has in matters of this sort, and to follow it.

If some citation from other source material were to intervene between the first and second citations from the May work, then the *ibid.* would be wrong, for "in the same" would point to the most recently cited work. The old scholarly usage would be

³May, *op. cit.,* p. 231.

This means, "From page 231 of the work by May which has already been cited." *"Opere citato"* is the unabbreviated Latin. Those who misgive Latin expressions might prefer to write any of four other forms:

³May, p. 231.

[3] May, *Man's Search,* p. 231.
[3] *Man's Search,* p. 231.
[3] P. 231.

The first-given form would serve if only one of May's books were being used as a source. If two or more were being used it would be necessary to mention the title and to mention the author's name also, as in the second-given form, unless May's name were mentioned in the text. If the text mentioned May, but not the book title, the third-given form would be sufficient documentation. The last-given and briefest form would be correct and sufficient if the text language made clear what book and author were being considered.

When these English shortened forms are to be used, it is a frequent and helpful practice to tell the reader so in the first full footnote. Thus, after citing the source in full, you would add, perhaps: "This will here-(in)after be cited as May," or ". . . as May, *Man's Search.*"

## CITATIONS AFTER THE FIRST— MAGAZINE ARTICLES

The short expression *op. cit.* is not used when the source cited is a magazine article or other work not independent and complete in itself, such as an article in a symposium, an encyclopedia entry, or a newspaper story. For such sources, instead of *op. cit.* the footnote Latin is *loc. cit.* for *locus citatus,* Englished as "the place cited" or "the passage cited." Thus several alternative entries for the later footnote to a magazine article:

[3] Kirstein, *loc. cit.*
[3] Kirstein, p. 55.
[3] Kirstein, "Future," p. 55.
[3] "Future," p. 55.
[3] P. 55.

These five forms of short documentation correspond in function to the similar five forms for books. But note that *loc. cit.* cannot be followed by a page number; such is the convention. The other forms may therefore be preferable as more specific.

## CITING WORKS BY NUMEROUS AUTHORS

A Latin expression that often appears in documentation is the abbreviation combination *et al.* for *et alii,* which means "and others." Writers who are not alert in their Latin often punctuate this expression improperly;

those who choose to use it need to remember that *et* is a word and that *al.* is an abbreviation.

The proper use of this expression is to save writing or repeating the names of two or more co-authors of a cited source. Thus a first and later footnote might be:

¹ Francis M. Boddy, Frank E. Childs, Wendell R. Smith, O. H. Brownlee, Alvin E. Coons, and Virgil Salera, *Applied Economic Analysis*, New York, 1948, p. 363.

³ Boddy *et al., op. cit.*, p. 370.

Instead of *et al.*, those who object to Latin would use "and others":

³ Boddy and others, p. 370.

If the names of the junior authors are not important for the citation, even the first footnote may have them packaged into *et al.* or "and others":

¹ Francis M. Boddy *et al., Applied Economic Analysis*, New York, 1948.

It is not courteous to use *et al.* in substitution for the name of a single author.

## DOCUMENTATION WITHOUT FOOTNOTES

In some people's view the footnote is the most useful and explicit form of specific documentation, the least likely to be misconstrued, and the minimum civil acknowledgment that a writer can make to his source. With all these merits, footnotes are disliked by other people as obtrusive, over-formal, distracting, and an extreme nuisance for the typist. Their preference is to put some or all of the specific documentation into the text itself.

In-text documentation for books, magazine articles, and other sources requires the same information that is given in footnotes. A writer citing a statement from a book might therefore write:

. . . A definition of Rollo May (*Man's Search for Himself*, New York, 1953, p. 224) describes courage as ". . . the capacity to meet the anxiety which arises as one achieves freedom." Seen as such, courage is demanded . . .

The parenthetical documentation would be worded to accord with the text language. If it were to follow the quoted passage rather than precede it:

"The capacity to meet the anxiety which arises as one achieves freedom" (Rollo May, *Man's Search for Himself*, New York,

1953, p. 224) is a definition of courage as it is demanded from all of us. . . .

A writer uses footnote or in-text documentation as he and his readers prefer. If his readers are instructors who grade his research papers, their preference may well overrule the writer's. The general documentation is needed, in the usual bibliography form, to support either style of specific documentation.

Some writers attempt to have the best features of both kinds of documentation by using a footnote for the first mention of a source, then using brief parenthetical notes for later references. This practice might give:

. . . May found that "the greatest block to a person's development of courage is his having to take on a way of life which is not rooted in his own powers" (*Man's Search,* p. 231). . . .

Or it might give:

. . . May (p. 231) found that . . .

Either of these two parenthetical documentations might be replaced by the more traditional "*op cit.,* p. 231" or if proper by "*ibid.,* p. 231."

## BRIEF DOCUMENTATION

It is often unnecessary to give a complete footnote for every citation from a source, yet necessary to document the citation. It seems redundant, when a text has mentioned an author's name or his book's title, or both, to repeat them in a footnote. The footnote then need contain only those facts not given in the text; but all the documenting facts must be given in one place or the other. For examples:

. . . Rollo May, in his *Man's Search for Himself,*[1] defines courage . . .

[1] New York, 1953, p. 224.

. . . Rollo May[1] defines courage as . . .

[1] *Man's Search for Himself* (New York, 1953), p. 224.

Specific documentation can be kept brief by using the general documentation, the bibliography, after notifying the reader that footnotes or in-text references identify the names of sources given in full in the bibliography. Thus a writer might refer to Rollo May's book thus, even on first mention:

... Courage is "the capacity to meet the anxiety which arises as one achieves freedom" (May, p. 224). Seen as such, ...

The reader is then expected to understand that he will find the source given in full in the bibliography, thus:

May, Rollo. *Man's Search for Himself.* New York, 1953.

If several books by May were in the bibliography, the brief documentation would have to be explicit enough to prevent confusion. To this end, "May, *Man's Search*" would be used rather than "May" alone.

Sometimes the entries in the bibliography are numbered. If in such a bibliography the May book were to be numbered 221, then the citing note might read "221, p. 224."

## DIVERSE PRACTICE IN DOCUMENTATION

Custom and agreement have not established uniform practice as to correct documentation. Readers' needs differ; scholars in different fields have different kinds of source material to identify and describe; and editors, teachers, and research directors have strong preferences which they can enforce on their contributors, students, and staff. The student writer who goes beyond this discussion in exploring documentation can find some additional and different recommendations in any of four books especially:

ELINOR YAGGY, *How to Write Your Term Paper.* Chandler Publishing Company, 660 Market Street, San Francisco 4, California. Contains a thorough discussion of documentation forms, with numerous examples. Primarily for undergraduate writers.

BLANCHE ELLSWORTH, *English Simplified.* Chandler Publishing Company, 660 Market Street, San Francisco 4, California. An appendix on Writing the Research Paper contains directions for preparing a bibliography and for using footnotes, with a chart of model footnotes and corresponding bibliography entries in parallel columns. Primarily for undergraduate writers.

KATE L. TURABIAN, *A Manual for Writers of Term Papers, Theses, and Dissertations.* The University of Chicago Press, Chicago 37, Illinois. Has chapters on footnotes and bibliography, with numerous examples. Primarily for graduates and advanced undergraduate writers.

WILLIAM RILEY PARKER, compiler, *The MLA Style Sheet.* The Modern Language Association of America, 6 Washington Square North, New

York 3, New York. Primarily for writers of material to be published in Modern Language Association periodicals. This has a supplement dealing with the preparation of masters' theses and doctors' dissertations. Widely accepted and authoritative, especially for papers on literary subjects.

## THE DOCUMENTATION OF MATERIAL IN THIS COLLECTION

This collection, being a book of special character compiled for the convenience of students writing research papers, differs from general books and periodicals that might be found in a library. Footnotes and bibliographical entries describing sources in this collection must identify both the source and the collection. Acceptable forms for these are given at the ends of most selections. These name the original source and its author (if known), giving facts of publication, and also name this collection and its editors. They are models for documentation of materials from similar sources.

There would be some question of propriety, or even of honesty, if a writer were to name an original source in a documentary citation without making it clear that he examined the material in a collection—whether this collection or another. A reader has the right to know whether a writer is working from original or secondary sources: whether for instance he has seen George Washington's actual diary or has seen only an edited version of the diary in print. For edited versions, even carefully and scrupulously edited versions, may depart from originals.